Contents at a Glance

Contents

About the Authors

 **Josh Juneau** has been developing software since the mid-1990s. Database application programming has been the focus of his career since the beginning. He became an Oracle Database administrator and adopted the PL/SQL language for performing administrative tasks and developing applications for Oracle Database. As his skills evolved, he began to incorporate Java into his PL/SQL applications and later began to develop stand-alone applications in Java. During his tenure as a developer, he has combined his knowledge of PL/SQL and Java to develop robust Oracle Database applications that harness the great features offered by both technologies. He has extended his knowledge of the JVM by learning and developing applications with other JVM languages such as Jython and Groovy. His interest in learning new languages that run on the JVM led to his interest in Jython. Since 2006, Josh has been the editor and publisher for the *Jython Monthly* newsletter. In late 2008, he began a podcast dedicated to the Jython programming language. Josh was the lead author for *The Definitive Guide to Jython*, which was published in early 2010 by Apress. He has most recently become the lead for the Django-Jython project (http://code.google.com/p/django-jython/), after developing the project's implementation for the Oracle Database. To hear more from Josh, follow his blog at http://jj-blogger.blogspot.com. You can also follow him on Twitter via @javajuneau.

 **Matt Arena** has been developing Oracle Database applications for 25 years. He's focused on web-based applications since the Web was first developed. Matt has worked in every phase of the project development life cycle but enjoys database modeling and programming the most.

About the Technical Reviewer

 **Bob Bryla** is an Oracle 9*i*, 10*g*, and 11*g* Certified Professional with more than 20 years of experience in database design, database application development, training, and database administration. He is an Internet database analyst and Oracle DBA at Lands' End, Inc., in Dodgeville, Wisconsin. He is the author of several other Oracle DBA books for both novice and seasoned professionals.

Acknowledgments

This book is dedicated to my wife and kids...we made it through another one. I would like to thank my wife Angela for always being so great, even when there were days that I had to work on it instead of spending time with my family. Happy anniversary, Angela; this has been the best ten years of my life, and I look forward to growing old with you and watching our children grow up.

Thank you to my children, Kaitlyn, Jacob, Matthew, and Zachary, for understanding when I needed to work on this book. There were many times throughout the production of this book that I had to work late on Saturday mornings or take time out of the day to read and write for the book. Thanks for being patient with me; I hope that you will read this book someday and understand why my eyes were plastered to the computer screen for many hours on end. I know that at least two of you will follow in my footsteps and become developers!

I want to thank my family for supporting me throughout my career and for taking an interest in my work. I hope that you will enjoy reading it, and maybe you can learn why I am such an Oracle and Java enthusiast. I also want to thank my friends and co-workers for their support, especially Roger Slisz and Kent Collins, for trusting me to be the brains behind application development for our section.

I owe the Jython and Java communities a huge thanks for keeping me involved. Even when times are slow, the community keeps me moving forward to learn new and useful things. A big thank-you to Jim Baker who was responsible for getting me started in the field of writing books.

Thanks to Jonathan Gennick for providing me with the opportunity to write this book. I look forward to working with you again on future projects. I also thank Bob Bryla, John Osborne, and Adam Heath for the useful feedback they provided throughout the authoring of this book. I especially want to thank my coauthor, Matt Arena, for stepping in and lending me a hand with the book; your material is excellent. Matt, you showed me the ropes in PL/SQL, and it has been a privilege to work with you on authoring this book. I hope to work on many more projects together.

Lastly, thanks to the Oracle community and readers of this book. We enjoy the privilege of working with the number-one database. This book is my contribution to the community, and I hope it inspires many to utilize PL/SQL and Oracle to its full potential.

-   *Josh Juneau*

Prayerful thanks to God for all the blessings He has given me in life, especially Pat, my loving wife. I want to thank Michael, my terrific son, for whom this book is dedicated, for being an amazing person and for giving me a sweet daughter-in-law Anna and wonderful grandchildren, Michael and Kyra (and for the future grandchildren). I also thank my parents, John and Jane, and my siblings John, Mark, Kathi and Cindy for many sacrifices, wisdom and support throughout my life.

Josh Juneau, respected friend, colleague and lead author of this book, my sincere thanks for giving me the opportunity to contribute to your work. It has been a great pleasure and I hope to work with you again.

I thank Jonathan Gennick, Adam Heath, Bob Bryla, John Osborn and the entire editorial staff at Apress for their guidance and support throughout the process of writing this book.

I'd like to Dr. Paul Kaiser, Dr. Steven Berger and Brother Joseph Ninh of Lewis University for teaching me the foundations of computer programming and instilling in me the passion to learn.

Finally, to KLN angel in Heaven ~ I will always remember you.

-    *Matt Arena*

Introduction

Oracle Database is one of the most advanced relational databases available. It includes technologies that empower you to work with your data in ways that no other database offers. In the early days of Oracle Database, Structured Query Language (SQL) was used to work directly with the data, but as time went on, people turned to other languages outside the database for performing more sophisticated tasks with data. Although these procedural languages offered a powerful way to harness data, developers and database administrators wanted a language that was easier to use and bound more closely to the data. Oracle Corporation addressed that need by introducing Procedural Language/Structured Query Language (PL/SQL) into Oracle Database in release 7. This language offered the best of both worlds, allowing developers and database administrators to work directly with data via SQL and perform routine programming tasks within the database.

The PL/SQL programming language was influenced by the Ada programming language. In fact, the syntax is much the same as Ada. When PL/SQL was originated, it contained many constructs that are available in other languages, including variables and arrays. In Oracle Database 8, the language began to take on more of an object-oriented dialect, allowing developers to create types and develop applications in a way that was more in tune with other modern-day languages. The language continues to grow, adding new features with each release of Oracle Database and making PL/SQL an essential tool for anyone programming against an Oracle Database.

PL/SQL can be quite powerful for performing routine database tasks such as creating, returning, updating, and deleting records. However, its capabilities go far beyond performing the routine tasks. Database administrators can use PL/SQL to create powerful database procedures and queries among other things, and developers can use it for developing sophisticated web-based applications, working with stored Java classes, and much more.

The Recipe Approach

Although plenty of PL/SQL references are available today, this book takes a different approach. You'll find an example-based approach in which each chapter is built of sections containing solutions to specific, real-life programming problems. When faced with a problem, you can turn to the section for that problem and find a proven solution that you can modify and implement.

Each recipe contains a problem statement, a solution, and a detailed explanation of how the solution works. Some of the recipes contain more than one solution, and many of those recipes will also contain more than one section explaining how the solutions work.

The problem statements have been written so that you can easily identify with the topics. We've tried to make it obvious from the titles exactly what recipe you need to look at in order to get the job at hand completed.

The chapters have been organized in a fashion that allow for concepts to build upon each other as the book progresses. Yet we've taken care to write the recipes without assuming that you have read all the preceding content in the book. We've designed the book so that you can "dip in" randomly to whatever recipe addresses the problem you are facing at a given moment.

Many of the examples have been written and tested using Oracle's SQL*Plus environment, but the examples can also be ported to other environments such as Oracle SQL Developer and Oracle Application Express. In fact, Chapter 12 is devoted to learning the concepts and strategies behind using Oracle SQL Developer for working with PL/SQL.

We have been using PL/SQL for several years, and over that time we have watched the language mature. We think PL/SQL is the best language to use for working directly with Oracle Database. We also think it can be advantageous when used in combination with other languages such as Java to develop applications that take advantage of the strengths offered by each technology.

Many of the recipes in this book focus on learning how to use the language features in a way that applies each feature to a particular problem scenario. Other recipes in this book contain solutions that we used to resolve many of the problems that we have encountered over the years.

We have used the PL/SQL language for running database administrative tasks, writing entire web applications, developing web services, working in conjunction with Java and other languages, and much more. This book will provide you with the knowledge that we have picked up along the way in using the language for different solutions.

We hope that you will enjoy this book and that you will embrace the power of PL/SQL and learn to take full advantage of what Oracle Database has to offer. We have had a great time writing this book, and we look forward to updating it as the technology changes and new recipes are formed. We encourage you to post suggestions or feedback for this book at Apress.com. Thanks for reading this book. We hope you will enjoy using PL/SQL and find it to be as powerful as we do.

Audience

This book is intended for all audiences, beginners and advanced developers alike. We cover a wide gamut of problems and solutions. Beginners will find solutions to some of the most common PL/SQL programming tasks, such as trapping errors, writing loops, and retrieving data. Intermediate and advanced users will find solutions to more advanced problems such as those encountered when developing web applications and working with dynamic languages.

Example Code

Source code is available for many of the examples shown in this book. You can download that source code from the book's catalog page on the Apress web site. Here is the URL for that page:

```
http://apress.com/book/view/1430232072
```

Once there, look under the book's cover image for the catalog page section entitled Book Resources. You'll see a Source Code link. Click that link to download a zip archive containing the example code for this book.

To get started with the source code, please install the HR tables using the scripts that are contained within the hr folder in the source download. These tables can be added to the schema of your choice. Once you have added these tables, then you will be ready to run the examples provided with the book.

CHAPTER 1

PL/SQL Fundamentals

The Oracle PL/SQL language is important for database administrators and developers of Oracle Database products. Developing PL/SQL code requires a fundamental knowledge of the database, but there are also some key components that each program will need to use. This chapter embarks on a short journey through some recipes to get you better acquainted with those fundamental components.

This chapter is targeted as a starting point for those who are new to PL/SQL. However, those who are very familiar with the language may also want to glance through these recipes as a refresher. Who knows, you may even find a solution or two that you haven't ever seen before!

As stated in the introduction, this book focuses on Oracle Database 11g Release 2. However, many of the recipes will work in other versions of Oracle Database without any changes. All the recipes in this particular chapter are fundamental and should work unchanged in any version of Oracle Database that you're likely to encounter.

1-1. Creating a Block of Code

Problem

You are interested in creating an executable block of PL/SQL code.

Solution

Write the keywords BEGIN and END. Place your lines of code between those two keywords. Here's an example:

```
BEGIN
    Executable statements go here…
END;
```

If you want to introduce variables for your PL/SQL block, you must precede your block with a DECLARE section. Here's an example:

```
DECLARE
    One or more variable declarations
BEGIN
    One or more PL/SQL statements
END;
```

How It Works

A block of code is an executable program that performs a unit of work. The minimum executable block of code starts with the keyword BEGIN and ends with the keyword END. In between those two keywords there should be one or more PL/SQL statements that comprise your code block.

In practice, you'll find that you most often want to work with variables. That's why you need the DECLARE...BEGIN...END pattern in the solution's second example. One or more variable or constant declarations can be made within the declaration section, and they will then be available for use within your code block.

A PL/SQL application may consist of one or more code blocks, and some of them may even be recursively nested within each other. Variables that are defined within the DECLARE section can be used by the code block(s) immediately following, until the outer END keyword is reached.

1-2. Executing a Block of Code in SQL*Plus

Problem

You want to execute a block of PL/SQL code within the SQL*Plus command-line utility.

Solution

The solution to this recipe is multitiered, in that executing a block of code in SQL*Plus incorporates at least two steps:

Enter the PL/SQL code into the SQL*Plus utility.

Execute the code block by simply placing a backslash (/) as the last line of code, and then press the Enter key.

The following is an example displaying a code block that has been typed into SQL*Plus:

```
SQL> BEGIN
  2  DBMS_OUTPUT.PUT_LINE('HELLO WORLD');
  3  END;
  4  /
```

How It Works

To execute code within SQL*Plus, you simply type the executable block and place a forward slash (/) after the closing END. The code will be executed by the SQL*Plus interpreter when the slash is encountered. Once the code has been executed, control will be returned to the user at the SQL*Plus prompt. This differs from the execution of a query within SQL*Plus because when you write a SELECT statement, it can be executed by simply placing a semicolon at the end and hitting the Enter key.

■ **Note** Be sure to put the forward slash on a line by itself and to make it the first character on that line.

If the code you are executing contains a DECLARE section, then its execution will resemble the following:

```
SQL> DECLARE
  2     -- Some cursor and variable declarations
  3   BEGIN
  4     DBMS_OUTPUT.PUT_LINE('Hello World');
  5   END;
  6   /
Hello World

PL/SQL procedure successfully completed.
```

You also follow a similar syntax when creating stored procedures, packages, and functions. To create or replace stored code, write a CREATE statement and use a trailing slash, followed by pressing the Enter key. For example, then you can use the following code to create a simple stored procedure that prints a line of text. Notice how it contains a trailing slash character.

```
SQL> CREATE OR REPLACE PROCEDURE hello_world AS
  2   BEGIN
  3       DBMS_OUTPUT.PUT_LINE('Hello World');
  4   END;
  5   /

Procedure created.
```

Most likely, you will use SQL*Plus for much of your development life cycle. It is easy to execute code blocks and create stored code using the syntax discussed in this recipe. The same syntax can also be carried over to the Oracle Application Express environment. The Oracle Application Express environment contains an embedded SQL*Plus interpreter that can be used for performing the same tasks that you would perform using the standard client. For more information about using Oracle Application Express for building and maintaining web applications, please see the online Oracle documentation at http://download.oracle.com/docs/cd/E11882_01/appdev.112/e11946/toc.htm.

1-3. Storing Code in a Script

Problem

Rather than typing your PL/SQL code into the SQL*Plus utility each time you want to run it, you want to store the code in an executable script.

Solution

Open your favorite text editor or development environment; type the PL/SQL code into a new file, and save the file using the .sql extension. The script can contain any number of PL/SQL statements, but the last line of the script must be a forward slash (/).

For example, you could place the following lines into a file named count_down.sql:

```
SET SERVEROUTPUT ON;
DECLARE
```

```
  counter    NUMBER;
BEGIN
  FOR counter IN REVERSE 0..10 LOOP
    DBMS_OUTPUT.PUT_LINE (counter);
  END LOOP;
END;
```

Now you have a file that you can execute from SQL*Plus any time you want to count down from ten to zero.

How It Works

You can basically use any text editor or development environment to create and save your script. The key is to ensure that the file extension on the saved script is `.sql` so that SQL development environments and other developers recognize it as a stored SQL script. SQL Developer supports a number of additional extensions for more specific types of PL/SQL. To learn more about using SQL Developer, please see Chapter 12. Once the script has been stored, it can be executed within SQL*Plus. See the next recipe for details on doing that.

■ **Note** The line SET SERVEROUTPUT ON at the beginning of the script is an important detail. That command instructs SQL*Plus to look for and display any output from DBMS_OUTPUT.PUT_LINE. A common mistake is to omit the SET SERVEROUTPUT ON command and then be left wondering why you don't see any output.

1-4. Executing a Stored Script

Problem

You have stored an SQL script to your file system and want to execute it in SQL*Plus.

Solution

Assume you have a stored script named `my_stored_script.sql` and that it is saved within a directory named `/Oracle/scripts/`. You can execute that script using any one of the following approaches:

- Traverse into the directory containing the script, then connect to a database via SQL*Plus, and finally issue the following command:

```
@my_stored_script.sql
```

- Open the command line or terminal, connect to the database via SQL*Plus, and issue the following command:

```
@/Oracle/scripts/my_stored_script.sql
```

- Open command line or terminal, and issue the following command:

```
sqlplus username/password@database my_stored_script.sql
```

How It Works

Notice that the first two solutions involved an @ symbol before the script's file name. If you are already connected and have an open SQL*Plus session, then you must place an @ symbol before the path/script name in order for the script to be executed. Otherwise, if you are invoking both SQL*Plus and the script from the operating-system command line, then you do not need the leading @ command. The @ command is a SQL*Plus command that tells the interpreter to execute the code contained in the specified SQL file.

Oftentimes, database administrators will create one or more stored scripts to be executed to complete a task. An administrator will then set up a separate script containing the database connection information followed by one or more scripts to be executed. Such a script can then be executed by the operating system to invoke SQL*Plus, which in turn executes the scripts that contain the actual code to perform the work. If there is only one script to be executed, then an administrator will usually opt to use the third option from the solution to connect and execute a script. We will learn more about configuring PL/SQL jobs in Chapter 11.

1-5. Accepting User Input from the Keyboard

Problem

You want to write a script that prompts the user for some input. You want your PL/SQL code to then use that input to generate some results.

Solution

SQL*Plus provides a facility to accept user input. Use ampersand (&) character to indicate that a particular value should be entered from the keyboard. Here's an example:

```
DECLARE
  emp_count    NUMBER;
BEGIN
  SELECT count(*)
  INTO emp_count
  FROM employees
  WHERE department_id = &department_id;
END;
```

If the previous block is executed from SQL*Plus, you will see the following text, which prompts you to enter a department ID. In this case, the department ID of 40 is used.

```
Enter value for department_id: 40
old   7:    WHERE department_id = &department_id;
new   7:    WHERE department_id = 40;
```

How It Works

SQL*Plus uses the ampersand (&) character to indicate a value should be prompted for at the command line or terminal and assigned to the variable name immediately following the ampersand. The text immediately following the ampersand is the variable to which the input will be assigned, and it will be displayed as the prompt.

The variable following the & character is known as a *substitution variable*. It is important to note that a substitution variable is meaningful to SQL*Plus. Substitution variables are not "seen" by the database engine. SQL*Plus actually replaces the variable reference with the text that the user entered. As far as the database is concerned, the solution code contains the following WHERE clause:

```
WHERE department_id = 40;
```

If you want to reference the same substitution variable at a different point in your code, you can place two ampersands in front of the first to tell SQL*Plus that you want to retain that value for use at a later time. For instance, the following code block first obtains the value from the keyboard using &&variable_name, and then it prints that value out using &variable_name:

```
DECLARE
  emp_count    NUMBER;
BEGIN
  SELECT count(*)
  INTO emp_count
  FROM employees
  WHERE department_id = &&department_id;

  DBMS_OUTPUT.PUT_LINE('The employee count is: ' || emp_count ||
        ' for the department with an ID of: ' || &department_id);
END;
```

You can also use substitution variables in the DECLARE section of an anonymous code block to immediately assign an initial value to a variable. An anonymous code block is a block of code that is not stored in the database. It cannot be called by name, and it is executed only once unless it is stored into a script. Placing substitution variables into the DECLARE section may be useful if a particular variable will be used more than once throughout a code block. Here's an example:

```
DECLARE
  dept_id_var  NUMBER(4) := &department_id;
  dept_name    VARCHAR2(30);
  emp_count    NUMBER;
BEGIN
  SELECT count(*)
  INTO emp_count
  FROM employees
  WHERE department_id = dept_id_var;

  SELECT department_name
  INTO dept_name
  FROM departments
  WHERE department_id = dept_id_var;

  DBMS_OUTPUT.PUT_LINE('There are ' || emp_count || ' employees ' ||
        'in the ' || dept_name || ' department.');
END;
```

In this example, the substitution variable department_id will be assigned to the variable dept_id_var, at which point dept_id_var can be used anywhere in the code block.

When using substitution variables, it is imperative to pay attention to the type of value the user will be entering at the keyboard. If a value will be a variable character (VARCHAR2) type, then the substitution variable must be surrounded by single quotes, or you will receive an error when the input is processed. Similarly, if a value should be a numeric (NUMBER) type, then there should not be single quotes placed around the substitution variable. Here's an example:

```
DECLARE
    first    varchar2(20);
    last     varchar2(25);
    emp_last VARCHAR2(25) := '&last_name';
    emp_count NUMBER;
BEGIN
  SELECT count(*)
  INTO emp_count
  FROM employees
  WHERE last_name = emp_last;

  IF emp_count > 1 THEN
    DBMS_OUTPUT.PUT_LINE('More than 1 employee exists with that name.');
  ELSE
    SELECT first_name, last_name
    INTO first, last
    FROM employees
    WHERE last_name = emp_last;

    DBMS_OUTPUT.PUT_LINE('The matching employee is: ' ||
          first ||' ' || last);
  END IF;
EXCEPTION
  WHEN NO_DATA_FOUND THEN
    DBMS_OUTPUT.PUT_LINE('Please enter a different last name.');
END;
```

Of course, the previous assumes that there is only one person in the EMPLOYEES table that will match the provided last_name. If there were possibly more than one person with a given age, then we would have to begin looping through rows from a query. See Recipe 2-2 for an example of such looping. For now, we simply print out a message if more than one employee with the same last name exists.

1-6. Displaying Results in SQL*Plus

Problem

You want to display query results at the SQL*Plus prompt.

Solution

Use the DBMS_OUTPUT package to assist in displaying query results or lines of text. The following example depicts both of these use cases:

```
DECLARE
   first        VARCHAR2(20);
   last         VARCHAR2(25);
 BEGIN
  SELECT first_name, last_name
  INTO first, last
  FROM employees
  WHERE email = 'VJONES';
  DBMS_OUTPUT.PUT_LINE('The following employee matches your query:');
  DBMS_OUTPUT.PUT_LINE(first || ' ' || last);
 END;
```

The previous example uses DBMS_OUTPUT.PUT_LINE to print a line of text as well as the values of the variables first and last.

How It Works

The DBMS_OUTPUT package contains several useful procedures. By far, the most widely used is PUT_LINE for the purposes noted in the solution to this recipe. As you've seen, you can use the DBMS_OUTPUT.PUT_LINE procedure to display the contents of a stored variable or any arbitrary text. Before any lines of output will be displayed in SQL*Plus, you must first tell SQL*Plus to display server output by issuing this command:

```
SET SERVEROUTPUT ON;
```

Once issued, any lines of output created by DBMS_OUTPUT.PUT_LINE will be displayed. In a similar fashion, the interpreter will no longer display output once the following command is issued:

```
SET SERVEROUTPUT OFF;
```

One important note to remember is that if you plan to print many lines, it may be a good idea to resize the print buffer. When SET SERVEROUTPUT ON is issued, then the default buffer size is 20,000 bytes. Any content that surpasses that size will be cut off. To increase the buffer, simply set the size of buffer you'd like to use when turning the SERVEROUTPUT on:

```
SET SERVEROUTPUT ON SIZE 1000000;
```

The DBMS_OUTPUT package also has a buffer size limit. The buffer can be set from 2,000 to 1,000,000 bytes in size. The buffer can be set by passing the size to DBMS_ENABLE. If you attempt to exceed the size, then an Oracle exception will be raised.

1-7. Commenting Your Code

Problem

You want to document your code with inline and multiline comments.

Solution

Place two dashes before any text to create a one-line comment. For example, in the following code there is a comment placed before the query to describe its functionality:

```
-- The following query obtains a count of rows from the employees table
SELECT COUNT(*)
FROM EMPLOYEES;
```

Multiline comments can be created beginning with a slash and asterisk (/*) and ending with an asterisk and slash (*/). The following lines depict a multiple-line comment for a given code block:

```
/* This comment describes the functionality
      in the following code block. */
```

How It Works

Comments play a crucial role in code development. Not only are they useful for commenting inline code to tip off future developers who may see the code, but they can also be useful to you when trying to debug some code you authored several years ago. It can be useful to place comments before any lines of code that may require some interpretation, and in some cases it is useful to place comments on the same line as code itself. The double dashes can be placed at any position in a line of code, and any text following the dashes becomes a comment. Here's an example:

```
DECLARE
  emp_count     NUMBER;
BEGIN
  SELECT COUNT(*)
  INTO emp_count    -- Local variable
  FROM EMPLOYEES;
END;
```

When PL/SQL sees a double dash, it ignores any text that follows for the remainder of the line. Similarly, when a /* sequence is encountered, the interpreter ignores any lines of text until it encounters a closing */.

1-8. Referencing a Block of Code

Problem

You want to reference a block of code within a code segment later in your program.

Solution

Assign a *label* to the block of code that you want to reference. A PL/SQL label consists of a unique identifier surrounded by double angle brackets. For example, in the following code, you see that the block has been labeled dept_block:

```
<<dept_block>>
DECLARE
  dept_name     varchar2(30);
BEGIN
  SELECT department_name
  INTO dept_name
  FROM departments
```

```
  WHERE department_id = 230;
  DBMS_OUTPUT.PUT_LINE(dept_name);
END;
```

This code block can now be referenced by the label dept_block. See Recipe 1-9 for one example of code block labels.

How It Works

Any block of code can be labeled with a unique identifier for readability purposes or for referencing at a later point. The label can appear at the beginning of the code block and again at the end. The following code is a representation of the same block that was listed in the solution, but the label has been placed at the end as well.

```
<<dept_block>>
DECLARE
  dept_name      varchar2(30);
BEGIN
  SELECT department_name
  INTO dept_name
  FROM departments
  WHERE department_id = 230;
  DBMS_OUTPUT.PUT_LINE(dept_name);
END dept_block;
```

Labeling can be useful for a variety of reasons. It is often useful to place a label on a block for documentation and readability purposes. Furthermore, a label can be useful for referencing variables that are part of a particular code block from outside the block, elsewhere in the program. The labeling technique is useful for referencing variables from within nested loops. Labels can also assist in program control by referencing blocks of code with such keywords as GOTO and EXIT.

1-9. Referring to Variables from Nested Blocks

Problem

A variable that is defined in an outer code block needs to be used within an inner block. However, there is also a variable of the same name within the inner block. Thus, two variables with the same name are in scope, and you need a mechanism for differentiating between them.

Solution

Label the code blocks, and use the labels to qualify the variable references. For instance, if a variable dept_name is defined in an outer code block, which is labeled outer_block, then you can use the fully qualified name outer_block.dept_name to reference that variable. Let's take a look at an example:

```
<<outer_block>>
DECLARE
  mgr_id NUMBER(6) := '&current_manager_id';
  dept_count  number := 0;
BEGIN
```

```
SELECT count(*)
INTO dept_count
FROM departments
WHERE manager_id = outer_block.mgr_id;

IF dept_count > 0 THEN
    <<inner_block>>
    DECLARE
        dept_name VARCHAR2(30);
        mgr_id  NUMBER(6):= '&new_manager_id';
    BEGIN
        SELECT department_name
        INTO dept_name
        FROM departments
        WHERE manager_id = outer_block.mgr_id;

        UPDATE departments
        SET manager_id = inner_block.mgr_id
        WHERE manager_id = outer_block.mgr_id;
            DBMS_OUTPUT.PUT_LINE
                ('Department manager ID has been changed for ' || dept_name);

    END inner_block;
    ELSE
        DBMS_OUTPUT.PUT_LINE('There are no departments listed for the manager');
    END IF;
EXCEPTION
    WHEN NO_DATA_FOUND THEN
        DBMS_OUTPUT.PUT_LINE('There are no departments listed for the manager');
END outer_block;
```

When the previous example is executed, SQL*Plus will prompt you for the current_manager_id and new_manager_id values before execution begins. The database is then queried for the supplied current_manager_id. If the manager_id is a valid department manager for a department contained within the DEPARTMENTS table, then it is changed to match the value provided by new_manager_id.

How It Works

As you can see from the example, blocks can be nested within one another. An identifier can be used within the block of code that defines it. If a block of code is nested within another block, those identifiers that are declared within the outer block are visible from within the inner block. On the other hand, any identifier declared within the inner block is not visible from the outer block. As you can see, nested blocks are a great way to control the scope of identifier use.

Although it is not recommended that you use the same name for variables contained within different blocks of code, labels can be very useful in the event that such name conflicts occur. If the solution hadn't contained block labels, then the outer block variable mgr_id identifier would not have been accessible from within the inner block, since the inner block also contains an identifier by the same name. Of course, the cleanest way to write code such as this is to use different identifier names for all the variables. In that case, the outer block variable would be visible within the inner block without fully qualifying the name, and block labels would not be required.

1-10. Ignoring Substitution Variables

Problem

You want to execute a script in SQL*Plus that contains elements that appear to be substitution variables, but you do not intend them to be substitution variables. You want the interpreter to ignore them instead of prompting the user for input.

Solution #1

One solution is to precede the & character with an escape character. The escape character tells SQL*Plus that what follows is not intended to be a variable reference.

In the following code, an escape character is used to tell SQL*Plus to ignore the & character when it is encountered and to treat "& Receiving" as simple text within a string:

```
SQL> SET ESCAPE '\'
SQL> INSERT INTO DEPARTMENTS VALUES(
  2  departments_seq.nextval,
  3  'Shipping \& Receiving',
  4  null,
  5  null);

1 row created.
```

Solution #2

Another solution is to completely disable the substitution variable feature. The next example uses the SET DEFINE OFF command to tell SQL*Plus that it should ignore all substitution variables:

```
SQL> SET DEFINE OFF
INSERT INTO DEPARTMENTS VALUES(
departments_seq.nextval,
'Importing & Exporting',
null,
null);

1 row created.
```

How It Works

Oftentimes you will encounter a situation where you need to tell SQL*Plus to ignore substitution variables for processing. As shown in the examples, there are a couple of different solutions in these cases. It is up to you to decide which method works best for you. Usually the method that is chosen depends upon the scenario.

Setting up an escape character via the SET ESCAPE command actually tells SQL*Plus to treat the designated character as the escape character for all scenarios, so whenever that character is encountered, then the character immediately following it should be ignored by the interpreter. By "ignored," I mean that the character will not trigger the normal functionality that you would expect, such as prompting a user for input.

Using the SET DEFINE OFF method will cause all substitution variables to be ignored. In effect, this solution will affect only substitution variables and does not cause the interpreter to escape in any other scenario. Since this method only escapes substitution variables, it is better suited for use when running scripts. For instance, suppose you have a script named display_department_info.sql that contains the following SQL:

```
SELECT department_id
FROM departments
WHERE department_name = 'Importing & Exporting';
```

If you execute the script via SQL*Plus without using one of the solutions provided in this recipe, you will see the following message:

```
SQL> @display_department_id.sql
Enter value for exporting:
```

The reason this message occurs is because SQL*Plus is treating the ampersand in "Importing & Exporting" as a substitution variable, which prompts the user to enter text. Now, try executing the same script again, and this time issue the SET DEFINE OFF command first:

```
SQL> SET DEFINE OFF
SQL> @display_department_id.sql


DEPARTMENT_ID
-------------
          360
```

Using SET DEFINE OFF gives you the expected results.

1-11. Changing the Substitution Variable Character

Problem

You are interested in changing the substitution variable from & to some other character.

Solution

Issue the SET DEFINE command to set the new character. For example, say you want the substitution character to be a caret (^). To that end, you can issue the SET DEFINE command shown in the following example:

```
SQL> SET DEFINE ^
SQL> SELECT department_name
  2  FROM departments
  3  WHERE department_id = ^dept_id;
Enter value for dept_id: 150
old   3: where department_id = ^dept_id
new   3: where department_id = 150


DEPARTMENT_NAME
------------------------------
Shareholder Services
```

As shown in the example, the substitution variable dept_id is prefaced with the ^ symbol. That works, since the SET DEFINE command specifies that symbol as the one to use.

How It Works

Issue the SET DEFINE command when you want to change the substitution variable character recognized by SQL*Plus. The syntax for using the SET DEFINE command is as follows:

```
SET DEFINE character
```

The character can be any valid character. Any statement within the same SQL*Plus session will utilize that character to denote a substitution variable after this command is issued.

The solution in this recipe can be most useful if you are working with a piece of code that contains many occurrences of the default DEFINE character (&) in various string literals.

1-12. Creating a Variable to Match a Database Column Type

Problem

You are querying the database for a particular column, and you are interested in saving the column's value into a local variable. In doing so, you want to create the local variable with the same type as the column being queried.

Solution

Make use of the %TYPE attribute of the column name in order to create the new variable. In the following example, you will see that the dept_name variable is given the same type as the department_name database table column.

```
DECLARE
  dept_name    departments.department_name%TYPE;
  dept_id      NUMBER(6) := &department_id;
BEGIN
  SELECT department_name
  INTO dept_name
  FROM departments
  WHERE department_id = dept_id;
  DBMS_OUTPUT.PUT_LINE('The department with the given ID is: ' || dept_name);
EXCEPTION
  WHEN NO_DATA_FOUND THEN
    DBMS_OUTPUT.PUT_LINE('No department for the given ID');
END;
```

How It Works

The %TYPE attribute of a database column returns the column's datatype. That type can then be used to declare a variable, therefore providing a nice way to declare variables in your programs that are consistent with the columns in your database.

The advantage of declaring variables using %TYPE is that if the original database column type is ever modified, then all the variables that rely on that column will also change type accordingly. Hence, code will be easier to maintain.

CHAPTER 2

■■■

Essential SQL

SQL is an essential part of any database application. From queries to update statements to inserts and deletes, database transactions consume much of a database application developer's time. The PL/SQL language is unmatched by any other in providing seamless integration between SQL and procedural language for the Oracle Database. PL/SQL is based around database transactions, so the seamless language characteristics help to provide ease of use and increased developer productivity.

This chapter will focus on some of the more widely used PL/SQL techniques for working directly with the database. If you are looking for some great ways to insert, update, create, or delete records with your application, then this is the chapter that you'll want to read. The recipes will begin with showing how to retrieve data and work with it. After that, you will find some recipes for updating data, deleting rows, and more advanced topics such as removing duplicate rows from the database.

2-1. Retrieving a Single Row from the Database

Problem

You are interested in returning one row from a database table via a query that searches for an exact match.

Solution #1

Use the `SELECT…INTO` syntax in order to retrieve the row from the database. You can choose to retrieve one or more columns of data from the matching row. The following example depicts a scenario in which a table is queried to return multiple columns from a single row:

```
DECLARE
  first   VARCHAR2(20);
  last    VARCHAR2(25);
  email   VARCHAR2(25);
BEGIN
  SELECT first_name, last_name, email
  INTO first, last, email
  FROM employees
  WHERE employee_id = 100;

  DBMS_OUTPUT.PUT_LINE(
      'Employee Information for ID: ' || first || ' ' || last || ' - ' || email);
EXCEPTION
  WHEN NO_DATA_FOUND THEN
    DBMS_OUTPUT.PUT_LINE('No employee matches the given ID');
```

```
WHEN TOO_MANY_ROWS THEN
    DBMS_OUTPUT.PUT_LINE('More than one employee matches the given ID');
END;
```

The example in this solution shows how you can retrieve a row from the database when given an employee ID. Once the data is retrieved, then some formatted information regarding that employee is printed to the command line via DBMS_OUTPUT. The following result shows what the response will look like if a user enters an employee ID of 100:

```
Employee Information for ID: Steven King - SKING

PL/SQL procedure successfully completed.
```

As you can see, the employee Steven King has an employee ID of 100. You could modify this example to retrieve any data columns from the EMPLOYEES table. For instance, if you wanted to return the column HIRE_DATE, then you could do so by declaring one more variable and adjusting the SELECT INTO statement accordingly.

Solution #2

It is also possible to use a cursor for selecting a single row from the database, although this technique is not used quite as often as SELECT INTO. One particular use case for retrieving a single row via a cursor would be if you were working with a dynamic query where the query string stored in a variable may change. You will learn more about dynamic queries in Chapter 8. In the meantime, the following example shows the use of a cursor that is expected to retrieve a single row of data with an explicit SELECT statement:

```
DECLARE

  CURSOR emp_cursor IS
  SELECT first_name, last_name, email
  FROM employees
  WHERE employee_id = &emp_id;

  first   VARCHAR2(20);
  last    VARCHAR2(25);
  email   VARCHAR2(25);

BEGIN
  OPEN emp_cursor;
  FETCH emp_cursor INTO first, last, email;
  IF emp_cursor%NOTFOUND THEN
    RAISE NO_DATA_FOUND;
  ELSE
      -- Perform second fetch to see if more than one row is returned
    FETCH emp_cursor INTO first, last, email;
    IF emp_cursor%FOUND THEN
      RAISE TOO_MANY_ROWS;
    ELSE
      DBMS_OUTPUT.PUT_LINE(
      'Employee Information for ID: ' || first || ' ' || last || ' - ' || email);
```

```
    END IF;
  END IF;

  CLOSE emp_cursor;


EXCEPTION
  WHEN NO_DATA_FOUND THEN
    DBMS_OUTPUT.PUT_LINE('No employee matches the given ID');
  WHEN TOO_MANY_ROWS THEN
    DBMS_OUTPUT.PUT_LINE('More than one employee matches the given ID');
END;
```

How It Works

There are two possible solutions to the problem in this recipe. One is to issue a SELECT…INTO statement, which is a statement designed to return just one row. The other approach is to open a cursor, fetch the one row, and close the cursor. Some argue that a cursor-based approach is always better. We keep a more open mind on that point. Either approach is acceptable. If your application is predicated on exactly one row being returned, it is actually easier to trap the exceptions of zero or multiple rows being returned when using SELECT…INTO. Ultimately, the approach to use comes down to your own preference and possibly to the question of which approach you are most familiar with.

Comments on Solution #1

The SELECT…INTO statement is a convenient way to return a single row from the database. It allows the database to be queried and then returns values into local variables based upon a single-row query. The format for using SELECT…INTO is as follows:

```
SELECT column_1, column_2
INTO variable_1, variable2
FROM table_name
WHERE filters;
```

The solution to this recipe queries the database using a SELECT…INTO statement in order to obtain some information on a particular employee from the EMPLOYEES database table. The results are stored into local variables and then printed out using DBMS_OUTPUT.PUT_LINE. There can be one or more columns queried, and their values will be returned into the local variables that are listed within the INTO clause in sequential order.

To provide an informative message to the end user when no data is found or if more than one row of data is found, you can use an exception handler. Exception handlers allow you to recover from fatal errors so that an application can continue to run as expected but provide meaningful details to the user of the application. PL/SQL will immediately transfer control of execution to the exception block when an exception is raised. Therefore, if the SELECT statement fails to find a row, then control is passed to the exception block, and the NO_DATA_FOUND exception is raised. Similarly, PL/SQL throws the TOO_MANY_ROWS exception when the query results in more than one row being returned.

■ **Note** Chapter 9 gives more details on exception handling, including showing you how to create your own exceptions.

A well-formulated application will be coded to ensure that corner cases and unexpected conditions do not result in the application failing in front of the user. Proper exception handling is thus instrumental to the success of an application in the real world. While retrieving rows from the database, always ensure that you have provided proper handling for any possible outcome.

Comments on Solution #2

Some would suggest that the cursor approach is best, because it will not return an error in the event that the SELECT statement returns multiple rows. We keep an open mind on that point. Consider that if you are expecting exactly one row to be returned, getting multiple rows back represents an exception case that you must somehow deal with. The cursor-based solution makes it easy to simply ignore that exception case, but ignoring a condition that you do not expect to occur does not change the fact that it has occurred.

Although a cursor is used, the cases where no data is returned or where too many rows are returned given the user-supplied EMPLOYEE_ID still remain a reality. However, since cursors are specifically designed to deal with zero rows or more than one row coming back from a query, no exceptions will be raised if these situations occur. For this reason, Solution #2 contains some conditional logic that is used to manually raise the desired exceptions. In the event that the user supplies the block with an invalid EMPLOYEE_ID, the cursor will not fetch any data. The %NOTFOUND attribute of the cursor will be checked to see whether the cursor successfully fetched data. If not, then the NO_DATA_FOUND exception is raised. If the cursor is successful in retrieving data, then a second FETCH statement is issued to see whether more than one row will be returned. If more than one row is returned, then the TOO_MANY_ROWS exception is raised; otherwise, the expected output is displayed. In any event, the output that is displayed using either of the solutions will be the same whether successful or not.

2-2. Qualifying Column and Variable Names

Problem

You have a variable and a column sharing the same name. You want to refer to both in the same SQL statement.

For example, you decide that you'd like to search for records where LAST_NAME is not equal to a last name that is provided by a user via an argument to a procedure call. Suppose you have declared a variable LAST_NAME, and you want to alter the query to read as follows:

```
SELECT first_name, last_name, email
INTO first, last, email
FROM employees
WHERE last_name = last_name;
```

How does PL/SQL know which LAST_NAME you are referring to since both the table column name and the variable name are the same? You need a way to differentiate your references.

Solution

You can use the dot notation to fully qualify the local variable name with the procedure name so that PL/SQL can differentiate between the two. The altered query, including the fully qualified procedure_name.variable solution, would read as follows:

```
CREATE OR REPLACE PROCEDURE retrieve_emp_info(last_name IN VARCHAR2) AS
   first    VARCHAR2(20);
   last     VARCHAR2(25);
   email    VARCHAR2(25);

BEGIN
  SELECT first_name, last_name, email
  INTO first, last, email
  FROM employees
  WHERE last_name = retrieve_emp_info.last_name;

  DBMS_OUTPUT.PUT_LINE(
      'Employee Information for ID: ' || first || ' ' || last_name || ' - ' || email);
EXCEPTION
  WHEN NO_DATA_FOUND THEN
    DBMS_OUTPUT.PUT_LINE('No employee matches the last name ' || last_name);
END;
```

How It Works

PL/SQL name resolution becomes very important in circumstances such as these, and by fully qualifying the names, you can be sure that your code will work as expected. The solution used dot notation to fully qualify the variable name.

The column name could have been qualified with the table name, as in EMPLOYEES.LAST_NAME. However, there's no need to qualify the column name in this case. Because the reference occurs within a SELECT, the closest resolution for LAST_NAME becomes the table column of that name. So, in this particular case, it is necessary only to qualify references to variable names in the enclosing PL/SQL block.

If you are executing a simple BEGIN...END block, then you also have the option of fully qualifying the variable using the dot notation along with the block label. For the purposes of this demonstration, let's say that the code block shown in the solution was labeled <<emp_info>>. You could then fully qualify a variable named description as follows:

```
<<emp_info>>
DECLARE
  last_name    VARCHAR2(25) := 'Fay';
  first  VARCHAR2(20);
  last   VARCHAR2(25);
  email  VARCHAR2(25);
BEGIN
  SELECT first_name, last_name, email
  INTO first, last, email
  FROM employees
  WHERE last_name = emp_info.last_name;
END;
```

In this example, the LAST_NAME that is declared in the code block is used within the SELECT..INTO query, and it is fully qualified with the code block label.

2-3. Declaring Variable Types That Match Column Types

Problem

You want to declare some variables in your code block that match the same datatypes as some columns in a particular table. If the datatype on one of those columns changes, you'd like the code block to automatically update the variable type to match that of the updated column.

■ **Note** Sharp-eyed readers will notice that we cover this problem redundantly in Chapter 1. We cover this problem here as well, because the solution is fundamental to working in PL/SQL, especially to working with SQL in PL/SQL. We don't want you to miss what we discuss in this recipe. It is that important.

Solution

Use the %TYPE attribute on table columns to identify the types of data that will be returned into your local variables. Instead of providing a hard-coded datatype for a variable, append %TYPE to the database column name. Doing so will apply the datatype from the specified column to the variable you are declaring.

In the following example, the same SELECT INTO query is issued, as in the previous problem, to retrieve an employee record from the database. However, in this case, the variables are declared using the %TYPE attribute rather than designating a specified datatype for each.

```
DECLARE
  first               employees.first_name%TYPE;
  last                employees.last_name%TYPE;
  email               employees.email%TYPE;
BEGIN
  SELECT first_name, last_name, email
  INTO first, last, email
  FROM employees
  WHERE employee_id = &emp_id;
  DBMS_OUTPUT.PUT_LINE('Employee Information for ID: ' ||
 first || '   ' || last || ' - ' || email);
EXCEPTION
  WHEN NO_DATA_FOUND THEN
    DBMS_OUTPUT.PUT_LINE('No matching employee was found, please try again.');
  WHEN OTHERS THEN
    DBMS_OUTPUT.PUT_LINE('An unknown error has occured, please try again.');
END;
```

As you can see from the solution, the code block looks essentially the same as the one in the previous recipe. The only difference is that here the %TYPE attribute of each database column is being used in order to declare your local variable types.

How It Works

The %TYPE attribute can become a significant time-saver and savior for declaring variable types, especially if the underlying database column types are subject to change. This attribute enables the local variable to assume the same datatype of its corresponding database column type at runtime. Retrieving several columns into local application variables can become tedious if you need to continually verify that the datatypes of each variable are the same as those of the columns whose data they will consume.

The %TYPE attribute can be used when defining variables, constants, fields, and parameters. Using %TYPE assures that the variables you declare will always remain synchronized with the datatypes of their corresponding columns.

2-4. Returning Queried Data into a PL/SQL Record

Problem

Instead of retrieving only a select few columns via a database query, you'd rather return the entire matching row. It can be a time-consuming task to replicate each of the table's columns in your application by creating a local variable for each along with selecting the correct datatypes. Although you can certainly make use of the %TYPE attribute while declaring the variables, you'd rather retrieve the entire row into a single object. Furthermore, you'd like the object that the data is going to be stored into to have the ability to assume the same datatypes for each of the columns being returned just as you would by using the %TYPE attribute.

Solution

Make use of the %ROWTYPE attribute for the particular database table that you are querying. The %ROWTYPE attribute returns a record type that represents a database row from the specified table. For instance, the following example demonstrates how the %ROWTYPE attribute can store an entire employee table row for a cursor:

```
DECLARE
  CURSOR emp_cur IS
  SELECT *
  FROM employees
  WHERE employee_id = &emp_id;
  -- Declaring a local variable using the ROWTYPE attribute
  -- of the employees table
  emp_rec     employees%ROWTYPE;
BEGIN
  OPEN emp_cur;
  FETCH emp_cur INTO emp_rec;
  IF emp_cur%FOUND THEN

    DBMS_OUTPUT.PUT_LINE('Employee Information for ID: ' || emp_rec.first_name || '   ' ||
                emp_rec.last_name || ' - ' || emp_rec.email);
  ELSE
```

```
      DBMS_OUTPUT.PUT_LINE('No matching employee for the given ID');
    END IF;
    CLOSE emp_cur;
  EXCEPTION
    WHEN NO_DATA_FOUND THEN
      DBMS_OUTPUT.PUT_LINE('No employee matches the given emp ID');
END;
```

If the employee ID that is provided to the program in the example correlates to an employee record in the database, then the cursor is able to FETCH the entire row into the emp_rec record type.

How It Works

The %ROWTYPE attribute represents an entire database table row as a record type. Each of the corresponding table columns is represented within the record as a variable, and each variable in the record inherits its type from the respective table column.

Using the %ROWTYPE attribute offers several advantages to declaring each variable individually. For starters, declaring a single record type is much more productive than declaring several local variables to correspond to each of the columns of a table. Also, if any of the table columns' datatypes is ever adjusted, then your code will not break because the %ROWTYPE attribute works in much the same manner as the %TYPE attribute of a column in that it will automatically maintain the same datatypes as the corresponding table columns. Therefore, if a column with a type of VARCHAR2(10) is changed to VARCHAR2(100), that change will ripple through into your record definition.

Using %ROWTYPE also makes your code much easier to read because you are not littering local variables throughout. Instead, you can use the dot notation to reference each of the different columns that the record type returned by %ROWTYPE consists of. For instance, in the solution, the first_name, last_name, and email columns are referenced from the emp_rec record type.

2-5. Creating Your Own Records to Receive Query Results

Problem

You want to query the database, return several columns from one or more tables, and store them into local variables of a code block for processing. Rather than placing the values of the columns into separate variables, you want to create a single variable that contains all the values.

Solution

Create a database RECORD containing variables to hold the data you want to retrieve from the database. Since a RECORD can hold multiple variables of different datatypes, they work nicely for grouping data that has been retrieved as a result of a query.

In the following example, the database is queried for the name and position of a player. The data that is returned is used to populate a PL/SQL RECORD containing three separate variables: first name, last name, and position.

```
DECLARE
  TYPE emp_info IS RECORD(first    employees.first_name%TYPE,
                          last     employees.last_name%TYPE,
                          email    employees.email%TYPE);
```

```
  emp_info_rec   emp_info;
BEGIN
  SELECT first_name, last_name, email
  INTO emp_info_rec
  FROM  employees
  WHERE last_name = 'Vargas';

  DBMS_OUTPUT.PUT_LINE('The queried employee''s email address is ' || emp_info_rec.email);
  EXCEPTION
  WHEN NO_DATA_FOUND THEN
    DBMS_OUTPUT.PUT_LINE('No employee matches the last name provided');
END;
```

As you can see, the record is defined as its own TYPE, and then a variable named emp_info_rec is declared using the record type. The queried data is then assigned to emp_info_rec, and its individual values can later be accessed using the dot notation.

How It Works

Records are useful for passing similar data around within an application, but they are also quite useful for simply retrieving data and organizing it nicely as is the case with the solution to this recipe. To create a record, you first declare a record TYPE. This declaration can consist of one or more different datatypes that represent columns of one or more database tables. Once the record type is declared, you create a variable and define it as an instance of the record type. This variable is then used to populate and work with the data stored in the record.

■ **Note** It is possible to create a record that matches the columns of a particular table exactly by using the %ROWTYPE attribute of a database table. See the preceding Recipe 2-4 for details on doing that.

Cursors work very well with records of data. When declaring a cursor, you can select particular columns of data to return into your record. The record variable then takes on the type of cursor%ROWTYPE. In the following example, a cursor is used to determine which fields you want to return from EMPLOYEES. That cursor's %ROWTYPE attribute is then used to define a record variable that is used for holding the queried data.

```
DECLARE
    CURSOR emp_cur IS
    SELECT first_name, last_name, email
    FROM employees
    WHERE employee_id = 100;

    emp_rec      emp_cur%ROWTYPE;
BEGIN
  OPEN emp_cur;
  FETCH emp_cur INTO emp_rec;
  IF emp_cur %FOUND THEN
  CLOSE emp_cur;
```

```
      DBMS_OUTPUT.PUT_LINE(emp_rec.first_name || ' ' || emp_rec.last_name ||
                                      '''s email is ' || emp_rec.email);
   ELSE
      DBMS_OUTPUT.PUT_LINE('No employee matches the provided ID number');
   END IF;
EXCEPTION
   WHEN NO_DATA_FOUND THEN
      DBMS_OUTPUT.PUT_LINE('No employee matches the last name provided');
END;
```

As you can see in this example, the cursor %ROWTYPE attribute creates a record type using the columns that are queried by the cursor. The result is easy-to-read code that gains all the positive effects of declaring record types via the %ROWTYPE attribute.

2-6. Looping Through Rows from a Query

Problem

A query that you are issuing to the database will return many rows. You want to loop through those rows and process them accordingly.

Solution #1

There are a couple of different solutions for looping through rows from a query. One is to work directly with a SELECT statement and use a FOR loop along with it. In the following example, you will see this technique in action:

```
SET SERVEROUTPUT ON;
BEGIN
  FOR emp IN
  (
    SELECT first_name, last_name, email
    FROM employees
    WHERE commission_pct is not NULL
  )
  LOOP
    DBMS_OUTPUT.PUT_LINE(emp.first_name || ' ' || emp.last_name || ' - ' || emp.email);
  END LOOP;
END;
```

Solution #2

Similarly, you can choose to use a FOR loop along with a cursor. Here's an example:

```
SET SERVEROUTPUT ON;
DECLARE
  CURSOR emp_cur IS
  SELECT first_name, last_name, email
    FROM employees
    WHERE commission_pct is not NULL;
```

```
  emp_rec    emp_cur%ROWTYPE;
BEGIN
  FOR emp_rec IN emp_cur LOOP
      DBMS_OUTPUT.PUT_LINE(
          emp_rec.first_name || ' ' || emp_rec.last_name || ' - ' || emp_rec.email);
  END LOOP;
END;
```

Either of the two solutions demonstrated in this recipe will work fine. However, the second technique using the cursor allows for more reusable code and is the more standard technique.

How It Works

The loop that is used in the first solution is also known as an *implicit cursor FOR loop*. No variables need to be explicitly defined in that solution, because the FOR loop will automatically create a record using the results of the query. That record will take the name provided in the FOR variable_name IN clause. That record variable can then be used to reference the different columns that are returned by the query.

As demonstrated in the second solution to this recipe, a cursor is also a very useful way to loop through the results of a query. This technique is also known as an *explicit cursor FOR loop*. This technique is very similar to looping through the results of an explicitly listed query.

Neither solution requires you to explicitly open and close a cursor. In both cases, the opening and closing is done on your behalf by the FOR loop processing.

As you can see, the FOR loop with the SELECT query in the first example is a bit more concise, and there are fewer lines of code. The first example also contains no declarations. In the second example, with the cursor, there are two declarations that account for more lines of code. However, using the cursor is a standard technique that provides for more reusable code. For instance, you can elect to use the cursor any number of times, and you'll need to write the query only once when declaring the cursor. On the contrary, if you wanted to reuse the query in the first example, then you would have to rewrite it, and having to write the same query multiple times opens the door to errors and inconsistencies. We recommend Solution #2.

2-7. Obtaining Environment and Session Information

Problem

You want to obtain environment and session information such as the name and IP address of the current user so that the values can be stored into local variables for logging purposes.

Solution

Make use of the SYS_CONTEXT built-in function to query the database for the user's information. Once you have obtained the information, then store it into a local variable. At that point, you can do whatever you'd like with it, such as save it in a logging table. The following code block demonstrates this technique:

```
<<obtain_user_info>>
DECLARE
  username      varchar2(100);
  ip_address    varchar2(100);
```

```
BEGIN
  SELECT SYS_CONTEXT('USERENV','SESSION_USER'), SYS_CONTEXT('USERENV','IP_ADDRESS')
  INTO username, ip_address
  FROM DUAL;

  DBMS_OUTPUT.PUT_LINE('The connected user is: ' || username || ', and the IP address↵
  is ' ||
                                                    ip_address);
END;
```

Once this code block has been run, then the user's information should be stored into the local variables that have been declared within it.

How It Works

You can use the SYS_CONTEXT function to obtain important information regarding the current user's environment, among other things. It is oftentimes used for auditing purposes so that a particular code block can grab important information about the connected user such as you've seen in the solution to this recipe. The SYS_CONTEXT function allows you to define a namespace and then place parameters within it so that they can be retrieved for use at a later time. The general syntax for the use of SYS_CONTEXT is as follows:

```
SYS_CONTEXT('namespace','parameter'[,length])
```

A namespace can be any valid SQL identifier, and it must be created using the CREATE_CONTEXT statement. The parameter must be a string or evaluate to a string, and it must be set using the DBMS_SESSION.SET_CONTEXT procedure. The call to SYS_CONTEXT with a valid namespace and parameter will result in the return of a value that has a VARCHAR2 datatype. The default maximum length of the returned value is 256 bytes. However, this default maximum length can be overridden by specifying the length when calling SYS_CONTEXT. The length is an optional parameter. The range of values for the length is 1 to 4000, and if you specify an invalid value, then the default of 256 will be used.

The USERENV namespace is automatically available for use because it is a built-in namespace provided by Oracle. The USERENV namespace contains session information for the current user. Table 2-1 lists the parameters that are available to use with the USERENV namespace.

Table 2-1. USERENV Parameter Listing

Parameter	Description
ACTION	Identifies the position in the application name.
AUDITED_CURSORID	Returns the cursor ID of the SQL that triggered the audit.
AUTHENTICATED_DATA	Returns the data being used to authenticate the user.
AUTHENTICATION_TYPE	Identifies how the user was authenticated.

Parameter	Description
BG_JOB_ID	If an Oracle Database background process was used to establish the connection, then this returns the job ID of the current session. If no background process was established, then NULL is returned.
CLIENT_IDENTIFIER	Returns identifier that is set by the application.
CLIENT_INFO	Returns up to 64 bytes of user session information that can be stored by an application using the DBMS_APPLICATION_INFO package.
CURRENT_SCHEMA	Returns the current session's default schema.
CURRENT_SCHEMAID	Returns the current schema's identifier.
CURRENT_SQL	Returns the first 4KB of the triggering SQL.
DB_DOMAIN	Returns the value specified in the DB_DOMAIN parameter.
DB_NAME	Returns the value specified in the DB_NAME parameter.
DB_UNIQUE_NAME	Returns the value specified in the DB_UNIQUE_NAME parameter.
ENTRYID	Returns the current audit entry number.
EXTERNAL_NAME	Returns the external name of the database user.
FG_JOB_ID	If an Oracle Database foreground process was used to establish the connection, then this returns the job ID of the current session. If no foreground process was established, then NULL is returned.
GLOBAL_CONTEXT_MEMORY	Returns the number being used by the globally accessed context in the System Global Area.
HOST	Returns the host name of the machine from which the client has connected.
INSTANCE	Returns the instance ID number of the current instance.
IP_ADDRESS	Returns the IP address of the machine from which the client has connected.
ISDBA	Returns TRUE if the user was authenticated as a DBA.
LANG	Returns the ISO abbreviation of the language name.
LANGUAGE	Returns the language and territory used by the session, along with the character set.

Parameter	Description
MODULE	Returns the application name. This name has to be set via the DBMS_APPLICATION_INFO package.
NETWORK_PROTOCOL	Returns the network protocol being used for communication.
NLS_CALENDAR	Returns the current calendar of the current session.
NLS_CURRENCY	Returns the currency of the current session.
NLS_DATE_FORMAT	Returns the date format for the session.
NLS_DATE_LANGUAGE	Returns the language being used for expressing dates.
NLS_SORT	Returns the BINARY or linguistic sort basis.
NLS_TERRITORY	Returns the territory of the current session.
OS_USER	Returns the operating system user name of the client that initiated the session.
PROXY_USER	Returns the name of the database that opened the current session on behalf of SESSION_USER.
PROXY_USERID	Returns the identifier of the database user who opened the current session on behalf of the SESSION_USER.
SERVICE_NAME	Returns the name of the service to which a given session is connected.
SESSION_USER	Returns the database user name through which the current user is authenticated.
SESSION_USERID	Returns the identifier of the database user name by which the current user is authenticated.
SESSIONID	Returns the auditing session identifier.
STATEMENTID	Returns the auditing statement identifier.
TERMINAL	Returns the operating system identifier for the client of the current session.

When SYS_CONTEXT is used within any query, it is most commonly issued against the DUAL table. The DUAL table is installed along with the data dictionary when the Oracle Database is created. This table is really a dummy table that contains one column that is appropriately named DUMMY. This column contains the value X.

```
SQL> desc dual;
 Name        Null?    Type
 --------------------------------------- -------- ----------------------------
 DUMMY                VARCHAR2(1)
```

Among other things, DUAL is useful for obtaining values from the database when no actual table is needed. Our solution case is such a situation.

2-8. Formatting Query Results

Problem

Your boss asks you to print the results from a couple of queries in a nicely formatted manner.

Solution

Use a combination of different built-in formatting functions along with the concatenation operator (||) to create a nice-looking basic report. The RPAD and LPAD functions along with the concatenation operator are used together in the following example that displays a list of employees from a company:

```
DECLARE
   CURSOR emp_cur IS
   SELECT first_name, last_name, phone_number
   FROM employees;

   emp_rec     employees%ROWTYPE;

BEGIN
   FOR emp_rec IN emp_cur LOOP
      IF emp_rec.phone_number IS NOT NULL THEN
         DBMS_OUTPUT.PUT_LINE(RPAD(emp_rec.first_name || ' ' || emp_rec.last_name, 35,'.') ||
                           emp_rec.phone_number);
      ELSE
         DBMS_OUTPUT.PUT_LINE(emp_rec.first_name || ' ' || emp_rec.last_name ||
                              ' does not have a phone number.');
      END IF;
   END LOOP;
END;
```

The following is another variant of the same report, but this time dashes are used instead of using dots to space out the report:

```
DECLARE
   CURSOR emp_cur IS
   SELECT first_name, last_name, phone_number
   FROM employees;

   emp_rec     employees%ROWTYPE;

BEGIN
   FOR emp_rec IN emp_cur LOOP
```

```
    IF emp_rec.phone_number IS NOT NULL THEN
       -- CHECK FOR INTERNATIONAL PHONE NUMBERS
       IF length(emp_rec.phone_number) > 12 THEN
          DBMS_OUTPUT.PUT_LINE(RPAD(emp_rec.first_name || ' ' || emp_rec.last_name, 20)||
                          ' - ' || LPAD(emp_rec.phone_number,18));
       ELSE
          DBMS_OUTPUT.PUT_LINE(RPAD(emp_rec.first_name || ' ' || emp_rec.last_name, 20)||
                          ' - ' || LPAD(emp_rec.phone_number,12));
       END IF;
    ELSE
          DBMS_OUTPUT.PUT_LINE(emp_rec.first_name || ' ' || emp_rec.last_name ||
                          ' does not have a phone number.');
    END IF;
  END LOOP;
END;
```

How It Works

The RPAD and LPAD functions are used to return the data in a formatted manner. The RPAD function takes a string of text and pads it on the right by the number of spaces provided by the second parameter. The syntax for the RPAD function is as follows:

```
RPAD(input_text, n, character)
```

In this syntax, *n* is the number of spaces used to pad. Similarly, the LPAD function pads on the left of the provided string. The syntax is exactly the same as RPAD; the only difference is the direction of the padding. The combination of these two functions, along with the concatenation operator (||), provides for some excellent formatting options.

It is important to look at the data being returned before you try to format it, especially to consider what formatting options will look best when generating output for presentation. In the case of the examples in this recipe, the latter example would be the most reasonable choice of formatting for the data being returned, since the phone number includes dots in it. The first example uses dots to space out the report, so too many dots may make the output difficult to read. Know your data, and then choose the appropriate PL/SQL built-ins to format accordingly.

■ **Note** When using DBMS_OUTPUT to display data, please be sure to pay attention to the size of the buffer. You can set the buffer size from 2,000 to 1,000,000 bytes by passing the size you desire to the DBMS_OUTPUT.ENABLE procedure. If you attempt to display content over this size limit, then Oracle will raise an exception.

Oracle provides a number of built-in functions to use when formatting strings. Two others that are especially useful are LTRIM(<string>) and RTRIM(<string>). These remove leading and trailing spaces, respectively. See your *Oracle SQL Reference* manual for a complete list of available string functions.

2-9. Updating Rows Returned by a Query

Problem

You've queried the database and retrieved a row into a variable. You want to update some values contained in the row and commit them to the database.

Solution

First, retrieve the database row that you want to update. Second, update the values in the row that need to be changed, and then issue an UPDATE statement to modify the database with the updated values. In the following example, a procedure is created that queries a table of employees for a particular employee. The resulting employee's department ID is then updated with the new one unless the employee is already a member of the given department.

```
CREATE OR REPLACE PROCEDURE change_emp_dept(emp_id   IN   NUMBER,
                                            dept_id  IN   NUMBER) AS
  emp_row            employees%ROWTYPE;
  dept               departments.department_name%TYPE;
  rec_count          number := 0;
BEGIN

  SELECT count(*)
  INTO rec_count
  FROM employees
  WHERE employee_id = emp_id;

  IF rec_count = 1 THEN
     SELECT *
     INTO emp_row
     FROM employees
     WHERE employee_id = emp_id;

    IF emp_row.department_id != dept_id THEN

        emp_row.department_id := dept_id;

        UPDATE employees SET ROW = emp_row
        WHERE employee_id = emp_id;

        SELECT department_name
        INTO dept
        from departments
        WHERE department_id = dept_id;

        DBMS_OUTPUT.PUT_LINE('The employee ' || emp_row.first_name || ' ' ||
                         emp_row.last_name  || ' is now in department: ' || dept);
    ELSE
        DBMS_OUTPUT.PUT_LINE('The employee is already in that department...no change');
    END IF;
  ELSIF rec_count > 1 THEN
```

31

```
      DBMS_OUTPUT.PUT_LINE('The employee ID you entered is not unique');
    ELSE
      DBMS_OUTPUT.PUT_LINE('No employee records match the given employee ID');
    END IF;
EXCEPTION
    WHEN NO_DATA_FOUND THEN
      DBMS_OUTPUT.PUT_LINE('Invalid employee or department ID, try again');
    WHEN OTHERS THEN
      DBMS_OUTPUT.PUT_LINE('Unsuccessful change, please check ID numbers and try again');
END;
```

As you can see, the example queries the database into a record declared using the %ROWTYPE attribute. The value that needs to be updated is then modified using the data contained in the record. Lastly, using the SET ROW clause updates the table with the modified record.

How It Works

As you've seen in the solution to the recipe, it is possible to update the values of a row returned by a query using the UPDATE...SET ROW syntax. In many cases, using a single UPDATE statement can solve this type of transaction. However, in some scenarios where you need to evaluate the current value of a particular column, then this solution is the correct choice.

Using the UPDATE ROW statement, you can update entire database rows with a single variable of either the %ROWTYPE or RECORD type. The UPDATE statement also allows you to return values after the update by adding the RETURNING clause to the end of the statement followed by the column names to return and the variables that will receive their values. Take a look at this next example:

```
DECLARE
  first                 employees.first_name%TYPE;
  last                  employees.last_name%TYPE;
  new_salary            employees.salary%TYPE;
BEGIN

  UPDATE employees
  SET salary = salary + (salary * .03)
  WHERE employee_id = 100
  RETURNING first_name, last_name,salary INTO first, last, new_salary;

  DBMS_OUTPUT.PUT_LINE('The employee ' || first || ' ' || last  || ' now has a salary of:
  ' || new_salary);
END;
```

As you can see, the example outputs the new values that are the result of the update statement. Using the RETURNING clause saves a step in that you are not required to requery the table after the update in order to display the updated results.

2-10. Updating Rows Returned by a Cursor

Problem

You've created a cursor to use for querying your data. You want to loop through the results using a cursor for loop and update the data as needed.

Solution

Use the WHERE_CURRENT_OF clause within your loop to update the current data row in the iteration. In the following example, the EMPLOYEES table is queried for all employees in a particular department. The results of the query are then iterated using a FOR loop, and the salary is increased for each employee record that is returned.

```
DECLARE
  CURSOR emp_sal_cur IS
  SELECT *
  FROM employees
  WHERE department_id = 60
  FOR UPDATE;

  emp_sal_rec   emp_sal_cur%ROWTYPE;

BEGIN
    FOR emp_sal_rec IN emp_sal_cur LOOP
      DBMS_OUTPUT.PUT_LINE('Old Salary: ' || emp_sal_rec.last_name ||
                  ' - ' || emp_sal_rec.salary);

      UPDATE employees
      SET salary = salary + (salary * .025)
      WHERE CURRENT OF emp_sal_cur;

    END LOOP;

    -- Display the updated salaries
    FOR emp_sal_rec IN emp_sal_cur LOOP
      DBMS_OUTPUT.PUT_LINE('New Salary: ' || emp_sal_rec.last_name ||
                  ' - ' || emp_sal_rec.salary);
    END LOOP;
END;
```

An update on the EMPLOYEES table occurs with each iteration of the loop. The second loop in this example simply displays the new salary result for each employee that was returned by the cursor query.

How It Works

Updating values when iterating a cursor can be handy, especially when working with a number of rows. There is one main difference between a cursor that allows updating and one that does not. That difference is the addition of the FOR UPDATE clause in the cursor declaration. By using the FOR UPDATE clause of the SELECT statement, you are causing the database to lock the rows that have been read by the query. This lock is to ensure that nobody else can modify the rows while you are working with them. The lock creates a read-only block on the table rows so that if someone else attempts to modify them while you have them locked, then they will have to wait until you have performed either a COMMIT or a ROLLBACK.

The FOR UPDATE clause has an optional NOWAIT keyword. By including this keyword, you will ensure that your query does not block your transaction if someone else already has the rows that you are querying blocked. The NOWAIT keyword tells Oracle not to wait if the requested rows are already locked, and control is immediately passed back to your program so that it can continue to run. If the NOWAIT keyword is omitted and the rows are already locked, then your program will stop and wait until the lock has been released.

You can use the cursor with any style of loop, as you've seen in previous recipes. No matter which type of loop you choose, the UPDATE must be coded using the WHERE CURRENT OF clause to update the current row in the cursor iteration. You will need to be sure to commit the changes after this block has been run, and in many circumstances the COMMIT statement can be coded into this block once it has been tested and verified to work correctly. As with any UPDATE statement, if you fail to COMMIT your changes, then the UPDATE will not save any changes to the database, and the updated data will be visible to your schema only until you disconnect. Issuing a COMMIT after your UPDATE statements have been issued is also a good practice in this case because it will release the lock on the rows you had queried via the cursor so that someone else can update them if needed. If you determine the data that was updated by the code block is incorrect, then a ROLLBACK will also release the lock.

2-11. Deleting Rows Returned by a Cursor

Problem

There are a series of database rows that you'd like to delete. You've created a cursor FOR LOOP, and you want to delete some or all rows that have been queried with the cursor.

Solution

Use a DELETE statement within a FOR loop to delete the rows that are retrieved by the cursor. If you create a cursor using the FOR UPDATE clause, then you will be able to use the WHERE CURRENT OF clause along with the DELETE statement to eliminate the current row within each iteration of the cursor. The following example shows how this can be done to remove all job history for a given department ID:

```
CREATE OR REPLACE PROCEDURE remove_job_history(dept_id IN NUMBER) AS
  CURSOR job_history_cur IS
  SELECT *
  FROM job_history
  WHERE department_id = dept_id
  FOR UPDATE;

  job_history_rec  job_history_cur%ROWTYPE;

BEGIN

    FOR job_history_rec IN job_history_cur LOOP

      DELETE FROM job_history
      WHERE CURRENT OF job_history_cur;
```

```
        DBMS_OUTPUT.PUT_LINE('Job history removed for department ' ||
                    dept_id);
    END LOOP;
END;
```

Using this technique, the job history for the department with the given ID will be removed from the JOB_HISTORY table.

How It Works

Much like updating rows using a cursor, the deletion of rows uses the WHERE CURRENT OF clause within the DELETE statement to remove each row. The cursor query must contain the FOR UPDATE clause in order to lock the rows that you are reading until a COMMIT or ROLLBACK has been issued. As mentioned in the previous recipe, the NOWAIT keyword is optional, and it can be used to allow control to be immediately returned to your program if someone else already has locks on the rows that you are interested in updating.

In each iteration of the loop, the DELETE statement is used along with the WHERE CURRENT OF clause to remove the current cursor record from the database. Once the loop has been completed, then all the rows that had been queried via the cursor should have been deleted. This technique is especially useful if you are going to be performing some further processing on each of the records and then deleting them. One such case would be if you wanted to write each of the records to a history table prior to deleting them. In any case, the cursor FOR loop deletion technique is a great way to remove rows from the database and work with the data along the way.

2-12. Performing a Transaction

Problem

You need to complete a series of INSERT or UPDATE statements in order to process a complete transaction. In doing so, you need to ensure that if one of the statements fails, that all of the statements are canceled so that the transaction is not partially processed.

Solution

Use the transaction control mechanisms that are part of PL/SQL, as well as SQL itself, in order to control your transactions. When all your statements have been completed successfully, issue a COMMIT to make them final. On the other hand, if one of the statements does not complete successfully, then perform a ROLLBACK to undo all the other changes that have been made and bring the database back to the state that it was in prior to the transaction occurring.

In the following example, the code block entails the body of a script that is to be executed in order to create a new department and add some employees to it. The department change involves an INSERT and UPDATE statement to complete.

```
DECLARE

    -- Query all programmers who make more than 4000
    -- as they will be moved to the new 'Web Development' department
    CURSOR new_dept_cur IS
    SELECT *
    FROM employees
```

```
       WHERE job_id = 'IT_PROG'
       AND salary > 4000
       FOR UPDATE;

    new_dept_rec          new_dept_cur%ROWTYPE;
    current_department    departments.department_id%TYPE;

BEGIN

    -- Create a new department
    INSERT INTO departments values(
      DEPARTMENTS_SEQ.nextval,       -- Department ID (sequence value)
      'Web Development',             -- Department Title
      103                                    -- Manager ID
      1700);                                 -- Location ID

    -- Obtain the current department ID…the new department ID
    SELECT DEPARTMENTS_SEQ.currval
    INTO current_department
    FROM DUAL;

    -- Assign all employees to the new department
    FOR new_dept_rec IN new_dept_cur LOOP

      UPDATE employees
      SET department_id = current_department
      WHERE CURRENT OF new_dept_cur;

    END LOOP;

    COMMIT;
    DBMS_OUTPUT.PUT_LINE('The transaction has been successfully completed.');

END;
```

As you can see, a transaction was performed in this block of code. It is important to roll back changes if errors occur along the way so that the transaction is not partially completed.

How It Works

Transaction control is built into the Oracle Database. Any database changes that are made within a code block are visible to the current session only until a COMMIT has been made. The changes that have been made by the statements can be rolled back via the ROLLBACK command up until the point that a COMMIT is issued. Oracle uses table and row locks to ensure that data that has been updated in one session cannot be seen in another session until a COMMIT occurs.

A transaction is started when the first statement after the last COMMIT or ROLLBACK is processed or when a session is created. It ends when a COMMIT or ROLLBACK occurs. A transaction is not bound to a single code block, and any code block may contain one or more transactions. Oracle provides a SAVEPOINT command, which places a marker at the current database state so as to allow you to roll back to that point in time in a transaction. Oracle Database automatically issues a SAVEPOINT prior to processing the first statement in any transaction.

As a rule of thumb, it is always a good idea to have exception handling in place in case an exception occurs. However, if an unhandled exception occurs, then the database will roll back the statement that caused the exception, not the entire transaction. Therefore, it is up to the program to handle exceptions and issue the ROLLBACK command if the entire transaction should be undone. If a database crashes and goes down during a transaction, then when the database is restarted, all uncommitted statements are rolled back. All transactions are completed when a COMMIT or ROLLBACK is issued.

2-13. Ensuring That Multiple Queries "See" the Same Data

Problem

You are issuing a set of queries against the database, and you need to ensure that none of the table rows change throughout the course of the queries being made.

Solution

Set up a read-only transaction in which the current transaction will see the data only as an unchanged snapshot in time. To do so, use the SET TRANSACTION statement to begin a read-only transaction and establish a snapshot of the data so it will be consistent and unchanged from all other updates being made. For instance, the following example displays a block that sets up read-only queries against the database for dollar values from a bank account:

```
DECLARE
    daily_atm_total    NUMBER(12,2);
    weekly_atm_total   NUMBER(12,2);
BEGIN
    COMMIT; -- ends previous transaction
    SET TRANSACTION READ ONLY NAME 'ATM Weekly Summary';
    SELECT SUM (wd_amt) INTO daily_atm_total FROM atm_withdrawals
      WHERE to_char(wd_date, 'MM-DD-YYYY') = to_char(SYSDATE, 'MM-DD-YYYY');
    SELECT SUM (weekly_total) INTO weekly_atm_total FROM atm_withdrawals
      WHERE to_char(wd_date, 'MM-DD-YYYY') = to_char(SYSDATE - 7, 'MM-DD-YYYY');
    DBMS_OUTPUT.PUT_LINE(daily_atm_total || ' - ' || weekly_atm_total);
    COMMIT; -- ends read-only transaction

END;
```

Querying the database using read-only transactions will ensure that someone will see the correct values in a situation such as the one depicted in this example.

How It Works

Oftentimes there are situations when you need to ensure that the data being queried throughout a transaction's life cycle is unchanged by other users' updates. The classic case is when someone goes to withdraw money from the bank and their spouse is at an ATM machine depositing into the account at the same time. If read consistency were not in place, the individual may view their account balance and see that there was plenty of money to withdraw, and then they'd go to take the money out and receive an error because the spouse had canceled the deposit instead. A read-only transaction allows for read consistency until a COMMIT has been issued. If the spouse had confirmed the deposit, then the next query on the account would reflect the additional funds (assuming that the bank were to release them to the account in real time).

Situations such as these require that you provide an environment that is essentially isolated from the outside world. You can use the SET TRANSACTION command to start a read-only transaction, set an isolation level, and assign the current transaction to a rollback segment. The SET TRANSACTION statement must be the first statement in a read-only transaction, and it can appear only once in the transaction. Note that there are some statement restrictions when using a read-only transaction. Only SELECT INTO, OPEN, FETCH, CLOSE, LOCK TABLE, COMMIT, and ROLLBACK statements can be used; other statements are not allowed.

2-14. Executing One Transaction from Within Another

Problem

You are executing a transaction, and you are faced with the need to suspend your current work, issue a completely separate transaction, and then pick up your current work. For example, say you want to log entries into a log table. The log entries should be persisted separately from the current transaction such that if the transaction fails or is rolled back, the log entries will still be completed.

Solution

Start an autonomous transaction to make the log entry. This will ensure that the log entry is performed separately from the current transaction. In the following example, an employee is deleted from the EMPLOYEES table. Hence, a job is ended, and the job history must be recorded into the JOB_HISTORY table. In the case that something fails within the transaction, the log entry into the JOB_HISTORY table must be intact. This log entry cannot be rolled back because it is performed using an autonomous transaction.

The code to encapsulate the autonomous transaction needs to be placed into a named block that can be called when the logging needs to be performed. The following piece of code creates a PL/SQL procedure that performs the log entry using an autonomous transaction. (You will learn more about procedures in Chapter 4.) Specifically notice the declaration of PRAGMA AUTONOMOUS_TRANSACTION. That pragma specifies that the procedure executes as a separate transaction, independent of any calling transaction.

```
CREATE OR REPLACE PROCEDURE log_job_history (emp_id IN
employees.employee_id%TYPE,
Job_id IN jobs.job_id%TYPE,
Department_id IN employees.department_id%TYPE,
 employee_start    IN DATE) AS
    PRAGMA AUTONOMOUS_TRANSACTION;
BEGIN
    INSERT INTO job_history
    VALUES (emp_id,
            employee_start,
            sysdate,
            job_id,
            department_id);
    COMMIT;
END;
```

The LOG_JOB_HISTORY procedure inserts an entry into the log table separately from the transaction that is taking place in the calling code block. The following code performs the job termination, and it calls the log_substitution procedure to record the history:

```
DECLARE
   CURSOR dept_removal_cur IS
   SELECT *
   FROM employees
   WHERE department_id = 10
   FOR UPDATE;

   dept_removal_rec            dept_removal_cur%ROWTYPE;

BEGIN
   -- Delete all employees from the database who reside in department 10
   FOR dept_removal_rec IN dept_removal_cur LOOP
       DBMS_OUTPUT.PUT_LINE('DELETING RECORD NOW');
    DELETE FROM employees
    WHERE CURRENT OF dept_removal_cur;

    -- Log the termination
    log_job_history(dept_removal_rec.employee_id,
                        dept_removal_rec.job_id,
                        dept_removal_rec.department_id,
                        dept_removal_rec.hire_date);
   END LOOP;

   DBMS_OUTPUT.PUT_LINE('The transaction has been successfully completed.');

EXCEPTION
   -- Handles all errors
   WHEN NO_DATA_FOUND THEN
     DBMS_OUTPUT.PUT_LINE
       ('The transaction has been rolled back due to errors, please try again.');

     ROLLBACK;

END;
```

If this code block is executed and then rolled back, the entry into the job history table remains, because it is performed as a separate, autonomous transaction.

How It Works

An autonomous transaction is a transaction that is called by another transaction and that runs separately from the calling transaction. Autonomous transactions commit or roll back without affecting the calling transaction. They also have the full functionality of regular transactions; they merely run separately from the main transaction. They allow parallel activity to occur. Even if the main transaction fails or is rolled back, the autonomous transaction can be committed or rolled back independently of any other transactions in progress.

An autonomous transaction must be created with a top-level code block, trigger, procedure, function, or stand-alone named piece of code. In the solution, you saw that a procedure was created to run as an autonomous transaction. That is because it is not possible to create an autonomous transaction within a nested code block. To name a transaction as autonomous, you must place the statement PRAGMA AUTONOMOUS_TRANSACTION within the declaration section of a block encompassing the transaction. To end the transaction, perform a COMMIT or ROLLBACK.

2-15. Finding and Removing Duplicate Table Rows

Problem

You have found that for some reason your database contains a table that has duplicate records. You are working with a database that unfortunately does not use primary key values, so you must manually enforce data integrity. You need a way to remove the duplicate records. However, any query you write to remove one record will also remove its duplicate.

Solution

The solution to this issue involves two steps. First you need to query the database to find all duplicate rows, and then you need to run a statement to delete one of each duplicate record that is found.

The following code block queries the EMPLOYEES table for duplicate rows. When a duplicate is found, it is returned along with a count of duplicates found.

```
<<duplicate_emp_qry>>
DECLARE
  CURSOR emp_cur IS
  SELECT *
  FROM    employees
  ORDER BY employee_id;

  emp_count        number := 0;
  total_count         number := 0;

BEGIN
  DBMS_OUTPUT.PUT_LINE('You will see each duplicated employee listed more ');
  DBMS_OUTPUT.PUT_LINE('than once in the list below.  This will allow you to ');
  DBMS_OUTPUT.PUT_LINE('review the list and ensure that indeed...there are more ');
  DBMS_OUTPUT.PUT_LINE('than one of these employee records in the table.');

  DBMS_OUTPUT.PUT_LINE('Duplicated Employees: ');

-- Loop through each player in the table
  FOR emp_rec IN  emp_cur LOOP

-- Select the number of records in the table that have the same ID as the current record
    SELECT count(*)
    INTO emp_count
    FROM employees
    WHERE employee_id = emp_rec.employee_id;
```

```
-- If the count is greater than one then a duplicate has been found, so print it out.
    IF emp_count > 1 THEN
        DBMS_OUTPUT.PUT_LINE(emp_rec.employee_id || ' - ' || emp_rec.first_name ||
                ' ' || emp_rec.last_name || ' - ' || emp_count);
                    total_count := total_count + 1;
    END IF;

  END LOOP;
END;
```

If the table includes a duplicate, then it is printed out as follows:

```
You will see each duplicated employee listed more
than once in the list below.  This will allow you to
review the list and ensure that indeed...there are more
than one of these employees in the table.
Duplicated Employees:
100 - Steven King - 2
100 - Steven King - 2
PL/SQL procedure successfully completed.
```

Next, you need to delete the duplicated rows that have been found. The following DELETE statement will ensure that one of the duplicates is removed:

```
DELETE FROM employees A WHERE ROWID > (
SELECT min(rowid) FROM employees B
WHERE A.employee_id = B.employee_id);
```

How It Works

Usually using primary keys prohibits the entry of duplicate rows into a database table. However, many legacy databases still in use today do not include such constraints. In rare situations, a duplicate key and values are entered into the database that can cause issues when querying data or assigning values. The method shown in the solution for finding duplicate rows is very basic. The solution loops through each record in the table, and during each pass, it queries the table for the number of records found that match the current record's EMPLOYEE_ID. If the number found is greater than one, then you know that you have found a duplicate.

The solution presented here for finding duplicates will work on any table provided that you have a column of data that *should* contain logically unique values. In the example, each record should contain a different EMPLOYEE_ID, so if there is more than one record with the same EMPLOYEE_ID value, then a duplicate is found. If the table you are working with does not contain any unique columns, then you can concatenate a number of columns in order to obtain a unique combination. For instance, if EMPLOYEES did not contain an EMPLOYEE_ID column, then you could concatenate the FIRST_NAME, LAST_NAME, and EMAIL columns to obtain a unique combination. More likely than not, there will not be two employees in the table with the same name and e-mail address.

The second part of the solution involves removing one or more duplicate records from the set. To do so, you have to look at a pseudocolumn known as the ROWID. The ROWID is a pseudocolumn (invisible column) that is found in each table in an Oracle Database that uniquely identifies each row. By comparing these unique ROWID values, you can delete just one of the records, not both. The DELETE statement actually finds the rows that contain the same uniquely identified column(s) and then removes the row with the larger ROWID value.

CHAPTER 3

■ ■ ■

Looping and Logic

Any substantial program always contains some conditional logic or looping. Oftentimes, both looping and logic are combined to make powerful solutions. The recipes in this chapter will show you some examples using basic conditional logic. Once you've mastered the art of conditional logic, then you will learn how to perform all the loop types that are available in PL/SQL. Lastly, you will see some useful examples that put these concepts into action.

For the purposes of this chapter, it is important to note that a condition is any variable or expression that evaluates to a boolean. Conditions can contain one or more variables or expressions, but they must always evaluate to either TRUE, FALSE, or NULL.

3-1. Choosing When to Execute Code

Problem

Your code contains a condition, and you are interested in executing code to perform specific actions if the condition evaluates to TRUE, FALSE, or NULL.

Solution

Use an IF-THEN statement to evaluate an expression (or condition) and determine which code to execute as a result.

The following example depicts a very simple IF-THEN statement that evaluates one variable to see whether it contains a larger value than another variable. If so, then the statements contained within the IF-THEN statement are executed; otherwise, they are ignored.

```
DECLARE
  value_one    NUMBER := &value_one;
  value_two    NUMBER := &value_two;
BEGIN
  IF value_one > value_two THEN
    DBMS_OUTPUT.PUT_LINE('value_one is greater than value_two');
  END IF;
END;
```

As you can see from the example, if value_one is greater than value_two, a line of output will be printed stating so. Otherwise, the IF statement is bypassed, and processing continues.

How It Works

As shown in the solution, the general format for the IF-THEN statement is as follows:

```
IF condition THEN
   Statements to be executed
   ...
END IF;
```

The IF-THEN statement is one of the most frequently used conditional statements. If a given condition evaluates to TRUE, then the code contained within the IF-THEN statement is executed. If the condition evaluates to FALSE or NULL, then the statement is exited. However, it is possible to incorporate a different set of statements if the condition is not satisfied. Please see Recipe 3-2 for an example.

Any number of IF-THEN statements can be nested within one another. The statements within the IF-THEN will be executed if the condition that is specified evaluates to TRUE.

3-2. Choosing Between Two Mutually Exclusive Conditions

Problem

You have two conditions that are mutually exclusive. You want to execute one set of statements if the first condition evaluates to TRUE. Otherwise, if the first condition is FALSE or NULL, then execute a different set of statements.

Solution

Use an IF-ELSE statement to evaluate the condition and execute the statements that correspond to it if the condition evaluates to TRUE. In the following example, a given employee ID is used to query the EMPLOYEES table. If that employee exists, then the employee record will be retrieved. If not found, then a message will be displayed stating that no match was found.

```
DECLARE
  employee              employees%ROWTYPE;
  emp_count             number := 0;
BEGIN
  SELECT count(*)
  INTO emp_count
  FROM employees
  WHERE employee_id = 100;

  IF emp_count > 0  THEN
    SELECT *
    INTO employee
    FROM employees
    WHERE employee_id = 100;

    IF employee.manager_id IS NOT NULL THEN
      DBMS_OUTPUT.PUT_LINE(employee.first_name || ' ' || employee.last_name ||
          ' has an assigned manager.');
    ELSE
      DBMS_OUTPUT.PUT_LINE(employee.first_name || ' ' || employee.last_name ||
          ' does not have an assigned manager.');
    END IF;
```

```
  ELSE
    DBMS_OUTPUT.PUT_LINE('The given employee ID does not match any records, '||
                ' please try again');
  END IF;
EXCEPTION
  WHEN NO_DATA_FOUND THEN
    DBMS_OUTPUT.PUT_LINE('Try another employee ID.');
END;
```

Here are the results:

```
Steven King does not have an assigned manager.

PL/SQL procedure successfully completed.
```

In the real world, the employee ID would not be hard-coded into the example. However, this example provides a good scenario for evaluating mutually exclusive conditions and also nesting IF statements.

How It Works

The IF-ELSE statement syntax is basically the same as the IF-THEN syntax, except that a different set of statements is executed in the ELSE clause when the condition evaluates to FALSE or NULL. Therefore, if the first condition is FALSE or NULL, then the control automatically drops down into the statements contained within the ELSE clause and executes them.

3-3. Evaluating Multiple Mutually Exclusive Conditions

Problem

Your application has multiple conditions to evaluate, and each of them is mutually exclusive. If one of the conditions evaluates to FALSE, you'd like to evaluate the next one. You want that process to continue until there are no more conditions.

Two solutions are possible: one using IF and the other using CASE.

Solution #1

Use an IF-ELSIF-ELSE statement to perform an evaluation of all mutually exclusive conditions. The following example is a SQL*Plus script that queries how many countries are in a specified region.

■ **Note** The following example uses SQL*Plus substitution variables. Be sure to execute the example from an environment such as SQL*Plus or SQL Developer that recognizes such variables.

If the region that is typed as input when the following example executes matches any of the regions specified by the conditions in the IF statement, then subsequent statements are executed. However, a default message is displayed if the input does not match any region.

```
DECLARE
  Region                regions.region_name%TYPE := '&region';
  country_count         number := 0;
BEGIN

  IF upper(region) = 'EUROPE' THEN
    SELECT count(*)
    INTO country_count
    FROM countries
    WHERE region_id = 1;

    DBMS_OUTPUT.PUT_LINE('There are ' || country_count || ' countries in ' ||
            'the Europe region.');
  ELSIF upper(region) = 'AMERICAS' THEN
    SELECT count(*)
    INTO country_count
    FROM countries
    WHERE region_id = 2;

    DBMS_OUTPUT.PUT_LINE('There are ' || country_count || ' countries in ' ||
            'the Americas region.');
  ELSIF upper(region) = 'ASIA' THEN
    SELECT count(*)
    INTO country_count
    FROM countries
    WHERE region_id = 3;

    DBMS_OUTPUT.PUT_LINE('There are ' || country_count || ' countries in ' ||
        'the Asia region.');
  ELSIF upper(region) = 'MIDDLE EAST AND AFRICA' THEN
    SELECT count(*)
    INTO country_count
    FROM countries
    WHERE region_id = 4;

    DBMS_OUTPUT.PUT_LINE('There are ' || country_count || ' countries in ' ||
        'the Middle East and Africa region.');
  ELSE
    DBMS_OUTPUT.PUT_LINE('You have entered an invaid region, please try again');
  END IF;

END;
```

Solution #2

You can use the searched CASE statement to evaluate a boolean expression to determine which statements to execute among multiple, mutually exclusive conditions. The next example is a SQL*Plus script that performs the same tasks as Solution #1 but this time using a searched CASE statement:

```
DECLARE
  region                  regions.region_name%TYPE := '&region';
  country_count           number := 0;
BEGIN

  CASE
    WHEN upper(region) = 'EUROPE' THEN
        SELECT count(*)
        INTO country_count
        FROM countries
        WHERE region_id = 1;

        DBMS_OUTPUT.PUT_LINE('There are ' || country_count || ' countries in ' ||
                'the Europe region.');
    WHEN upper(region) = 'AMERICAS' THEN
        SELECT count(*)
        INTO country_count
        FROM countries
        WHERE region_id = 2;

        DBMS_OUTPUT.PUT_LINE('There are ' || country_count || ' countries in ' ||
                'the Americas region.');
    WHEN upper(region) = 'ASIA' THEN
        SELECT count(*)
        INTO country_count
        FROM countries
        WHERE region_id = 3;

        DBMS_OUTPUT.PUT_LINE('There are ' || country_count || ' countries in ' ||
                'the Asia region.');
    WHEN upper(region) = 'MIDDLE EAST AND AFRICA' THEN
        SELECT count(*)
        INTO country_count
        FROM countries
        WHERE region_id = 4;

        DBMS_OUTPUT.PUT_LINE('There are ' || country_count || ' countries in ' ||
                'the Middle East and Africa region.');
    ELSE
      DBMS_OUTPUT.PUT_LINE('You have entered an invaid region, please try again');
    END CASE;

END;
```

How It Works

IF-ELSIF-ELSE can be used to evaluate any number of conditions. It functions such that if the first condition in the IF-ELSIF-ELSE statement evaluates to TRUE, then the statements within its block are executed, and all others are bypassed. Similarly, if the first condition evaluates to FALSE and the second condition evaluates to TRUE, then the second condition's statements will be executed, others will be ignored, and so on.

Like the `IF-ELSE` statement, you can include an `ELSE` clause that will cause a set of statements to be executed if none of the conditions is met. If you do not include an `ELSE` clause on your `IF` statement and none of the conditions is met, then the entire statement will be completely bypassed.

The second solution to this recipe entails the use of a searched `CASE` statement. Technically, the searched `CASE` has the same functionality of an `IF-ELSIF-ELSE` statement, but it is oftentimes easier to follow. The format for a searched `CASE` statement is as follows:

```
CASE
  WHEN <<boolean_expression>> THEN <<statements>>
[ELSE statements];
```

In this statement, a boolean expression is evaluated, and if the result is `TRUE`, then the statements following `THEN` will be executed. Otherwise, execution will continue to the next `WHEN` clause in the statement. If there are no boolean expressions within the `CASE` statement that evaluate to `TRUE`, then the statements contained within the optional `ELSE` clause are executed.

3-4. Driving from an Expression Having Multiple Outcomes

Problem

You have a single expression that yields multiple outcomes. You are interested in evaluating the expression and performing a different set of statements depending upon the outcome.

Solution

Use a `CASE` statement to evaluate your expression, and decide which set of statements to execute depending upon the outcome. In the following example, a SQL*Plus script accepts a region entry, which is being evaluated to determine the set of statements to be executed. Based upon the value of the region, the corresponding set of statements is executed, and once those statements have been executed, then the control is passed to the statement immediately following the `CASE` statement.

```
DECLARE
  region                  regions.region_name%TYPE := '&region';
  country_count           number := 0;
BEGIN

  CASE upper(region)
    WHEN 'EUROPE' THEN
        SELECT count(*)
        INTO country_count
        FROM countries
        WHERE region_id = 1;

        DBMS_OUTPUT.PUT_LINE('There are ' || country_count || ' countries in ' ||
                'the Europe region.');
    WHEN 'AMERICAS' THEN
        SELECT count(*)
        INTO country_count
        FROM countries
        WHERE region_id = 2;
```

```
        DBMS_OUTPUT.PUT_LINE('There are ' || country_count || ' countries in ' ||
                'the Americas region.');
   WHEN 'ASIA' THEN
        SELECT count(*)
        INTO country_count
        FROM countries
        WHERE region_id = 3;

        DBMS_OUTPUT.PUT_LINE('There are ' || country_count || ' countries in ' ||
                'the Asia region.');
   WHEN 'MIDDLE EAST AND AFRICA' THEN
        SELECT count(*)
        INTO country_count
        FROM countries
        WHERE region_id = 4;

        DBMS_OUTPUT.PUT_LINE('There are ' || country_count || ' countries in ' ||
                'the Middle East and Africa region.');
   ELSE
     DBMS_OUTPUT.PUT_LINE('You have entered an invaid region, please try again');
   END CASE;

END;
```

How It Works

There are two different types of CASE statements that can be used—those being the searched CASE and the simple CASE statement. The solution to this recipe demonstrates the simple CASE. For an example of a searched CASE statement, please see Recipe 3-3.

The simple CASE statement begins with the keyword CASE followed by a single expression called a *selector*. The selector is evaluated one time, and it can evaluate to any PL/SQL type other than BLOB, BFILE, an object type, a record, or a collection type. The selector is followed by a series of WHEN clauses. The WHEN clauses are evaluated sequentially to determine whether the value of the selector equals the result from any of the WHEN clause expressions. If a match is found, then the corresponding WHEN clause is executed.

The CASE statement can include any number of WHEN clauses, and much like an IF statement, it can be followed with a trailing ELSE clause that will be executed if none of the WHEN expressions matches. If the ELSE clause is omitted, a predefined exception will be raised if the CASE statement does not match any of the WHEN clauses. The END CASE keywords end the statement.

3-5. Looping Until a Specified Condition Is Met

Problem

You want to loop through a set of statements until a specified condition evaluates to true.

Solution

Use a simple LOOP statement along with an EXIT clause to define a condition that will end the iteration. The following example shows a simple LOOP that will print out each employee with a department_id equal to 90:

```
DECLARE
  CURSOR emp_cur IS
  SELECT *
  FROM employees
  WHERE department_id = 90;
  emp_rec employees%ROWTYPE;
BEGIN
  OPEN emp_cur;
  LOOP
  FETCH emp_cur into emp_rec;
  IF emp_cur%FOUND THEN
    DBMS_OUTPUT.PUT_LINE(emp_rec.first_name || ' ' || emp_rec.last_name ||
        ' - ' || emp_rec.email);
  ELSE
    EXIT;
   END IF;
  END LOOP;
  CLOSE emp_cur;
END;
```

As you can see from the example, the cursor is opened prior to the start of the loop. Inside the loop, the cursor is fetched into emp_rec, and emp_rec is evaluated to see whether it contains anything using the cursor %FOUND attribute. If emp_cur%FOUND is FALSE, then the loop is exited using the EXIT keyword.

How It Works

The simple LOOP structure is very easy to use for generating a loop in your code. The LOOP keyword is used to start the loop, and the END LOOP keywords are used to terminate it. Every simple loop must contain an EXIT or GOTO statement; otherwise, the loop will become infinite and run indefinitely.

You can use a couple of different styles for the EXIT. When used alone, the EXIT keyword causes a loop to be terminated immediately, and control is passed to the first statement following the loop. You can use the EXIT-WHEN statement to terminate the loop based upon the evaluation of a condition after the WHEN statement. If the condition evaluates to TRUE, then the loop is terminated; otherwise, it will continue.

The following example shows the same LOOP as the example in the solution, but instead of using an IF statement to evaluate the content of emp_rec, the EXIT-WHEN statement is used:

```
DECLARE
  CURSOR emp_cur IS
  SELECT *
  FROM employees
  WHERE department_id = 90;
  emp_rec employees%ROWTYPE;
BEGIN
  OPEN emp_cur;
```

```
  LOOP
     FETCH emp_cur into emp_rec;
     EXIT WHEN emp_cur%NOTFOUND;
     DBMS_OUTPUT.PUT_LINE(emp_rec.first_name || ' ' || emp_rec.last_name ||
        ' - ' || emp_rec.email);
  END LOOP;
  CLOSE emp_cur;
END;
```

You can use a loop to iterate over any number of things including cursors or collections of data. As you will see in some of the coming recipes, different forms of loops work better in different circumstances.

3-6. Iterating Cursor Results Until All Rows Have Been Returned

Problem

You have created a cursor and retrieved a number of rows from the database. As a result, you want to loop through the results and do some processing on them.

Solution

Use a standard FOR loop to iterate through the records. Within each iteration of the loop, process the current record. The following code shows the use of a FOR loop to iterate through the records retrieved from the cursor and display each employee name and e-mail. Each iteration of the loop returns an employee with the job_id of 'ST_MAN', and the loop will continue to execute until the cursor has been exhausted.

```
DECLARE
  CURSOR emp_cur IS
  SELECT *
  FROM employees
  WHERE job_id = 'ST_MAN';
  emp_rec employees%ROWTYPE;
BEGIN
  FOR emp_rec IN emp_cur LOOP
    DBMS_OUTPUT.PUT_LINE(emp_rec.first_name || ' ' || emp_rec.last_name ||
        ' - ' || emp_rec.email);
  END LOOP;
END;
```

Here are the results:

```
Matthew Weiss - MWEISS
Adam Fripp - AFRIPP
Payam Kaufling - PKAUFLIN
Shanta Vollman - SVOLLMAN
Kevin Mourgos - KMOURGOS

PL/SQL procedure successfully completed.
```

As you can see, the employee records that meet the specified criteria are displayed.

How It Works

The FOR...IN loop works by iterating over a collection of data such as a cursor. The loop begins with the FOR keyword followed by a variable that will be used to contain the current value or values from the collection of data you are iterating. In this case, the variable is a record that will contain the current row. Next, the IN collection clause is used to denote the collection of data being iterated. The loop is terminated just like all other PL/SQL loops, using the END LOOP keywords. There is no need to evaluate a condition in a FOR loop because the collection or range that is used to define the loop determines its scope. However, it is possible to use the EXIT keyword to escape from a loop prematurely. For more information regarding the use of EXIT, please see Recipe 3-5.

The benefit of using a FOR loop is decreased lines of code and better readability. Rather than opening the cursor prior to the loop, fetching a row into a record with each iteration, and then closing the cursor after the loop, you simply fetch the row into the record within the LOOP definition itself.

3-7. Iterating Until a Condition Evaluates to FALSE

Problem

You want to iterate over a series of statements until a specified condition no longer evaluates to TRUE.

Solution

Use a WHILE statement to test the condition, and execute the series of statements if the condition evaluates to TRUE; otherwise, skip the statements completely. The following example shows a WHILE statement evaluating the current value of a variable and looping through until the value of the variable reaches ten. Within the loop, this variable is being multiplied by two and printing out its current value.

```
DECLARE
  myValue     NUMBER := 1;
BEGIN
WHILE myValue < 10 LOOP
      DBMS_OUTPUT.PUT_LINE('The current value is: ' || myValue);
      myValue := myValue * 2;
  END LOOP;
END;
```

Here are the results:

```
The current value is: 1
The current value is: 2
The current value is: 4
The current value is: 8

PL/SQL procedure successfully completed.
```

The important thing to note in this example is that the value of myValue is increased with each iteration of the loop as to eventually meet the condition specified in the WHILE loop.

How It Works

The WHILE loop tests a condition at the top of the loop, and if it evaluates to TRUE, then the statements within the loop are executed, and control is returned to the start of the loop where the condition is tested again. If the condition does not evaluate to TRUE, the loop is bypassed, and control goes to the next statement after the END LOOP. If the condition never fails, then an infinite loop is formed, so it is important to ensure that the condition will eventually evaluate to FALSE.

It is important to note that the statements in the loop will never be executed if the condition evaluates to FALSE during the first pass. This situation is different from the simple loop that always iterates at least once because the EXIT condition is usually evaluated elsewhere in the loop.

To ensure that a WHILE loop is always executed at least one time, you must ensure that the condition evaluates to TRUE at least once. One way to do this is to use a flag variable that is evaluated with each iteration of the loop. Set the flag equal to FALSE prior to starting the loop, and then set it to TRUE when a certain condition is met inside the loop. The following pseudocode depicts such a solution:

```
BEGIN
  flag = FALSE;
  WHILE flag = TRUE LOOP
    Perform statements
    flag = Boolean expression;
  END LOOP;
END;
```

As mentioned previously, the boolean expression that is assigned to the flag in this case must eventually evaluate to FALSE; otherwise, an infinite loop will occur.

3-8. Bypassing the Current Loop Iteration

Problem

If a specified conditional statement evaluates to TRUE, you want to terminate the current loop iteration of the loop early and start the next iteration immediately.

Solution

Use a CONTINUE statement along with a condition to end the current iteration.

In the following example, a loop is used to iterate through the records in the employees table. The primary reason for the loop is to print out a list of employees who receive a salary greater than 15,000. If an employee does not receive more than 15,000, then nothing is printed out, and the loop continues to the next iteration.

```
DECLARE
  CURSOR emp_cur is
  SELECT *
  FROM employees;

  emp_rec      emp_cur%ROWTYPE;

BEGIN
  DBMS_OUTPUT.PUT_LINE('Employees with salary > 15000: ');
```

```
   OPEN emp_cur;
   LOOP
     FETCH emp_cur INTO emp_rec;
     EXIT WHEN emp_cur%NOTFOUND;
     IF emp_rec.salary < 15000 THEN
       CONTINUE;
     ELSE
       DBMS_OUTPUT.PUT_LINE('Employee: ' || emp_rec.first_name || ' ' ||
             emp_rec.last_name);
     END IF;

   END LOOP;
   CLOSE emp_cur;

END;
```

Here are some sample results:

```
Employees with salary > 15000:
Employee: Steven King
Employee: Neena Kochhar
Employee: Lex De Haan

PL/SQL procedure successfully completed.
```

How It Works

You can use the CONTINUE statement in any loop to unconditionally halt execution of the current iteration of the loop and move to the next. As shown in the solution, the CONTINUE statement is usually encompassed within some conditional statement so that it is invoked only when that certain condition is met.

You can use the CONTINUE statement along with a label in order to jump to a specified point in the program. Rather than merely using CONTINUE to bypass the current loop iteration, specifying a label will allow you to resume programming in an outer loop. For more information regarding the use of the CONTINUE statement along with labels in nested loops, please see Recipe 3-13.

As an alternative to specifying CONTINUE from within an IF statement, you can choose to write a CONTINUE WHEN statement. For example, the following two approaches yield identical results:

```
   IF team_rec.total_points < 10 THEN
   CONTINUE;
```

or

```
   CONTINUE WHEN rec.total_points < 10;
```

Using the CONTINUE WHEN format, the loop will stop its current iteration if the condition in the WHEN clause is met. Otherwise, the iteration will ignore the statement altogether.

3-9. Iterating a Fixed Number of Times

Problem

You are interested in executing the contents of a loop a specified number of times. For example, you are interested in executing a loop ten times, and you need to number each line of output in the range by the current loop index.

Solution

Write a FOR loop. Use a variable to store the current index of the loop while looping through a range of numbers from one to ten in ascending order. The following lines of code will iterate ten times through a loop and print out the current index in each pass:

```
BEGIN
  FOR idx IN 1..10 LOOP
    DBMS_OUTPUT.PUT_LINE('The current index is: ' || idx);
  END LOOP;
END;
```

Here is the result:

```
The current index is: 1
The current index is: 2
The current index is: 3
The current index is: 4
The current index is: 5
The current index is: 6
The current index is: 7
The current index is: 8
The current index is: 9
The current index is: 10

PL/SQL procedure successfully completed.
```

How It Works

The FOR loop will increment by one through the given range for each iteration until it reaches the end. The loop is opened using the keyword FOR, followed by a variable that will be used as the index for the loop. Following the index variable is the IN keyword, which is used to signify that the index variable should increment one by one through the given range, which is listed after the IN keyword. The loop is terminated using the END LOOP keywords.

Each statement contained within the loop is executed once for each iteration of the loop. The index variable can be used within the loop, but it cannot be changed. As shown in the solution, you may use the index for printing purposes, and it is oftentimes used in calculations as well.

3-10. Iterating Backward Through a Range

Problem

You are working with a range of numbers and want to iterate backward through the range, from the upper bound to the lower bound.

Solution

Use a FOR loop along with the REVERSE keyword to iterate backward through the range. In this example, the same solution that was shown in Recipe 3-9 has been modified to iterate backward through the range of numbers.

```
BEGIN
  FOR idx IN REVERSE 1..10 LOOP
    DBMS_OUTPUT.PUT_LINE('The current index is: ' || idx);
  END LOOP;
END;
```

Here is the result:

```
The current index is: 10
The current index is: 9
The current index is: 8
The current index is: 7
The current index is: 6
The current index is: 5
The current index is: 4
The current index is: 3
The current index is: 2
The current index is: 1

PL/SQL procedure successfully completed.
```

How It Works

The REVERSE keyword causes a FOR loop to iterate backward through the specified range of numbers. This is the only way to loop backward through a sequence of numbers because it is not possible to simply list the numbers in a different order to loop a different direction.

For example, the following loop would never be executed since the lower bound and upper bound values have been swapped:

```
BEGIN
  FOR idx IN 10..1 LOOP
  --These statements will never be executed
  END LOOP;
END;
```

The REVERSE keyword should be placed directly after the IN keyword and before the range that you specify. The REVERSE keyword has no effect when working with cursors. If you need to iterate through cursor results in a specific order, then specify an ORDER BY clause in your SELECT statement.

3-11. Iterating in Increments Other Than One

Problem

Rather than iterating through a range of numbers one at a time, you want to increment by some other value. For example, you might want to increment through even values such as 2, 4, 6, and so forth.

Solution

Multiply the loop index by two (or by whatever other multiplier you need) to achieve the effect of incrementing through all even numbers. As you can see in the following example, an even number is always generated when the index is multiplied by two:

```
BEGIN
  FOR idx IN 1..5 LOOP
    DBMS_OUTPUT.PUT_LINE('The current index is: ' || idx*2);
  END LOOP;
END;
```

Here is the result:

```
The current index is: 2
The current index is: 4
The current index is: 6
The current index is: 8
The current index is: 10

PL/SQL procedure successfully completed.
```

How It Works

Unlike some other languages, PL/SQL does not include a STEP clause that can be used while looping. To work around that limitation, you will need to write your own stepping algorithm. In the solution to this recipe, you can see that the algorithm was quite easy; you simply multiply the index by two to achieve the desired result. In this solution, assigning the range of 1..5 as the index produces the effect of iterating through all even numbers from 2..10 when the current index is multiplied by two.

Using similar techniques, you can increment through ranges of numbers in various intervals. However, sometimes this can become troublesome if you are attempting to step by anything other than even numbers. You can see an example of this in the next recipe.

3-12. Stepping Through a Loop Based on Odd-Numbered Increments

Problem

Rather than iterating through a range of numbers by even increments, you prefer to loop through the range using odd increments.

Solution

Use the built-in MOD function to determine whether the current index is odd. If it is odd, then print out the value; otherwise, continue to the next iteration. The following example shows how to implement this solution:

```
BEGIN
  FOR idx IN 1..10 LOOP
    IF MOD(idx,2) != 0 THEN
      DBMS_OUTPUT.PUT_LINE('The current index is: ' || idx);
    END IF;
  END LOOP;
END;
```

    Results:

```
The current index is: 1
The current index is: 3
The current index is: 5
The current index is: 7
The current index is: 9

PL/SQL procedure successfully completed.
```

How It Works

The solution depicts one possible workaround for a STEP replacement. Using the MOD function to determine whether a number is odd works quite well. The MOD function, otherwise known as the *modulus function*, is used to return the remainder from the division of the two numbers that are passed into the function. Therefore, this function is useful for determining even or odd numbers. In this case, if any value is returned from MOD, then the number is assumed to be odd, and the statements within the IF statement will be executed.

Such a technique may be useful in the case of iterating through a collection of data such as a table. If you want to grab every other record from the collection, then performing a stepping solution such as this or the solution from Recipe 3-11 will allow you to achieve the desired result. You could easily use the resulting index from this technique as the index for a collection.

3-13. Exiting an Outer Loop Prematurely

Problem

Your code contains a nested loop, and you want the inner loop to have the ability to exit from both loops and stop iteration completely.

Solution

Use loop labels for both loops and then reference either loop within an EXIT statement by following the EXIT keyword with a loop label. The following example prints out a series of numbers. During each iteration, the inner loop will increment until it reaches an odd number. At that point, it will pass control to the outer loop again. The outer loop will be exited when the index for the inner loop is greater than or equal to the number ten.

```
BEGIN
  <<outer>> for idx1 in 1 .. 10 loop
    <<inner>> for idx2 in 1 .. 10 loop
      dbms_output.put(idx2);
      exit inner when idx2 > idx1 * 2;
      exit outer when idx2 = 10;
    END LOOP;
    DBMS_OUTPUT.NEW_LINE;
  END LOOP;
  DBMS_OUTPUT.NEW_LINE;
END;
```

    Results:

```
123
12345
1234567
123456789
12345678910
```

```
PL/SQL procedure successfully completed.
```

How It Works

Any loop in PL/SQL can be labeled using a similar style to labels for code blocks. The label can be any valid identifier surrounded by angle brackets before the loop, and optionally the identifier can be placed at the end after the END LOOP clause. The result of such a labeling mechanism is that you will have a distinct start and end to the loops and more control over loop execution.

In the solution to this recipe, the label helps identify the outer loop so that it can be terminated with the EXIT clause. Without a label, the EXIT will terminate the innermost FOR loop. However, the label can also be used to help identify the loop's index. In the solution, this is not necessary because the outer loop index was named differently than the inner loop index. If both indexes were named the same, then you could use the loop label along with the index name to fully qualify the index. The following example demonstrates this technique:

```
BEGIN
  <<outer>> FOR idx IN 1 .. 10 LOOP
    <<inner>> FOR idx IN 1 .. 10 LOOP
      DBMS_OUTPUT.PUT(inner.idx);
      EXIT inner WHEN inner.idx > outer.idx * 2;
      EXIT outer WHEN inner.idx = 10;
    END LOOP;
    DBMS_OUTPUT.NEW_LINE;
  END LOOP;
  DBMS_OUTPUT.NEW_LINE;
END;
```

This code will display the same results as the example given in the solution to this recipe. The only difference is that in this example the index name is the same in both the inner and outer loops. An alternative technique to end the current iteration of an inner loop is to use the CONTINUE statement. A CONTINUE statement can reference the label of a loop that is within the same scope. Therefore, an inner loop can exit its current iteration and proceed to an outer loop, as the following example demonstrates:

```
BEGIN
  <<outer>> for idx1 in 1 .. 10 loop
    <<inner>> for idx2 in 1 .. 10 loop
      dbms_output.put(idx2);
      exit inner when idx2 > idx1 * 2;
      exit outer when idx2 = 10;
    END LOOP;
    CONTINUE outer;
  END LOOP;
  DBMS_OUTPUT.NEW_LINE;
END;
```

In this example, the same code that is used in the solution to this recipe is rewritten to incorporate a CONTINUE statement. This statement is used to move control of execution back to the outer loop. When the CONTINUE statement is reached, execution of the current loop is immediately halted, and processing continues to the loop designated by the label.

3-14. Jumping to a Designated Location in Code

Problem

You want your code to stop executing and jump to a different, designated location.

Solution

Use a GOTO statement along with a label name to cause code execution to jump into the position where the label is located.

The following example shows the GOTO statement in action. The user is prompted to enter a numeric value, and that value is then evaluated to determine whether it is greater than ten. In either case, a message is printed, and then the code jumps to the end_msg label. If the number entered is a negative number, then the code jumps to the bad_input label where an error message is printed.

```
DECLARE
  in_number    number := 0;
BEGIN

    in_number := '&input_number';
    IF in_number > 10 THEN
      DBMS_OUTPUT.PUT_LINE('The number you entered is greater than ten');
      GOTO end_msg;
    ELSIF in_number <= 10 and in_number > 0 THEN
      DBMS_OUTPUT.PUT_LINE('The number you entered is less than or equal to ten');
      GOTO end_msg;
    ELSE
      -- Entered a negative number
      GOTO bad_input;
    END IF;

    << bad_input >>
    DBMS_OUTPUT.PUT_LINE('Invalid input.  No negatives allowed.');

    << end_msg >>
    DBMS_OUTPUT.PUT_LINE('Thank you for playing..');

END;
```

How It Works

The GOTO statement is used to branch code unconditionally. Code can be branched to any label within the same scope as the GOTO. In the solution, the GOTO statement causes the code to branch to a parent code block. You could just as easily branch to a loop within the current or outer block. However, you cannot branch to a label within a subblock, IF statement, or LOOP.

You should use this statement sparingly because arbitrary branching makes code difficult to read. Use conditional statements to branch whenever possible, because that's why they were put into the language. As you can see from the solution, the same code could have been written printing the "Invalid number" message within the ELSE clause. There are usually better alternatives to using GOTO.

■ ■ ■

CHAPTER 4

Functions, Packages, and Procedures

PL/SQL applications are composed of functions, procedures, and packages. *Functions* are PL/SQL programs that accept zero or more parameters and always return a result. *Procedures* are similar to functions, but they are not required to return a result. *Packages* are a combination of related functions, procedures, types, and variables. Each of these PL/SQL components helps formulate the basis for small and large applications alike. They differ from anonymous blocks that have been covered in previous recipes because they are all named routines that are stored within the database. Together, they provide the advantage of reusable code that can be called from any schema in the database to which you've granted the appropriate access.

Let's say you have a few lines of code that perform some calculations on a number and return a result. Will these calculations help you anywhere else? If so, then you should probably encapsulate this code in a function. Maybe you have a nightly script that you use as a batch job to load and execute. Perhaps this script can be turned into a stored procedure and Oracle Scheduler can kick it off each night. What about tasks that use more than one procedure or function? Can these be combined at all? A PL/SQL package would probably be a good choice in this case. After reading through the recipes in this chapter, you should be able to answer these questions at the drop of a hat.

■ **Note** We mention job scheduling in our introduction to this chapter. However, we actually address that topic in Chapter 11, which is an entire chapter dedicated to running PL/SQL jobs, whether for application purposes or for database maintenance.

4-1. Creating a Stored Function

Problem

One of your programs is using a few lines of code repeatedly for performing a calculation. Rather than using the same lines of code numerous times throughout your application, it makes more sense to encapsulate the functionality into a common routine that can be called and reused time and time again.

Solution

Create a stored function to encapsulate your code, and save it into the database. Once stored in the database, any user with execution privileges can invoke the function. Let's take a look at a function to give you an idea of how they work.

In this example, the function is used to round a given number to the nearest quarter. This function works well for accepting a decimal value for labor hours and rounding to the nearest quarter hour.

```
CREATE OR REPLACE FUNCTION CALC_QUARTER_HOUR(HOURS IN NUMBER) RETURN NUMBER AS
  CALCULATED_HOURS NUMBER := 0;
BEGIN

    -- if HOURS is greater than one, then calculate the decimal portion
•   -- based upon quarterly hours
 IF HOURS > 1 THEN
   -- calculate the modulus of the HOURS variable and compare it to •
   -- fractional values
    IF MOD(HOURS, 1) <=.125 THEN
        CALCULATED_HOURS := substr(to_char(HOURS),0,1);
     ELSIF MOD(HOURS, 1) > .125 AND MOD(HOURS,1) <= .375 THEN
        CALCULATED_HOURS := substr(to_char(HOURS),0,1) + MOD(.25,1);
     ELSIF MOD(HOURS, 1) > .375 AND MOD(HOURS,1) <= .625 THEN
        CALCULATED_HOURS := substr(to_char(HOURS),0,1) + MOD(.50,1);
     ELSIF MOD(HOURS, 1) > .63 AND MOD(HOURS,1) <= .825 THEN
        CALCULATED_HOURS := substr(to_char(HOURS),0,1) + MOD(.75,1);
     ELSE
        CALCULATED_HOURS := ROUND(HOURS,1);

    END IF;

  ELSE
    -- if HOURS is less than one, then calculate the entire value•
    -- based upon quarterly hours
    IF HOURS > 0 AND HOURS <=.375 THEN
        CALCULATED_HOURS := .25;
     ELSIF HOURS > .375 AND HOURS <= .625 THEN
        CALCULATED_HOURS := .5;
     ELSIF HOURS > .625 AND HOURS <= .825 THEN
        CALCULATED_HOURS := .75;
     ELSE
        CALCULATED_HOURS := ROUND(HOURS,1);
    END IF;

  END IF;

  RETURN CALCULATED_HOURS;

END CALC_QUARTER_HOUR;
```

This function accepts one value as input, a decimal value representing a number of hours worked. The function then checks to see whether the value is greater than one, and if so, it performs a series of manipulations to round the value to the nearest quarter hour. If the value is not greater than one, then the function rounds the given fraction to the nearest quarter.

■ **Note** See Recipe 4-2 for an example showing the execution of this function.

How It Works

A function is a named body of code that is stored within the database and returns a value. Functions are often used to encapsulate logic so that it can be reused. A function can accept zero or more parameters and always returns a value. A function is comprised of a header, an execution section containing statements, and an optional exception block.

For example, the header for our solution function is as follows:

```
CREATE OR REPLACE FUNCTION CALC_QUARTER_HOUR(HOURS IN NUMBER) RETURN NUMBER AS
```

The OR REPLACE clause is optional, but in practice it is something you'll most always want. Specifying OR REPLACE will replace a function that is already under the same name in the same schema. (A function name must be unique within its schema.)

Functions can take zero or more parameters, which can be any datatype including collections. You will learn more about collections in Chapter 10. Our example function takes one parameter, a NUMBER representing some number of hours.

The parameters that can be passed to a function can be declared in three different ways, namely, as IN, OUT, and IN OUT. The difference between these three declaration types is that parameters declared as IN are basically read-only, OUT parameters are write-only, and IN OUT parameters are read-write. The value of an OUT parameter is initially NULL but can contain a value after the function has returned. Similarly, the value of an IN OUT can be modified within the function, but IN parameters cannot.

■ **Note** Typically you want only IN parameters for a function. If you find yourself creating a function with OUT or IN OUT parameters, then reconsider and think about creating a stored procedure instead. This is not a hard-and-fast requirement, but it is generally good practice for a function to return only one value.

The declaration section of the function begins directly after the header, and unlike the anonymous block, you do not include the DECLARE keyword at the top of this section. Just like the anonymous block, the declaration section is where you will declare any variables, types, or cursors for your function. Our declaration section defines a single variable:

```
CALCULATED_HOURS NUMBER := 0;
```

Following the declaration is the executable section, which is laid out exactly like that of an anonymous block. The only difference with a function is that it always includes a RETURN statement. It can return a value of any datatype as long as it is the same datatype specified in the RETURN clause of the header.

Following the return clause can be an optional EXCEPTION block to handle any errors that were encountered in the function. The following example is the same function that was demonstrated in the solution to this recipe, except that it has an added EXCEPTION block.

```
CREATE OR REPLACE FUNCTION CALC_QUARTER_HOUR(HOURS IN NUMBER)
 RETURN NUMBER AS
  CALCULATED_HOURS NUMBER := 0;
BEGIN

   -- if HOURS is greater than one, then calculate the decimal portion

  -- based upon quarterly hours
 IF HOURS > 1 THEN
  -- calculate the modulus of the HOURS variable and compare it to

  -- fractional values
   IF MOD(HOURS, 1) <=.125 THEN
      CALCULATED_HOURS := substr(to_char(HOURS),0,1);
   ELSIF MOD(HOURS, 1) > .125 AND MOD(HOURS,1) <= .375 THEN
      CALCULATED_HOURS := substr(to_char(HOURS),0,1) + MOD(.25,1);
   ELSIF MOD(HOURS, 1) > .375 AND MOD(HOURS,1) <= .625 THEN
      CALCULATED_HOURS := substr(to_char(HOURS),0,1) + MOD(.50,1);
   ELSIF MOD(HOURS, 1) > .63 AND MOD(HOURS,1) <= .825 THEN
      CALCULATED_HOURS := substr(to_char(HOURS),0,1) + MOD(.75,1);
   ELSE
      CALCULATED_HOURS := ROUND(HOURS,1);

   END IF;

  ELSE
    -- if HOURS is less than one, then calculate the entire value

    -- based upon quarterly hours
    IF HOURS > 0 AND HOURS <=.375 THEN
       CALCULATED_HOURS := .25;
    ELSIF HOURS > .375 AND HOURS <= .625 THEN
       CALCULATED_HOURS := .5;
    ELSIF HOURS > .625 AND HOURS <= .825 THEN
       CALCULATED_HOURS := .75;
    ELSE
       CALCULATED_HOURS := ROUND(HOURS,1);
    END IF;

  END IF;

  RETURN CALCULATED_HOURS;

EXCEPTION
  WHEN VALUE_ERROR THEN
    DBMS_OUTPUT.PUT_LINE('VALUE ERROR RAISED, TRY AGAIN');
    RETURN -1;
  WHEN OTHERS THEN
```

```
      DBMS_OUTPUT.PUT_LINE('UNK ERROR RAISED, TRY AGAIN');
      RETURN -1;
END CALC_QUARTER_HOUR;
```

Again, don't fret if you are unfamiliar with how to handle exceptions, because they will be discussed in detail later in the book. At this point, it is important to know that you have the ability to declare exceptions that can be caught by code so that your program can process abnormalities or errors accordingly.

Functions are important not only for encapsulation but also for reuse. As a matter of fact, the function defined within the solution uses other built-in PL/SQL functions within them. There are entire libraries that consist of functions that are helpful for performing various transactions. Functions are a fundamental part of PL/SQL programming, just as they are in any other language. It is up to you to ensure that your database is stocked with plenty of useful functions that can be used in your current and future applications.

4-2. Executing a Stored Function from a Query

Problem

You want to invoke a function from an SQL query. For example, you want to take the quarter-hour rounding function from Recipe 4-1 and invoke it on hourly values in a database table.

Solution

Write a query and invoke the function on values returned by the SELECT statement. In the following lines, the function that was written in the previous recipe will be called. The results of calling the function from within a query are as follows:

```
SQL> select calc_quarter_hour(.17) from dual;

CALC_QUARTER_HOUR(.17)
----------------------
   .25

SQL> select calc_quarter_hour(1.3) from dual;

CALC_QUARTER_HOUR(1.3)
----------------------
  1.25
```

How It Works

There are a few ways in which a function can be called, one of which is via a query. A function can be executed inline via a SELECT statement, as was the case with the solution to this recipe. A function can also be executed by assigning it to a variable within an anonymous block or another function/procedure. Since all functions return a value, this works quite well. For instance, the following QTR_HOUR variable can be assigned the value that is returned from the function:

```
DECLARE
  qtr_hour          NUMBER;
BEGIN
  qtr_hour := calc_quarter_hour(1.3);
  DBMS_OUTPUT.PUT_LINE(qtr_hour);
END;
```

You can also execute a function as part of an expression. In the following statement, you can see that TOTAL_HOURS is calculated by adding the bill total to the value returned from the function:

```
DECLARE
  total_hours        NUMBER;
  hours              NUMBER := 8;
BEGIN
  total_hours := hours + calc_quarter_hour(3.2);
  DBMS_OUTPUT.PUT_LINE(total_hours);
END;
```

The way in which your program calls a function depends on its needs. If you need to simply return some results from the database and apply a function to each of the results, then use a query. You may have an application that needs to pass a value to a function and use the result at some later point, in which case assigning the function to a variable would be a good choice for this case. Whatever the case may be, functions provide convenient calling mechanisms to cover most use cases.

4-3. Optimizing a Function That Will Always Return the Same Result for a Given Input

Problem

You want to create a function that will return the same result whenever a given input, or set of inputs, is presented to it. You want the database to optimize based upon that *deterministic* nature.

Solution

Specify the DETERMINISTIC keyword when creating the function to indicate that the function will always return the same result for a given input. For instance, you want to return a specific manager name based upon a given manager ID. Furthermore, you want to optimize for the fact that any given input will always return the same result. The following example demonstrates a function that does so by specifying the DETERMINISTIC keyword:

```
CREATE OR REPLACE FUNCTION manager_name(mgr_id IN NUMBER)
RETURN VARCHAR2
DETERMINISTIC IS
  first_name       employees.first_name%TYPE;
  last_name        employees.last_name%TYPE;
BEGIN
  IF mgr_id IS NOT NULL THEN
    SELECT first_name, last_name
    INTO first_name, last_name
```

```
    FROM EMPLOYEES
    WHERE employee_id = mgr_id;

    RETURN first_name || ' ' || last_name;
  ELSE
    RETURN 'N/A';
  END IF;
EXCEPTION
  WHEN NO_DATA_FOUND THEN
    RETURN 'N/A';
END;
```

This function will return the manager name for a matching EMPLOYEE_ID. If there are no matches for the EMPLOYEE_ID found, then N/A will be returned.

How It Works

A deterministic function is one that always returns the same resulting value as long as the parameters that are passed in are the same. This type of function can be useful for improving performance. The function will be executed only once for any given set of parameters. This means that if the same parameters are passed to this function in subsequent calls, then the function will be bypassed and return the cached value from the last execution using those parameters. This can really help in cases where calculations are being performed and repeated calls to the function may take a toll on performance.

The DETERMINISTIC clause is required in a couple of cases. In the event that you are calling a function in an expression of a function-based index, you need to write the function as DETERMINISTIC, or you will receive errors. Similarly, a function must be made DETERMINISTIC if it is being called in an expression of a materialized view query or if the view is marked as ENABLE QUERY REWRITE or REFRESH FAST.

4-4. Creating a Stored Procedure

Problem

There is a database task that you are performing on a regular basis. Rather than executing a script that contains lines of PL/SQL code each time you execute the task, you want to store the code in the database so that you can simply execute the task by name or so that you can schedule it to execute routinely via Oracle Scheduler.

■ **Note** See Chapter 11 for information on scheduling PL/SQL jobs using Oracle Scheduler.

Solution

Place the code that is used to perform your task within a stored procedure. The following example creates a procedure named INCREASE_WAGE to update the employee table by giving a designated employee a pay increase. Of course, you will need to execute this procedure for each eligible employee in your department. Storing the code in a procedure makes the task easier to perform.

69

```
CREATE OR REPLACE PROCEDURE INCREASE_WAGE (empno_in IN NUMBER,
                                           pct_increase IN NUMBER,
                                           upper_bound IN NUMBER) AS
  emp_count    NUMBER := 0;
  emp_sal      employees.salary%TYPE;

  Results   VARCHAR2(50);

BEGIN

    SELECT salary
    INTO emp_sal
    FROM employees
    WHERE employee_id = empno_in;

    IF emp_sal < upper_bound
    AND round(emp_sal + (emp_sal * pct_increase), 2) < upper_bound THEN

        UPDATE employees
        SET salary = round(salary + (salary * pct_increase),2)
        WHERE employee_id = empno_in;

        results := 'SUCCESSFUL INCREASE';
    ELSE
        results := 'EMPLOYEE MAKES TOO MUCH, DECREASE RAISE PERCENTAGE';
    END IF;

  DBMS_OUTPUT.PUT_LINE(results);
EXCEPTION
  WHEN NO_DATA_FOUND THEN
    RAISE_APPLICATION_ERROR(-20001, 'No employee match for the given ID');
END;
```

The following are the results from executing the procedure for employee number 198. In the example, the employee is being given a 3 percent increase and an upper bound of $5,000.

```
BEGIN
  increase_wage(198,.03,5000);
END;

SUCCESSFUL INCREASE
Statement processed.
```

How It Works

In the example, the procedure accepts three parameters: the employee number, the percent of increase they will receive, and an upper salary bound. You can then invoke the procedure by name, passing in the required parameters.

The procedure first searches the database for the provided employee number. If a record for that employee is found, then the employee record is queried for the current salary. If the salary is less than the upper bound and the resulting new salary will still be less than the upper bound, then the increase will be applied via an UPDATE statement. If the employee is not found, then an alert message will be displayed. As you can see, this procedure can be called for any individual employee, and it will increase their wage accordingly as long as the increase stays within the bound.

Stored procedures can be used to encapsulate functionality and store code in the database data dictionary. Much like a function, they can accept zero or more values as parameters, including collections. A stored procedure is structured in much the same way as a function in that it includes a header, an executable section, and an optional exception-handling block. However, a procedure cannot include a RETURN clause in the header, and it does not return a value.

For example, in the solution to this recipe, the procedure contains the following header:

```
CREATE OR REPLACE PROCEDURE INCREASE_WAGE (empno_in IN NUMBER,
                                pct_increase IN NUMBER,
                                upper_bound IN NUMBER) AS
```

The header uses the OR REPLACE clause to indicate that this procedure should replace any procedure with the same name that already exists. The procedure accepts three parameters, and although all of them are NUMBER type, any datatype can be accepted as a parameter. The declaration section comes after the header, and any cursors, variables, or exceptions that need to be declared should be taken care of in that section. Next, the actual work that the procedure will do takes place between the BEGIN and END keywords. Note that the header does not contain a RETURNS clause since procedures cannot return any values.

The advantage of using procedures is that code can be encapsulated into a callable named routine in the data dictionary and can be called by many users. To create a procedure in your schema, you must have the CREATE PROCEDURE system privilege. You can create a stored procedure in another schema if you have the CREATE ANY PROCEDURE system privilege.

4-5. Executing a Stored Procedure

Problem

You want to execute a stored procedure from SQL*Plus.

Solution

Open SQL*Plus, and connect to the database schema that contains the procedure you are interested in executing. Execute the procedure by issuing the following command:

```
EXEC procedure_name([param1, param2,...]);
```

For instance, to execute the procedure that was created in Recipe 4-3, you would issue the following command:

```
EXEC increase_wage(198, .03, 5000);
```

This would invoke the INCREASE_WAGE procedure, passing three parameters: EMPLOYEE_ID, a percentage of increase, and an upper salary bound.

You can also execute a stored procedure by creating a simple anonymous block that contains the procedure call, as depicted in the following code:

```
BEGIN
  procedure_name([param1, param2,…]);
END;
```

Using this technique, invoking the stored procedure that was created in Recipe 4-3 would resemble the following:

```
BEGIN
  increase_wage(198,.03,5000);
END;
```

Both techniques work equally well, but the latter would be better to use if you wanted to execute more than one procedure or follow up with more PL/SQL statements. If you are running a single procedure from SQL*Plus, then using EXEC is certainly a good choice.

How It Works

A stored procedure can be executed using the EXEC keyword. You can also type EXECUTE entirely. Both the long and shortened versions will work.

It is also possible to execute a procedure that is contained within other schemas, if the current user has execute privileges on that procedure. In such a scenario, use dot notation to qualify the procedure name. Here's an example:

```
EXEC different_schema.increase_wage(emp_rec.employee_id, pct_increase, upper_bound);
```

■ **Note** To learn more about privileges regarding stored programs, please take a look at Recipe 4-11.

A procedure can also be invoked from within another procedure by simply typing the name and placing the parameters inside parentheses, if there are any. For instance, the following lines of code demonstrate calling a procedure from within another procedure. The procedure in this example invokes the procedure that was shown in Recipe 4-3.

```
CREATE OR REPLACE PROCEDURE grant_raises (pct_increase IN NUMBER,

upper_bound IN NUMBER) as
  CURSOR emp_cur is
  SELECT employee_id, first_name, last_name
  FROM employees;
BEGIN
  -- loop through each record in the employees table
  FOR emp_rec IN emp_cur LOOP
      DBMS_OUTPUT.PUT_LINE(emp_rec.first_name || ' ' || emp_rec.last_name);
      increase_wage(emp_rec.employee_id, pct_increase, upper_bound);
  END LOOP;
END;
```

The procedure GRANT_RAISES applies an increase across the board to all employees. It loops through all employee records, and the INCREASE_WAGE procedure is called with each iteration. The procedure is called without the use of the EXEC keyword since it is being invoked by another procedure rather than directly from the SQL*Plus command line.

4-6. Creating Functions Within a Procedure or Code Block

Problem

You want to create some functions within a stored procedure. You want the functions to be local to the procedure, available only from the procedure's code block.

Solution

Create a stored procedure, and then create functions within the declaration section. The internal functions will accept parameters and return values just as an ordinary stored function would, except that the scope of the functions will be constrained to the outer code block or to the procedure. The procedure that is demonstrated in this solution embodies two functions. One of the functions is used to calculate the federal tax for an employee paycheck, while the other calculates the state tax.

```
CREATE OR REPLACE PROCEDURE calc_employee_paycheck(emp_id IN NUMBER) as
  emp_rec          employees%ROWTYPE;
  paycheck_total   NUMBER;

-- function for state tax
  FUNCTION calc_state (sal IN NUMBER)
    RETURN NUMBER IS
  BEGIN
    RETURN sal *  .08;
  END;

-- function for federal tax
 FUNCTION calc_federal (sal IN NUMBER)
    RETURN NUMBER IS
  BEGIN
    RETURN sal *  .12;
  END;

BEGIN
  DBMS_OUTPUT.PUT_LINE('Calculating paycheck with taxes');
  SELECT *
  INTO emp_rec
  FROM employees
  WHERE employee_id = emp_id;

  paycheck_total := emp_rec.salary - calc_state(emp_rec.salary) -
                   calc_federal(emp_rec.salary);

 DBMS_OUTPUT.PUT_LINE('The paycheck total for ' || emp_rec.last_name ||
    ' is ' || paycheck_total);
```

```
EXCEPTION
  WHEN NO_DATA_FOUND THEN
    RAISE_APPLICATION_ERROR(-20001,
    'No matching employee for the given ID');
END;
```

How It Works

Functions—and procedures too—can be contained within other bodies of code. Creating a function within a declaration section will make the function accessible to the block that contains it. The declaration of the function is the same as when you are creating a stored function, with the exception of the CREATE OR REPLACE keywords. Any variables that are declared inside the function will be accessible only to that function, not to the containing object.

Creating a function or procedure inside a PL/SQL code block can be useful when you want to make a function that is only to be used by the containing object. However, if you find that the body of the embedded function may change frequently, then coding a separate stored function may prove to be more efficient.

4-7. Passing Parameters by Name

Problem

You have a procedure in your database that accepts a large number of parameters. When calling the procedure, you would rather not worry that the positioning of the parameters is correct.

Solution

Rather than trying to pass all the parameters to the procedure in the correct order, you can pass them by name. The code in this solution calls a procedure that accepts six parameters, and it passes the parameters by name rather than in order.

Procedure Declaration:

```
PROCEDURE process_emp_paycheck(EMP_ID IN NUMBER,
    PAY_CODE IN NUMBER,
    SICK_USED IN NUMBER,
    VACATION_USED IN NUMBER,
    FEDERAL_TAX IN NUMBER,
    STATE_TAX IN NUMBER);
```

Procedure Execution:

```
EXEC process_emp_paycheck(EMP_ID=>10,
    PAY_CODE=>10,
    VACATION_USED=>8.0,
    SICK_USED=>8.0,
    STATE_TAX=>.06,
    FEDERAL_TAX=>.08);
```

As you can see, by passing the parameters by name, they do not need to follow the same positional ordering as they do within the declaration of the procedure.

How It Works

To pass a parameter by name, you list the parameter name followed by an arrow (consisting of an equal sign and a greater-than symbol) pointing to the value you are passing. The following pseudocode depicts this technique:

```
procedure_name(parameter=>value);
```

Although it can be more verbose to use named parameters, passing parameters by name can be very handy when there are several parameters to pass because you do not need to worry about passing them in the correct order. It is also helpful because it increases readability.

Both procedures and functions can accept positional and named parameters. Neither notation is superior to the other, so which one you choose to use is completely dependant upon the procedure or function that is currently being called. However, named parameters are a safe choice if trying to maintain consistency with procedure calls throughout your application or your organization.

Although not recommended, you can use both positional and named notation when passing parameters within the same call. When doing so, you need to place the parameters that you want to pass using positional notation first, followed by the parameters that you want to pass using named notation. The following execution illustrates using both positional and named notation while passing parameters to the PROCESS_EMP_PAYCHECK procedure:

```
EXEC process_emp_paycheck(198, 10, 0,
   SICK_USED=>4.0,
   STATE_TAX=>.05,
   FEDERAL_TAX=> .04);
```

This particular call passed both of the first parameters by position, those being EMP_ID and PAY_CODE. The last three parameters are passed by named notation.

4-8. Setting Default Parameter Values

Problem

You want to create a procedure that accepts several parameters. However, some of those parameters should be made optional and contain default values.

Solution

You can allow the procedure caller to omit the parameters if default values are declared for the variables within the procedure. The following example shows a procedure declaration that contains default values:

```
PROCEDURE process_emp_paycheck(EMP_ID IN NUMBER,
   PAY_CODE IN NUMBER,
   SICK_USED IN NUMBER,
   VACATION_USED IN NUMBER,
   FEDERAL_TAX IN NUMBER DEFAULT .08,
```

```
     STATE_TAX IN NUMBER DEFAULT .035);
```

And here is an example execution:

```
EXEC process_emp_paycheck(EMP_ID=>10,
                          PAY_CODE=>10,
                          VACATION_USED=>8.0,
                          SICK_USED=>8.0);
```

Since the procedure contains default values, the parameters can be omitted when the procedure is called.

How It Works

The ability to provide a default value for a variable declaration is optional. To do so, you must provide the declaration of the variable with the keyword DEFAULT followed by the value, as shown in the solution to this recipe. If a default value is declared, then you needn't specify a value for the parameter when the function or procedure is called. If you do specify a value for a parameter that has a default value, the specified value overrides the default.

4-9. Collecting Related Routines into a Single Unit

Problem

You have a number of procedures and functions that formulate an entire application when used together. Rather than defining each subprogram individually, you prefer to combine all of them into a single, logically related entity.

Solution

Create a PL/SQL package that in turn declares and defines each of the procedures together as an organized entity. You declare each of the subprograms in the package specification (otherwise known as a *header*) and define them in the package body.

The following example shows the creation of a PL/SQL package containing two procedures and a variable.

First, you create the package specification:

```
CREATE OR REPLACE PACKAGE process_employee_time IS
  total_employee_salary           NUMBER;
  PROCEDURE grant_raises(pct_increase IN NUMBER,
                                      upper_bound IN NUMBER);
  PROCEDURE increase_wage (empno_in IN NUMBER,
                           pct_increase IN NUMBER,
                           upper_bound IN NUMBER) ;
END;
```

The specification lists the procedures, functions, and variables that you want to be visible from outside the package. Think of the specification as the external interface to your package.

Next, create the package body:

```
CREATE OR REPLACE PACKAGE BODY process_employee_time IS
  PROCEDURE grant_raises (pct_increase IN NUMBER,
                          upper_bound IN NUMBER) as
  CURSOR emp_cur is
  SELECT employee_id, first_name, last_name
  FROM employees;
BEGIN
  -- loop through each record in the employees table
  FOR emp_rec IN emp_cur LOOP
      DBMS_OUTPUT.PUT_LINE(emp_rec.first_name || ' ' || emp_rec.last_name);
      increase_wage(emp_rec.employee_id, pct_increase, upper_bound);
  END LOOP;
END;

 PROCEDURE INCREASE_WAGE (empno_in IN NUMBER,
                          pct_increase IN NUMBER,
                          upper_bound IN NUMBER) AS
  emp_count     NUMBER := 0;
  emp_sal       employees.salary%TYPE;

  Results    VARCHAR2(50);

BEGIN

  SELECT count(*)
  INTO emp_count
  FROM employees
  WHERE employee_id = empno_in;

  IF emp_count > 0 THEN
    -- IF EMPLOYEE FOUND, THEN OBTAIN RECORD
    SELECT salary
    INTO emp_sal
    FROM employees
    WHERE employee_id = empno_in;

    IF emp_sal < upper_bound AND round(emp_sal + (emp_sal * pct_increase), 2) <↵
  upper_bound THEN

        UPDATE employees
        SET salary = round(salary + (salary * pct_increase),2)
        WHERE employee_id = empno_in;

        results := 'SUCCESSFUL INCREASE';
    ELSE
        results := 'EMPLOYEE MAKES TOO MUCH, DECREASE RAISE PERCENTAGE';
    END IF;

  ELSE
    Results := 'NO EMPLOYEE FOUND';
  END IF;
```

```
DBMS_OUTPUT.PUT_LINE(results);

  END;
END;
```

The package in this example declares a global variable and two procedures within the package specification. The package body then defines both of the procedures and assigns a value to the variable that was declared in the specification. Procedures defined within the package body are defined in the same manner as they would be if they were stand-alone procedures. The difference is that now these two procedures are contained in a single package entity and are therefore related to each other and can share variables declared globally within the package.

How It Works

A PL/SQL package can be useful for organizing code into a single construct. Usually the code consists of a grouping of variables, types, cursors, functions, and procedures that perform actions that are logically related to one another. Packages consist of a specification and a body, both of which are stored separately in the data dictionary. The specification contains the declarations for each of the variables, types, subprograms, and so on, that are defined in the package. The body contains the implementations for each of the subprograms and cursors that are included in the specification, and it can also include implementations for other functions and procedures that are not in the specification. You'll learn more about this in other recipes.

Most packages contain both a specification and a body, and in these cases the specification acts as the interface to the constructs implemented within the body. The items that are included in the specification are available to the public and can be used outside the package. Not all packages contain a body. If there are only declarations of variables or constants in the package, then there is no need for a body to implement anything. Other PL/SQL objects outside the package can reference any variables that are declared in the specification. In other words, declaring a variable within a PL/SQL package specification essentially creates a global variable.

■ **Note** Global variables should be used wisely. The use of global variables can complicate matters when tracking down problems or debugging your code. If global variables are used, then it can be hard to determine where values have been set and where initialization of such variables occurs. Following the rules of encapsulation and using local variables where possible can make your life easier.

Procedures and functions defined within the package body may call each other, and they can be defined in any order as long as they have been declared within the package specification. If any of the procedures or functions have not been declared in the specification, then they must be defined in the package body prior to being called by any of the other procedures or functions.

You can change any implementations within a package body without recompiling the specification. This becomes very important when you have other objects in the database that depend on a particular package because it is probably not a good idea to change a package specification during normal business hours when a package is in use by others. Doing so may result in unusable objects, and the package users could begin to see errors. However, if changes need to be made to the code within the package body, then you can change that code without affecting public-facing constructs of a package.

Packages are one of the most important constructs that you can create in PL/SQL. You will use packages to combine common code objects for almost any significant application that you write. It is possible to create entire applications without the use of a package, but doing so can create a maintenance nightmare because you will begin to see a pool of procedures and functions being created within your database, and it will be difficult to remember which constructs are used for different tasks. Packages are especially handy when writing PL/SQL web applications, and you will learn all about doing this in Chapter 14.

4-10. Writing Initialization Code for a Package

Problem

You want to execute some code each time a particular PL/SQL package is instantiated in a session.

Solution

Create an initialization block for the package in question. By doing so, you will have the ability to execute code each time the package is initialized. The following example shows the same package that was constructed in Recipe 4-7. However, this time the package contains an initialization block.

```
CREATE OR REPLACE PACKAGE BODY process_employee_time IS

  PROCEDURE grant_raises (pct_increase IN NUMBER,
                          upper_bound IN NUMBER) as
  CURSOR emp_cur is
  SELECT employee_id, first_name, last_name
  FROM employees;
  BEGIN
  -- loop through each record in the employees table
   FOR emp_rec IN emp_cur LOOP
      DBMS_OUTPUT.PUT_LINE(emp_rec.first_name || ' ' || emp_rec.last_name);
      increase_wage(emp_rec.employee_id, pct_increase, upper_bound);
   END LOOP;
  END grant_raises;


  PROCEDURE increase_wage (empno_in IN NUMBER,
                           pct_increase IN NUMBER,
                           upper_bound IN NUMBER) AS
  emp_count     NUMBER := 0;
  emp_sal       employees.salary%TYPE;

  Results     VARCHAR2(50);

  BEGIN

  SELECT count(*)
  INTO emp_count
  FROM employees
  WHERE employee_id = empno_in;
```

```
   IF emp_count > 0 THEN
     -- IF EMPLOYEE FOUND, THEN OBTAIN RECORD
     SELECT salary
     INTO emp_sal
     FROM employees
     WHERE employee_id = empno_in;

     IF emp_sal < upper_bound AND round(emp_sal + (emp_sal * pct_increase), 2) <↵
   upper_bound THEN

         UPDATE employees
         SET salary = round(salary + (salary * pct_increase),2)
         WHERE employee_id = empno_in;

         results := 'SUCCESSFUL INCREASE';
     ELSE
         results := 'EMPLOYEE MAKES TOO MUCH, DECREASE RAISE PERCENTAGE';
     END IF;

   ELSE
     Results := 'NO EMPLOYEE FOUND';
   END IF;

   DBMS_OUTPUT.PUT_LINE(results);

   END increase_wage;


BEGIN
   DBMS_OUTPUT.PUT_LINE('EXECUTING THE INITIALIZATION BLOCK');
END;
```

The initialization block in this example is the last code block within the package body. In this case, that block lies in the final three lines.

How It Works

The initialization block for the package in the solution displays a line of text to indicate that the initialization block has been executed. The initialization block will execute once per session, the first time the package is used in that session. If you were to create this package in your session and invoke one of its members, you would see the message print. Although an initialization message is not very useful, there are several good reasons to use an initialization block. One such reason is to perform a query to obtain some data for the session.

4-11. Granting the Ability to Create and Execute Stored Programs

Problem

You want to grant someone the ability to create and execute stored programs.

Solution

To grant the ability for a user to create a procedure, function, or package, you must log in to the database with a privileged account and grant the CREATE PROCEDURE privilege to the user. Here's an example:

```
GRANT CREATE PROCEDURE TO user;
```

Similarly, to grant permissions for execution of a procedure, package, or function, you must log in with a privileged account and grant the user EXECUTE permissions on a particular procedure, function, or package. Here's an example:

```
GRANT EXECUTE ON schema_name.program_name TO schema;
```

How It Works

Before a user can create stored code, the user must be given permission to do so. The solution shows the straightforward approach. The database administrator logs in and grants CREATE PROCEDURE to the schema owner. The schema owner can then log in and create stored code in their schema.

A schema owner can always execute stored code in the schema. However, application users do not generally log in as schema owners because of the security risks inherent in doing so. Thus, you will commonly be faced with the need to grant other users execute access on stored code. You do that by granting EXECUTE privileges, as shown in the second solution example.

4-12. Executing Packaged Procedures and Functions

Problem

You want to execute one of the procedures or functions contained within a package.

Solution

Use the package_name.object_name notation to execute a particular code object within a package. For instance, the following block of code executes the GRANT_RAISES procedure that is contained within the PROCESS_EMPLOYEE_TIME package.

```
BEGIN
   process_employee_time.grant_raises(.03,4000);
END;
```

The previous code block executes the GRANT_RAISES function, passing .03 for the percentage of increase and 4000 for the upper bound.

How It Works

Dot notation is used for accessing members of a package. Similar to other languages such as Java, dot notation can be used to access any publically accessible member of the package. Any variable, function, or procedure that is contained in the package specification can be accessed using the dot notation. Therefore, if your package contained a constant variable within its specification that you wanted to access, it would be possible to do so from outside the package.

For a schema to access and execute package members, it must have the appropriate permissions. To grant EXECUTE permission on a package that you own, use the following syntax:

```
GRANT EXECUTE ON package_name TO user_name;
```

Dot notation works from within other procedures or functions. It can also be used from the SQL*Plus command line using the EXEC command.

■ **Note** In most cases, if a package is being used by another schema, then it is a good idea to create a public synonym for that package within the database. This will help decrease issues while attempting to reference the package and its programs from the different schema because you will not need to specify the schema name in order to qualify the call. Please see Recipe 4-13 for more information regarding public synonyms.

4-13. Creating a Public Name for a Stored Program

Problem

You want to allow for any schema to have the ability to reference a particular stored program that is contained within your schema. For instance, the CALC_EMPLOYEE_PAYCHECK procedure should be executable for any of the administrative users of the database. You want these users to have the ability to simply call the procedure rather than preceding the procedure name with the schema using the dot notation.

Solution

Create a public synonym for the function, procedure, or package. This will allow any user that has EXECUTE privileges on the stored program to call it without specifying the schema name first. Instead, the invoker need only reference the synonym.

In the following example, the user AdminUser does not have direct access to the CALC_EMPLOYEE_PAYCHECK procedure, so they must fully qualify the name of the package using the schema name for which the procedure resides.

```
SQL> exec application_account.calc_employee_paycheck(200);
Calculating paycheck with taxes
The paycheck total for Whalen is 5200.8

PL/SQL procedure successfully completed.
```

Next, the database administrator will create a public synonym for the procedure:

```
SQL> CREATE PUBLIC SYNONYM calc_employee_paycheck
         FOR application_user.calc_employee_paycheck;
```

Now any user with execute privileges on the procedure can invoke it without fully qualifying the name since a public synonym named CALC_EMPLOYEE_PAYCHECK has been created. This is demonstrated in the next lines of code. Again, the user AdminUser is now logged into the system and executes the procedure.

```
SQL> exec calc_employee_paycheck(206);
Calculating paycheck with taxes
The paycheck total for Gietz is 6640.8

PL/SQL procedure successfully completed.
```

As you can see, the procedure name no longer requires the schema name to fully qualify it before being invoked.

How It Works

Creating public synonyms is a useful technique for allowing any user to have access to a stored piece of code without knowing which schema the code belongs to. Any user who has EXECUTE privileges on the code can invoke it without fully qualifying the name. Instead, the invoker specifies the synonym name.

An account must be granted the CREATE PUBLIC SYNONYM privilege in order to create a public synonym. It's actually common for database administrators to take care of creating such synonyms.

To create a synonym, execute the following statement, replacing the PUB_SYNONYM_NAME identifier with the name of your choice and replacing SCHEMA.STORED_PROGRAM with the schema name and program that you want to make publically accessible:

```
CREATE PUBLIC SYNONYM pub_synonym_name FOR schema.stored_program;
```

The public synonym name does not have to be the same as the actual stored program name, but it is conventional to keep them the same, and it makes things consistent and the names easier to remember. If you begin to have synonym names that differ from the actual program names, then confusion will eventually set in.

■ **Note** Creating a synonym does not give execute access. Creating a public synonym provides only a global name that avoids the need for dot notation. Invokers of a procedure or function still must be granted EXECUTE access, as shown in Recipe 4-11.

4-14. Executing Package Programs in Sequence

Problem

You have created a package that contains all the necessary procedures and functions for your program. Although you can invoke each of these subprograms individually using the package_name.subprogram_name notation, it would be beneficial to execute all of them at the same time by issuing a single statement.

Solution

Create a driver procedure within your PL/SQL package that will be used to initiate all the subprograms in turn, and run your entire program. In the following example, a procedure named driver is created inside a package, and it will invoke all the other package subprograms in turn:

First, create the specification:

```
CREATE OR REPLACE PACKAGE synchronize_data IS
  PROCEDURE driver;
END;
```

Then, create the body:

```
CREATE OR REPLACE PACKAGE BODY synchronize_data IS
  PROCEDURE query_remote_data IS
    BEGIN
      --statements go here
      DBMS_OUTPUT.PUT_LINE('QUERYING REMOTE DATA');
    END query_remote_data;

  PROCEDURE obtain_new_record_list IS
    BEGIN
      --statements go here
      DBMS_OUTPUT.PUT_LINE('NEW RECORD LIST');
    END obtain_new_record_list;

  PROCEDURE obtain_updated_record_list IS
    BEGIN
      --statements go here
      DBMS_OUTPUT.PUT_LINE('UPDATED RECORD LIST');
    END obtain_updated_record_list;

  PROCEDURE sync_local_data IS
    BEGIN
      --statements go here
      DBMS_OUTPUT.PUT_LINE('SYNC LOCAL DATA');
    END sync_local_data;

  PROCEDURE driver IS
  BEGIN
    query_remote_data;
    obtain_new_record_list;
    obtain_updated_record_list;
    sync_local_data;
  END driver;
END synchronize_data;
```

The driver procedure initiates all the other procedures in the order that they should be executed. To initiate the packaged program, you now make a call to the driver procedure as follows:

```
BEGIN
  synchronize_data.driver;
```

```
END;
```

One statement invokes the driver procedure. That procedure in turn invokes the other procedures in the proper sequence.

How It Works

By creating a single procedure that can be called in order to execute all the other subprograms in turn, you eliminate the potential for calling subprograms in the incorrect order. This will also allow you the convenience of making one call as opposed to numerous calls each time you want to execute the task(s) involved. And, if you create the other subprograms as private procedures and functions, then you eliminate the risk of a developer invoking them out of order. That's because you only make the driver procedure public, and you know that the driver invokes in the correct sequence.

Oftentimes, packages are used to hold all the database constructs that make up an entire process. In the solution to this recipe, the package entails a database synchronization process, and each procedure within performs a separate piece of the synchronization. When executed in the correct order, the procedures together perform the complete synchronization task.

One could just as easily create a script or manually invoke each package program separately just as the `driver` procedure does in this case. However, you open the door to error when you write the logic of invoking the sequence of procedures from multiple places. Another important factor is that the driver can also be used to perform any additional initialization that must be done prior to executing each procedure. Similarly, additional processing can be done in between each procedure call, such as printing out the current status of the program. The `driver` procedure essentially provides another layer of abstraction that you can take advantage of. The package can be initialized using the default package initialization; then additional initialization or statements can be provided within the `driver` procedure, and the program caller doesn't need to know about them.

4-15. Implementing a Failure Flag

Problem

You want to create a boolean variable to determine whether one of the subprograms in the package has generated an error. If an error has been generated by one of the subprograms, then the variable will be set to TRUE. This flag will be evaluated in the driver procedure to determine whether the updates performed by the package should be committed or rolled back.

Solution

Declare a global variable at the package level, and it will be accessible to all objects within. You can do this by declaring the variable within the package body. The following package illustrates such a variable, where the variable has been declared within the package body so that it is available for all objects in the package only.

```
CREATE OR REPLACE PACKAGE synchronize_data
PROCEDURE driver;
END;

CREATE OR REPLACE PACKAGE BODY synchronize_data IS
  error_flag BOOLEAN := FALSE;
```

```
PROCEDURE query_remote_data is
   Cursor remote_db_query is
   SELECT *
   FROM my_remote_data@remote_db;

   remote_db_rec employees%ROWTYPE;

BEGIN
  OPEN remote_db_query;
  LOOP
    FETCH remote_db_query INTO remote_db_rec;
    EXIT WHEN remote_db_query%NOTFOUND;
  IF remote_db_query%NOTFOUND THEN
    error_flag := TRUE;
  ELSE
    -- PERFORM PROCESSING
    DBMS_OUTPUT.PUT_LINE('QUERY REMOTE DATA');
  END IF;
  END LOOP;
  CLOSE remote_db_query;
END query_remote_data;

PROCEDURE obtain_new_record_list IS
  BEGIN
    --statements go here
    DBMS_OUTPUT.PUT_LINE('NEW RECORD LIST');
  END obtain_new_record_list;

PROCEDURE obtain_updated_record_list IS
  BEGIN
    --statements go here
    DBMS_OUTPUT.PUT_LINE('UPDATED RECORD LIST');
  END obtain_updated_record_list;

PROCEDURE sync_local_data IS
  BEGIN
    --statements go here
    DBMS_OUTPUT.PUT_LINE('SYNC LOCAL DATA');
  END sync_local_data;


PROCEDURE driver IS
BEGIN
  query_remote_data;
  IF error_flag = TRUE THEN
    GOTO error_check;
  END IF;

  obtain_new_record_list;
  IF error_flag = TRUE THEN
    GOTO error_check;
  END IF;
```

```
   obtain_updated_record_list;
   IF error_flag = TRUE THEN
     GOTO error_check;
   END IF;

   sync_local_data;

   -- If any errors were found then roll back all updates
   <<error_check>>
   DBMS_OUTPUT.PUT_LINE('Checking transaction status');
   IF error_flag = TRUE THEN
     ROLLBACK;
     DBMS_OUTPUT.PUT_LINE('The transaction has been rolled back.');
   ELSE
     COMMIT;
     DBMS_OUTPUT.PUT_LINE('The transaction has been processed.');
   END IF;

 END driver;
END;
```

How It Works

Declaring variables in the package body outside any procedures or functions allows them to become accessible to all subprograms within the package. If one or more of the subprograms changes such a variable's value, then the changed value will be seen throughout the entire package.

As depicted in the example, you can see that the variable is referenced several times throughout the package. If you had a requirement to make a variable global to all PL/SQL objects outside the package as well, then you can declare the variable within the package specification. As mentioned in Recipe 4-8, anything declared in the package specification is publically available to any PL/SQL object outside as well as within the package body.

4-16. Forcing Data Access to Go Through Packages

Problem

You have defined all subprograms and packages for a particular application, and you want to allow other users to access these constructs and execute the program but not have access to any data tables directly.

Solution

Define all the packages, procedures, and functions for your program within a single schema that has access to all the data. All user access should be made from separate schemas, and they should be granted execute privileges on the PL/SQL objects but not access to the tables themselves.

For instance, if you want to control access to a package named PROCESS_EMPLOYEE_TIME, that package along with all required tables, types, and sequences should be loaded into an application schema that has the appropriate permissions required to access the data. For the purposes of this recipe, the application schema name is EMP.

Next, create a role by which to manage the privileges needed to invoke the package's procedures and functions. Grant EXECUTE privileges to that role. Grant that role to application users.

Your application users will now be able to execute the procedures and functions within the package. Those procedures and functions can in turn update the database tables in the package's schema. However, users will not have direct access to those tables. All updates must flow through the package.

How It Works

To control an application's data, it is important to restrict access to the tables. The solution in this recipe shows how to create a package in the same schema that contains the application tables. The package thus has access to those tables. Users, however, do not have table-level access.

After creating the package, you can grant EXECUTE access on the package to application users. Users can then invoke packaged procedures and functions, and those procedures and functions in turn can modify the data in the tables. However, users have no direct access to the tables.

By forcing users to go through packaged procedures and functions, you limit users to using a defined interface that remains under your control. You now have some amount of freedom to modify the underlying tables. So long as you do not change the package interface, you can make changes to the underlying tables without disrupting the application.

4-17. Executing Stored Code Under Your Own Privilege Set

Problem

You have loaded all of an application's objects into a single application schema. However, you do not want packages, procedures, and functions to execute as the schema owner. Instead, you want stored code to execute with the privileges and access of the user who is invoking that code.

Solution

Use invoker's rights by providing the AUTHID property within the declaration of your program. If the AUTHID property is specified when defining a package, procedure, or function, then you have the ability to specify whether the program should be invoked using the CURRENT_USER privileges or the DEFINER privileges. In the case of this solution, you would rather use the CURRENT_USER privileges to ensure that the user does not have the same level of access as the schema owner. The default is DEFINER.

The following code shows how to create a procedure for changing a password, and it uses the AUTHID property to ensure that the procedure will be run using the CURRENT_USER's privilege set. This particular procedure uses dynamic SQL to create a SQL statement. To learn more about using dynamic SQL, please see Chapter 8.

```
CREATE OR REPLACE PROCEDURE change_password(username IN VARCHAR2,

new_password IN VARCHAR2)
AUTHID CURRENT_USER IS

  sql_stmt VARCHAR2(100);

BEGIN
    sql_stmt := 'ALTER USER ' || username || ' IDENTIFIED BY ' || new_password;

    EXECUTE IMMEDIATE sql_stmt;
```

```
END;
```

When the user executes this procedure, it will be executed using their own set of permissions. This will prevent them from changing anyone else's password unless they have the ability to do so under their allotted permission set.

How It Works

Invoker's rights are a great way to secure your application if you are planning to limit access to the CURRENT_USER's privilege set. To allow for invoker's rights to be set into place, the AUTHID property must be used with the CURRENT_USER keyword in the definition of a stored PL/SQL unit. This property affects the name resolution and privilege set for that unit. You can find the value of the AUTHID property if you take a look at the USER_PROCEDURES data dictionary view.

Using the invoker's rights methodology is a great way to protect a program as long as the users access the program with their own database account. If each user within the database has their own account, then they can be granted the required level of access via database roles. The AUTHID property can constrain the execution of code to the current user's privilege set. Because of that, if a user does not have the privileges that are required to execute a particular program, then they will not have access. Simply put, invoker's rights are a good means of securing your code as long as the approach is used correctly.

4-18. Accepting Multiple Parameter Sets in One Function

Problem

You want to give a function the ability to accept multiple parameter types instead of being constrained to a particular datatype or number of parameters. For example, you want to create a single function that can accept either one or two parameters and that will perform a slightly different action depending upon the number of parameters you pass it.

Solution

Use overloading to create multiple functions that are named the same and perform similar functionality but accept a different number of parameters, different ordering of parameters, or parameters of different types. In this recipe, you will see a function named squared that takes a number and returns its value squared. Similarly, there is another function also named squared that accepts two numbers instead of one. This second function is the overloaded version of the original squared. Here is the code for the two functions:

```
-- Returns the square of the number passed in
CREATE OR REPLACE FUNCTION squared (in_num IN NUMBER)
    RETURN NUMBER AS
BEGIN
  RETURN in_num * in_num;
END;

 -- Returns the squared sum of two numbers
CREATE OR REPLACE FUNCTION squared (in_num IN NUMBER,
                                    in_num_two IN NUMBER)
    RETURN NUMBER AS
```

```
BEGIN
  RETURN (in_num + in_num_two) * (in_num + in_num_two);
END;
```

You can see that each of the previous functions accepts a different number of parameters, but they both perform similar tasks. This is a good illustration for using function overloading because someone using this function would expect a similar result to be returned whether calling the function with one parameter or two.

How It Works

Like many other programming languages, PL/SQL offers an overloading of functions. This makes it possible to name more than one function by the same name but give each of them different parameter types, different parameter ordering, or a different number of parameters. This is also known as changing the function signature. A signature for a function consists of the object name and its parameter list. By overloading, you have the ability to allow more flexibility to those using the function. For instance, if you place both of the squared functions into a package named MATH_API, then someone using this package can simply call the function passing whatever they require and still receive a usable result without actually knowing the implementation details.

Using overloading to create multiple functions or procedures by the same name can become troublesome if overused. Be careful that your package is not littered with too many overloaded procedures or functions because maintenance on such a code base can become a nightmare. Overloading has its good use cases, but if it can be avoided by using technique that is easier to follow, then it is a good idea to go the simpler route.

4-19. Listing the Functions, Procedures, and Packages in a Schema

Problem

Your team has defined a number of functions, procedures, and packages within a schema. You want to generate a listing of all functions, procedures, and packages at the end of each day to evaluate productivity.

Solution

Use the USER_OBJECTS table to return the program list and prefix packages, procedures, and functions for the same program with the same first word to make them easier to find.

This first example will return a list of all procedure names that reside within the EMP schema and that have a name that is prefixed with EMPTIME:

```
SELECT OBJECT_NAME
FROM USER_OBJECTS
WHERE OBJECT_TYPE = 'PROCEDURE;
WHERE OBJECT_NAME like 'EMPTIME%';
```

The next query will return a list of all function names that reside within the schema:

```
SELECT OBJECT_NAME
FROM USER_OBJECTS
WHERE OBJECT_TYPE = 'FUNCTION';
```

Lastly, the following query will return a listing of all package names that reside within the schema:

```
SELECT OBJECT_NAME
FROM USER_OBJECTS
WHERE OBJECT_TYPE = 'PACKAGE';
```

How It Works

Oracle Database contains many views that contain data useful for application development. Using the USER_OBJECTS table can be very handy when searching for objects within the database. By prefixing like objects with the same first word, it can make searching for a particular selection of objects rather easy.

USER_OBJECTS provides the ability to find a certain object type by specifying the OBJECT_TYPE within the query. If no OBJECT_TYPE is specified, then all objects for the schema will be returned.

4-20. Viewing Source Code for Stored Programs

Problem

You want to retrieve the code for your stored functions, procedures, triggers, and packages.

Solution

Use the DBMS_METADATA package to assist you in fetching the information. In this case, you will use the DBMS_METADATA.GET_DDL procedure to obtain the code for a stored function. In the following code, the DBMS_METADATA package is used to return the DDL for the CALC_QUARTER_HOUR function:

```
SELECT DBMS_METADATA.GET_DDL('FUNCTION','CALC_QUARTER_HOUR') FROM DUAL;
```

The query illustrated previously should produce results that are similar to the following as long as you have the CALC_QUARTER_HOUR function loaded in your database:

```
CREATE OR REPLACE FUNCTION "MY_SCHEMA"."CALC_QUARTER_HOUR" (HOURS IN NUMBER)
 RETURN NUMBER AS
    CALCULATED_HOURS NUMBER := 0;
 BEGIN
   IF HOURS > 1 THEN
       IF MOD(HOURS, 1) <=.125 THEN
          CALCULATED_HOURS := substr(to_char(HOURS),0,1);
        ELSIF MOD(HOURS, 1) > .125 AND MOD(HOURS,1) <= .375 THEN
          CALCULATED_HOURS := substr(to_char(HOURS),0,1) + MOD(.25,1);
      ELSIF MOD(HOURS, 1) > .375 AND MOD(HOURS,1) <= .625 THEN
          CALCULATED_HOURS := substr(to_char(HOURS),0,1) + MOD(.50,1);
      ELSIF MOD(HOURS, 1) > .63 AND MOD(HOURS,1) <= .825 THEN
          CALCULATED_HOURS := substr(to_char(HOURS),0,1) + MOD(.75,1);
      ELSE
          CALCULATED_HOURS := ROUND(HOURS,1);
      END IF;
   ELSE
       IF HOURS > 0 AND HOURS <=.375 THEN
```

```
         CALCULATED_HOURS := .25;
       ELSIF HOURS > .375 AND HOURS <= .625 THEN
         CALCULATED_HOURS := .5;
       ELSIF HOURS > .625 AND HOURS <= .825 THEN
         CALCULATED_HOURS := .75;
       ELSE
         CALCULATED_HOURS := ROUND(HOURS,1);
       END IF;
   END IF;
   RETURN CALCULATED_HOURS;
 END CALC_QUARTER_HOUR;
```

The GET_DDL function returns the code that can be used to re-create the procedure or function. This can be a good way to debug code that you may not have authored and do not have on hand.

■ **Note** The GET_DDL function will not format the code. Rather, it will be returned as a single string of text. By default, the buffer will not be large enough to display all of the DDL. You can change the buffer size by issuing the SET LONG buffersize within SQL*Plus, substituting buffersize with a large integer value.

How It Works

You can use the DBMS_METADATA package to retrieve various pieces of information from the database. The solution to this recipe demonstrated how to fetch the DDL for a function. There is an abundance of information that can be obtained by using the DBMS_METADATA package, and GET_DDL barely scratches the surface.

The GET_DDL function can return the code for each different type of object. To retrieve a the code for an object using GET_DDL, use the following syntax:

```
SELECT DBMS_METADATA.GET_DDL('object_type','object_name', 'schema') FROM DUAL;
```

The OBJECT_TYPE can be the name of any database object type, including TABLE. For the purposes of PL/SQL code, the OBJECT_TYPE can be FUNCTION, PROCEDURE, PACKAGE, or TRIGGER. The SCHEMA parameter is optional and does not have to be specified if the object resides within the caller's schema.

Using DBMS_METADATA, you can obtain complete database object definitions from the database dictionary via the retrieval subprograms. To learn more about the DBMS_METADATA package and obtain a listing of available subprograms, please refer to the online Oracle documentation at http://download.oracle.com/docs/cd/B28359_01/appdev.111/b28419/d_metada.htm#ARPLS640, which goes into detail regarding each of the subprogram functionalities.

CHAPTER 5

■ ■ ■

Triggers

Triggers play an important role in any database developer's or database administrator's career. They provide the ability to execute code upon the occurrence of defined database, schema, or system events. Triggers can be useful for enhancing applications by providing database capabilities when a table event occurs, providing alerts on system event occurrences, and so much more. Triggers are an enormous topic because they are very intricate constructs. However, even though triggers can open up a world of possibilities, they are easy to use.

In this chapter, you will see recipes demonstrating the many different capabilities that triggers provide to you. If you are interested in learning how to create code that executes upon a database table–level event, then this is the chapter for you. If you want to learn how to create an intricate alerting system that will send e-mail and create logs upon system events, then look at the recipes in this chapter. Triggers are intricate building blocks that can provide an enormous benefit to our databases and applications as a whole. By learning how to incorporate these recipes into your applications, you will be able to solve many issues and enhance a number of your application features. Triggers can be one of the most useful tools to add to a DBA or application developer's arsenal.

5-1. Automatically Generating Column Values

Problem

You want to automatically generate certain column values for newly inserted rows. For example, one of your tables includes a date field that you want to have populated with the current date when a record is inserted.

Solution

Create a trigger that executes BEFORE INSERT on the table. The trigger will capture the system date and populate this date field with it prior to inserting the row into the database. The following code demonstrates how to create a trigger that provides this type of functionality for your application. In the example, the EMPLOYEES table is going to have its HIRE_DATE populated with the current date when a record is inserted into the EMPLOYEES table.

```
CREATE or REPLACE TRIGGER populate_hire_date
BEFORE INSERT•    ON employees
    FOR EACH ROW
DECLARE
BEGIN
    :new.hire_date := sysdate;
END;
```

A `BEFORE INSERT` trigger has access to data before it is inserted into the table. This example demonstrates a useful technique for using this type of trigger.

How It Works

You can use triggers to execute code when a DML statement, DDL statement, or system event occurs. This recipe demonstrates a trigger that executes when a DML event occurs. Specifically, the trigger that was created for this recipe is fired `BEFORE` a row is inserted into the `EMPLOYEES` table. Any DDL event trigger can be created to fire `BEFORE` or `AFTER` a row is inserted, updated, or deleted from a database table. This flexibility allows a developer or DBA the luxury of executing code either before or directly after the values are inserted into the database.

The syntax for creating a trigger that will execute before an insert on a particular table is as follows:

```
CREATE or REPLACE TRIGGER trigger_name
BEFORE INSERT
    ON table_name
    [ FOR EACH ROW ]
DECLARE
    -- variable declarations
BEGIN
    -- trigger code
EXCEPTION
    WHEN ...
    -- exception handling
END;
```

The `CREATE OR REPLACE TRIGGER` statement will do just what it says, either create the trigger in the current schema if none is specified or replace it if another trigger by that name already exists. The trigger name must be unique among other triggers within the same schema. Although it is possible to name a trigger the same as an existing table, we do not recommend doing so. Different triggers by the same name can coexist in the same database if they are in different schemas.

The `BEFORE INSERT` clause is what tells Oracle when the trigger should be executed before a row is inserted into the table. The other option for insert triggers is `AFTER INSERT`, which causes the trigger to be executed after a row is inserted into the table. You will learn more about `AFTER INSERT` triggers in another recipe within this chapter. The optional `FOR EACH ROW` clause determines whether the trigger will be executed once for each row that is affected or once when the statement is executed. Essentially this clause determines whether it will become a row-level trigger or a statement level-trigger. The `FOR EACH ROW` clause can have a significant impact on the outcome of an `UPDATE` trigger. You will learn more about `UPDATE` triggers in the next recipe.

The code that follows the optional `FOR EACH ROW` clause is the `DECLARE` section. Much like that of a procedure, this section of the trigger is used to declare any variables, types, or cursors that will be used by the trigger body. The body of the trigger also resembles that of a procedure. The trigger body is a standard code block that opens with the `BEGIN` keyword and ends with the `END` keyword. Any of the keywords and constructs that can be used within other PL/SQL code blocks can also be used in triggers.

There are a couple of differences between the trigger and other code blocks in PL/SQL. First, a trigger is limited to 32KB in size. This is a bit of a limitation; however, it does not prevent a trigger from invoking other named code blocks. For example, you can write a trigger to invoke stored procedures and functions that are much longer than 32KB in size.

Second, the `INSERT` trigger has access to data values prior to insertion in the database via the `:NEW` qualifier. This qualifier is what provides the power to the trigger construct. Using the `:NEW` qualifier along with a table column name allows you to access the value that is going to be placed into that column via the INSERT statement that has just occurred. In the solution to is recipe, using :NEW.FIRST_NAME and :NEW.LAST_NAME allows you to reference the values that are going to be inserted into the FIRST_NAME and LAST_NAME columns before it occurs. This provides the ability to change the values or check the values for error prior to insertion.

In the case of the solution to this recipe, the HIRE_DATE will always be made the same as the date in which the record is inserted into the database. Even if the HIRE_DATE is set to some date in the past, this trigger will automatically assign SYSDATE to it and override the original value. Now, this may not be very practical example because the data entry clerk may not be inputting the data on the same day as the hire, but it does provide an effective learning tool for this type of situation. If you wanted to modify the trigger to be more realistic, then you could add an IF statement to check and see whether :NEW.HIRE_DATE already had a value. If it does, then that value is inserted into the database, but if left blank, then SYSDATE could be used. Such an example would be a more practical real-life solution.

5-2. Keeping Related Values in Sync

Problem

You want to keep related values in sync that happen to be stored in separate tables. For example, say you are updating the salary level for a number of jobs within the JOBS table. However, in doing so, you will need to update the salaries within the EMPLOYEES table for employees having those jobs. In short, if you update the salary range for a job, then you want to automatically update salaries to ensure that they fall within the new range.

■ **Note** When we use the term *related* in this problem description, we do not necessarily mean related in the relational sense that one commonly thinks about. There is no referential integrity issue in our scenario. Rather, we are instituting a business rule that says that employees automatically get salary bumps in response to changing salary ranges. Not all businesses would choose to institute such a rule. In fact, we suspect most businesses would not do such a thing.

Solution

Create an AFTER UPDATE trigger on the primary table. In our example, create such a trigger to be executed after the JOBS table has been updated. This trigger will obtain the updated salary from the JOBS table and modify the data within the EMPLOYEES table accordingly.

```
CREATE OR REPLACE TRIGGER job_salary_update
AFTER UPDATE
    ON jobs
FOR EACH ROW
DECLARE

  CURSOR emp_cur IS
  SELECT * FROM employees
  WHERE job_id = :new.job_id
  AND salary < :new.min_salary FOR UPDATE;

  emp_rec  emp_cur%ROWTYPE;
```

```
BEGIN

    FOR emp_rec IN emp_cur LOOP
        UPDATE employees
        SET salary = :new.min_salary
        WHERE CURRENT OF emp_cur;
    END LOOP;

END;
```

Since this example uses an AFTER UPDATE trigger, you have access to both the :NEW and :OLD data value qualifiers. This can be very advantageous, as you'll learn in the next section.

How It Works

The update trigger provides the same type of functionality as an INSERT trigger. The syntax for an update trigger is almost identical to that of an insert trigger, other than the BEFORE UPDATE or AFTER UPDATE clause. A BEFORE UPDATE trigger is executed prior to an update on a database table. On the contrary, the AFTER UPDATE executes after an update has been made to a table.

The optional FOR EACH ROW clause can make a great deal of difference when issuing an update trigger. If used, this clause tells Oracle to execute the trigger one time for every row that is updated. This is quite useful for capturing or modifying data as it is being updated. If the FOR EACH ROW clause is omitted, the trigger is executed one time either prior to or after the UPDATE has taken place. Without the FOR EACH ROW clause, the trigger is not executed once for each row but rather one time only for each UPDATE statement that is issued.

As mentioned previously in this recipe, update triggers have access to the :OLD and :NEW qualifiers. The qualifiers allow the trigger to obtain the values of data that are being updated prior to (:OLD) and after (:NEW) the update has been made. Generally, update triggers are most useful for obtaining and modifying data values as the update is occurring. Update triggers, along with every other type of trigger, should be used judiciously because too many triggers on a table can become problematic.

For example, the solution to this recipe demonstrates a trigger in which a salary change in the JOBS table causes a trigger to execute. The trigger will be executed only if the JOBS table is updated. The cursor that is declared will select all the records within the EMPLOYEES table that contain a SALARY that is lower than the new MIN_SALARY for the corresponding JOB_ID. In the body of the trigger, the cursor result set is iterated, and each record is updated so that the SALARY is adjusted to the new MIN_SALARY amount for that job.

If that trigger contains another update statement that modifies values in the EMPLOYEES table, then you must be sure that the EMPLOYEES table does not contain an update trigger that modifies values within the JOBS table. Otherwise, a vicious cycle could occur in which one trigger is causing another trigger to execute, which in turn causes the initial trigger to execute again, and so on. This may even cause an ORA-xxxxx error if Oracle detects a recursive loop.

Update triggers can provide the best of both worlds because you have access to data values before and after they have been updated.

5-3. Responding to an Update of a Specific Table Column

Problem

You want to automatically update some particular values within a table based upon another update that has been made on a specific column of another table. For instance, assume that management has decided to change some positions around within your organization. A new manager is coming to one of the current manager positions, so several employees will receive a new manager. You need to find a way to update several employee records to change their manager from the old one to the new one.

Solution

Create an AFTER UPDATE trigger that will be executed only when the MANAGER_ID column is updated. The following trigger uses a cursor to obtain the employees that are supervised by the old manager. The trigger then determines whether the MANAGER_ID column has been updated, and if so, it loops through each employee who has the old manager in their record, and it updates the MANAGER_ID column to reflect the new manager's ID.

```
CREATE OR REPLACE TRIGGER dept_mgr_update
AFTER UPDATE OF manager_id
    ON departments
FOR EACH ROW
DECLARE
  CURSOR emp_cur IS
  SELECT *
  FROM EMPLOYEES
  WHERE manager_id = :old.manager_id
  FOR UPDATE;
BEGIN


    FOR emp_rec IN emp_cur LOOP
       UPDATE employees
       SET manager_id = :new.manager_id
       WHERE CURRENT OF emp_cur;
    END LOOP;

END;
```

This trigger will be executed only if the MANAGER_ID column of the DEPARTMENTS table is updated. Triggers that have this ability provide for better database performance, because the trigger is not executed each time the DEPARTMENTS table has been updated.

How It Works

Triggers can specify columns that must have their values updated in order to cause the trigger to execute. This allows the developer to have finer-grained control over when the trigger executes. You can take a few different strategies in order to cause a trigger to execute upon an update of a specified column. As is demonstrated in the solution to this recipe, you can specify the column in the trigger declaration. This is one of the easiest approaches to take, and it causes the trigger to execute only if that specified column is updated. Alternatively, you can use a conditional predicate in the trigger body to determine whether the row you had specified in the declaration is indeed being updated. A conditional predicate can be used along with a specified column name to determine whether a specified action is being performed on the named column. You can use three conditional predicates, INSERTING, UPDATING, and DELETING. Therefore, a conditional predicate such as the following can be used to determine whether a specified column is being updated by the current statement:

```
IF UPDATING ('my_column') THEN
   -- Some statements
END IF;
```

Using a conditional predicate ensures that the code in the THEN clause is executed only if a specified action is occurring against the named column. These predicates can also be used along with other conditions to have finer-grained control over your statements. For instance, if you want to ensure that a column was being updated and also that the current date does not match some end date, then you can combine those two conditions with an AND boolean operator. The following code demonstrates this type of conditional statement:

```
IF UPDATING ('my_column') AND end_date > SYSDATE THEN
   -- Some statements
END IF;
```

If you prefer to use the technique demonstrated in the solution to this recipe, then you can still check to ensure that the specified column is being updated by using the IF UPDATING predicate without the column name specified. This technique would look like the following statement:

```
IF UPDATING THEN
   --some statements
END IF;
```

As mentioned in the solution to this recipe, specifying a specific column can help decrease the amount of times that the trigger is fired because it is executed only when the specified column has been updated. Another advantage to using this level of constraint within your triggers is that you can add more triggers to the table if needed. For instance, if you needed to create another trigger to fire AFTER UPDATE on another column on the same table, then it would be possible to do so with less chance of a conflict. On the contrary, if you were using a simple AFTER UPDATE trigger, then chances of a conflict are more likely to occur.

5-4. Making a View Updatable

Problem

You are working with a database view, and it needs to be updated. However, the view is not a simple view and is therefore read-only. If you tried to update a column value on the view, then you would receive an error.

Solution

Use an INSTEAD OF trigger to specify the result of an update against the view, thus making the view updatable. For example, let's begin with the following view definition:

```
CREATE OR REPLACE VIEW EMP_JOB_VIEW AS
  SELECT EMP.employee_ID, EMP.first_name, EMP.last_name,
         EMP.email, JOB.job_title,
         DEPT.department_name
  FROM employees EMP,
       jobs JOB,
       departments DEPT
  WHERE JOB.job_id = EMP.job_id
  AND DEPT.department_id = EMP.department_id
  ORDER BY EMP.last_name;
```

Given the EMP_JOB_VIEW just shown, if you attempt to make an update to a column, then you will receive an error. The following demonstrates the consequences of attempting to update the DEPARTMENT_NAME column of the view.

```
SQL> update emp_job_view
  2   set department_name = 'dept'
  3   where department_name = 'Sales';
where department_name = 'Sales'
      *
ERROR at line 3:
ORA-01779: cannot modify a column which maps to a non key-preserved table
```

However, using the INSTEAD OF clause, you can create a trigger to implement the logic for an UPDATE statement issued against the view. Here's an example:

```
CREATE OR REPLACE TRIGGER update_emp_view
INSTEAD OF UPDATE ON emp_job_view
REFERENCING NEW AS NEW
FOR EACH ROW
DECLARE
  emp_rec                      employees%ROWTYPE;

  title                        jobs.job_title%TYPE;
  dept_name                    departments.department_name%TYPE;
BEGIN

    SELECT *
    INTO emp_rec
    FROM employees
    WHERE employee_id = :new.employee_id;

    UPDATE jobs
    SET job_title = :new.job_title
    WHERE job_id = emp_rec.job_id;

    UPDATE departments
    SET department_name = :new.department_name
    WHERE department_id = emp_rec.department_id;

    UPDATE employees
    SET email = :new.email,
```

```
       first_name = :new.first_name,
       last_name = :new.last_name
       WHERE employee_id = :new.employee_id;
EXCEPTION
 WHEN NO_DATA_FOUND THEN
      DBMS_OUTPUT.PUT_LINE('No matching record exists');

END;
```

The following are the results of issuing an update on the view when the UPDATE_EMP_VIEW trigger is in place. The UPDATE is issued, and the INSTEAD OF trigger executes instead of the database's built-in logic. The result is that the rows containing a DEPARTMENT_NAME of Sales will be updated in the view. Hence, the underlying row in the DEPARTMENTS table is updated to reflect the change.

```
SQL> update emp_job_view
  2   set department_name = 'Sales Dept'
  3   where department_name = 'Sales';

34 rows updated.
```

If you were to query the view after performing the update, then you would see that the view data has been updated to reflect the requested change. If you read through the code in the trigger body, you can see the magician behind the curtain.

How It Works

Oftentimes it is beneficial to have access to view data via a trigger event. However, there are some views that are read-only, and data manipulation is not allowed. Views that include any of the following constructs are not updatable and therefore require the use of an INSTEAD OF trigger for manipulation:

- SET

- DISTINCT

- GROUP BY, ORDER BY, CONNECT BY

- MODEL

- START WITH

- Subquery within a SELECT or containing the WITH READ ONLY clause

- Collection expressions

- Aggregate or analytic functions

A trigger that has been created with the INSTEAD OF clause allows you to declare a view name to be acted upon, and then once the specified event occurs, the trigger is fired, which causes the actual INSERT, UPDATE, or DELETE statement to occur. The trigger body actually acts upon the real tables behind the scenes using the values that have been specified in the action.

The format for the INSTEAD OF trigger is the same as any other trigger with the addition of the INSTEAD OF clause. You can see in the solution to this recipe that an additional clause has been specified, namely, REFERENCING NEW AS NEW. The REFERENCING clause can be used by triggers to specify how you want to prefix :NEW or :OLD values. This allows you to use any alias for :NEW or :OLD, so it is possible to reference a new value using :blah.my_value if you used the following clause when you declared your trigger:

```
REFERENCING NEW AS BLAH
```

Although there is no real magic at work behind an INSTEAD OF trigger, they do abstract some of the implementation details away from the typical user such that working with a view is no different from working with an actual table.

5-5. Altering the Functionality of Applications

Problem

You want to modify a third-party application, but you are not in a position to change the source code. Either you are not allowed to change the source or you simply do not have access to make changes.

As an example, let's consider a form in one application used to create jobs within the JOBS table. You want to enhance the application so that mail is sent to all the administrative staff members when a new job is created. However, your company does not own the license to modify the source code of the application.

Solution

You can often use triggers to add functionality to an application behind the scenes, without modifying application code. Sometimes you have to think creatively to come up with a trigger or blend of triggers that accomplishes your goal.

You can solve our example problem by creating a trigger that will execute after an insert has been made on the JOBS table. This trigger will obtain the information regarding the job that was just created and send an e-mail containing that information to all administrative personnel. In the following trigger, some necessary information regarding the new job entry is obtained and processed by the SEND_EMAIL procedure, which in turn sends the mail.

First, here is the code for the trigger:

```
CREATE OR REPLACE TRIGGER send_job_alert
  AFTER INSERT ON jobs
  FOR EACH ROW
DECLARE
  to_address                    varchar2(50)  := 'admin_list@mycompany.com';
  v_subject                     varchar2(100) := 'New job created: ' || :new.job_title;
  v_message                     varchar2(2000);
BEGIN

  v_message := 'There has been a new job created with an ID of ' || :new.job_id ||
               ' and a title of ' || :new.job_title || '.  The salary range is: ' ||
               :new.min_salary || ' - ' || :new.max_salary;
  -- Initiate the send_email procedure
  SEND_EMAIL(to_address, v_subject,  v_message);

END;
```

Next is the stored procedure that actually sends the e-mail:

```
CREATE OR REPLACE PROCEDURE send_email(to_address IN VARCHAR2,
                                       subject IN VARCHAR2,
                                       message IN VARCHAR2) AS
BEGIN
   UTL_MAIL.send(sender => 'me@address.com',
             recipients => to_address,
                subject => subject,
                message => message,
              mime_type => 'text; charset=us-ascii');
END;
```

A trigger has the ability to call any other PL/SQL named block as long as it is in the same schema or the schema that contains the trigger has the correct privileges to access the named block in the other schema.

How It Works

The ability to use triggers for altering third-party applications can be extremely beneficial. Using a DML trigger on INSERT, UPDATE, or DELETE of a particular table is a good way to control what occurs with application data once a database event occurs. This technique will be transparent to any application users because the trigger would most likely be executed when the user saves a record via a button that is built into the application.

Although creating database triggers to alter functionality can be beneficial, you must also be careful not to create a trigger that will have an adverse effect on the application. For instance, if you create a trigger that updates some data that has been entered and the application is expecting to do something different with the data, then the application may not work as expected. One way to remedy this issue would be to create an autonomous transaction. Autonomous transactions ensure that an application continues to run even if a dependent body of code fails. In this case, an autonomous transaction could prevent a failed trigger from crashing an application. To learn more about using autonomous transactions, please refer to Recipe 2-13.

Another issue that could arise is one where too many triggers are created on the same table for the same event. You must be careful when creating triggers and be aware of all other triggers that will be executed during the same event. By default, Oracle does not fire triggers in any specific order, and the execution order can vary each time the database event occurs. Do not create triggers that depend upon other triggers, because your application will eventually fail! If you must create two or more triggers that execute on the same table for the same event, then please ensure that you are using proper techniques to make the triggers execute in the correct order. For more information on this topic, please refer to Recipe 5-11.

The trigger in this particular recipe called a *stored procedure*. This was done so that the trigger body performed a specific task and remained concise. Triggers can call as many stored procedures as required, as long as the trigger itself is less than or equal to 32KB in size. The stored procedure in the solution to this recipe is used to send an e-mail. As such, maintaining a separate procedure to perform the task of sending e-mail will allow the trigger body to remain concise, and the procedure can also be used elsewhere if needed.

USING ORACLE'S UTL_MAIL PACKAGE

The e-mail in the solution to this recipe is sent using Oracle's UTL_MAIL package. You will learn more about using this package in a later chapter, but for the purposes of testing this recipe, it is important to know that the UTL_MAIL package is not enabled by default. To install it, you must log in as the SYS user and execute the utlmail.sql and prvtmail.plb scripts that reside within the $ORACLE_HOME/rdbms/admin directory.

An outgoing mail server must also be defined by setting the SMTP_OUT_SERVER initialization parameter prior to use.

5-6. Validating Input Data

Problem

You want to validate data before allowing it to be inserted into a table. If the input data does not pass your business-rules test, you want the INSERT statement to fail. For example, you want to ensure that an e-mail address field in the EMPLOYEE table never contains the domain portion of an e-mail address, in other words, that it never contains the @ character or anything following the @ character.

■ **Note** Recipe 5-7 presents an alternative solution to this same problem that involves silently cleansing erroneous data as it is inserted.

Solution

Generally speaking, do validation using BEFORE triggers, because that lets you trap errors prior to changes being made to the data. For this recipe, you can write a BEFORE INSERT trigger to examine the e-mail address for any new employee. Raise an error if that address contains an @ character. The following example demonstrates a trigger that uses this technique. If an attempt to enter an invalid e-mail address occurs, an error will be raised.

```
CREATE OR REPLACE TRIGGER check_email_address
BEFORE INSERT ON employees
FOR EACH ROW
BEGIN
  IF NOT INSTR(:new.email,'@') > 0 THEN
    RAISE_APPLICATION_ERROR(-20001, 'INVALID EMAIL ADDRESS');
  END IF;
END;
```

How It Works

A BEFORE INSERT trigger is useful for performing the validation of data before it is inserted into the database. In the solution to this recipe, a trigger is created that will check to ensure that a string that supposedly contains an e-mail address does indeed have an @ character within it. The trigger uses the Oracle built-in INSTR function inside a conditional statement to determine whether the @ character exists. If the character does not exist within the string, then the trigger will raise a user-defined error message. On the other hand, if the string does contain the character, then the trigger will not do anything.

Coding a trigger for validation of data is quite common. Although the solution to this recipe checks to ensure that an e-mail address is valid, you could write similar triggers to perform similar validation on other datatypes.

5-7. Scrubbing Input Data

Problem

You are interested in examining and correcting user input prior to it being inserted into a database table.

Solution

Use a BEFORE INSERT trigger to scrub the data prior to allowing it to be inserted into the table. By using a trigger, you will have access to the data before it is inserted, which will provide you with the ability to assess the data before it is persisted.

In this particular example, a trigger is being used to examine the data that was entered on a form for insertion into the EMPLOYEES table. The e-mail field is being validated to ensure that it is in a valid format. In particular, the e-mail field for the EMPLOYEES table includes only the address portion to the left of the @ symbol. This trigger ensures that even if someone had entered the entire e-mail address, then only the valid portion would be inserted into the database. The following example demonstrates this functionality:

```
CREATE OR REPLACE TRIGGER check_email_address
BEFORE INSERT ON employees
FOR EACH ROW
DECLARE
  temp_email              employees.email%TYPE := :new.email;
BEGIN
  IF INSTR(temp_email,'@') > 0 THEN
    temp_email := SUBSTR(:new.email, 0, INSTR(temp_email, '@')-1);
  END IF;
 :new.email := temp_email;
END;
```

The trigger in this example uses a couple of different PL/SQL built-in functions to ensure that the data being inserted into the EMPLOYEES.EMAIL table is formatted correctly.

How It Works

BEFORE INSERT triggers work very nicely for verifying data prior to inserting it into the database. Since insert triggers have access to the :NEW qualifier, the values that are going to be inserted into the database table can be tested to ensure that they conform to the proper standards and can then be manipulated if need be. When used in a BEFORE trigger, the :NEW value can be altered, allowing triggers to change values prior to when they are inserted. The :OLD qualifier will allow one to access the NULL old values, but they cannot be changed.

Validating data with triggers can be very useful if used appropriately. As a rule of thumb, you should not attempt to create triggers for validating data that can be performed declaratively. For instance, if you need to ensure that a column of data is never NULL, then you should place a NOT NULL constraint on that column. There are only a couple of circumstances where you are required to enforce constraints within triggers, and those are as follows:

- If you do not have access to the database objects to alter the table and add constraints because doing so would cause issues with a program that is in place

- If the business logic cannot be reflected in a simple, declarative trigger

- If your application requires a constraint to be enforced only part of the time

In all other circumstances, try to use database-level constraints because that is their job, and it can be done much more efficiently than using a trigger. However, trigger validation is perfect for situations such as those depicted in the solution to this recipe, where complex business rules must be validated that are not possible with built-in constraints.

5-8. Replacing a Column's Value

Problem

You want to verify that a column value is in the correct format when it is entered into the database. If it is not in the correct format, then you want to adjust the value so that it is in the correct format before inserting into the database. For example, upon creation of an employee record, it is essential that the e-mail address follows a certain format. If the e-mail address is not uniform with other employee e-mail addresses, then it needs to be adjusted. You want to write a trigger that ensures that the new employee EMAIL value will be in the correct format.

Solution

Check the format using a BEFORE trigger. For this recipe, use a BEFORE INSERT trigger to determine whether the new EMAIL value is in the correct format. If it is not, then adjust the value accordingly so that the new e-mail address will start with the first letter of the employee's first name, followed by the employee's last name. If the new e-mail address is not unique, then a number must be added to the end of it to ensure that it will be unique.

The following trigger demonstrates a BEFORE INSERT trigger that checks and updates the EMAIL value as described. This trigger will be fired whenever someone inserts values into the EMPLOYEES table.

```
CREATE OR REPLACE TRIGGER populate_emp_email
BEFORE INSERT ON employees
FOR EACH ROW
DECLARE
    email_count         NUMBER := 0;
    success_flag        BOOLEAN := FALSE;
    temp_email          employees.email%TYPE;
    email_idx           NUMBER := 0;
```

```
BEGIN
  -- check to see if the email address is in the correct format
  IF :new.email != UPPER(SUBSTR(:new.first_name,0,1) || :new.last_name) THEN
    -- check the database to ensure that the new email address will be unique
    temp_email := UPPER(SUBSTR(:new.first_name,0,1) || :new.last_name);
    WHILE success_flag = FALSE LOOP
        SELECT COUNT(*)
        INTO email_count
        FROM employees
        WHERE email = temp_email;

        -- if it is unique then end the loop
        IF email_count = 0 THEN
          success_flag := TRUE;
        -- if not unique, then add the index number to the end and check again
        ELSE
          temp_email := UPPER(SUBSTR(:new.first_name,0,1) || :new.last_name) || email_idx;
        END IF;
        email_idx := email_idx + 1;
    END LOOP;
    :new.email := temp_email;
  END IF;

END;
```

The value of the e-mail address must always follow the same format, and this trigger ensures that the any new EMAIL values will follow that format. If the new EMAIL value does follow the correct format, then it will be inserted into the database without changes, but if it does not follow the correct format, then this trigger will adjust the value accordingly.

How It Works

Another frequent usage of triggers is to replace a value that someone is trying to insert into the database with some other value. Much like ensuring data integrity, you must write to the :NEW qualifier value in order to replace another value that was entered. When the :NEW value is overwritten, then that new value is inserted into the database instead of the original value. The BEFORE trigger acts as an interceptor where the values that are entered are intercepted prior to reaching the database table. The trigger has full reign to change values as needed as long as the values that are changed by the trigger still maintain the necessary requirements to meet the database table constraints that have been defined.

Any DML trigger can include multiple trigger events, including INSERT, UPDATE, or DELETE events. Any combination of these three events can be used to fire a trigger. The events that are to be used for firing a trigger must be listed with the OR keyword between them. The following line of code is an example of using all three events on a BEFORE trigger:

```
BEFORE INSERT OR UPDATE OR DELETE ON employees
```

The events can be in any order within the BEFORE clause. Any combination of these three events can also be used with the AFTER trigger. The main difference between the BEFORE and AFTER triggers is what type of access each has to the :NEW and :OLD qualifiers. Table 4-1 lists the different types of triggers and their subsequent access to the qualifiers.

Table 4-1. Trigger Types and Qualifier Acccess

Trigger Type	:NEW	:OLD
BEFORE	Writeable	Always contains NULL
AFTER	Not writeable	Always contains populated values
INSERT	Contains values	Contains NULL
DELETE	Contains NULL	Contains populated values
UPDATE	Contains populated values	Contains populated values

A BEFORE trigger has write access to values using the :NEW qualifier, and AFTER triggers do not since the data has already been inserted or updated in the table. INSERT triggers have meaningful access to values with the :NEW qualifier only; variables using the :OLD qualifier will be NULL. UPDATE triggers have meaningful access to values using both the :NEW and :OLD qualifiers. DELETE triggers have meaningful access only to values using the :old qualifier; values using the :new qualifier will be NULL.

Performing tasks such as replacing values with triggers should be used only on an as-needed basis. This type of trigger can cause confusion for those who do not have access to the trigger code. It is also important to ensure that triggers do not act upon each other in order to avoid mutating table errors. This can occur if one trigger is updating the values of a table and another trigger is attempting to examine the values of the table at the same time.

5-9. Triggering on a System Event

Problem

You want to write a trigger that executes on a system event such as a login. For example, you want to increase security a bit for your database and ensure that users are logging into the database only during the week. In an effort to help control security, you want to receive an e-mail alert if someone logs into the database on the weekend.

Solution

Create a system-level trigger that will log an event into a table if anyone logs into the database during off-hours. To notify you as promptly as possible, it may also be a good idea to send an e-mail when this event occurs. To create a system-level trigger, use the AFTER LOGON ON DATABASE clause in your trigger definition.

The first step in creating this solution is to create an audit table. In the audit table you will want to capture the IP address of the user's machine, the time and date of the login, and the authenticated username. The following code will create a table to hold this information:

```
CREATE TABLE login_audit_table(
ID                      NUMBER PRIMARY KEY,   -- Populated by sequence number
login_audit_seq
AUDIT_DATE              DATE NOT NULL,
```

```
AUDIT_USER            VARCHAR2(50) NOT NULL,
AUDIT_IP              VARCHAR2(50) NOT NULL,
AUDIT_HOST            VARCHAR2(50) NOT NULL);
```

Now that the auditing table has been created, it is time to create the trigger. The following code demonstrates the creation of a logon trigger:

```
CREATE OR REPLACE TRIGGER login_audit_event
AFTER LOGON ON DATABASE
DECLARE
  v_subject                   VARCHAR2(100) := 'User login audit event triggered';
  v_message                   VARCHAR2(1000);
BEGIN
  INSERT INTO login_audit_table values(
    Login_audit_seq.nextval,
    Sysdate,
    SYS_CONTEXT('USERENV','SESSION_USERID'),
    SYS_CONTEXT('USERENV','IP_ADDRESS'),
    SYS_CONTEXT('USERENV','HOST'));
    v_message := 'User ' || SYS_CONTEXT('USERENV','SESSION_USERID') ||
                        ' logged into the database at ' || sysdate || ' from host ' ||
            SYS_CONTEXT('USERENV','HOST');


    SEND_email('DBA-GROUP@mycompany.com',
                    v_subject,
                    v_message);

END;
```

This simple trigger will fire each time someone logs into the database. To reduce the overhead of this trigger being initiated during normal business hours, this trigger should be disabled during normal business hours. It is possible to create a stored procedure that disables and enables the trigger and then schedule that procedure to be executed at certain times. However, if there are only a few users who will be logging into the database each day, then trigger controls such as these are not necessary.

How It Works

Triggers are a great way to audit system events on a database. There are several types of system triggers:

- AFTER STARTUP

- BEFORE SHUTDOWN

- AFTER LOGON

- BEFORE LOGOFF

- AFTER SUSPEND

- AFTER SERVERERROR

- AFTER DB_ROLE_CHANGE

Each of these system events can be correlated to a trigger when the trigger includes the ON DATABASE clause, as shown here:

```
CREATE OR REPLACE system_trigger
trigger_type ON DATABASE
…
```

System triggers fire once for each correlating system event that occurs. Therefore, if there is a system trigger defined for both the LOGON and LOGOFF events, each will be fired one time for every user who logs onto or off the database. System triggers are excellent tools for helping audit database system events. Notice that the different system events have access only to certain types of events. For instance, STARTUP triggers can be fired only after the event occurs. This is because the Oracle Database is not available before STARTUP, so it would be impossible to fire a trigger beforehand. Similarly, SHUTDOWN triggers have access to the BEFORE event only because the database is unavailable after SHUTDOWN.

In the solution to this recipe, the trigger is intended to execute once after each login to the database. The trigger will insert some values from the current session into an auditing table, and it will send an e-mail to the DBA group. It should be noted that Oracle Database provides some auditing capabilities to perform similar activities right out of the box. In fact, Oracle 11g turns on auditing by default for every database. However, the auditing options that are available via Oracle do not allow for sending e-mail as our solution does. You may prefer to use Oracle's internal auditing features for storing the audit trail and combine them with auditing triggers such as the one in this recipe for simply sending an e-mail when the event occurs.

The SERVERERROR event is fired whenever an Oracle server error occurs. The SERVERERROR event can be useful for detecting user SQL errors or logging system errors. However, there are a few cases in which an Oracle server error does not trigger this event. Those Oracle errors are as follows:

- ORA-01403: No data found

- ORA-01422: Exact fetch returns more than requested number of rows

- ORA-01423: Error encountered while checking for extra rows in exact fetch

- ORA-01034: ORACLE not available

- ORA-04030: Out of process memory when trying to allocate bytes

System event triggers can assist a DBA in administration of the database. These triggers can also help developers if SQL errors are triggering SERVERERROR events and notifying of possible SQL problems in the application.

5-10. Triggering on a Schema-Related Event

Problem

You want to trigger on an event related to a change in a database schema. For example, if someone drops a database table on accident, it could cause much time and grief attempting to restore and recover data to its original state. Rather than doing so, you want to place a control mechanism into the database that will ensure that administrators cannot delete essential tables.

Solution

Use a PL/SQL database trigger to raise an exception and send an alert to the DBA if someone attempts to drop a table. This will prevent any tables from inadvertently being dropped, and it will also allow the administrator to know whether someone is potentially trying to drop tables.

```
CREATE OR REPLACE TRIGGER ddl_trigger
BEFORE CREATE OR ALTER OR DROP
ON SCHEMA
DECLARE
  evt             VARCHAR2(2000);
  v_subject       VARCHAR2(100) := 'Drop table attempt';
  v_message       VARCHAR2(1000);
BEGIN
  SELECT ora_sysevent
  INTO evt
  FROM dual;

  IF evt = 'DROP' THEN
   RAISE_APPLICATION_ERROR(-20900, 'UNABLE TO DROP TABLE, ' ||
          'EVENT HAS BEEN LOGGED');
  END IF;
  v_message := 'Table drop attempted by: '||
    SYS_CONTEXT('USERENV','SESSION_USERID');
  SEND_EMAIL('DBA-GROUP@mycompany.com',
            v_subject,
            v_message);
END;
```

In this situation, both the user who attempts to drop the table and the members of the DBA-GROUP mailing list will be notified.

How It Works

You can use triggers to log or prevent certain database activities from occurring. In this recipe, you saw how to create a trigger that will prevent a table from being dropped. The trigger will be executed prior to any CREATE, ALTER, or DROP within the current schema. Within the body of the trigger, the event is checked to see whether it is a DROP, and actions are taken if so.

■ **Note** To be even more fine-grained, it is possible to specify a particular schema for the trigger to use. Doing so would look like the following:

```
BEFORE CREATE ALTER OR DROP ON HR.SCHEMA
...
```

There are several other DDL trigger operations that can be used to help administer a database or application. The following are these operations along with the type of trigger that can be used with it:

```
BEFORE / AFTER ALTER
BEFORE / AFTER ANALYZE
BEFORE / AFTER ASSOCIATE STATISTICS
BEFORE / AFTER AUDIT
BEFORE / AFTER COMMENT
BEFORE / AFTER CREATE
BEFORE / AFTER DDL
BEFORE / AFTER DISASSOCIATE STATISTICS
BEFORE / AFTER DROP
BEFORE / AFTER GRANT
BEFORE / AFTER NOAUDIT
BEFORE / AFTER RENAME
BEFORE / AFTER REVOKE
BEFORE / AFTER TRUNCATE
AFTER SUSPEND
```

All DDL triggers can be fired using either BEFORE or AFTER event types. In most cases, triggers that are fired before a DDL event occurs are used to prevent the event from happening. On the other hand, triggers that are fired after an event occurs usually log information or send an e-mail. In the solution to this recipe, a combination of those two situations exists. The BEFORE event type was used because the trigger is being used to prevent the tables from being dropped. However, logging or e-mailing can also occur to advise interested parties of the event. Typically a logging event occurs with an AFTER trigger so that the event has already occurred and the database is in a consistent state prior to the logging.

5-11. Firing Two Triggers on the Same Event

Problem

There is a requirement to create a trigger to enter the SYSDATE into the HIRE_DATE column of the LOCATIONS table. However, there is already a trigger in place that is fired BEFORE INSERT on the table, and you do not want the two triggers to conflict.

Solution

Use the FOLLOWS clause to ensure the ordering of the execution of the triggers. The following example shows the creation of two triggers that are to be executed BEFORE INSERT on the EMPLOYEES table.

First, we'll create a trigger to verify that a new employee's salary falls within range:

```
CREATE OR REPLACE TRIGGER verify_emp_salary
BEFORE INSERT ON employees
FOR EACH ROW
DECLARE
  v_min_sal      jobs.min_salary%TYPE;
  v_max_sal      jobs.max_salary%TYPE;
BEGIN
  SELECT min_salary, max_salary
  INTO v_min_sal, v_max_sal
```

```
    FROM JOBS
    WHERE JOB_ID = :new.JOB_ID;

    IF :new.salary > v_max_sal THEN
      RAISE_APPLICATION_ERROR(-20901,
        'You cannot give a salary greater than the max in this category');
    ELSIF :new.salary < v_min_sal THEN
      RAISE_APPLICATION_ERROR(-20902,
        'You cannot give a salary less than the min in this category');
    END IF;
END;
```

Next, you'll create a trigger to force the hire date to be the current date:

```
CREATE or REPLACE TRIGGER populate_hire_date
BEFORE INSERT
    ON employees
    FOR EACH ROW
FOLLOWS verify_emp_salary
DECLARE
BEGIN
    :new.hire_date := sysdate;
END;
```

Since it does not make sense to change the hire date if the record will not be inserted, you want the VERIFY_EMP_SALARY trigger to fire first. The FOLLOWS clause in the POPULATE_HIRE_DATE trigger ensures that this will be the case.

How It Works

Oracle 11g introduced the FOLLOWS clause into the Oracle trigger that allows you to specify the ordering in which triggers should execute. The FOLLOWS clause specifies the trigger that should fire prior to the trigger being created. In other words, if you specify the FOLLOWS clause when creating a trigger, then you should name a trigger that you want to have executed prior to your new trigger. Hence, if you specify a trigger in the FOLLOWS clause that does not already exist, you will receive a compile error.

■ **Note** The PRECEDES clause was introduced in Oracle 11g as well. You can use this clause to specify the opposite situation that is resolved using the FOLLOWS clause. If you specify PRECEDES instead of FOLLOWS, then the trigger being created will fire prior to the trigger that you specify after the PRECEDES clause.

By default, Oracle triggers fire in any arbitrary ordering. In the past, there was no way to guarantee the order in which triggers were to be executed. The addition of the FOLLOWS clause now allows you to do so. However, it is important that you do not make triggers dependent upon each other. Doing so could cause issues of one of the triggers were to be dropped for some reason. It is bad design to create a trigger that depends on the successful completion of another trigger, so the FOLLOWS clause should be used only in situations where there is no dependency.

5-12. Creating a Trigger That Fires on Multiple Events

Problem

You have logic that is very similar for two different events. Thus, you want to combine that logic into a single trigger that fires for both. For example, let's assume that we want to create a single trigger on the EMPLOYEES table with code to fire after each row that is inserted or modified and also with code to fire at the end of each of those statements' executions.

Solution

Use a compound trigger to combine all the triggers into a single body of code. The trigger in this solution will execute based upon various timing points. It will execute AFTER EACH ROW in the EMPLOYEES table has been updated, as well as AFTER the entire update statement has been executed. The AFTER EACH ROW section of the trigger will audit the inserts and updates made on the table, and the AFTER STATEMENT section of the trigger will send notification to the DBA regarding audits that have occurred on the table.

The following code shows the creation of a compound trigger that comprises each of these two triggers into one body of code:

```
CREATE OR REPLACE TRIGGER emp_table_auditing
  FOR INSERT OR UPDATE ON employees
    COMPOUND TRIGGER
  -- Global variable section
  table_upd_count       NUMBER := 0;
  table_id_start        employees.employee_id%TYPE;

  AFTER EACH ROW IS
  BEGIN
    SELECT MAX(employee_id)
    INTO table_id_start
    FROM employees;

    IF INSERTING THEN

      INSERT INTO update_access_log VALUES(
        update_access_seq.nextval,
        SYS_CONTEXT('USERENV','SESSION_USER'),
        sysdate,
        NULL,
        :new.salary,
        'EMPLOYEES - INSERT',
        'SALARY');
      table_upd_count := table_upd_count + 1;


    ELSIF UPDATING THEN
      IF :old.salary != :new.salary THEN
        INSERT INTO update_access_log VALUES(
          update_access_seq.nextval,
          SYS_CONTEXT('USERENV','SESSION_USER'),
```

```
            sysdate,
            :old.salary,
            :new.salary,
            'EMPLOYEES - UPDATE',
            'SALARY');
        table_upd_count := table_upd_count + 1;
      END IF;
    END IF;

  END AFTER EACH ROW;

  AFTER STATEMENT IS
    v_subject                    VARCHAR2(100) := 'Employee Table Update';
    v_message                    VARCHAR2(2000);
  BEGIN

    v_message := 'There have been ' || table_upd_count ||
      ' changes made to the employee table starting with ID #' ||
      table_id_start;

    SEND_EMAIL('DBA-GROUP@my_company.com',
              v_subject,
              v_message);
  END AFTER STATEMENT;

END emp_table_auditing;
```

The insert and update events are audited via the trigger that is coded using the AFTER EACH ROW clause, and then the AFTER STATEMENT trigger sends a notification to alert the DBA of each audit. The two triggers share a global variable that is declared prior to the code for the first trigger.

How It Works

Prior to Oracle 11g, there was no easy way to create multiple triggers that were able to share the same global variable. The compound trigger was introduced with the release of Oracle 11g, and it allows multiple triggers for the same table to be embodied within a single trigger. Compound triggers allow you to code different timing points within the same trigger; those different events are as follows in logical execution order:

- BEFORE STATEMENT

- BEFORE EACH ROW

- AFTER EACH ROW

- AFTER STATEMENT

Each of these timing points allows for the declaration of different trigger execution points. Using a compound trigger allows you to create a trigger that performs some actions: BEFORE INSERT on a table and AFTER INSERT on a table all within the same trigger body. In the case of the solution to this recipe, an AFTER UPDATE trigger is coded within the same compound trigger as an AFTER STATEMENT trigger. The logical order of execution allows you to code triggers that depend upon others using this technique. In other recipes within this chapter, you have learned that it is not good programming practice to code triggers that depend upon each other. This is mainly because if one trigger is invalidated or dropped, then the other trigger that depends on it will automatically be invalidated. Since a compound trigger is one body of code, either the entire trigger is valid or invalid. Therefore, the failure points between two trigger bodies are removed.

In the solution, the AFTER STATEMENT trigger depends upon the AFTER EACH ROW trigger. If the AFTER EACH ROW trigger does not audit anything, then the AFTER STATEMENT trigger will still fire, but it will send an e-mail that signifies zero rows have been changed. The two trigger bodies are able to share access to global variables, types, and cursors via the use of the global declaration section. Anything declared within this section is visible to all triggers within the compound trigger body, so in the case of this solution, you can use the first AFTER EACH ROW to update the value of the global variable, which is then in turn used within the AFTER STATEMENT trigger. The overall compound trigger structure is as follows:

```
CREATE OR REPLACE TRIGGER trigger-name
   FOR trigger-action ON table-name
      COMPOUND TRIGGER
      -- Global declaration section
   global_variable VARCHAR2(10);
    BEFORE STATEMENT IS
    BEGIN
      NULL;
  -- Statements go here.
    END BEFORE STATEMENT;
    BEFORE EACH ROW IS
    BEGIN
      NULL;
-- Statements go here.    END BEFORE EACH ROW;
      AFTER EACH ROW IS
  BEGIN
      NULL;
-- Statements go here.
    END AFTER EACH ROW;
      AFTER STATEMENT IS
      BEGIN
      NULL;
  -- Statements go here.
    END AFTER STATEMENT;
  END trigger-name;
```

Compound triggers can be very useful for incorporating several different timed events on the same database table. Not only do they allow for easier maintenance because all code resides within one trigger body, but they also allow for shared variables among the trigger events as well as more robust dependency management.

5-13. Creating a Trigger in a Disabled State

Problem

After a planning meeting, your company has decided that it would be a great idea to create a trigger to send notification of updates to employee salaries. Since the trigger will be tied into the system-wide database application, you want to ensure that it compiles before enabling it so that it will not affect the rest of the application.

Solution

Create a trigger that is in a disabled state by default. This will afford you the opportunity to ensure that the trigger has compiled successfully before you enable it. Use the new DISABLE clause to ensure that your trigger is in DISABLED state by default.

The following trigger sends messages to employees when their salary is changed. The trigger is disabled by default to ensure that the application is not adversely affected if there is a compilation error.

```
CREATE OR REPLACE TRIGGER send_salary_notice
AFTER UPDATE OF SALARY ON employees
FOR EACH ROW
DISABLE
DECLARE
  v_subject      VARCHAR2(100) := 'Salary Update Has Occurrred';
  v_message      VARCHAR2(2000);
BEGIN
  v_message := 'Your salary has been increased from ' ||
               :old.salary || ' to ' || :new.salary || '.'   ||
               'If you have any questions or complaints, please ' ||
               'do not contact the DBA.';

  SEND_EMAIL(:new.email || '@mycompany.com',
             v_subject,
             v_message);
END;
```

On an annual basis, this trigger can be enabled via the following syntax:

```
ALTER TRIGGER send_salary_notice ENABLE;
```

It can then be disabled again using the same syntax:

```
ALTER TRIGGER send_salary_notice DISABLE;
```

How It Works

Another welcome new feature with Oracle 11g is the ability to create triggers that are DISABLED by default. The syntax for creating a trigger in this fashion is as follows:

```
CREATE OR REPLACE TRIGGER trigger_name
ON UPDATE OR INSERT OR DELETION OF table_name
[FOR EACH ROW]
DISABLED
DECLARE
  -- Declarations go here.
BEGIN
  -- Statements go here.
END;
```

The new DISABLED clause is used upon creation of a trigger. By default, a trigger is ENABLED by creation, and this clause allows for the opposite to hold true.

■ ■ ■

CHAPTER 6

Type Conversion

Type conversion takes place in almost every PL/SQL program. It is important to know how to convert from one datatype to another so that your applications can contain more versatility. Not only are datatype conversions important to developers, but they can also be a godsend to database administrators. Type conversion can occur when moving data around from one table to another. It is also very common when obtaining data from input forms and performing calculations upon it.

Whatever your use may be, this chapter will get you headed into the right direction with a handful of useful recipes. If your application works with dates or numbers, you will most likely find this chapter useful. There are two forms of datatype conversion: explicit conversion and implicit conversion. Explicit datatype conversion is what you will learn about in the following recipes. Using explicit conversion, you tell Oracle how you want types to be converted. Implicit conversion is automatically performed by Oracle. There are many datatypes that can be converted using implicit type conversion. However, it is not recommended that you rely on implicit conversion, because you never know exactly how Oracle will convert something. The recipes in this chapter will show you more reliable explicit conversion techniques that will give you the ability to convert types in such a way that your application will be rock solid.

6-1. Converting a String to a Number

Problem

You need to convert some strings into numbers. For instance, your application contains several strings that are entered via a user input screen. These strings need to be converted into numbers so that they can be used to perform calculations.

Solution

Use the TO_NUMBER function to explicitly convert the VARCHAR2 field into a NUMBER. The following examples demonstrate the use of TO_NUMBER by showing how to convert some currency values taken from the user interface into numbers for storage in the database.

The first example demonstrates the conversion of a variable with a datatype of VARCHAR2 into a NUMBER:

```
DECLARE
  in_dollars              VARCHAR2(10) := &dollars;
  dollars_formatted  NUMBER;
BEGIN
  -- Assume that IN_DOLLARS is the user input in VARCHAR2 format
  dollars_formatted := TO_NUMBER(in_dollars, '9G999D99');
  DBMS_OUTPUT.PUT_LINE(dollars_formatted);
```

```
END;
```

The TO_NUMBER function returns a number from a VARCHAR2 format. The previous example demonstrates the typical usage of this function.

How It Works

The TO_NUMBER function provides an explicit way to convert strings into NUMBER format in PL/SQL. Although most string to NUMBER conversion is implicit via Oracle Database, it is always a best practice to explicitly use the TO_NUMBER function to ensure that your code will not break at some point in the future. The format for using the function is as follows:

```
TO_NUMBER(expression [, format [, 'nls' ] ])
```

The expression can be a value of type BINARY_DOUBLE, CHAR, VARCHAR2, NCHAR, or NVARCHAR2. The optional format is a mask that can be used to help format the expression value into a number. The mask is a string of characters that represents the format of the string value that is contained in the expression value. Table 6-1 shows the most commonly used format mask characters:

Table 6-1. Common Formatting Mask Characters

Character	Description
9	Represents a numeric character
D	Represents a decimal point
G	Represents a comma

Although the use of a formatting mask is optional, it is a good idea to include it if you know the format of the string. Doing so will help Oracle convert your value into a number more accurately. Lastly, you can use the optional nls settings to set the NLS_LANGUAGE that is to be used to convert the string, the NLS_CURRENCY, or any of the other NLS session parameters. Use of the nls parameter is not very common.

■ **Note** For a complete listing of available session NLS parameters, issue the following query: SELECT * FROM NLS_SESSION_PARAMETERS.

It is also possible to convert strings into numbers using the CAST function. However, for direct string to number conversion, the TO_NUMBER function is the best tool for the job since it is straightforward and easy to maintain. For more information on the CAST function, please take a look at Recipe 6-5.

6-2. Converting a String to a Date

Problem

You need to convert some strings into DATE types. Let's say you have a requirement to insert date types into a database table column from one of your applications. The user is allowed to enter a date using your application's web page, but it is in a string format after the user submits the page. You need to convert this date from a string to a date type.

Solution

Use the TO_DATE function to convert the string values into the DATE type. This will allow your application to accept the date string in any format and convert it to a DATE type for you. The next example shows how to use the TO_DATE function:

```
my_val      DATE := TO_DATE('06/12/2010','MM/DD/YYYY');
```

You can convert the string through assignment, as shown in the preceding example, or directly within a query, as shown in the next example:

```
SELECT TO_DATE('December 31, 2010', 'Month DD, YYYY') FROM DUAL;
```

As you can see, it is possible to convert multiple string formats into DATE types.

How It Works

The TO_DATE function is arguably the most widely used conversion function in Oracle. Whether you are using the function to convert dates for proper formatting within a SQL query or you are accepting and converting user input, this function is extremely helpful for getting your data into the Oracle DATE format. The syntax for using this function is as follows:

```
TO_DATE(expression[, format[,'nls']])
```

The syntax is much like that of the other Oracle conversion functions in that it accepts a required expression or string and two optional parameters. The optional format is used to specify the format of the string and to assist Oracle in converting the value into a DATE type. Table 6-2 shows many of the more common characters that can be used to specify the date format. See the *Oracle SQL Reference* for a complete list of formatting characters.

Table 6-2. Date Formatting Characters

Character	Description
MM	Represents the numeric month.
MON	Represents an abbreviated month name.
MONTH	Represents the entire month name.

Character	Description
DD	Represents the numeric day of the month.
DY	Abbreviation representing the day of the week.
YY	Represents the two-digit year.
YYYY	Represents the four-digit year.
RR	Represents the rounded two-digit year. The year is rounded in the range 1950 to 2049 to assist with two-digit years such as 10. A two-digit year less than 50 will result in a four-digit year such as 2010.
AM or PM	Represents the meridian indicator.
HH	Represents the hour of the day in 12-hour time format.
HH24	Represents the hour of the day in 24-hour time format.
MI	Represents the minutes in time.
SS	Represents the seconds in time.

The standard, or default, date format in Oracle is DD-MON-YY, though your database administrator does have the ability to change that default format. If you want to convert a string that is in the default format into a DATE type, then the mask is not required. The following example demonstrates this capability:

```
TO_DATE('27-MAY-10');
```

On the contrary, if you want to convert a string that is in a format that is different from the standard, then you must make use of a mask. The solution to this recipe depicts this type of behavior. Dates are also in care of time in Oracle, so if you want to display the time in your date, then it is possible to do so using the proper format mask. The following conversion will include both the date and the time:

```
TO_DATE('05/25/2010 07:35AM','MM/DD/YYYY HH:MIAM')
```

The TO_DATE conversion function is most often used when inserting or updating data. If you have a table column that has a DATE type, then you cannot place a string into that column unless it is in the standard date format. To get the data from an entry screen into the database, the TO_DATE function is usually used to convert the string into a date while the value is being inserted or updated.

It is also possible to convert strings to dates using the CAST function. For more information on the use of the CAST function, please see Recipe 6-5.

6-3. Converting a Number to a String

Problem

You need to alter some numbers into a currency format for display. Given a set of numbers, your application will perform a calculation and then convert the outcome into currency format, which will be a string type.

Solution

Use the TO_CHAR conversion function to obtain a nicely formatted currency string. The following code block accepts a number, performs a calculation, and then converts the number to a string:

```
CREATE OR REPLACE FUNCTION CALCULATE_BILL(bill_amount IN NUMBER)
  RETURN VARCHAR2 AS
  tax                    NUMBER  := .12;
  tip                    NUMBER  := .2;
  total_bill             NUMBER  := 0;
BEGIN
  total_bill := bill_amount + (bill_amount * tax);
  total_bill := total_bill + (total_bill * tip);
  return to_char(total_bill, '$999.00');
END;
```

When a bill amount is passed to the CALCULATE_BILL function, a nicely formatted dollar amount will be returned. If you were to pass 24.75 to the function, it would return $33.26.

How It Works

The TO_CHAR function works much like the other Oracle TO_ conversion functions in that it accepts a number value along with an optional format mask and nls language value. Table 6-3 describes the more commonly used formatting mask characters for numbers.

Table 6-3. Common Formatting Mask Characters

Character	Description
9	Represents a numeric character that displays only if a value is present
.	Represents a decimal point
,	Represents a comma
$	Represents a dollar sign
0	Represents a numeric character that will always display, even if null

As you can see from the solution to this recipe, the format mask of $999.00 is chosen. Why not use the mask of $999.99 for the conversion? By using the 0 instead of the 9, you ensure that the cents value will always be present. Even if the cents value is zero, you will still get a .00 at the end of your string. Essentially, the 0 character forces Oracle to pad with zeros rather than spaces.

You can also pad with zero characters to the left of the decimal. Here's an example:

```
select to_char(82,'0000099') from dual;
```

That results in the following:

```
0000082
```

It is also possible to convert numbers to strings using the CAST function, although TO_CHAR makes for code that is easier to read and maintain. For more information on the use of the CAST function, please see recipe 6-5.

6-4. Converting a Date to a String

Problem

You want to convert a date into a nicely formatted string value. For example, you are converting a legacy application from another database vendor into a web-based Oracle application. A few of the fields on the web form are dates. The users of the application expect to see the dates in a specific format, so you need the dates to be formatted in a particular manner for display.

Solution

Use the TO_CHAR function using the date masks. The TO_CHAR function offers many formatting options for returning a string from a DATE value. The following function accepts an EMPLOYEE_ID value and returns a representation of the HIRE_DATE spelled out.

```
CREATE OR REPLACE PROCEDURE obtain_emp_hire_date(emp_id IN NUMBER)
  AS
  emp_hire_date     employees.hire_date%TYPE;
  emp_first         employees.first_name%TYPE;
  emp_last          employees.last_name%TYPE;
BEGIN
  SELECT hire_date, first_name, last_name
  INTO emp_hire_date, emp_first, emp_last
  FROM employees
  WHERE employee_id = emp_id;

  DBMS_OUTPUT.PUT_LINE(emp_first || ' ' || emp_last ||
        ' was hired on: ' ||
        TO_CHAR(emp_hire_date, 'DAY MONTH DDTH YYYY'));
EXCEPTION
  WHEN NO_DATA_FOUND THEN
    DBMS_OUTPUT.PUT_LINE('No employee found for the given ID');
END;
```

If you pass the employee ID of 200 to this function, then it will return a result in the following format:

```
Jennifer Whalen was hired on: THURSDAY    SEPTEMBER 17TH 1987

PL/SQL procedure successfully completed.
```

How It Works

As shown in the previous recipe, the TO_CHAR function accepts a NUMBER or DATE value and returns a nicely formatted string. Using the many formatting masks that are available, you can return a string-based representation in a number of ways. As demonstrated in the solutions to this recipe and the previous one, the TO_CHAR function works a bit differently than the other conversion functions because the formatting mask is used to help produce the final string. Other conversion functions use the formatting mask to represent the format of the string you are passing in. In other words, TO_CHAR produces the formatted strings, whereas the other conversion functions accept them and produce a different datatype.

Table 6-4 lists some of the most commonly used characters for converting dates into strings.

Table 6-4. *Date Formatting Mask Characters*

Characters	Description
YYYY	Represents the four-digit year
YEAR	Represents the spelled-out year
YYY	Represents the last three digits of the year
YY	Represents the last two digits of the year
Y	Represents the last digit of the year
IYY	Represents the last three digits of the ISO year
IY	Represents the last two digits of the ISO year
I	Represents the last digit of the ISO year
Q	Represents the quarter of the year
MM	Represents the month of the year
MON	Represents the abbreviated month name
MONTH	Represents the spelled-out month name padded with blanks
RM	Represents the Roman numeral month
WW	Represents the week of the year

Characters	Description
W	Represents the week of the month
IW	Represents the ISO week of the year
D	Represents the day of the week
DAY	Represents the name of the day
DD	Represents the day of the month
DDD	Represents the day of the year
DY	Represents the abbreviated name of the day
J	Represents the Julian day
HH	Represents the hour of the day (1–12)
HH12	Represents the hour of the day (1–12); same as HH
HH24	Represents the hour of the day (0–23)
MI	Represents the minute of the hour (0–59)
SS	Represents the second (0–59)
SSSSS	Represents the seconds past midnight (0–86399)
FF	Represents the fractional seconds

There are several formatting options, as you can see. It is best to spend some time with each of the different combinations to decide upon which one works best for your solution.

PL/SQL can make date formatting easy, because it is possible to create your own function that returns a date formatted per your application's requirements. Sometimes it is difficult to remember all the different formatting options that are available for dates. It can also be quite painful to reference a table such as Table 6-4 each time you want to format a date string. You can instead create your own conversion function to support just the formats that you use, and no others. Such a function greatly reduces the possibility for error, thus enhancing consistency in how your application formats dates.

The function in the following example accepts two parameters: the date to be converted and a string that specifies the output format. The second argument is limited to only four, easy-to-remember values: LONG, SHORT, STD, and DASH.

```
-- Returns a date string formatted per the style
-- that is passed into it.  The possible style strings
-- are as follows:
```

```
--    LONG => The spelled out date
--    SHORT => The abbreviated date
--    STD or blank => The standard date format mm/dd/yyyy
--    DASH => The standard format with dashes mm-dd-yyyy
CREATE OR REPLACE FUNCTION FORMAT_DATE(in_date IN DATE,
                                       style IN VARCHAR2)
 RETURN VARCHAR2 AS
 formatted_date     VARCHAR2(100);
BEGIN
  CASE style
    WHEN 'LONG' THEN
        formatted_date := TO_CHAR(in_date, 'DAY MONTH DDTH YYYY');
    WHEN 'SHORT' THEN
        formatted_date := TO_CHAR(in_date, 'DY MON DDTH YYYY');
    WHEN 'DASH' THEN
        formatted_date := TO_CHAR(in_date, 'MM-DD-YYYY');
    ELSE
        formatted_date := TO_CHAR(in_date, 'MM/DD/YYYY');
  END CASE;
  RETURN formatted_date;
END;
```

This function is nice because you only need to remember a short string that is used to represent the date format that you'd like to return.

It is also possible to convert dates to strings using the CAST function. For more information on the use of the CAST function, please see Recipe 6-5.

6-5. Converting Strings to Timestamps

Problem

You are working with a series of strings. You want to convert them into timestamps.

Solution

Use the TO_TIMESTAMP function to convert the strings into timestamps. In this example, a trigger is created that will log an INSERT into the JOBS table. The logging table consists of two columns. The first column is used to store the date of the transaction, and it is of type TIMESTAMP WITH LOCAL TIME ZONE. The second column is used to contain a DESCRIPTION of type VARCHAR2. The trigger that performs the logging needs to combine a sysdate and a time zone value into a string prior to converting it into a TIMESTAMP.

First, let's create the table that will be used to log the changes on the JOBS table:

```
CREATE TABLE time_log
(job_time                TIMESTAMP WITH LOCAL TIME ZONE,
 description             VARCHAR2(2000));
```

Next, a simple function is created that will return the time zone for a given city code. The function will return time zones for Chicago, Orlando, or San Jose because these are the different cities where our imaginary industry has offices.

```
CREATE OR REPLACE FUNCTION find_tz (city IN VARCHAR2)
RETURN NUMBER IS
  tz            NUMBER := 0;
BEGIN
  IF city = 'CHI' THEN
    tz := -5;
  ELSIF city = 'ORD' THEN
    tz := -4;
  ELSIF city = 'SJ' THEN
    tz := -7;
  END IF;
  RETURN tz;
END;
```

The last piece of code is the trigger that performs the INSERT on the logging table. This trigger performs a conversion of a string to a TIMESTAMP using the TO_TIMESTAMP_TZ function.

```
CREATE OR REPLACE TRIGGER log_job_history
AFTER INSERT ON jobs
FOR EACH ROW
DECLARE
  my_ts  VARCHAR2(25) := to_char(sysdate, 'YYYY-MM-DD HH:MI:SS');
BEGIN
  my_ts := my_ts || ' ' || find_tz('CHI');

  INSERT INTO time_log values(
    TO_TIMESTAMP_TZ(my_ts, 'YYYY-MM-DD HH:MI:SS TZH:TZM'),
    'INSERT'
  );

END;
```

In this example, the trigger is hard-coded to assume a Chicago entry, but in reality this information would have been obtained from the user's session. However, since that code is out of scope for this recipe, the hard-coded city does the trick.

How It Works

Similar to other Oracle conversion functions, the TO_TIMESTAMP_TZ and TO_TIMESTAMP functions accept two arguments. The first argument is a string value containing a date value in text form. The second argument is a format model that is used to coerce the given string value into the TIMESTAMP or TIMESTAMP WITH LOCAL TIME ZONE datatype. The TO_TIMESTAMP_TZ conversion will accept and convert a time zone along with the TIMESTAMP, whereas the TO_TIMESTAMP function will not account for a time zone.

The format model is very similar to that of the TO_CHAR and TO_DATE functions. The format model will differ depending upon the format of the date that you want to convert. In the solution to this recipe, the format included a standard Oracle date along with a time zone. For a complete listing of all possible format model characters, please refer to the *Oracle SQL Reference* manual.

6-6. Writing ANSI-Compliant Conversions

Problem

You want to convert strings to dates using an ANSI-compliant methodology.

Solution

Use the CAST function, because it is ANSI-compliant. In this example, a procedure is written that will select each of the rows within the JOB_HISTORY table that fall within a specified date range. The dates will be converted into strings, and other information will be appended to the converted dates. This procedure will produce a simple report to display the JOB_HISTORY.

```
CREATE OR REPLACE PROCEDURE job_history_rpt(in_start_date IN DATE,
                                            in_end_date IN DATE) AS
  CURSOR job_history_cur IS
  SELECT CAST(hist.start_date AS VARCHAR2(12)) || ' - ' ||
         CAST(hist.end_date AS VARCHAR2(12)) || ': ' ||
         emp.first_name || ' ' || emp.last_name || ' - ' ||
         job_title || ' ' || department_name as details
  FROM jobs jobs,
       job_history hist,
       employees emp,
       departments dept
  WHERE hist.start_date >= in_start_date
  AND hist.end_date <= in_end_date
  AND jobs.job_id = hist.job_id
  AND emp.employee_id = hist.employee_id
  AND dept.department_id = hist.department_id;


  job_history_rec     job_history_cur%ROWTYPE;

BEGIN
  DBMS_OUTPUT.PUT_LINE('JOB HISTORY REPORT FOR ' ||
    in_start_date || ' to ' || in_end_date);
  FOR job_history_rec IN job_history_cur LOOP
    DBMS_OUTPUT.PUT_LINE(job_history_rec.details);
  END LOOP;
END;
```

Given the start date of September 1, 1989, the resulting output from this procedure will resemble the following:

```
SQL> exec job_history_rpt(to_date('01-SEP-1989','DD-MON-YYYY'),sysdate);
JOB HISTORY REPORT FOR 01-SEP-89 to 01-SEP-10
13-JAN-93 - 24-JUL-98: Lex De Haan - Programmer IT
21-SEP-89 - 27-OCT-93: Neena Kochhar - Public Accountant Accounting
28-OCT-93 - 15-MAR-97: Neena Kochhar - Accounting Manager Accounting
17-FEB-96 - 19-DEC-99: Michael Hartstein - Marketing Representative Marketing
```

```
24-MAR-98 - 31-DEC-98: Jonathon Taylor - Sales Representative Sales
01-JAN-99 - 31-DEC-99: Jonathon Taylor - Sales Manager Sales
01-JUL-94 - 31-DEC-98: Jennifer Whalen - Public Accountant Executive

PL/SQL procedure successfully completed.
```

How It Works

The CAST function can be used to easily convert datatypes. However, there is no real benefit to using CAST as opposed to TO_NUMBER or TO_CHAR in most cases. The format for the CAST function is as follows:

```
CAST(expression AS type_name)
```

You can use this function to convert between different datatypes. Table 6-5 lists the different to and from datatypes that the CAST function can handle.

Table 6-5. CAST Function Converstion Table

CAST from Datatype	To Datatype
CHAR, VARCHAR2	CHAR, VARCHAR2 NUMBER DATETIME/INTERVAL RAW ROWID, UROWID
NUMBER	CHAR, VARCHAR2 NUMBER NCHAR, NVARCHAR2
DATETIME/INTERVAL	CHAR, VARCHAR2 DATETIME/INTERVAL NCHAR, NVARCHAR2
RAW	CHAR, VARCHAR2 RAW NCHAR, NVARCHAR2
ROWID, UROWID	CHAR, VARCHAR2 ROWID, UROWID NCHAR, NVARCHAR2
NCHAR, NVARCHAR2	NCHAR, NVARCHAR2

The CAST function offers advantages to the TO_ conversion functions in some cases. For instance, if you are attempting to write SQL that is 100 percent ANSI-compliant, then you should use the CAST function because the Oracle conversion functions are not compliant. However, PL/SQL itself is not ANSI-compliant, so the CAST function offers no advantages while writing PL/SQL code.

The following are a few more examples of using the CAST function:

```
-- Convert date to VARCHAR2
SELECT CAST('05-MAY-2010' AS VARCHAR2(15)) FROM DUAL;

-- Convert string to NUMBER
SELECT CAST('1024' AS NUMBER) FROM DUAL;

-- Convert string to ROWID
SELECT CAST('AAYyVSADsAAAAFLAAA' AS ROWID) FROM DUAL;
```

If you prefer to have more control over your conversions, the Oracle TO_ conversion functions are the way to go. They allow you to provide a format mask to control the conversion formatting.

6-7. Implicitly Converting Between PLS_INTEGER and NUMBER

Problem

You want to convert a number to PLS_INTEGER datatype so that calculations can be performed.

Solution

In this case, allow Oracle to do the footwork and implicitly convert between the two datatypes. In the following example, the function accepts a NUMBER, converts it to PLS_INTEGER, and performs a calculation returning the result. The function converts to PLS_INTEGER in order to gain a performance boost.

```
CREATE OR REPLACE FUNCTION mass_energy_calc (mass IN NUMBER,
                                            energy IN NUMBER)
RETURN PLS_INTEGER IS
  new_mass    PLS_INTEGER := mass;
  new_energy  PLS_INTEGER := energy;
BEGIN
  RETURN ((new_mass * new_energy) * (new_mass * new_energy));
EXCEPTION
  WHEN OTHERS THEN
    RETURN -1;
END;
```

The function will accept NUMBER values, automatically convert them into PLS_INTEGER, and return a PLS_INTEGER type.

How It Works

Implicit conversion occurs when Oracle automatically converts from one datatype to another. Oracle will implicitly convert some datatypes but not others. As per the solution to this recipe, one of the datatypes that supports implicit conversion is PLS_INTEGER. As a matter of fact, PLS_INTEGER cannot be converted using the TO_NUMBER function; so in this case, implicit is the best way to convert a PLS_INTEGER datatype to anything else. However, if there is a way to explicitly convert the datatype from one to another, then that is the recommended approach. You cannot be certain of the results when Oracle is automatically converting for you; explicit conversion allows you to have more control.

The PLS_INTEGER datatype can be advantageous over using a NUMBER in some cases. For instance, a PLS_INTEGER has performance advantages when compared to a NUMBER for doing calculations because they use machine arithmetic as opposed to library arithmetic. Additionally, the PLS_INTEGER datatype requires less storage than its counterparts. In the solution to this recipe, the function takes advantage of the faster calculation speed that is possible using PLS_INTEGER.

CHAPTER 7

■ ■ ■

Numbers, Strings, and Dates

Every PL/SQL program uses one or more datatypes. This chapter focuses on some details that you should know when working with data in the form of numbers, strings, and dates. Each recipe in this chapter provides a basic tip for working with these datatypes. From basic string concatenation to more advanced regular expression processing, you'll learn some techniques for getting things done in an effective manner. You'll learn about date calculations as well. When you're done with this chapter, you'll be ready to move on to the more advanced recipes later in the chapters to follow.

7-1. Concatenating Strings

Problem

You have two or more text strings, or variables containing strings, that you want to combine.

Solution

Use the concatenation operator to append the strings. In the following example, you can see that two variables are concatenated to a string of text to form a single string of text:

```
DECLARE
  CURSOR emp_cur IS
  SELECT employee_id, first_name, last_name
  FROM EMPLOYEES
  WHERE HIRE_DATE > TO_DATE('01/01/2000','MM/DD/YYYY');

  emp_rec        emp_cur%ROWTYPE;
  emp_string     VARCHAR2(150);
BEGIN
  DBMS_OUTPUT.PUT_LINE('EMPLOYEES HIRED AFTER 01/01/2000');
  DBMS_OUTPUT.PUT_LINE('=================================');
  FOR emp_rec IN emp_cur LOOP
      emp_string := emp_rec.first_name || ' ' ||
                    emp_rec.last_name || ' - ' ||
                    'ID #: ' || emp_rec.employee_id;

      DBMS_OUTPUT.PUT_LINE(emp_string);
  END LOOP;
END;
```

You can see that the example uses the concatenation operator ‖ to formulate a string of text that contains each employee's first name, last name, and employee ID number.

How It Works

As you have seen in the solution to this recipe, the concatenation operator is used for concatenating strings within your PL/SQL applications. When the concatenation operator is used to concatenate numbers with strings, the numbers are automatically converted into strings and then concatenated. Similarly, an automatic conversion occurs with dates before being concatenated.

7-2. Adding Some Number of Days to a Date

Problem

You want to add a number of days to a given date. For example, you are developing an application that calculates shipping dates for a company's products. In this case, your application is processing shipments, and you need to calculate a date that is 14 days from the current date.

Solution

Treat the number of days as an integer, and add that integer to your DATE value. The following lines of code show how this can be done:

```
DECLARE
  ship_date     DATE := SYSDATE + 14;
BEGIN
  DBMS_OUTPUT.PUT_LINE('The shipping date for any products '||
                       'that are ordered today is ' || ship_date);
END;
```

The result that is displayed for this example will be 14 days past your current date.

If you wanted to encapsulate this logic within a function, then it would be easy to do. The following function takes a date and a number as arguments. The function will perform simple mathematics and return the result.

```
CREATE OR REPLACE FUNCTION calculate_days(date_to_change  IN DATE,
                                          number_of_days  IN NUMBER)
RETURN DATE IS
BEGIN
  RETURN date_to_change + number_of_days;
END;
```

Notice that the name of the function does not include the word *add*, such as ADD_DAYS. That was done on purpose because this function not only allows addition of days to a date, but if a negative number is passed in as an argument, then it will also subtract the number of days from the given date.

How It Works

Since calculations such as these are the most common date calculations performed, Oracle makes them easy to do. If a number is added to or subtracted from a DATE value, Oracle Database will add or subtract that number of days from the date value. DATE types can have numbers added to them, and they can also have numbers subtracted from them. Multiplication and division do not work because it is not possible to perform such a calculation on a date. For example, it doesn't mean anything to speak of multiplying a date by some value.

If you are developing an application that always performs an addition or subtraction using the same number of days, it may be helpful to create a function such as the one demonstrated in the solution to this recipe. For instance, if you were developing a billing application and always required a date that was 30 days into the future of the current date, then you could create a function named BILLING_DATE and hard-code the 30 days into it. This is not necessary, but if your business or application depended upon it, then it may be a good idea to encapsulate logic to alleviate possible data entry errors.

7-3. Adding a Number of Months to a Date

Problem

You want to add some number of months to a date. For example, you are developing a payment application for a company, and it requires payments every six months. You need to enable the application to calculate the date six months in the future of the current date.

▓ **Note** This recipe's solution also works for subtracting months. Simply "add" a negative number of months.

Solution

Use the ADD_MONTHS function to add six months onto the given date. Doing so will enable your application to create bills for future payments. This technique is demonstrated in the following example:

```
DECLARE
  new_date     DATE;
BEGIN
  new_date := ADD_MONTHS(sysdate,6);
  DBMS_OUTPUT.PUT_LINE('The newly calculated date is: ' || new_date);
END;
```

This simple technique will enable you to add a number of months to any given date. As with any other logic, this could easily be encapsulated into a function for the specific purpose of producing a billing date that was six months into the future of the current date. Such a function may look something like the next example:

```
CREATE OR REPLACE FUNCTION calc_billing_date IS
BEGIN
  RETURN ADD_MONTHS(sysdate, 6);
END;
```

Although this function does not do much besides encapsulate logic, it is a good idea to code such functions when developing a larger application where this type of calculation may be performed several times. It will help to maintain consistency and alleviate maintenance issues if the date calculation ever needs to change. You could simply make the change within the function rather than visiting all the locations in the code that use the function.

How It Works

Oracle provides the ADD_MONTHS function to assist with date calculations. This function has two purposes—to add or subtract a specified number of months from the given date. The syntax for use of the ADD_MONTHS function is as follows:

```
ADD_MONTHS(date, integer)
```

You can also use the function to subtract months from the given date. If the function is passed a negative integer in place of the month's argument, then that number of months will be subtracted from the date. The following example demonstrates this functionality:

```
DECLARE
  new_date     DATE;
BEGIN
  new_date := ADD_MONTHS(sysdate,-2);
  DBMS_OUTPUT.PUT_LINE('The newly calculated date is: ' || new_date);
END;
```

As you can see from the example in Figure 7-3, the negative integer is the only change made to the code in order to achieve a subtraction of months rather than an addition. As a result, the example in this figure will return the current date minus two months.

In the case that you are attempting to add months to a date that represents the last day of the month, the ADD_MONTHS function works a bit differently than you might expect. For instance, if it is August 31 and you want to add one month, then you would expect the calculation to resolve to September 31, which is not possible. However, ADD_MONTHS is smart enough to return the last day of September in this case. The following code provides a demonstration:

```
DECLARE
  new_date     DATE;
BEGIN
  new_date := ADD_MONTHS(to_date('08/31/2010','MM/DD/YYYY'),1);
  DBMS_OUTPUT.PUT_LINE('The last day of next month is: ' || new_date);
END;
```

The following is the resulting output:

```
The last day of next month is: 30-SEP-10
```

PL/SQL procedure successfully completed.

In general, if your source date is the late day of its month, then your result date will be forced to the last day of its respective month. Adding one month to September 30, for example, will yield October 31.

7-4. Adding Years to a Date

Problem

You are developing an application that requires date calculations to be performed. You need to determine how to add to a specified date. You may also want to subtract years.

Solution

Create a function that will calculate a new date based upon the number of years that you have specified. If you want to subtract a number of years from a date, then pass a negative value for the number of years. The following code implements this functionality:

```
CREATE OR REPLACE FUNCTION calculate_date_years (in_date DATE,
                                    in_years NUMBER)
RETURN DATE AS
  new_date    DATE;
BEGIN
  IF in_date is NULL OR in_years is NULL THEN
    RAISE NO_DATA_FOUND;
  END IF;
  new_date := ADD_MONTHS(in_date, 12 * in_years);
  RETURN new_date;
END;
```

The example function expects to receive a date and a number of years to add or subtract as arguments. If one of those arguments is left out, then PL/SQL will raise an ORA-06553 error, and the example also raises a special NO_DATA_FOUND error if one or both of the arguments are NULL. The return value will be the input date but in the newly calculated year.

How It Works

Oracle provides a couple of different ways to calculate dates based upon the addition or subtraction of years. One such technique is to use the ADD_MONTHS function that was discussed in Recipe 7-3, as the solution to this recipe demonstrates. Simple mathematics allow you to multiply the number of years passed into the ADD_MONTHS function by 12 since there are 12 months in the year. Essentially this technique exploits the ADD_MONTHS function to return a date a specified number of dates into the future.

■ **Note** See Recipe 7-3 for discussion of a corner case involving the use of ADD_MONTHS on a date that represents the final day of that date's month.

You can use this same technique to subtract a number of years from the specified date by passing a negative integer value that represents the number of years you want to subtract. For instance, if you wanted to subtract five years from the date 06/01/2000, then pass a -5 to the function that was created in the solution to this recipe. The following query demonstrates this strategy.

```
select calculate_date_years(to_date('06/01/2000','MM/DD/YYYY'),-5) from dual;
```

Here's the result:

```
06/01/1995
```

Using the `ADD_MONTHS` function works well for adding or subtracting a rounded number of years. However, if you wanted to add one year and six months, then it would take another line of code to add the number of months to the calculated date. The function in the next example is a modified version of the `CALCULATE_DATE_YEARS` function that allows you to specify a number of months to add or subtract as well:

```
CREATE OR REPLACE FUNCTION calculate_date_years (in_date DATE,
                                              in_years IN NUMBER,
                                              in_months IN NUMBER DEFAULT 0)
RETURN DATE AS
  new_date     DATE;
BEGIN
  IF in_date is NULL OR in_years is NULL THEN
    RAISE NO_DATA_FOUND;
  END IF;
  new_date := ADD_MONTHS(in_date, 12 * in_years);
  -- Additional code to add the number of months to the calculated date
  IF in_months != 0 THEN
    new_date := ADD_MONTHS(new_date, in_months);
  END IF;
  RETURN new_date;
END;
```

Using the new function, you can pass positive integer values for the number of years and the number of months to add years or months to the date, or you can pass negative values for each to subtract years or months from the date. You can also use a combination of positive and negative integers for each to obtain the desired date. Since the modified function contains a `DEFAULT` value of 0 for the number of months, it is possible to not specify a number of months, and you will achieve the same result as the function in the solution to the recipe.

As you can see, this function is a bit easier to follow, but it does not allow for one to enter a negative value to subtract from the date. All the techniques described within this section have their own merit. However, it is always a good rule of thumb to write software so that it is easy to maintain in the future. Using this rule of thumb, the most favored technique of the three would be to use the `ADD_MONTHS` function as demonstrated in the solution. Not only is this function easy to understand but also widely used by others within the Oracle community.

7-5. Determining the Interval Between Two Dates

Problem

You want to determine the number of days between two dates. For example, working on an application to calculate credit card late fees, you are required to determine the number of days between any two given dates. The difference in days between the two dates will produce the number of days that the payment is overdue.

Solution

Subtract the two dates using simple math to find the interval in days. In this solution, the example code subtracts the current date from the due date to obtain the number of days that the payment is past due:

```
CREATE OR REPLACE FUNCTION find_interval(from_date IN DATE,
                                         to_date IN DATE)
RETURN NUMBER AS
BEGIN
  RETURN abs(trunc(to_date) - trunc(from_date));
END;
```

This function will return the difference between the two dates passed as arguments. Note that the number of days will be a decimal value. Although it is just as easy to subtract one date from another without the use of a helper function, sometimes it is useful to encapsulate the logic. This is especially true if the same calculation will be performed multiple times throughout the application.

How It Works

Oracle includes the ability to subtract dates in order to find the difference between the two. You can use this functionality within PL/SQL code or SQL queries. The result of the calculation is the number of fractional days between the two dates. That number can be rounded in order to find the number of days, or it can be formatted to determine the number of days, hours, minutes, and seconds.

As it stands, the result from the subtraction of two will return the number of days between the given dates. If you were interested in returning the number of hours, minutes, or seconds between the two dates, then you could do so by applying some simple mathematics to the result of the subtraction. For instance, to find an interval in minutes, multiply the result by 24 * 60. The following functions show how this technique can be used to create separate functions for returning each time interval:

```
CREATE OR REPLACE FUNCTION find_interval_hours(from_date IN DATE,
                          to_date IN DATE)
RETURN NUMBER AS
BEGIN
 RETURN abs(trunc(from_date) - trunc(to_date) )* 24;
END;
```

```
CREATE OR REPLACE FUNCTION find_interval_minutes(from_date IN DATE,
                                                 to_date IN DATE)
RETURN NUMBER AS
BEGIN
  RETURN (from_date - to_date) * 24 * 60;
END;
```

```
CREATE OR REPLACE FUNCTION find_interval_seconds(from_date IN DATE,
                                                 to_date IN DATE)
RETURN NUMBER AS
BEGIN
  RETURN (from_date - to_date) * 24 * 60 * 60;
END;
```

Each of these functions will return a decimal number that can be rounded. Now you can mix and match these functions as needed to return the desired time interval between two dates.

7-6. Adding Hours, Minutes, Seconds, or Days to a Given Date

Problem

One of your applications requires that you have the ability to add any number of days, hours, minutes, or seconds to a given date and time to produce a new date and time.

Solution

Create functions that add each of these time values to TIMESTAMP dataypes that are passed as an argument. Each of these functions will return the given time plus the amount of time that is passed in as argument. The following three functions will provide the ability to add hours, minutes, seconds, or days to a given time. Each of these functions returns the calculated date and time using the TIMESTAMP datatype.

```
CREATE OR REPLACE FUNCTION calc_hours(time_to_change IN TIMESTAMP,
                     timeval IN NUMBER)
RETURN TIMESTAMP AS
  new_time    TIMESTAMP;
BEGIN

  new_time := time_to_change + NUMTODSINTERVAL(timeval,'HOUR');

  RETURN new_time;
END;

CREATE OR REPLACE FUNCTION calc_minutes(time_to_change IN TIMESTAMP,
                     timeval IN NUMBER)
RETURN TIMESTAMP AS
  new_time    TIMESTAMP;
BEGIN

  new_time := time_to_change + NUMTODSINTERVAL(timeval,'MINUTE');

  RETURN new_time;
END;

CREATE OR REPLACE FUNCTION calc_seconds(time_to_change IN TIMESTAMP,
                     timeval IN NUMBER)
RETURN TIMESTAMP AS
  new_time    TIMESTAMP;
BEGIN

  new_time := time_to_change + NUMTODSINTERVAL(timeval,'SECOND');

  RETURN new_time;
END;
```

```
CREATE OR REPLACE FUNCTION calc_days(time_to_change IN TIMESTAMP,
                        timeval IN NUMBER)
RETURN TIMESTAMP as
  new_time  TIMESTAMP;
BEGIN
  new_time := time_to_change + timeval;
  RETURN new_time;
END;
```

All of these functions operate in a similar fashion. You must input a date in the form of a TIMESTAMP, and the calculated TIMESTAMP will be returned.

How It Works

When performing the calculation of times and dates in Oracle, you have plenty of options. Over the years, Oracle Database has introduced newer functions to help alleviate some of the difficulties that were encountered when attempting date and time calculations in earlier versions of the database. Date and time calculations can be as simple as adding an integer to the DATE or TIMESTAMP. They can also be difficult when many multiplications and divisions occur within the same calculation. The solution to this recipe provides you with an easy way to add time to a given date using the NUMTODSINTERVAL function. The syntax for this function is as follows:

```
NUMTODSINTERVAL(number, expression)
```

The expression that is passed to the function must be one of the following: HOUR, MINUTE, SECOND, or DAY. Technically, the functions created in the solution are capable of subtracting the time or day values from the given date as well. If you were to pass a negative number to the functions, then the NUMTODSINTERVAL would subtract that many units from the given date and time and return the result. The functions in the solution also do not lock you into using a TIMESTAMP; if you were to pass a DATE type in as an argument, then it would work just as well.

In the past, you used to only have the ability to use fractions to add or subtract hours, minutes, and seconds to a date. Over the next few examples, I will show you the sort of fractional mathematics that you may see in legacy code. You can add a fraction to a date or TIMESTAMP as both will return a result. To add hours to a date, use the fraction x/24, where x is the number of hours (1–24) you want to add. You can subtract hours by using a negative value for x. This works because there are of course 24 hours in one day. The following example shows how you may see some legacy code using fractions to add hours.

```
-- Add 1 hour to the current date
result := SYSDATE + 1/24;

-- Add 5 hours to the current date
result := CURRENT_TIMESTAMP + 5/24;
```

It is possible to add minutes to a date using a similar technique with fractions. To add minutes, use the fraction x/24/60, where x is the number of minutes (1–60) that you would like to add. Again, use a negative value in place of x in order to subtract that number of minutes from a date. This fraction works because it divides the number assigned to x by the hours in the day and then divides that result by the number of minutes in an hour. The next figure shows an example of this technique.

```
-- Add 10 mintes to the current date
result := SYSDATE + 10/24/60;
```

```
-- Add 30 minutes to the current date
result := CURRENT_TIMESTAMP + 30/24/60;
```

Similarly, you can add seconds to a date by using the fraction x/24/3600. In this fraction, x is the number of seconds (1–60) that you want to add. Subtraction of seconds is possible by using a negative number for the x value. Just as with the other fractional calculations, this works because there are 3,600 seconds in one hour. Therefore, the number assigned to x is divided by the number of hours in the day, and then that result is divided by the number of seconds in one hour. The next figure demonstrates adding seconds to the date using this technique:

```
-- Add 10 seconds to the current date
result := SYSDATE + 10/24/3600;
```

```
-- Add 45 seconds to the current date
result := CURRENT_TIMESTAMP + 45/24/3600;
```

Using the fractional mathematics, you can add each of the different fractions to the given date and achieve the same result. It is not uncommon for legacy code using fractional mathematics for date calculation to look like the following:

```
-- Add 2 hours, 5 minutes, and 30 seconds to the current date
result := SYSDATE + 2/24 + 5/24/60 + 30/24/3600;
```

There are a number of ways to add time intervals to a given date. I recommend using NUMTODSINTERVAL for performing mathematics on time values. In the past, this function was not available, so using fractional mathematics was the only way to add or subtract time from a given date. As shown in the solution to this recipe, it is possible to encapsulate the logic inside of a PL/SQL function. If this is done, then you could change the implementation inside the function and someone using it would never know the difference. Date and time calculations can be made even easier to use by writing functions to encapsulate the logic.

7-7. Returning the First Day of a Given Month

Problem

You want to have the ability to obtain the name of the first day for a given month.

Solution

Write a PL/SQL function that accepts a date and applies the necessary functions to return the first day of month for the given date.

```
CREATE OR REPLACE FUNCTION first_day_of_month(in_date DATE)
RETURN VARCHAR2 IS
BEGIN
  RETURN to_char(trunc(in_date,'MM'), 'DD-MON-YYYY');
END;
```

The function created in this solution will return the first day of the month that is passed into it because it is passed into the TRUNC function.

How It Works

The TRUNC function can be useful for returning information from a DATE type. In this case, it is used to return the first day of the month from the given date. The solution then converts the truncated date value to a character format and returns the result.

The TRUNC function accepts two arguments, the first being the date that is to be truncated and the second being the format model. The format model is a series of characters that specifies how you want to truncate the given date. Table 7-1 lists the format models along with a description of each.

Table 7-1. Format Models for TRUNC

Format Model	Description
MI	Returns the nearest minute
HH, HH12, HH24	Returns the nearest hour
D, DY, DAY	Returns the first day of the week
W	Returns the same day of the week as the first day of the month
IW	Returns the same day of the week as the first day of ISO year
WW	Returns the same day of the week as the first day of the year
RM, MM, MON, MONTH	Rounds to the nearest first day of the month
Q	Rounds to the nearest quarter
I, IY, IYYY	Returns the ISO year
Y, YY, YYY, SYEAR, YEAR, YYYY	Rounds to the nearest first day of the year
CC, SCC	Returns one greater than the first two digits of a given four-digit year

The solution to this recipe returns the first day of the given month using the format model MM.

7-8. Returning the Last Day of a Given Month

Problem

You want to have the ability to obtain the last day for a given month.

Solution

Use the Oracle built-in LAST_DAY function to return the last day of the month for the date that you pass into it. The following example demonstrates a code block in which the LAST_DAY function is used to return the last day of the current month:

```
DECLARE
  last_day  VARCHAR2(20);
BEGIN
  select LAST_DAY(sysdate)
  INTO last_day
  FROM DUAL;
  DBMS_OUTPUT.PUT_LINE(last_day);
END;
```

How It Works

The LAST_DAY function is an easy way to retrieve the date for the last day of a given date. To use the function, pass in any date, and the last day of the month for the given date will be returned. The function can be useful in combination with other functions, especially for converting strings into dates and then determining the last day of the given month for the date given in string format. For example, the following combination is used quite often:

```
LAST_DAY(to_date(string_based_date,'MM/DD/YYYY'))
```

7-9. Rounding a Number

Problem

You are interested in rounding a given number. For example, let's say you are working on employee timecards, and you want to round to the nearest tenth of an hour for every given hour amount.

Solution

Use the Oracle built-in ROUND function to return the result that you desire. For this solution, you are working with hours on employee timecards. To round to the nearest tenth, you would write a small PL/SQL function that uses the ROUND function and returns the result. The following example demonstrates this technique:

```
CREATE OR REPLACE FUNCTION emp_labor_hours(time IN NUMBER)
RETURN NUMBER IS
BEGIN
  RETURN ROUND(time, 1);
END;
```

The time will be rounded to the nearest tenth in this example because a 1 is passed as the second argument to the ROUND function.

How It Works

The Oracle built-in ROUND function can be used for rounding numbers based upon a specified precision level. To use the ROUND function, pass a number that you would like to round as the first argument, and pass the optional precision level as the second argument. If you do not specify a precision level, then the number will be rounded to the nearest integer. If the precision is specified, then the number will be rounded to the number of decimal places specified by the precision argument.

In the case of this solution, a 1 was specified for the precision argument, so the number will be rounded to one decimal place. The precision can be up to eight decimal places. If you specify a precision larger than eight decimal places, then the precision will default to eight.

7-10. Rounding a Datetime Value

Problem

Given a particular date and time, you want the ability to round the date.

Solution

Use the ROUND function passing the date you want to round along with the format model for the unit you want to round. For example, suppose that given a date and time, you want to the nearest day. To do this, you would pass in the date along with the DD format model. The following code block demonstrates this technique:

```
BEGIN
  DBMS_OUTPUT.PUT_LINE(to_char(ROUND (SYSDATE, 'DD'),'MM/DD/YYYY - HH12:MI:SS'));
  END;
```

The previous code block will return the current date and time rounded to the nearest day. For example, if it is before 12 p.m., then it will round the given date back to 12 a.m. on that date; otherwise, it will round forward to 12 a.m. on the next date.

How It Works

You can also use the ROUND function for working with DATE types. To round a date using this function, you must specify the date you want to have rounded as the first argument along with the format parameter for the type of rounding you want to perform. Table 7-2 lists the different format parameters for performing DATE rounding.

Table 7-2. Format Parameters for DATE Rounding

Format Parameter	Description
Y, YYY, YYYY, YEAR, SYEAR, SYYYY	Rounds to the nearest year
I, IY, IYYY	Rounds to the nearest ISO year
Q	Rounds to the nearest quarter
RM, MM, MON, MONTH	Rounds to the nearest month
WW	Rounds to the same day of the week as the first day of the year
IW	Rounds to the same day of the week as the first day of the ISO year
W	Rounds to the same day of the week as the first day of the month
J, DD, DDD	Rounds to the nearest day
D, DY, DAY	Rounds to the start day of the week
HH, HH12, HH24	Rounds to the nearest hour
MI	Rounds to the nearest minute

If you find that you are using the same date conversion in many places throughout your application, then it may make sense to create a function to encapsulate the call to the ROUND function. Doing so would enable a simple function call that can be used to return the date value you require rather than remembering to use the correct format parameter each time.

7-11. Tracking Time to a Millisecond

Problem

You are interested in tracking time in a finely grained manner to the millisecond. For example, you want to determine the exact time in which a particular change is made to the database.

Solution

Perform simple mathematics with the current date time in order to determine the exact time down the millisecond. The following function accepts a timestamp and returns the |milliseconds:

```
CREATE OR REPLACE FUNCTION capture_milliseconds(in_time TIMESTAMP)
RETURN NUMBER IS
  milliseconds    NUMBER;
```

```
BEGIN
select sum(
    (extract(hour from in_time))*3600+
    (extract(minute from in_time))*60+
    (extract(second from in_time)))*1000
into MILLISECONDS from dual;
RETURN milliseconds;

END;
```

How It Works

If your application requires a fine-grained accuracy for time, then you may want to track time in milliseconds. Performing a calculation such as the one demonstrated in the solution to this recipe on a given DATE or TIMESTAMP can do this. By combining the EXTRACT function with some calculations, the desired milliseconds result can be achieved.

The EXTRACT function is used to extract YEAR, MONTH, or DATE units from a DATE type. It can extract HOUR, MINUTE, or SECOND from a TIMESTAMP. Milliseconds can be calculated by obtaining the sum of the hours multiplied by 3600, the minutes multiplied by 60, and the seconds multiplied by 1000 from a given TIMESTAMP. If you need to use milliseconds in your program, then I recommend creating a function such as the one demonstrated in the solution to this recipe to encapsulate this logic.

7-12. Associating a Time Zone with a Date and Time

Problem

You want to associate a time zone with a given date and time in order to be more precise.

Solution

Create a code block that declares a field as type TIMESTAMP WITH TIME ZONE. Assign a TIMESTAMP to the newly declared field within the body of the code block. After doing so, the field that you declared will contain the date and time of the TIMESTAMP that you assigned along with the associated time zone. The following example demonstrates a code block that performs this technique using the SYSTIMESTAMP:

```
DECLARE
  time    TIMESTAMP WITH TIME ZONE;
 BEGIN
  time := SYSTIMESTAMP;
  DBMS_OUTPUT.PUT_LINE(time);
 END;
```

The results that will be displayed via the call to DBMS_OUTPUT should resemble something similar to the following:

```
29-AUG-10 10.27.58.639000 AM -05:00

PL/SQL procedure successfully completed.
```

How It Works

Prior to the `TIMESTAMP` datatype being introduced in Oracle 9i, the `DATE` type was the only way to work with dates. There were limited capabilities provided, and later the `TIMESTAMP` was created to fill those gaps. For those needing to make use of time zones, Oracle created the `TIMESTAMP WITH TIME ZONE` and `TIMESTAMP WITH LOCAL TIME ZONE` datatypes. Both of these datatypes provide a time zone to be associated with a given date, but they work a bit differently. When you specify the `WITH TIME ZONE` option, the time zone information is stored within the database along with the hours, minutes, and so on. However, if you specify the `WITH LOCAL TIME ZONE` option, the time zone information is not stored within the database, but rather it is calculated each time against a baseline time zone, which determines the time zone of your current session.

In the solution to this recipe, the time zone information is stored within the database along with the rest of the date and time associated with the `TIMESTAMP`.

7-13. Finding a Pattern Within a String

Problem

You want to find the number of occurrences of a particular pattern within a given string. For instance, you want to search for email addresses within a body of text.

Solution

Use a regular expression to match a given string against the body of text and return the resulting count of matching occurrences. The following example searches through a given body of text and counts the number of email addresses it encounters. Any email address will be added to the tally because a regular expression is used to compare the strings.

```
CREATE OR REPLACE PROCEDURE COUNT_EMAIL_IN_TEXT(text_var      IN VARCHAR2) AS
  counter    NUMBER := 0;
  mail_pattern     VARCHAR2(15) := '\w+@\w+(\.\w+)+';
BEGIN
  counter := REGEXP_COUNT(text_var, mail_pattern);

  IF COUNTER = 1 THEN
    DBMS_OUTPUT.PUT_LINE('This passage provided contains 1 email address');
  ELSIF counter > 1 THEN
    DBMS_OUTPUT.PUT_LINE('This passage provided contains '||
                    counter || ' email addresses');
  ELSE
    DBMS_OUTPUT.PUT_LINE('This passage provided contains ' ||
            'no email addresses');
  END IF;
END;
```

The function in this example provides a single service because it counts the number of occurrences of an email address in a given body of text and returns the result.

How It Works

You can use regular expressions to help match strings of numbers, text, or alphanumeric values. They are sequences of characters and symbols that assimilate a pattern that can be used to match against strings of text. A regular expression is similar to using the % symbol as a wildcard within a query, except that a regular expression provides a pattern that text must match against. Please refer to online Oracle documentation for a listing of the different options that can be used for creating regular expression patterns.

Oracle introduced the REGEXP_COUNT function in Oracle 11g, which provides the functionality of counting the number of occurrences of a given string within a given body of text. The syntax for the REGEXP_COUNT function is as follows:

```
REGEXP_COUNT(source_text, pattern, position, options)
```

The source text for the function can be any string literal, variable, or column that has a datatype of VARCHAR2, NVARCHAR2, CHAR, NCHAR, CLOB, or NCLOB. The pattern is a regular expression or a string of text that will be used to match against. The position specifies the placement within the source text where the search should begin. By default, the position is 1. The options include different useful matching modifiers; please refer to the Oracle regular expression support documentation at http://download.oracle.com/docs/cd/E14072_01/server.112/e10592/ap_posix.htm#g693775 for a listing of the pattern matching modifiers that can be used as options.

The REGEXP_COUNT function can be used within any Oracle SQL statement or PL/SQL program. The following are a few more examples of using this function:

```
-- Count all occurrences of the letter 'l' in the word Hello
result := REGEXP_COUNT('hello','l');

Returns:  2

-- Count the number of occurrences of the pattern 'ells' beginning at
-- the fifth character.
result := REGEXP_COUNT('she sells sea shells by the sea shore',
                       'ells',7,'c');

Returns: 1

-- Count the number of words in the line
result := REGEXP_COUNT('she sells sea shells by the sea shore',
                       '\w+');

Returns: 8
```

As you can see from these examples, the REGEXP_COUNT function is a great addition to the Oracle regular expression function family

7-14. Determining the Position of a Pattern Within a String

Problem

You want to return the position of a matching string within a body of text. Furthermore, you are want to pattern match and therefore must invoke a regular expression function. For example, you need to find a way to determine the position of a string that matches the pattern of a phone number.

Solution

Use the REGEXP_INSTR function to use a regular expression to search a body of text to find the position of a phone number. The following code block demonstrates this technique by looping through each of the rows in the EMPLOYEES table and determining whether the employee phone number is USA or international:

```
DECLARE
  CURSOR emp_cur IS
  SELECT *
  FROM employees;

  emp_rec        emp_cur%ROWTYPE;

  position       NUMBER := 0;
  counter        NUMBER := 0;
  intl_count     NUMBER := 0;
BEGIN
  FOR emp_rec IN emp_cur LOOP
  position := REGEXP_INSTR(emp_rec.phone_number,
  '([[:digit:]]{3})\.([[:digit:]]{3})\.([[:digit:]]{4})');

  IF position > 0 THEN
    counter := counter + 1;
  ELSE
    intl_count := intl_count + 1;
  END IF;
  END LOOP;

  DBMS_OUTPUT.PUT_LINE('Numbers within USA: ' || counter);
  DBMS_OUTPUT.PUT_LINE('International Numbers: ' || intl_count);

END;
```

Result:

```
Numbers within USA: 72
International Numbers: 35

PL/SQL procedure successfully completed.
```

How It Works

In the solution to this recipe, the function uses REGEXP_INSTR to find all telephone numbers that match the U.S. telephone number format. The field passed into REGEXP_INSTR is always going to return a telephone number, but that number may be in an international format or a U.S. format. If the pattern of the telephone number matches that of a U.S. format, then the counter for U.S. numbers is increased by one. Otherwise, the counter for the international numbers is increased by one. The reasonable assumption is that if a number is not a U.S. number, that it is an "international" number. Using REGEXP_INSTR makes this a very easy function to implement.

REGEXP_INSTR will return the position of the first or last character of the matching string depending upon the value of the return option argument. This function provides the same functionality of INSTR except that it also allows the ability to use regular expression patterns. The syntax for this function is as follows:

```
REGEXP_INSTR(source_text, pattern, position, occurrence,
                    return_option, match parameter, subexpression)
```

All but the source_text and pattern parameters are optional. The source_text is the string of text to be searched. The pattern is a regular expression or string that will be matched against the source_text. The optional position argument is an integer that specifies on which character Oracle should start the search. The optional occurrence parameter specifies which occurrence of the pattern will have its position returned. The default occurrence argument is 1, which means that the position of the first matching string will be returned

The optional return_option is used to specify special options that are outlined within the Oracle regular expression documentation that can be found at http://download.oracle.com/docs/cd/E11882_01/server.112/e10592/ap_posix.htm#g693775. The optional match_parameter allows you to change the default matching behavior. The subexpression parameter is optional, and it is an integer from 0 to 9 that indicates which subexpression in the source_text will be the target of the function.

7-15. Finding and Replacing Text Within a String

Problem

You want to replace each occurrence of a given string within a body of text.

Solution

Use the REGEXP_REPLACE function to match a pattern of text against a given body of text, and replace all matching occurrences with a new string. In the following function, the REGEXP_REPLACE function is used to replace all occurrences of the JOB_TITLE 'Programmer' with the new title of 'Developer.'

```
DECLARE
  CURSOR job_cur IS
  SELECT *
  FROM jobs;

  job_rec        job_cur%ROWTYPE;
  new_job_title  jobs.job_title%TYPE;
BEGIN
```

```
   FOR job_rec IN job_cur LOOP
     IF REGEXP_INSTR(job_rec.job_title,'Programmer') > 0 THEN
       new_job_title := REGEXP_REPLACE(job_rec.job_title, 'Programmer',
                                      'Developer');

       UPDATE jobs
       SET job_title = new_job_title
       WHERE job_id = job_rec.job_id;

       DBMS_OUTPUT.PUT_LINE(job_rec.job_title || ' replaced with ' ||
           new_job_title);
     END IF;
   END LOOP;

END;
```

Although this particular example does not use any regular expression patterns, it could be adjusted to do so. To find more information and tables specifying the options that are available for creating patterns, please refer to the online Oracle documentation.

The solution to this recipe prints out the revised text. Each occurrence of the 'Programmer' text is replaced with 'Developer', and the newly generated string is returned into the NEW_REVIEW variable.

How It Works

The REGEXP_REPLACE function is a great way to find and replace strings within a body of text. The function can be used within any Oracle SQL statement or PL/SQL code. The syntax for the function is as follows:

```
REGEXP_REPLACE(source_text, pattern, replacement_string, position, occurrence, options)
```

The source text for the function can be any string literal, variable, or column that has a datatype of VARCHAR2, NVARCHAR2, CHAR, NCHAR, CLOB, or NCLOB. The pattern is a regular expression or a string of text that will be used to match against. The replacement string is will replace each occurrence of the string identified by the source text. The optional position specifies the placement within the source text where the search should begin. By default, the position is 1. The optional occurrence argument is a nonnegative integer that indicates the occurrence of the replace operation. If a 0 is specified, then all matching occurrences will be replaced. If a positive integer is specified, then Oracle will replace the match for that occurrence with the replacement string. The optional options argument includes different useful matching modifiers; please refer to the online Oracle documentation for a listing of the pattern matching modifiers that can be used as options.

■ **Note** Do not use REGEXP_REPLACE if the replacement can be performed with a regular UPDATE statement. Since REGEXP_REPLACE uses regular expressions, it can be slower than a regular UPDATE.

The following examples demonstrate how this function can be used within a PL/SQL application or a simple query. This next bit of code demonstrates how to replace numbers that match those within the given set.

```
select REGEXP_REPLACE('abcdefghi','[acegi]','x') from dual;
```

Returns: xbxdxfxhx

Next, we replace a Social Security Number with Xs.

```
new_ssn := REGEXP_REPLACE('123-45-6789','[[:digit:]]{3}-[[:digit:]]{2}-[[:digit:]]{4}','xxx-
xxx-xxxx');
```

Returns: xxx-xxx-xxxx

The REGEXP_REPLACE function can be most useful when attempting to replace patterns of strings within a given body of text such as the two previous examples have shown. As noted previously, if a standard UPDATE statement can be used to replace a value, then that should be the first choice, because regular expressions perform slightly slower.

■ ■ ■

CHAPTER 8

Dynamic SQL

Oracle provides dynamic SQL as a means for generating DML or DDL at runtime. It can be useful when the full text of a SQL statement or query is not known until application runtime. Dynamic SQL can help overcome some of the limitations of static SQL, such as generating a full SQL query based upon some user-provided information or inserting into a specific table depending upon a user action within your application. Simply put, the ability to use dynamic SQL within PL/SQL applications provides a level of flexibility that is not attainable with the use of static SQL alone.

Oracle allows dynamic SQL to be generated in two different ways: native dynamic SQL and through the use of the DBMS_SQL package. Each strategy has its own benefits as well as drawbacks. In comparison, native dynamic SQL is easier to use, it supports user-defined types, and it performs better than DBMS_SQL. On the other hand, DBMS_SQL supports some features that are not currently supported in native dynamic SQL such as the use of the SQL*Plus DESCRIBE command and the reuse of SQL statements. Each of these methodologies will be compared under various use cases within this chapter. By the end of the chapter, you should know what advantages each approach has to offer and which should be used in certain circumstances.

8-1. Executing a Single Row Query That Is Unknown at Compile Time

Problem

You need to query the database for a single row of data matched by the primary key value. However, you are unsure of what columns will need to be returned at runtime.

Solution #1

Use a native dynamic query to retrieve the columns of data that are determined by your application at runtime. After you determine what columns need to be returned, create a string that contains the SQL that is needed to query the database. The following example demonstrates the concept of creating a dynamic SQL query and then using native dynamic SQL to retrieve the single row that is returned.

```
CREATE OR REPLACE PROCEDURE obtain_emp_detail(emp_info IN VARCHAR2) IS
  emp_qry                 VARCHAR2(500);
  emp_first               employees.first_name%TYPE;
  emp_last                employees.last_name%TYPE;
  email                   employees.email%TYPE;

  valid_id_count          NUMBER := 0;
  valid_flag              BOOLEAN := TRUE;
  temp_emp_info           VARCHAR2(50);
```

```
BEGIN
  emp_qry := 'SELECT FIRST_NAME, LAST_NAME, EMAIL FROM EMPLOYEES ';
  IF emp_info LIKE '%@%' THEN
    temp_emp_info := substr(emp_info,0,instr(emp_info,'@')-1);
    emp_qry := emp_qry || 'WHERE EMAIL = :emp_info';
  ELSE
    SELECT COUNT(*)
    INTO valid_id_count
    FROM employees
    WHERE employee_id = emp_info;

    IF valid_id_count > 0 THEN
        temp_emp_info := emp_info;
        emp_qry := emp_qry || 'WHERE EMPLOYEE_ID = :id';
    ELSE
        valid_flag := FALSE;
    END IF;
  END IF;

  IF valid_flag = TRUE THEN
    EXECUTE IMMEDIATE emp_qry
    INTO emp_first, emp_last, email
    USING temp_emp_info;

    DBMS_OUTPUT.PUT_LINE(emp_first || ' ' || emp_last || ' - ' || email);
  ELSE
    DBMS_OUTPUT.PUT_LINE('THE INFORMATION YOU HAVE SPECIFIED DOES ' ||
                        'NOT MATCH ANY EMPLOYEE RECORD');
  END IF;
END;
```

At runtime, the procedure creates a SQL query based upon the criteria that are passed into the procedure by the invoking program. That query is then executed using the EXECUTE IMMEDIATE statement along with the argument that will be substituted into the query WHERE clause.

Solution #2

Use the DBMS_SQL package to create a query based upon criteria that are specified at runtime. The example in this solution will query the employee table and retrieve data based upon the parameter that has been passed into the procedure. The procedure will accept either a primary key ID or an employee e-mail address. The SQL statement that will be used to query the database will be determined at runtime based upon what type of argument is used.

```
CREATE OR REPLACE PROCEDURE obtain_emp_detail(emp_info IN VARCHAR2) IS
  emp_qry                 VARCHAR2(500);
  emp_first               employees.first_name%TYPE := NULL;
  emp_last                employees.last_name%TYPE := NULL;
  email                   employees.email%TYPE := NULL;

  valid_id_count          NUMBER := 0;
  valid_flag              BOOLEAN := TRUE;
```

```
    temp_emp_info              VARCHAR2(50);

    cursor_name                INTEGER;
    row_ct                     INTEGER;

BEGIN

    emp_qry := 'SELECT FIRST_NAME, LAST_NAME, EMAIL FROM EMPLOYEES ';
    IF emp_info LIKE '%@%' THEN
      temp_emp_info := substr(emp_info,0,instr(emp_info,'@')-1);
      emp_qry := emp_qry || 'WHERE EMAIL = :emp_info';
    ELSE
      SELECT COUNT(*)
      INTO valid_id_count
      FROM employees
      WHERE employee_id = emp_info;

      IF valid_id_count > 0 THEN
          temp_emp_info := emp_info;
          emp_qry := emp_qry || 'WHERE EMPLOYEE_ID = :emp_info';
      ELSE
          valid_flag := FALSE;
      END IF;
    END IF;

    IF valid_flag = TRUE THEN
      cursor_name := DBMS_SQL.OPEN_CURSOR;
      DBMS_SQL.PARSE(cursor_name, emp_qry, DBMS_SQL.NATIVE);
      DBMS_SQL.BIND_VARIABLE(cursor_name, ':emp_info', temp_emp_info);
      DBMS_SQL.DEFINE_COLUMN(cursor_name, 1, emp_first, 20);
      DBMS_SQL.DEFINE_COLUMN(cursor_name, 2, emp_last, 25);
      DBMS_SQL.DEFINE_COLUMN(cursor_name, 3, email, 25);
      row_ct := DBMS_SQL.EXECUTE(cursor_name);
    IF DBMS_SQL.FETCH_ROWS(cursor_name) > 0 THEN
        DBMS_SQL.COLUMN_VALUE (cursor_name, 1, emp_first);
        DBMS_SQL.COLUMN_VALUE (cursor_name, 2, emp_last);
        DBMS_SQL.COLUMN_VALUE (cursor_name, 3, email);
        DBMS_OUTPUT.PUT_LINE(emp_first || ' ' || emp_last || ' - ' || email);

    END IF;

    ELSE
      DBMS_OUTPUT.PUT_LINE('THE INFORMATION YOU HAVE SPECIFIED DOES ' ||
                           'NOT MATCH ANY EMPLOYEE RECORD');
    END IF;
    DBMS_SQL.CLOSE_CURSOR(cursor_name);
    EXCEPTION
      WHEN OTHERS THEN
        DBMS_OUTPUT.PUT_LINE('THE INFORMATION YOU HAVE SPECIFIED DOES ' ||
                             'NOT MATCH ANY EMPLOYEE RECORD');

END;
```

How It Works #1

Native dynamic SQL allows you to form a string of SQL text and then execute it via the EXECUTE IMMEDIATE statement. This is very useful when the columns, table names, or WHERE clause text is not known at runtime. The program can build the SQL string as it needs to, and then the EXECUTE IMMEDIATE statement will execute it. The format for the EXECUTE IMMEDIATE statement is as follows:

```
EXECUTE IMMEDIATE sql_string
[INTO variable_name1[, variable_name2, . . .]
USING variable_name1[, variable_name2, . . .]];
```

The EXECUTE IMMEDIATE statement requires only one parameter, which is a SQL string to execute. The remainder of the statement is optional. The INTO clause lists all the variables that a SQL query would return values into. The variables should be listed in the same order within the SQL string as they are listed within the INTO clause. The USING clause lists all the variables that will be bound to the SQL string at runtime. Bind variables are arguably one of the most valuable features of the PL/SQL language. Each variable listed in the USING clause is bound to a bind variable within the SQL string. The order in which the variables are listed in the USING clause is the same order in which they will be bound within the string. Take a look at the following example that uses two bind variables:

```
EXECUTE IMMEDIATE 'select email from employees ' ||
                              'where last_name =:last ' ||
                              'and first_name = :first'
INTO v_email
USING v_last, v_first;
```

In the example query, the variables contained within the USING clause are bound in order to the bind variables within the SQL string. Bind variables are the cornerstone to developing robust, secure, and well-performing software.

How It Works #2

The DBMS_SQL package can also be used to perform the same task. Each of the different techniques, native dynamic SQL and DBMS_SQL, have their advantages and disadvantages. The major difference between the use of DBMS_SQL and native dynamic SQL is how the dynamic SQL string is executed. In this example, DBMS_SQL package functions are used to process the SQL rather than EXECUTE IMMEDIATE. As you can see, the code is quite a bit lengthier than using EXECUTE IMMEDIATE, and it essentially returns the same information. In this case, DBMS_SQL is certainly not the best choice. DBMS_SQL can become useful in situations where you do not know the SELECT list until runtime or when you are unsure of which variables must be bound to a SELECT or DML statement. On the other hand, you must use native dynamic SQL if you intend to use the cursor variable attributes %FOUND, %NOTFOUND, %ISOPEN, or %ROWCOUNT when working with your cursor.

■ **Note** Native dynamic SQL was introduced in Oracle 9i, because DBMS_SQL was overly complex for many of the routine tasks that programmers perform. We consider use of native dynamic SQL as the technique of choice for working with dynamic SQL. Use DBMS_SQL only when you have a specific need to do so.

8-2. Executing a Multiple Row Query That Is Unknown at Compile Time

Problem

Your application requires a database table to be queried, but the filters for the WHERE clause are not known until runtime. You have no idea how many rows will be returned by the query.

Solution #1

Create a native dynamic query using a SQL string that will be built at application runtime. Declare the query using REF CURSOR, execute it by issuing an OPEN statement, and loop through the records using a standard loop, fetching the fields within each iteration of the loop. This technique is illustrated via the code in the following example:

```
DECLARE
  emp_qry                  VARCHAR2(500);
  TYPE                     cur_type IS REF CURSOR;
  cur                      cur_type;
  emp_first                employees.first_name%TYPE;
  emp_last                 employees.last_name%TYPE;
  email                    employees.email%TYPE;

  dept_id                  employees.department_id%TYPE := &department_id;

BEGIN
  -- DEPARTMENT_ID WILL NOT UNIQUELY DEFINE ANY ONE EMPLOYEE

  emp_qry := 'SELECT FIRST_NAME, LAST_NAME, EMAIL FROM EMPLOYEES ' ||
             ' WHERE DEPARTMENT_ID = :id';

  OPEN cur FOR emp_qry USING dept_id;
  LOOP
    FETCH cur INTO emp_first, emp_last, email;
   EXIT WHEN cur%NOTFOUND;
    DBMS_OUTPUT.PUT_LINE(emp_first || ' ' || emp_last || ' - ' || email);
  END LOOP;
  CLOSE cur;
END;
```

This example accepts a DEPARTMENT_ID as input, and it uses a bind variable to substitute the value within the SQL string. Although the actual SQL string in this example does not require the use of a dynamic query, it is a useful example to demonstrate the technique.

Solution #2

This same procedure can also be performed using the DBMS_SQL package. Although the native dynamic SQL solution is easier to understand and implement, the DBMS_SQL alternative offers some different options that are not available when using the native method. The following example is a sample of a procedure that performs the same functionality as Solution #1 of this recipe. However, the procedure in the following example uses the DBMS_SQL package to parse and execute the dynamic query rather than native dynamic SQL.

```
CREATE OR REPLACE PROCEDURE obtain_emp_detail(dept_id IN NUMBER) IS
  emp_qry                   VARCHAR2(500);
  emp_first                 employees.first_name%TYPE := NULL;
  emp_last                  employees.last_name%TYPE := NULL;
  email                     employees.email%TYPE := NULL;

  cursor_name               INTEGER;
  row_ct                    INTEGER;

BEGIN

 emp_qry := 'SELECT FIRST_NAME, LAST_NAME, EMAIL FROM EMPLOYEES ' ||
             ' WHERE DEPARTMENT_ID = :id';

    cursor_name := DBMS_SQL.OPEN_CURSOR;
    DBMS_SQL.PARSE(cursor_name, emp_qry, DBMS_SQL.NATIVE);
    DBMS_SQL.BIND_VARIABLE(cursor_name, ':id', dept_id);
    DBMS_SQL.DEFINE_COLUMN(cursor_name, 1, emp_first, 20);
    DBMS_SQL.DEFINE_COLUMN(cursor_name, 2, emp_last, 25);
    DBMS_SQL.DEFINE_COLUMN(cursor_name, 3, email, 25);
    row_ct := DBMS_SQL.EXECUTE(cursor_name);
    LOOP
    IF DBMS_SQL.FETCH_ROWS(cursor_name) > 0 THEN
      DBMS_SQL.COLUMN_VALUE (cursor_name, 1, emp_first);
      DBMS_SQL.COLUMN_VALUE (cursor_name, 2, emp_last);
      DBMS_SQL.COLUMN_VALUE (cursor_name, 3, email);
     DBMS_OUTPUT.PUT_LINE(emp_first || ' ' || emp_last || ' - ' || email);
    ELSE
      EXIT;
    END IF;
    END LOOP;

DBMS_SQL.CLOSE_CURSOR(cursor_name);
EXCEPTION
    WHEN OTHERS THEN
      DBMS_OUTPUT.PUT_LINE('THE INFORMATION YOU HAVE USED DOES ' ||
                           'NOT MATCH ANY EMPLOYEE RECORD');
END;
```

How It Works

The use of native dynamic SQL in this solution is more or less equivalent to that which was performed in the previous recipe. The largest difference lies in the use of the REF CURSOR as opposed to the EXECUTE IMMEDIATE statement. The REF CURSOR is used to create a cursor using a dynamic SQL string.

Cursor variables can be either weakly typed or strongly typed. The cursor variable demonstrated in the solution to this example of a weakly typed REF CURSOR, since the SQL string is not known until runtime. A strongly typed cursor variable must be known at runtime. In this sense, a strongly typed cursor variable is very similar to a regular cursor.

The REF CURSOR type must be declared first, and then the actual cursor variable that will be used in your code should be declared using the REF CURSOR as its type. Next you have the OPEN statement. To tell Oracle what SQL to use for the cursor, the OPEN statement should include a FOR clause indicating the SQL string that the cursor should use. If there are any variables to bind into the query, the optional USING clause should follow at the end of the OPEN statement.

The subsequent cursor loop should work with the REF CURSOR in the same manner that you would use with regular cursor variables. Always FETCH the current record or its contents into a local record or separate local variables. Next, perform the tasks that need to be completed. Lastly, ensure that you include an EXIT statement to indicate that the loop should be terminated after the last record has been processed. The final step in the process is to close the cursor. After the cursor has been closed, it can be assigned a new SQL string since you are working with weakly typed REF CURSORs.

As you can see, the example of using DBMS_SQL in Solution #2 of this recipe as opposed to the example in Recipe 8-1 differs only because of the addition of a LOOP construct. Instead of displaying only one value, this example will loop through all the records that are returned from the query, and the loop will exit when there are no remaining rows in the result. The example in Recipe 8-1 could entail the same loop construct as the one shown in Solution #2 of this recipe, but it is only expected to return one row since the query is based upon a primary and unique key value.

The choice for using DBMS_SQL as opposed to native dynamic SQL (NDS) depends on what you are trying to achieve. DBMS_SQL will allow you to use a SQL string that is greater than 32KB in size, whereas native dynamic SQL will not. However, there are other options for creating large SQL text strings and parsing them with native dynamic SQL. Please see Recipe 8-11 for more details.

8-3. Writing a Dynamic INSERT Statement

Problem

Your application must insert data into a table, but you don't know until runtime which columns you will insert. For example, you are writing a procedure that will be used for saving records into the EMPLOYEES table. However, the exact content to be saved is not known until runtime because the person who is calling the procedure can decide whether they are including a DEPARTMENT_ID. If a DEPARTMENT_ID is included, then the department will be included in the INSERT.

Solution

Create a string at runtime that will contain the INSERT statement text to be executed. Use bind variables to substitute the values that are to be inserted into the database table. The following procedure accepts user input for entry of a new employee record. Bind variables are used to substitute those values into the SQL.

```
CREATE OR REPLACE PROCEDURE new_employee (  first   IN VARCHAR2,
                                            last    IN VARCHAR2,
                                            email   IN VARCHAR2,
                                            phone   IN VARCHAR2,
                                            hired   IN DATE,
                                            job     IN VARCHAR2,
                                            dept    IN NUMBER DEFAULT 0) AS
                                            v_sql   VARCHAR2(1000);
BEGIN
```

```
   IF dept != 0 THEN
     v_sql := 'INSERT INTO EMPLOYEES ( ' ||
                   'employee_id, first_name, last_name, email, ' ||
                   'phone_number, hire_date, job_id, department_id) ' ||
                   'VALUES( ' ||
                   ':id, :first, :last, :email, :phone, :hired, ' ||
                   ':job_id, :dept)';

     EXECUTE IMMEDIATE v_sql
     USING employees_seq.nextval, first, last, email, phone, hired, job, dept;

   ELSE
     v_sql := 'INSERT INTO EMPLOYEES ( ' ||
                   'employee_id, first_name, last_name, email, ' ||
                   'phone_number, hire_date, job_id) ' ||
                   'VALUES( ' ||
                   ':id, :first, :last, :email, :phone, :hired, ' ||
                   ':job_id)';

     EXECUTE IMMEDIATE v_sql
     USING employees_seq.nextval, first, last, email, phone, hired, job;

   END IF;

  DBMS_OUTPUT.PUT_LINE('The employee has been successfully entered');
EXCEPTION
  WHEN NO_DATA_FOUND THEN
    DBMS_OUTPUT.PUT_LINE('YOU MUST SUPPLY A VALUE FOR DEPARTMENT');
  WHEN TOO_MANY_ROWS THEN
    DBMS_OUTPUT.PUT_LINE('EMPLOYEE_ID ALREADY EXISTS');
END;
```

If the data entry clerk includes a department ID number for the employee when executing the NEW_EMPLOYEE procedure, then the INSERT statement will differ slightly than it would if no department ID were provided. The basic native dynamic SQL in this example does not differ much from those examples demonstrated in Recipe 8-1 or Recipe 8-2 of this chapter.

Solution #2

The DBMS_SQL API can also be used to execute dynamic INSERT statements. Although dynamic DML is not usually performed with DBMS_SQL very often, it can still be useful in some circumstances. The following example performs the same task as Solution #1 to this recipe. However, it has been rewritten to use DBMS_SQL instead of native dynamic SQL.

```
CREATE OR REPLACE PROCEDURE new_employee(first     IN VARCHAR2,
                                         last      IN VARCHAR2,
                                         email     IN VARCHAR2,
                                         phone     IN VARCHAR2,
                                         hired     IN DATE,
                                         job       IN VARCHAR2,
                                         dept      IN NUMBER DEFAULT 0)
```

```
AS
  v_sql      VARCHAR2(1000);

  cursor_var               NUMBER := DBMS_SQL.OPEN_CURSOR;
  rows_compelete NUMBER := 0;
  next_emp                 NUMBER := employee_seq.nextval;
BEGIN


  IF dept != 0 THEN
    v_sql := 'INSERT INTO EMPLOYEES ( ' ||
                   'employee_id, first_name, last_name, email, ' ||
                   'phone_number, hire_date, job_id, department_id) ' ||
                   'VALUES( ' ||
                   ':id, :first, :last, :email, :phone, :hired, ' ||
                   ':job_id, :dept)';


  ELSE
    v_sql := 'INSERT INTO EMPLOYEES ( ' ||
                   'employee_id, first_name, last_name, email, ' ||
                   'phone_number, hire_date, job_id) ' ||
                   'VALUES( ' ||
                   ':id, :first, :last, :email, :phone, :hired, ' ||
                   ':job_id)';
  END IF;
  DBMS_SQL.PARSE(cursor_var, v_sql, DBMS_SQL.NATIVE);
  DBMS_SQL.BIND_VARIABLE(cursor_var, 1, ':id', next_emp);
  DBMS_SQL.BIND_VARIABLE(cursor_var, 2, ':first', first);
  DBMS_SQL.BIND_VARIABLE(cursor_var, 3, ':last', last);
  DBMS_SQL.BIND_VARIABLE(cursor_var, 4, ':email', email);
  DBMS_SQL.BIND_VARIABLE(cursor_var, 5, ':phone', phone);
  DBMS_SQL.BIND_VARIABLE(cursor_var, 6, ':hired');
  DBMS_SQL.BIND_VARIABLE(cursor_var, 7, ':job', job);
  IF dept != 0 then
    DBMS_SQL.BIND_VARIABLE(cursor_var, 8, ':dept', dept);
  END IF;
  rows_complete := DBMS_SQL.EXECUTE(cursor_var);
  DBMS_SQL.CLOSE_CURSOR(cursor_var);
  DBMS_OUTPUT.PUT_LINE('The employee has been successfully entered');
END;
```

How It Works

Using native dynamic SQL, creating an INSERT statement is almost identical to working with a query string. As a matter of fact, the only difference is that you will not be making use of the INTO clause within the EXECUTE IMMEDIATE statement. Standard PL/SQL can be used to create the SQL statement string in order to process an INSERT statement that contains column names, table names, or WHERE clause values that are not known until runtime.

■ **Note** If your SQL string contains any SQL that requires the use of single quotes, double up on the quotes. Placing a single quote immediately after another signals the parser to place a single quote into the string that you are creating.

Similarly to SQL queries using dynamic SQL, you should use bind variables to substitute values into the SQL statement string where needed. As a refresher, bind variables are used within SQL queries or statements to act as placeholders for values that are to be substituted at runtime. A bind variable begins with a colon and is then followed by the variable name. The EXECUTE IMMEDIATE statement implements the USING clause to list variables that contain values that will be substituted into the bind variables at runtime. The order in which the variables are listed in the USING clause must concur with the positioning of the bind variables within the SQL. The following is an example of an EXECUTE IMMEDIATE statement to be used with a SQL statement such as an INSERT:

```
EXECUTE IMMEDIATE sql_statement_string
[USING variable1, variable2, etc];
```

It is usually a good idea to include an EXCEPTION block at the end of any code block. This is especially true when working with dynamic queries or statements. An Oracle error will be raised if the INSERT statement within the SQL string is invalid. If an EXCEPTION block were added to catch OTHERS, then you could provide a well-written error message that describes the exact issue at hand. In most cases, users of your application would prefer to see such a nice summary message rather than a cryptic Oracle error message.

It is a good rule of thumb to maintain consistency throughout your application code. If you prefer to use native dynamic SQL, then try to use it in all cases where dynamic SQL is a requirement. Likewise, DBMS_SQL should be used throughout if you plan to make use of it instead. There are certain situations when you may want to mix the two techniques in order to obtain information or use features that are not available with one or the other. In Recipe 8-13, you will learn more about using both techniques within the same block of PL/SQL code.

8-4. Writing a Dynamic Update Statement

Problem

Your application needs to execute an update statement, and you are not sure of the columns to be updated until runtime. For example, your application will modify employee records. You would like to construct an update statement that contains only the columns that have updated values.

Solution

Use native dynamic SQL to execute a SQL statement string that you prepare at application runtime. The procedure in this example accepts employee record values as input. In this scenario, an application form allows user entry for many of the fields that are contained within the EMPLOYEES table so that a particular employee record can be updated. The values that are changed on the form should be included in the UPDATE statement. The procedure queries the employee record and checks to see which values have been updated. Only the updated values are included in the text of the SQL string that is used for the update.

```
CREATE OR REPLACE PROCEDURE update_employees(id   IN employees.employee_id%TYPE,
                                    first IN employees.first_name%TYPE,
                                    last  IN employees.last_name%TYPE,
                                    email IN employees.email%TYPE,
                                    phone IN employees.phone_number%TYPE,
                                    job   IN employees.job_id%TYPE,
                                    salary IN employees.salary%TYPE,
                                    commission_pct IN employees.commission_pct%TYPE,
                                    manager_id IN employees.manager_id%TYPE,
                                    department_id IN employees.department_id%TYPE)
    AS

    emp_upd_rec     employees%ROWTYPE;

    sql_string      VARCHAR2(1000);

    set_count       NUMBER := 0;
BEGIN

    SELECT *
    INTO emp_upd_rec
    FROM employees
    WHERE employee_id = id;

    sql_string := 'UPDATE EMPLOYEES SET ';

    IF first != emp_upd_rec.first_name THEN
      IF set_count > 0 THEN
        sql_string := sql_string ||', FIRST_NAME =' || first || '''';
      ELSE
        sql_string := sql_string || ' FIRST_NAME =' || first || '''';
        set_count := set_count + 1;
      END IF;
    END IF;

    IF last != emp_upd_rec.last_name THEN
      IF set_count > 0 THEN
        sql_string := sql_string ||', LAST_NAME =''' || last || '''';
      ELSE
        sql_string := sql_string ||' LAST_NAME =''' ||  last || '''';
        set_count := set_count + 1;
      END IF;
    END IF;

    IF upper(email) != emp_upd_rec.email THEN
      IF set_count > 0 THEN
        sql_string := sql_string ||', EMAIL =''' || upper(email) || '''';
      ELSE
        sql_string := sql_string ||' EMAIL =''' || upper(email) || '''';
        set_count := set_count + 1;
      END IF;
```

```
      END IF;

      IF upper(phone) != emp_upd_rec.phone_number THEN
        IF set_count > 0 THEN
          sql_string := sql_string ||', PHONE_NUMBER =''' ||
            upper(phone) || '''';
        ELSE
          sql_string := sql_string ||' PHONE_NUMBER =''' ||
            upper(phone) || '''';
          set_count := set_count + 1;
        END IF;
      END IF;

      IF job != emp_upd_rec.job_id THEN
        IF set_count > 0 THEN
          sql_string := sql_string ||', JOB_ID =''' || job || '''';
        ELSE
          sql_string := sql_string ||' JOB_ID =''' || job || '''';
          set_count := set_count + 1;
        END IF;
      END IF;

      IF salary != emp_upd_rec.salary THEN
        IF set_count > 0 THEN
          sql_string := sql_string ||', SALARY =' || salary;
        ELSE
          sql_string := sql_string ||' SALARY =' || salary;
          set_count := set_count + 1;
        END IF;
      END IF;

      IF commission_pct != emp_upd_rec.commission_pct THEN
        IF set_count > 0 THEN
          sql_string := sql_string ||', COMMISSION_PCT =' ||
                  commission_pct;
        ELSE
          sql_string := sql_string ||' COMMISSION_PCT =' ||
                  commission_pct;
          set_count := set_count + 1;
        END IF;
      END IF;

      IF manager_id != emp_upd_rec.manager_id THEN
        IF set_count > 0 THEN
          sql_string := sql_string ||', MANAGER_ID =' ||
            manager_id;
        ELSE
          sql_string := sql_string ||' MANAGER_ID =' ||
            manager_id;
          set_count := set_count + 1;
        END IF;
      END IF;
```

```
  IF department_id != emp_upd_rec.department_id THEN
    IF set_count > 0 THEN
      sql_string := sql_string ||', DEPARTMENT_ID =' ||
        department_id;
    ELSE
      sql_string := sql_string ||' DEPARTMENT_ID =' ||
        department_id;
      set_count := set_count + 1;
    END IF;
  END IF;

  sql_string := sql_string || ' WHERE employee_id = ' || id;

  IF set_count > 0 THEN
    EXECUTE IMMEDIATE sql_string;
  ELSE
    DBMS_OUTPUT.PUT_LINE('No update needed, ' ||
        'all fields match original values');
  END IF;

EXCEPTION
  WHEN NO_DATA_FOUND THEN
    DBMS_OUTPUT.PUT_LINE('No matching employee found');
  WHEN OTHERS THEN
    DBMS_OUTPUT.PUT_LINE('Data entry error has occurred, ' ||
                'please check values and try again' || sql_string);
END;
```

Execution and Results:

```
SQL> exec update_employees(187,
'Anthony',
'Cabrio',
'ACABRIO',
'650.509.4876',
 'SH_CLERK'
,6501,
.08,
121,
50);
No update needed, all fields match original values
```

As mentioned previously, this procedure accepts input from a user data entry form. The input pertains to an existing employee's database record. The values accepted as input are compared against those that already exist in the database, and if they are different, then they are added into the SQL UPDATE statement that is dynamically created. This code could be simplified by creating a separate function to take care of comparing values and building the SQL string, but this procedure gives you a good idea of how dynamic SQL can be used to EXECUTE an UPDATE statement.

How It Works

Dynamic SQL statement execution is straightforward when using native dynamic SQL. The procedure in the solution to this recipe creates a SQL string based upon certain criteria, after which it is executed with the use of the EXECUTE IMMEDIATE statement.

The EXECUTE IMMEDIATE statement works the same way for most DML statements. If you read Recipe 8-3 on creating and running a dynamic INSERT statement, then you can see that executing an UPDATE statement works in the same manner.

Any values that need to be substituted into the SQL string should be coded as bind variables. For more information regarding bind variables, please refer to Recipe 8-3. The format for executing an UPDATE statement with the EXECUTE IMMEDIATE statement is as follows:

```
EXECUTE IMMEDIATE update_statement_string
[USING variable1, variable2, etc];
```

Just as with the execution of the INSERT statement in Recipe 8-3, the EXECUTE IMMEDIATE statement requires the use of the USING clause only if there are variables that need to be substituted into the SQL statement at runtime.

■ **Note** If you are able to write a static SQL UPDATE statement for your application, then do so. Use of dynamic SQL will incur a small performance penalty.

The DBMS_SQL package can also be used to work with dynamic SQL updates. However, this technique is not used very much since the introduction of native dynamic SQL in Oracle 9i. For an example of using the DBMS_SQL package with DML statements, please refer to Recipe 8-3. Although the example in Recipe 8-3 demonstrates an INSERT statement, an UPDATE statement is processed the same way; only the SQL string needs to be changed.

8-5. Writing a Dynamic Delete Statement

Problem

You need to create a procedure that will delete rows from a table. However, the exact SQL for deleting the rows is not known until runtime. For instance, you need create a procedure to delete an employee from the EMPLOYEES table, but rather than limit the procedure to accepting only employee ID numbers for employee identification, you also want to accept an e-mail address. The procedure will determine whether an e-mail address or an ID has been passed and will construct the appropriate DELETE statement.

Solution

Use native dynamic SQL to process a string that is dynamically created based upon values that are passed into the procedure. In the following example, a procedure is created that will build a dynamic SQL string to delete an employee record. The DELETE statement syntax may vary depending upon what type of value is passed into the procedure. Valid entries include EMPLOYEE_ID values or EMAIL values.

```
CREATE OR REPLACE PROCEDURE delete_employee(emp_value IN VARCHAR2) AS

  is_number          NUMBER := 0;
  valid_flag         BOOLEAN := FALSE;
  sql_stmt           VARCHAR2(1000);
  emp_count          NUMBER := 0;
BEGIN
  sql_stmt := 'DELETE FROM EMPLOYEES ';

  -- DETERMINE IF emp_value IS NUMERIC, IF SO THEN QUERY
  -- DATABASE TO FIND OCCURRENCES OF MATCHING EMPLOYEE_ID
  IF LENGTH(TRIM(TRANSLATE(emp_value, ' +-.0123456789', ' '))) IS NULL THEN
    SELECT COUNT(*)
    INTO emp_count
    FROM EMPLOYEES
    WHERE EMPLOYEE_ID = emp_value;

    IF emp_count > 0 THEN
      sql_stmt := sql_stmt || 'WHERE EMPLOYEE_ID = :emp_val';
      valid_flag := TRUE;
    END IF;
  ELSE
    SELECT COUNT(*)
    INTO emp_count
    FROM EMPLOYEES
    WHERE EMAIL = upper(emp_value);

    IF emp_count > 0 THEN
      sql_stmt := sql_stmt || 'WHERE EMAIL = :emp_val';
      valid_flag := TRUE;
    ELSE
      valid_flag := FALSE;
    END IF;
  END IF;

  IF valid_flag = TRUE THEN

    EXECUTE IMMEDIATE sql_stmt
    USING emp_value;

    DBMS_OUTPUT.PUT_LINE('Employee has been deleted');
  ELSE
    DBMS_OUTPUT.PUT_LINE('No matching employee found, please try again');
  END IF;

END;
```

The procedure can be called by passing in either an EMPLOYEE_ID value or an EMAIL value. If a matching employee record is found, then it will be deleted from the database table.

How It Works

Dynamic SQL can be used to execute DELETE statements as well. In the solution to this recipe, a dynamic SQL string is built that will remove an employee entry that contains a matching EMPLOYEE_ID or EMAIL value that is passed into the procedure as a parameter. The parameter is checked to find out whether it is a numeric or alphanumeric value by using a combination of the LENGTH, TRIM, and TRANSLATE functions. If it is numeric, then it is assumed to be an EMPLOYEE_ID value, and the database is queried to see whether there are any matches. If the parameter is found to be alphanumeric, then it is assumed to be an EMAIL value, and the database is queried to see whether there are any matches. If matches are found in either case, then a dynamic SQL string is built to DELETE the matching record from the database.

In this example, native dynamic SQL is used to perform the database operation. The DBMS_SQL package can also be used to perform this task using the same techniques that were demonstrated in Recipe 8-3.

8-6. Returning Data from a Dynamic Query into a Record

Problem

You are writing a block of code that will need to use dynamic SQL to execute a query because the exact SQL string is not known until runtime. The query needs to return the entire contents of the table row so that all columns of data can be used. You want to return the columns into a record variable.

Solution

Create a native dynamic SQL query to accommodate the SQL string that is unknown until runtime. FETCH the data using BULK COLLECT into a table of records. Our solution example shows rows from the jobs table being fetched into records, after which the individual record columns of data can be worked with. The following code block demonstrates this technique:

```
CREATE OR REPLACE PROCEDURE obtain_job_info(min_sal  NUMBER DEFAULT 0,

max_sal  NUMBER DEFAULT 0)
AS
  sql_text        VARCHAR2(1000);
  TYPE job_tab IS TABLE OF jobs%ROWTYPE;
  job_list        job_tab;
  job_elem        jobs%ROWTYPE;
  max_sal_temp    NUMBER;
  filter_flag     BOOLEAN := FALSE;
  cursor_var      NUMBER;
  TYPE            cur_type IS REF CURSOR;
  cur             cur_type;
BEGIN
  sql_text := 'SELECT * ' ||
              'FROM JOBS WHERE ' ||
              'min_salary >= :min_sal ' ||
              'and max_salary <= :max_sal';
```

```
IF max_sal = 0 THEN
  SELECT max(max_salary)
  INTO max_sal_temp
  FROM JOBS;
ELSE
  max_sal_temp := max_sal;
END IF;

OPEN cur FOR sql_text USING min_sal, max_sal_temp;
FETCH cur BULK COLLECT INTO job_list;
CLOSE cur;

FOR i IN job_list.FIRST .. job_list.LAST LOOP
  DBMS_OUTPUT.PUT_LINE(job_list(i).job_id || ' - ' || job_list(i).job_title);
END LOOP;

END;
```

As the salaries are obtained from the user input, they are used to determine how the bind variables will be populated within the query. The SQL is then executed, and the results are traversed. Each record is fetched and returned into a PL/SQL table of job records using BULK_COLLECT, and then in turn, each record is used to process the results. In this example, the data is simply printed out using DBMS_OUTPUT.PUT_LINE, but any number of tasks could be completed with the data.

How It Works

Dynamic SQL can be processed in a number of ways. In this solution, a record type is created by using the %ROWTYPE attribute of the table that is being queried. In this case, the %ROWTYPE attribute of the JOBS table is being used as a record. The data that is returned from performing a SELECT * on the JOBS table will be stored within that record, and then it will be processed accordingly. The record is created using the following syntax:

```
record_name     table_name%ROWTYPE;
```

Using this format, the record_name is any name of your choice that complies with PL/SQL's naming conventions. The table_name is the name of the table from which you will be gathering the data for each column, and the %ROWTYPE attribute is a special table attribute that creates a record type.

To process each record, create a REF CURSOR using the dynamic SQL string and perform a BULK COLLECT to fetch each row of data into a record in the table of JOBS records. The BULK COLLECT will load all of the resulting records at once into a PL/SQL collection object. Once all the data has been retrieved into an object, it can be processed accordingly. The BULK COLLECT is much more efficient than fetching each row from the table one-by-one using a LOOP construct.

8-7. Executing a Dynamic Block of PL/SQL

Problem

You want to execute a specific stored procedure based upon events that occur within your application. Therefore, you need to provide the ability for your application to execute procedures that are unknown until runtime. In short, you want to execute PL/SQL in the same dynamic manner as SQL.

Solution #1

Native dynamic SQL can be used to create and execute a block of code at runtime. This strategy can be used to create a dynamic block of code that executes a given procedure when an event occurs. In this example, a procedure is created that accepts an *event identifier*. An event handler within the application can call upon this procedure passing an event identifier, and subsequently a procedure that can be determined via the identifier will be invoked.

```
-- Create first Procedure
CREATE OR REPLACE PROCEDURE TEST_PROCEDURE1 AS
BEGIN
  DBMS_OUTPUT.PUT_LINE('YOU HAVE EXECUTED PROCEDURE 1…');
END;

-- Create Second Procedure
CREATE OR REPLACE PROCEDURE TEST_PROCEDURE2 AS
BEGIN
  DBMS_OUTPUT.PUT_LINE('YOU HAVE EXECUTED PROCEDURE 2…');
END;

-- Create Event Handling Procedure
CREATE OR REPLACE PROCEDURE run_test(test_id  IN NUMBER DEFAULT 1) AS
  sql_text  VARCHAR2(200);
BEGIN
  sql_text := 'BEGIN ' ||
              '  TEST_PROCEDURE' || test_id || '; ' ||
              'END;';

  EXECUTE IMMEDIATE sql_text;

END;
```

When an event handler passes a given event number to this procedure, it dynamically creates a code block that is used to execute that procedure, passing the parameters the procedure needs. This solution provides the ultimate flexibility for creating an event handler within your applications.

Solution #2

DBMS_SQL can also be used to execute the same dynamic code. The following example demonstrates how this is done.

```
CREATE OR REPLACE PROCEDURE run_test(test_id  IN NUMBER DEFAULT 1) AS
  sql_text  VARCHAR2(200);
  cursor_var   NUMBER := DBMS_SQL.OPEN_CURSOR;
  rows       NUMBER;
BEGIN
  sql_text := 'BEGIN ' ||
              '  TEST_PROCEDURE' || test_id || '; ' ||
              'END;';

  DBMS_SQL.PARSE(cursor_var, sql_text, DBMS_SQL.NATIVE);
```

```
rows := DBMS_SQL.EXECUTE(cursor_var);
DBMS_SQL.CLOSE_CURSOR(cursor_var);

END;
```

How It Works

Native dynamic SQL allows processing of a SQL statement via the EXECUTE IMMEDIATE statement. This can be used to the advantage of the application and provide the ability to create dynamic blocks of executable code. By doing so, you can create an application that allows more flexibility, which can help ensure that your code is more easily manageable.

In the solution to this recipe, an unknown procedure name along with its parameters is concatenated into a SQL string that forms a code block. This code block is then executed using the EXECUTE IMMEDIATE statement.

Using native dynamic SQL, the array of parameters has to be manually processed to create the SQL string and assign each of the array values to the USING clause of the EXECUTE IMMEDIATE statement. This technique works quite well, but there is a different way to implement the same procedure.

As far as comparing native dynamic SQL and DBMS_SQL for dynamic code block execution, which code is better? That is up to you to decide. If you are using native dynamic SQL for all other dynamic SQL processing within your application, then it is probably a good idea to stick with it instead of mixing both techniques. However, if you are working with some legacy code that perhaps includes a mixture of both DBMS_SQL and native dynamic SQL, then you may prefer to write a dynamic code block using DBMS_SQL just to save some time and processing.

8-8. Creating a Table at Runtime

Problem

Your application needs to have the ability to create tables based upon user input. The user has the ability to add additional attributes to some of your application forms, and when this is done, a new attribute table needs to be created to hold the information.

Solution

Create a table at runtime using native dynamic SQL. Write a procedure that accepts a table name as an argument and then creates a SQL string including the DDL that is required for creating that table. The table structure will be hard-coded since the structure for an attribute table will always be the same within your application. The code that follows demonstrates this technique by creating a procedure named CREATE_ATTR_TABLE that dynamically creates attribute tables.

```
CREATE OR REPLACE PROCEDURE create_attr_table(table_name      VARCHAR2) AS
  BEGIN
    EXECUTE IMMEDIATE 'CREATE TABLE ' || table_name ||
                                  '(ATTRIBUTE_ID      NUMBER PRIMARY KEY,
                                   ATTRIBUTE_NAME   VARCHAR2(150) NOT NULL,
                                   ATTRIBUTE_VALUE  VARCHAR2(150))';
  END create_attr_table;
```

This procedure is invoked by the application whenever a user determines that additional attributes are required for a particular application form. That form will then have its own attribute table created, and the user can then provide additional fields/attributes to customize the form as needed.

How It Works

Dynamic SQL can be used to create database objects at runtime. In this recipe, it is used to create tables. Native dynamic SQL is used in this example, and the EXECUTE IMMEDIATE statement performs the work. When creating a table at runtime, generate a string that contains the necessary SQL to create the object. Once that task has been completed, issue the EXECUTE IMMEDIATE statement passing the generated SQL string. The format to use along with the EXECUTE IMMEDIATE statement to create objects is as follows:

```
EXECUTE IMMEDIATE SQL_string;
```

The SQL_string in this example is a dynamically created string that will create an object. In the case of creating objects, the USING clause is not used because you cannot use bind variables for substituting object names or attributes such as column names.

■ Please use care when concatenating user input variables with SQL text because the technique poses a security concern. Specifically, you open the door to the much-dreaded SQL injection attack. Refer to Recipe 8-14 for more details and for information on protecting yourself.

8-9. Altering a Table at Runtime

Problem

Your application provides the ability to add attributes to forms in order to store additional information. You need to provide users with the ability to make those attribute fields larger or smaller based upon their needs.

Solution

Create a procedure that will provide the ability to alter tables at runtime using native dynamic SQL. The procedure in this solution will accept two parameters, those being the table name to be altered and the column name along with new type declaration. The procedure assembles a SQL string using the arguments provided by the user and then executes it using native dynamic SQL. The following code demonstrates this solution:

```
CREATE OR REPLACE PROCEDURE modify_table(tab_name   VARCHAR2,
                                         tab_info   VARCHAR2) AS
                                         sql_text   VARCHAR2(1000);
BEGIN
  sql_text := 'ALTER TABLE ' || tab_name ||
              ' MODIFY ' || tab_info;
  DBMS_OUTPUT.PUT_LINE(sql_text);
```

```
  EXECUTE IMMEDIATE sql_text;
  DBMS_OUTPUT.PUT_LINE('Table successfully altered…');
EXCEPTION
  WHEN OTHERS THEN
    DBMS_OUTPUT.PUT_LINE('An error has occurred, table not modified');
END;
```

The procedure determines whether the user-defined data is valid. If so, then the EXECUTE IMMEDIATE statement executes the SQL string that was formed. Otherwise, the user will see an alert displayed.

How It Works

Similar to creating objects at runtime, Oracle provides the ability to alter objects using dynamic SQL. The same technique is used for constructing the SQL string as when creating an object, and that string is eventually executed via the EXECUTE IMMEDIATE statement. The EXECUTE IMMEDIATE statement for altering a table at runtime uses no clause, because it is not possible to use bind variables with an ALTER TABLE statement. If you try to pass in bind variable values, then you will receive an Oracle error.

The following format should be used when issuing the EXECUTE IMMEDIATE statement for SQL text containing an ALTER TABLE statement:

```
EXECUTE IMMEDIATE alter_table_sql_string;
```

The most important thing to remember when issuing a DDL statement using dynamic SQL is that you will need to concatenate all the strings and variables in order to formulate the final SQL string that will be executed. Bind variables will not work for substituting table names or column names/attributes.

8-10. Finding All Tables That Include a Specific Column Value

Problem

You are required to update all instances of a particular data column value across multiple tables within your database.

Solution

Search all user tables for the particular column you are interested in finding. Create a cursor that will be used to loop through all the results and execute a subsequent UPDATE statement in each iteration of the loop. The UPDATE statement will update all matching column values for the table that is current for that iteration of the cursor.

The following example shows how this technique can be performed. The procedure will be used to change a manager ID when a department or job position changes management.

```
CREATE OR REPLACE PROCEDURE change_manager(current_manager_id NUMBER,

new_manager_id  NUMBER)
AS

cursor manager_tab_cur is
select table_name
from user_tab_columns
```

```
    where column_name = 'MANAGER_ID'
    and table_name not in (select view_name from user_views);

    rec_count               number := 0;
    ref_count               number := 0;

BEGIN

    -- Print out the tables which will be updated

    DBMS_OUTPUT.PUT_LINE('Tables referencing the selected MANAGER ID#:' ||
  current_manager_id);

    FOR manager_rec IN manager_tab_cur LOOP
        EXECUTE IMMEDIATE 'select count(*) total ' ||
                          'from ' || manager_rec.table_name ||
                          ' where manager_id = :manager_id_num'
        INTO rec_count
        USING current_manager_id;

        if rec_count > 0 then
                    DBMS_OUTPUT.PUT_LINE(manager_rec.table_name || ': ' || rec_count);
                    ref_count := ref_count + 1;
        end if;

        rec_count := 0;

    END LOOP;

    if ref_count > 0 then
        DBMS_OUTPUT.PUT_LINE('Manager is referenced in ' || ref_count || ' tables.');
        DBMS_OUTPUT.PUT_LINE('...Now Changing the Manager Identifier...');
    end if;

    -- Perform the actual table updates

    FOR manager_rec IN manager_tab_cur LOOP
        EXECUTE IMMEDIATE 'select count(*) total ' ||
                                        'from ' || manager_rec.table_name ||
                                        ' where manager_id = :manager_id_num'
        INTO rec_count
        USING current_manager_id;

        if rec_count > 0 then

            EXECUTE IMMEDIATE 'update ' || manager_rec.table_name || ' ' ||
                                            'set manager_id = :new_manager_id ' ||
                                            'where manager_id = :old_manager_id'
            USING new_manager_id, current_manager_id;

        end if;
```

```
        rec_count := 0;

    END LOOP;

    -- Print out the tables which still reference the manager number.

    FOR manager_rec IN manager_tab_cur LOOP
        EXECUTE IMMEDIATE 'select count(*) total ' ||
                          'from ' || manager_rec.table_name ||
                          ' where manager_id = :manager_id'
        INTO rec_count
        USING current_manager_id;

        if rec_count > 0 then
                    DBMS_OUTPUT.PUT_LINE(manager_rec.table_name || ': ' || rec_count);
                    ref_count := ref_count + 1;
        end if;

        rec_count := 0;

    END LOOP;

    if ref_count > 0 then
        DBMS_OUTPUT.PUT_LINE('Manager #: ' || current_manager_id
                                || ' is now referenced in ' ||
                        ref_count || ' tables.');
        DBMS_OUTPUT.PUT_LINE('...There should be no tables listed above...');
    end if;

end;
```

Since MANAGER_ID depends upon a corresponding MANAGER_ID within the DEPARTMENTS table, you must first ensure that the MANAGER_ID that you want to change to is designated to a department within that table. In the following scenario, a manager is added to a department that does not have a manager. Afterward, the manager with ID of 205 is swapped for the newly populated manager.

```
SQL> update departments
  2   set manager_id = 241
  3   where department_id = 270;

1 row updated.

SQL> exec change_manager(205, 241);
Tables referencing the selected MANAGER ID#:205
DEPARTMENTS: 1
EMP: 1
EMPLOYEES: 1
Manager is referenced in 3 tables.
...Now Changing the Manager Identifier...
Manager #: 205 is now referenced in 3 tables.
...There should be no tables listed above...
```

```
PL/SQL procedure successfully completed.
```

> ■ **Note** If you attempt to swap a manager with one that is not associated with a department, then you will receive a foreign key error. This same concept holds true in the real world—ensure that constraints are reviewed before applying this technique.

If management decides to change a manager for a particular department, then this procedure will be called. The caller will pass in the old manager's ID number and the new manager's ID number. This procedure will then query all tables within the current schema for a matching current manager ID and update it to reflect the new ID number.

How It Works

To determine all instances of a specific column or database field, you must search all database tables for that column name. Of course, this assumes that the database was created using the same name for the same column in each different table. If columns containing the same data are named differently across tables, then this recipe's technique will not work.

> ■ **Note** Although most relational databases are set up with efficiency in mind and only populate data for a specific field value into one database table column, there are some legacy databases that still use the same fields across more than one table.

As the solution to this recipe entails, assume that a column name is coded into the procedure, and all tables will then be searched to find out whether that column exists. You can perform the search using the built-in USER_TAB_COLUMNS data dictionary view. This view is comprised of column information for all the tables within a particular schema. Querying any Oracle view that is prefixed with USER_ indicates that the view pertains to data contained within the current user's schema only. Querying the USER_TAB_COLUMNS view allows a table name and column name to be specified. In this case, since you need to find all tables that contain a specific column, query the USER_TAB_COLUMNS view to return all instances of TABLE_NAME where COLUMN_NAME is equal to the name that is passed into the procedure. This query should be defined as a cursor variable so that it can be parsed via a FOR loop in the code block.

> ■ **Warning** Be sure to exclude views from this process, or you may receive an error from attempting to update a value that is contained within a view if it is not an updatable view.

Now that the cursor is ready to parse all table names that contain a matching column, it is time to loop through the cursor and query each table that contains that column for a matching value. A user passes two values into the procedure: current manager ID and new manager ID. In the solution to this recipe, each table that contains a matching column is queried so that you can see how many matches were found prior to the updates taking place. A counter is used to tally the number of matches found throughout the tables. Next, looping through the cursor again performs the actual updates. This time, the tables are each queried to find matches again, but when a match is found, then that table will be updated so that the value is changed from the old value to the new value.

Lastly, the cursor is parsed again, and each table is queried to find existing matches once again. This last loop is done for consistency and to ensure that all matches have been found and updated to the current value. If any matches are found during this last loop, then all changes should be rolled back, and the changes should be manually processed instead.

This procedure can be updated to work with any column value change that may be needed. The code can also be shortened significantly if you do not want to perform verifications prior to and after performing an update.

8-11 Storing Dynamic SQL in Large Objects

Problem

The SQL code that you need to assemble at runtime is likely to exceed the 32KB limit that is bound to VARCHAR2 types. You need to be able to store dynamic SQL text in a type that will allow more for a large amount of text.

Solution #1

Declare a CLOB variable, and store your SQL string within it. After the CLOB has been created, execute the SQL. This can be done using either native dynamic SQL or the DBMS_SQL package. For the example, assume that a block of text is being read from an external file, and it will be passed to a procedure to be processed. That text will be the SQL string that will be dynamically processed within the procedure. Since the external text file can be virtually any size, this text must be read into a CLOB data type and then passed to the procedure in this example for processing. The following procedure processes the CLOB as dynamic SQL.

The first example demonstrates the parsing and execution of a dynamic SQL statement that has been stored in a CLOB using the DBMS_SQL package. Note that this procedure does not return any value, so it is not meant for issuing queries but rather for executing code.

```
CREATE OR REPLACE PROCEDURE execute_clob(sql_text CLOB) AS
  sql_string    CLOB;
  cur_var       BINARY_INTEGER;
  ret_var       INTEGER;
  return_value  VARCHAR2(100);
BEGIN
  sql_string := sql_text;
  cur_var := DBMS_SQL.OPEN_CURSOR;
  DBMS_SQL.PARSE(cur_var, sql_string, DBMS_SQL.NATIVE);
  ret_var := DBMS_SQL.EXECUTE(cur_var);
  DBMS_SQL.CLOSE_CURSOR(cur_var);
END;
```

Solution #2

The second example is the same procedure written to use native dynamic SQL. You will notice that the code is a bit shorter, and there is less work that needs to be done in order to complete the same transaction.

```
CREATE OR REPLACE PROCEDURE execute_clob_nds(sql_text    IN CLOB) AS
  sql_string    CLOB;

BEGIN
  sql_string := sql_text;
  EXECUTE IMMEDIATE sql_string;
END;
```

As noted previously, the native dynamic SQL is easier to follow and takes less code to implement. For the sake of maintaining a current code base, use of native dynamic SQL would be encouraged. However, DBMS_SQL is still available and offers different options as mentioned in the first recipes in this chapter.

How It Works

Oracle added some new features for working with dynamic SQL into the Oracle Database 11g release. Providing the ability to store dynamic SQL into a CLOB is certainly a useful addition. Prior to Oracle Database 11g, the only way to dynamically process a string that was larger than 32KB was to concatenate two VARCHAR types that were at or near 32KB in size. The largest string that could be processed by native dynamic SQL was 64KB. With the release of Oracle Database 11g, the CLOB (character large object) can be used in such cases, mitigating the need to concatenate two different variables to form the complete SQL.

Using DBMS_SQL and its PARSE function, SQL that is stored within a CLOB can be easily processed. The following lines of code are the lines from the first solution that read and process the CLOB:

```
cur_var := DBMS_SQL.OPEN_CURSOR;
DBMS_SQL.PARSE(cur_var, v_sql, DBMS_SQL.NATIVE);
ret_var := DBMS_SQL.EXECUTE(cur_var);
DBMS_SQL.CLOSE_CURSOR(cur_var);
```

The first line opens a new cursor using DBMS_SQL.OPEN_CURSOR. It assigns an integer to the cur_var variable, which is then passed to the DBMS_SQL.PARSE procedure. DBMS_SQL.PARSE also accepts the SQL CLOB and a constant DBMS_SQL.NATIVE that helps discern the dialect that should be used to process the SQL. The dialect is also referred to as the language_flag, and it is used to determine how Oracle will process the SQL statement. Possible values include V6 for version 6 behavior, V7 for Oracle database 7 behavior, and NATIVE to specify normal behavior for the database to which the program is connected. After the SQL has been parsed, it can be executed using the DBMS_SQL.EXECUTE function. This function will accept the cursor variable as input and execute the SQL. A code of 0 is returned if the SQL is executed successfully. Lastly, remember to close the cursor using DBMS_SQL.CLOSE_CURSOR and passing the cursor variable to it.

The example in Solution #2 of this recipe demonstrates the use of native dynamic SQL for execution of dynamic SQL text that is stored within a CLOB. Essentially no differences exist between the execution of SQL text stored in a VARCHAR data type as opposed to SQL text stored within a CLOB for native dynamic SQL. The code is short and precise, and it is easy to read.

8-12. Passing NULL Values to Dynamic SQL

Problem

You want to pass a NULL value to a dynamic query that you are using. For example, you want to query the EMPLOYEES table for all records that have a NULL MANAGER_ID value.

Solution

Create an uninitialized variable, and place it into the USING clause. In this example, a dynamic query is written and executed using native dynamic SQL. The dynamic query will retrieve all employees who do not currently have a manager assigned to their record. To retrieve the records that are required, the WHERE clause needs to filter the selection so that only records containing a NULL MANAGER_ID value are returned.

```
DECLARE
  TYPE cur_type IS REF CURSOR;
  cur                cur_type;
  null_value         CHAR(1);
  sql_string         VARCHAR2(150);
  emp_rec            employees%ROWTYPE;
BEGIN
  sql_string := 'SELECT * ' ||
                   'FROM EMPLOYEES ' ||
                   'WHERE MANAGER_ID IS :null_val';

  OPEN cur FOR sql_string USING null_value;
  LOOP
    FETCH cur INTO emp_rec;
    DBMS_OUTPUT.PUT_LINE(emp_rec.first_name || ' ' || emp_rec.last_name ||
                                           ' - ' || emp_rec.email);

    EXIT WHEN cur%NOTFOUND;
  END LOOP;
  CLOSE cur;
END;
```

In this solution, the bind variable :null_val has an uninitialized variable value substituted in its place. This will cause the query to evaluate the bind variable as a NULL value. All records that reside within the EMPLOYEES table and do not have a MANAGER_ID assigned to them should be printed by the DBMS_OUTPUT package.

How It Works

It is not possible to simply pass a NULL value using native dynamic SQL. At least, you cannot pass a NULL as a literal. However, oftentimes it is useful to initialize a bind variable to null.

An uninitialized variable in PL/SQL inherently has the value of NULL. Hence, if you do not initialize a variable, then it will contain a NULL value. Passing an uninitialized variable via the EXECUTE IMMEDIATE statement will have the same effect as substituting a NULL value for a bind variable.

8-13. Switching Between DBMS_SQL and Native Dynamic SQL

Problem

Your consulting company is currently migrating all its applications from using DBMS_SQL to native dynamic SQL. To help ensure that the migration can be done piecemeal, you want to provide the ability to switch between the two different techniques so that legacy code can coexist with the newer native dynamic SQL.

Solution

When you need both the DBMS_SQL package and native dynamic SQL, you can switch between them using the DBMS_SQL.TO_REFCURSOR and DBMS_SQL.TO_CURSOR_NUMBER APIs. The DBMS_SQL.TO_REFCURSOR API provides the ability to execute dynamic SQL using the DBMS_SQL package and then convert the DBMS_SQL cursor to a REF CURSOR. The DBMS_SQL.TO_CURSOR_NUMBER API allows for executing dynamic SQL via a REF CURSOR and then converting to DBMS_SQL for data retrieval.

The following example illustrates the usage of DBMS_SQL.TO_REFCURSOR. In the example, a simple dynamic query is being executed using DBMS_SQL, and the cursor is then being converted to a REF CURSOR.

```
DECLARE
  sql_string          CLOB;
  cur_var             BINARY_INTEGER := DBMS_SQL.OPEN_CURSOR;
  ref_cur             SYS_REFCURSOR;
  return_value        BINARY_INTEGER;
  cur_rec             jobs%ROWTYPE;
  salary              NUMBER := &salary;
BEGIN
  -- Formulate query
  sql_string := 'SELECT * FROM JOBS ' ||
                    'WHERE MAX_SALARY >= :sal';
  -- Parse SQL
  DBMS_SQL.PARSE(cur_var, sql_string, DBMS_SQL.NATIVE);

  -- Bind variable(s)
  DBMS_SQL.BIND_VARIABLE(cur_var, 'sal', salary);

  -- Execute query and convert to REF CURSOR

  return_value := DBMS_SQL.EXECUTE(cur_var);
  ref_cur := DBMS_SQL.TO_REFCURSOR(cur_var);
  DBMS_OUTPUT.PUT_LINE('Jobs that have a maximum salary over ' || salary);
  LOOP
    FETCH ref_cur INTO cur_rec;
    DBMS_OUTPUT.PUT_LINE(cur_rec.job_id || ' - ' || cur_rec.job_title);
    EXIT WHEN ref_cur%NOTFOUND;
  END LOOP;

  CLOSE ref_cur;

END;
```

The example prompts for the entry of a maximum salary via the :sal bind variable and the SQL*Plus &salary substitution variable. The DBMS_SQL API then binds the maximum salary that was entered to the dynamic SQL string and executes the query to find all jobs that have a maximum salary greater than the amount that was entered. Once the query is executed, the cursor is converted to a REF CURSOR using the DBMS_SQL.TO_REFCURSOR API. Native dynamic SQL is then used to process the results of the query. As you can see, the native dynamic SQL is much easier to read and process. The advantage of converting to a REF CURSOR is to have the ability to easily process code using native dynamic SQL but still have some of the advantages of using DBMS_SQL for querying the data. For instance, if the number of bind variables was unknown until runtime, then DBMS_SQL would be required.

A similar technique can be used if DBMS_SQL is required to process the results of a query. The DBMS_SQL.TO_CURSOR_NUMBER API provides the ability to convert a cursor from a REF CURSOR to DBMS_SQL. The following example shows the same query on the JOBS table, but this time native dynamic SQL is used to set up the query and execute it, and DBMS_SQL is used to describe the table structure. One of the nice features of the DBMS_SQL API is that it is possible to describe the columns of a query that will be returned.

```
DECLARE
   sql_string          CLOB;
   ref_cur             SYS_REFCURSOR;
   cursor_var          BINARY_INTEGER;
   cols_var            BINARY_INTEGER;
   desc_var            DBMS_SQL.DESC_TAB;
   v_job_id            NUMBER;
   v_job_title         VARCHAR2(25);
   salary              NUMBER(6) := &salary;
   return_val          NUMBER;

BEGIN
   -- Formulate query
   sql_string := 'SELECT * FROM JOBS ' ||
                              'WHERE MAX_SALARY >= :sal';
   -- Open REF CURSOR
   OPEN ref_cur FOR sql_string USING salary;

   cursor_var := DBMS_SQL.TO_CURSOR_NUMBER(ref_cur);
   DBMS_SQL.DESCRIBE_COLUMNS(cursor_var, cols_var, desc_var);
   DBMS_SQL.CLOSE_CURSOR(cursor_var);

   FOR x IN 1 .. cols_var LOOP
      DBMS_OUTPUT.PUT_LINE(desc_var(x).col_name || ' - ' ||
                           CASE desc_var(x).col_type
                                     WHEN 1 THEN 'VARCHAR2'
                                     WHEN 2 THEN 'NUMBER'
                           ELSE 'OTHER'
                           END);
   END LOOP;
END;
```

Each of these techniques has their place within the world of PL/SQL programming. Using this type of conversion is especially useful for enabling your application to use the features DBMS_SQL has to offer without compromising the ease and structure of native dynamic SQL.

How It Works

Oracle Database 11g added some new capabilities to dynamic SQL. One of those new features is the ability to convert between native dynamic SQL and DBMS_SQL. DBMS_SQL provides some functionality that is not offered by the newer and easier native dynamic SQL API. Now that Oracle Database 11g provides the ability to make use of native dynamic SQL but still gain the advantages of using DBMS_SQL, Oracle dynamic SQL is much more complete.

The DBMS_SQL.TO_REFCURSOR API is used to convert SQL that is using DBMS_SQL into a REF CURSOR, which allows you to work with the resulting records using native dynamic SQL. To convert SQL to a REF CURSOR, you will use DBMS_SQL to parse the SQL, bind any variables, and finally to execute it. Afterward, you call DBMS_SQL.TO_REFCURSOR and pass the original DBMS_SQL cursor as an argument. This will return a REF CURSOR that can be used to work with the results from the query. The statement that performs the conversion contains DBMS_SQL.EXECUTE. The EXECUTE function accepts a DBMS_SQL cursor as an argument. As a result, a REF CURSOR is returned, and it can be used to work with the results from the dynamic query.

Conversely, DBMS_SQL.TO_CURSOR_NUMBER can be used to convert a REF CURSOR into a DBMS_SQL cursor. You may choose to do this in order to use some additional functionality that DBMS_SQL has to offer such as the ability to DESCRIBE an object (DESCRIBE is a SQL*Plus feature). As you can see in the second example, native dynamic SQL is used to open the REF CURSOR and bind the variable to the SQL. Once this has been completed, the cursor is converted to DBMS_SQL using DBMS_SQL.TO_CURSOR_NUMBER and passing the REF CURSOR. After this conversion is complete, you can utilize the DBMS_SQL API to work with the resulting cursor.

8-14. Guarding Against SQL Injection Attacks

Problem

To provide the best security for your application, you want to ensure that your dynamic SQL statements are unable to be altered as a result of data entered from an application form.

Solution

Take care to provide security against SQL injection attacks by validating user input prior and using it in your dynamic SQL statements or queries. The easiest way to ensure that there are no malicious injections into your SQL is to make use of bind variables.

The following code is an example of a PL/SQL procedure that is vulnerable to SQL injection because it concatenates a variable that is populated with user input and does not properly validate the input prior:

```
CREATE OR REPLACE PROCEDURE check_password(username IN VARCHAR2) AS
  sql_stmt    VARCHAR2(1000);
  password    VARCHAR2(30);
BEGIN
 sql_stmt := 'SELECT password ' ||
                     'FROM user_records ' ||
                     'WHERE username = ''' || username || ''';
  EXECUTE sql_stmt
  INTO password;

  -- PROCESS PASSWORD
END;
```

To properly code this example to guard against SQL injection, use bind variables. The following is the same procedure that has been rewritten to make it invulnerable to SQL injection:

```
CREATE OR REPLACE PROCEDURE check_password(username IN VARCHAR2) AS
  sql_stmt    VARCHAR2(1000);
  password    VARCHAR2(30);
BEGIN
  sql_stmt := 'SELECT password ' ||
              'FROM user_records ' ||
              'WHERE username = :username';

  EXECUTE sql_stmt
  INTO password
  USING username;

  -- PROCESS PASSWORD
END;
```

Making just a couple of minor changes can significantly increase the security against SQL injection attacks.

How It Works

SQL injection attacks can occur when data that is accepted as input from an application form is concatenated into dynamic SQL queries or statements without proper validation. SQL injection is a form of malicious database attack that is caused by a user placing some code or escape characters into a form field so that the underlying application SQL query or statement becomes affected in an undesirable manner. In the solution to this recipe, all passwords stored in the USER_RECORDS table could be compromised if a malicious user were to place a line of text similar to the following into the form field for the USERNAME:

```
'WHATEVER '' OR username is NOT NULL--'
```

The strange-looking text that you see here can cause major issues because it essentially changes the query to read as follows:

```
SELECT password
FROM user_records
WHERE username = 'WHATEVER ' OR username is NOT NULL;
```

Bind variables can be used to guard against SQL injection attacks, because their contents are not interpreted at all by Oracle. The value of a bind variable is never parsed as part of the string containing the SQL query or statement to be executed. Thus, the use of bind variables provides absolute protection against SQL injection attacks.

Another way to safeguard your code against SQL injection attacks is to validate user input to ensure that it is not malicious. Only valid input should be used within a statement or query.

There are ways to validate user input depending upon the type of input you are receiving. For instance, to verify the integrity of user input, you can use regular expressions. If you are expecting to receive an e-mail address from a user input field, then the value that is passed into your code should be verified to ensure that it is in proper format of an e-mail address. Here's an example:

```
IF owa_pattern.match(email_variable,'^\w{1,}[.,0-9,a-z,A-Z,_]\w{1,}' ||
        '[.,0-9,a-z,A-Z,_]\w{1,}'||
        '@\w{1,}[.,0-9,a-z,A-Z,_]\' ||
        'w{1,}[.,0-9,a-z,A-Z,_]\w{1,}[.,0-9,a-z,A-Z,_]\w{1,}$') then
  -- Perform valid transaction
ELSE
  -- Raise an error message
```

It is imperative that you do not allow users of your applications to see the Oracle error codes that are returned by an error. Use proper exception handling (covered in Chapter 9) to ensure that you are catching any possible exceptions and returning a vaguely descriptive error message to the user. It is not wise to allow Oracle errors or detailed error messages to be displayed because they will most likely provide a malicious user with valuable information for attacking your database.

Using bind variables, validating user input, and displaying user-friendly and appropriate error messages can help ensure that your database is not attacked. It is never an enjoyable experience to explain to your users that all usernames and passwords were compromised. Time is much better spent securing your code than going back to clean up after a malicious attack.

■■■

CHAPTER 9

Exceptions

Exceptions are a fundamental part of any well-written program. They are used to display user-friendly error messages when an error is raised by an application, nondefault exception handling, and sometimes recovery so that an application can continue. Surely you have seen your fair share of ORA-XXXXX error messages. Although these messages are extremely useful to a developer for debugging and correcting issues, they are certainly foreign to the average application user and can be downright frightening to see.

Imagine that you are working with a significant number of updates via an application form, and after you submit your 150th update, an Oracle error is displayed. Your first reaction would be of panic, hoping that you haven't just lost all of the work you had completed thus far. By adding exception handling to an application, you can ensure that exceptions are handled in an orderly fashion so that no work is lost. You can also create a nicer error message to let the user know all changes have been saved up to this point so that sheer panic doesn't set in when the exception is raised.

Exceptions can also be raised as a means to provide informative detail regarding processes that are occurring within your application. They are not merely restricted to being used when Oracle encounters an issue. You can raise your own exceptions as well when certain circumstances are encountered in your application.

Whatever the case may be, exception handling should be present in any production-quality application code. This chapter will cover some basics of how to use exception handling in your code. Along the way, you will learn some key tips on how exception handling can make your life easier. In the end, you should be fully armed to implement exception handling for your applications.

9-1. Trapping an Exception

Problem

A procedure in your application has the potential to cause an exception to be raised. Rather than let the program exit and return control to the host machine, you want to perform some cleanup to ensure data integrity, as well as display an informative error message.

Solution

Write an exception handler for your procedure so that the exception can be caught and you can perform tasks that need to be completed and provide a more descriptive message. The following procedure is used to obtain employee information based upon a primary key value or an e-mail address. Beginning with the EXCEPTION keyword in the following example, an exception-handling block has been added to the end of the procedure in order to handle any exceptions that may occur when no matching record is found.

```
CREATE OR REPLACE PROCEDURE obtain_emp_detail(emp_info IN VARCHAR2) IS
  emp_qry             VARCHAR2(500);
  emp_first           employees.first_name%TYPE;
  emp_last            employees.last_name%TYPE;
  email               employees.email%TYPE;

  valid_id_count      NUMBER := 0;
  valid_flag          BOOLEAN := TRUE;
  temp_emp_info       VARCHAR2(50);

BEGIN
  emp_qry := 'SELECT FIRST_NAME, LAST_NAME, EMAIL FROM EMPLOYEES ';
  IF emp_info LIKE '%@%' THEN
    temp_emp_info := substr(emp_info,0,instr(emp_info,'@')-1);
    emp_qry := emp_qry || 'WHERE EMAIL = :emp_info';
  ELSE
    SELECT COUNT(*)
    INTO valid_id_count
    FROM employees
    WHERE employee_id = emp_info;

    IF valid_id_count > 0 THEN
        temp_emp_info := emp_info;
        emp_qry := emp_qry || 'WHERE EMPLOYEE_ID = :id';
    ELSE
        valid_flag := FALSE;
    END IF;
  END IF;

  IF valid_flag = TRUE THEN
    EXECUTE IMMEDIATE emp_qry
    INTO emp_first, emp_last, email
    USING temp_emp_info;

    DBMS_OUTPUT.PUT_LINE(emp_first || ' ' || emp_last || ' - ' || email);
  ELSE
    DBMS_OUTPUT.PUT_LINE('THE INFORMATION YOU HAVE USED DOES ' ||
                         'NOT MATCH ANY EMPLOYEE RECORD');
  END IF;

  EXCEPTION
    WHEN NO_DATA_FOUND THEN
      DBMS_OUTPUT.PUT_LINE('THE INFORMATION YOU HAVE USED DOES ' ||
                           'NOT MATCH ANY EMPLOYEE RECORD');
    WHEN INVALID_NUMBER THEN
      DBMS_OUTPUT.PUT_LINE('YOU MUST ENTER AN EMAIL ADDRESS INCLUDING ' ||
                           'THE @ OR A POSITIVE INTEGER VALUE FOR THE ' ||
                           'EMPLOYEE ID.');
END;
```

Here are the results of calling the procedure with various arguments:

```
SQL> EXEC OBTAIN_EMP_DETAIL(000);
THE INFORMATION YOU HAVE USED DOES NOT MATCH ANY EMPLOYEE RECORD

PL/SQL procedure successfully completed.

SQL> EXEC OBTAIN_EMP_DETAIL('TEST');
YOU MUST ENTER AN EMAIL ADDRESS INCLUDING THE @ OR A POSITIVE INTEGER VALUE FOR
THE EMPLOYEE ID.

PL/SQL procedure successfully completed.

SQL> EXEC OBTAIN_EMP_DETAIL(200);
Jennifer Whalen - JWHALEN

PL/SQL procedure successfully completed.
```

This procedure is essentially the same as the one demonstrated in Recipe 8-1. The difference is that when an exception is raised, the control will go into the exception block. At that time, the code you place within the exception block will determine the next step to take as opposed to simply raising an Oracle error and returning control to the calling procedure, calling function, or host environment.

How It Works

To perform remedial actions when an exception is raised, you should always make sure to code an exception handler if there is any possibility that an exception may be thrown. The sole purpose of an exception handler is to catch exceptions when they are raised and handle the outcome in a controlled fashion. There are two different types of exceptions that can be raised by a PL/SQL application: internally defined and user defined. Oracle Database has a defined set of internal exceptions that can be thrown by a PL/SQL application. Those exceptions are known as internally defined. It is also possible to define your own exceptions, which are known as user defined.

An exception-handling block is structured like a CASE statement in that a series of exceptions is listed followed by a separate set of statements to be executed for each outcome. The standard format for an exception-handling block is as follows:

```
EXCEPTION
  WHEN name_of_exception THEN
    -- One or more statements
```

Exception blocks begin with the EXCEPTION keyword, followed by a series of WHEN..THEN clauses that describe different possible exceptions along with the set of statements that should be executed if the exception is caught. The exception name can be one of the Oracle internally defined exceptions, or it can be the name of an exception that has been declared within your code. To learn more about declaring exceptions, please see Recipe 9-3 in this chapter. In the solution to this recipe, the internally defined NO_DATA_FOUND exception is raised if an unknown e-mail address is entered into the procedure because there will be no rows returned from the query. When the exception block encounters the WHEN clause that corresponds with NO_DATA_FOUND, the statements immediately following the THEN keyword are executed. In this case, an error message is printed using the DBMS_OUTPUT package. However, in a real-world application, this is where you will place any cleanup or error handling that should be done to help maintain the integrity of the data accessed by your application.

An exception block can contain any number of WHEN..THEN clauses, and therefore, any number of exceptions can each contain their own set of handler statements. Even if a simple message was to be displayed, as is the case with the solution to this recipe, a different and more descriptive error message can be coded for each different exception that may possibly be raised. This situation is reflected in the second exception handler contained within the solution because it returns a different error message than the first.

As mentioned previously, Oracle contains a number of internally defined exceptions. Table 9-1 provides a list of the internally defined exceptions, along with a description of their usage.

Table 9-1. Oracle Internal Exceptions

Exception	Code	Description
ACCESS_INTO_NULL	-6530	Values are assigned to an uninitialized object.
CASE_NOT_FOUND	-6592	No matching choice is available within CASE statement, and no ELSE clause has been defined.
COLLECTION_IS_NULL	-6531	Program attempts to apply collection methods other than EXISTS to varray or a nested table that has not yet been initialized.
CURSOR_ALREADY_OPEN	-6511	Program attempts to open a cursor that is already open.
DUP_VAL_ON_INDEX	-1	Program attempts to store duplicate values in a unique index column.
INVALID_CURSOR	-1001	Program attempts to use a cursor operation that is allowed.
INVALID_NUMBER	-1722	Conversion of string into number is incorrect because of the string not being a number.
LOGIN_DEINIED	-1017	Program attempts to log in to the database using an incorrect user name and/or password.
NO_DATA_FOUND	+100	SELECT statement returns no rows.
NOT_LOGGED_ON	-1012	Program attempts to issue a database call without being connected to the database.
PROGRAM_ERROR	-6501	Internal problem exists.
ROWTYPE_MISMATCH	-6504	Cursor variables are incompatible. A host cursor variable must have a compatible return type that matches a PL/SQL cursor variable.
SELF_IS_NULL	-30625	Instance of object type is not initialized.
STORAGE_ERROR	-6500	PL/SQL ran out of memory or was corrupted.

Exception	Code	Description
SUBSCRIPT_BEYOND_COUNT	– 6533	Program references nested table or varray element using an index number that goes beyond the number of elements within the object.
SYS_INVALID_ROWID	-1410	Conversion of character string into ROWID fails because character string does not represent a valid row ID.
TIMEOUT_ON_RESOURCE	-51	Oracle Database is waiting for resource, and timeout occurs.
TOO_MANY_ROWS	-1422	Attempts to select more than one row using a SELECT INTO statement.
VALUE_ERROR	-6502	Program attempts to perform an invalid arithmetic, conversion, or truncation operation.
ZERO_DIVIDE	-1476	Program attempts to divide a number by zero.

An exception handler's scope corresponds to its enclosing code block. They have the same scope as a variable would have within a code block. If your code contains a nested code block, an exception handler that is contained within the nested code block can only handle exceptions raised within that code block. The outer code block can contain an exception handler that will handle exceptions for both the outer code block and the nested code block. If an exception is raised within the nested code block and there is no corresponding handler for an exception that has been raised within the nested code block, then the exception is propagated to the outer code block to look for a corresponding handler there. If no handler is found, then runtime will be passed to the procedure or function that called it or the host system, which is what you do not want to have occur. The following code demonstrates an example of using an exception handler within a nested code block:

```
DECLARE
  CURSOR emp_cur IS
  SELECT *
  FROM EMPLOYEES;

  emp_rec emp_cur%ROWTYPE;
BEGIN
  FOR emp_rec IN emp_cur LOOP
    DBMS_OUTPUT.PUT_LINE(emp_rec.first_name || ' ' ||
        emp_rec.last_name);
    DECLARE
      emp_dept  departments.department_name%TYPE;
    BEGIN
      SELECT department_name
      INTO emp_dept
      FROM departments
      WHERE department_id = emp_rec.department_id;
      DBMS_OUTPUT.PUT_LINE('Department: ' || emp_dept);
    EXCEPTION
```

```
        WHEN NO_DATA_FOUND THEN
          DBMS_OUTPUT.PUT_LINE('EXCEPTION IN INNER BLOCK');
      END;
    END LOOP;
EXCEPTION
  WHEN NO_DATA_FOUND THEN
    DBMS_OUTPUT.PUT_LINE('EXCEPTION IN OUTER BLOCK');
END;
```

Multiple exceptions can be listed within the same exception handler if you want to execute the same set of statements when either of them is raised. You can do this within the WHEN clause by including two or more exception names and placing the OR keyword between them. Using this technique, if either of the exceptions that are contained within the clause is raised, then the set of statements that follows will be executed. Let's take a look at an exception handler that contains two exceptions within the same handler:

```
EXCEPTION
  WHEN NO_DATA_FOUND OR INVALID_EMAIL_ADDRESS THEN
    --  statements to execute
  WHEN OTHERS THEN
    --  statements to execute
END;
```

■ **Note** You cannot place the AND keyword in between exceptions because no two exceptions can be raised at the same time.

It is easy to include basic exception handling in your application. Code an exception-handling block at the end of each code block that may raise an exception. It is pertinent that you test your application under various conditions to try to predict which possible exceptions may be raised; each of those possibilities should be accounted for within the exception-handling block of your code.

9-2. Catching Unknown Exceptions

Problem

Some exceptions are being raised when executing one of your procedures and you want to ensure that all unforeseen exceptions are handled using an exception handler.

Solution

Use an exception handler, and specify OTHERS for the exception name to catch all the exceptions that have not been caught by previous handlers. In the following example, the same code from Recipe 9-1 has been modified to add an OTHERS exception handler:

```
CREATE OR REPLACE PROCEDURE obtain_emp_detail(emp_info IN VARCHAR2) IS
  emp_qry                  VARCHAR2(500);
```

```
  emp_first                     employees.first_name%TYPE;
  emp_last                      employees.last_name%TYPE;
  email                         employees.email%TYPE;

  valid_id_count                NUMBER := 0;
  valid_flag                    BOOLEAN := TRUE;
  temp_emp_info                 VARCHAR2(50);
BEGIN
  emp_qry := 'SELECT FIRST_NAME, LAST_NAME, EMAIL FROM EMPLOYEES ';
  IF emp_info LIKE '%@%' THEN
    temp_emp_info := substr(emp_info,0,instr(emp_info,'@')-1);
    emp_qry := emp_qry || 'WHERE EMAIL = :emp_info';
  ELSE
    SELECT COUNT(*)
    INTO valid_id_count
    FROM employees
    WHERE employee_id = emp_info;

    IF valid_id_count > 0 THEN
        temp_emp_info := emp_info;
        emp_qry := emp_qry || 'WHERE EMPLOYEE_ID = :id';
    ELSE
        valid_flag := FALSE;
    END IF;
  END IF;

  IF valid_flag = TRUE THEN
    EXECUTE IMMEDIATE emp_qry
    INTO emp_first, emp_last, email
    USING temp_emp_info;

    DBMS_OUTPUT.PUT_LINE(emp_first || ' ' || emp_last || ' - ' || email);
  ELSE
    DBMS_OUTPUT.PUT_LINE('THE INFORMATION YOU HAVE USED DOES ' ||
                         'NOT MATCH ANY EMPLOYEE RECORD');
  END IF;

  EXCEPTION
    WHEN NO_DATA_FOUND THEN
      DBMS_OUTPUT.PUT_LINE('THE INFORMATION YOU HAVE USED DOES ' ||
                           'NOT MATCH ANY EMPLOYEE RECORD');
    WHEN OTHERS THEN
      DBMS_OUTPUT.PUT_LINE('AN UNEXPECTED ERROR HAS OCCURRED, PLEASE ' ||
                           'TRY AGAIN');
END;
```

In this example, if an unexpected exception were to be raised, then the program control would transfer to the statements immediately following the WHEN OTHERS THEN clause.

■ **Note** In a real-world application, an exception should be manually reraised within the OTHERS handler. To learn more about determining the exception that was raised, please see Recipe 9-4.

How It Works

You can use the OTHERS handler to catch all the exceptions that have not been previously handled by any named exception handler. It is a good idea to include an OTHERS handler with any exception handler so that any unknown exceptions can be handled reasonably by your application. However, OTHERS should be used only to assist developers in finding application bugs rather than as a catchall for any exception. The format for using the OTHERS handler is the same as it is with other named exceptions; the only difference is that it should be the last handler to be coded in the exception handler. The following pseudocode depicts a typical exception handler that includes an OTHERS handler:

```
EXCEPTION
  WHEN named_exception1 THEN
    -- perform statements
  WHEN named_exception2 THEN
    -- perform statements
  WHEN OTHERS THEN
    -- perform statements
```

WHEN TO USE THE OTHERS HANDLER

It is important to note that the OTHERS handler is not used to avoid handling expected exceptions properly. Each exception that may possibly be raised should be handled within its own exception-handling block. The OTHERS handler should be used only to catch those exceptions that are not expected. Most often, the OTHERS handler is used to catch application bugs in order to assist a developer in finding and resolving issues.

As stated, the OTHERS handler will catch any exception that has not yet been caught by another handler. It is very important to code a separate handler for each type of named exception that may occur. However, if you have one set of statements to run for any type of exception that may occur, then it is reasonable to include only an OTHERS exception handler to catch exceptions that are unexpected. If no named exceptions are handled and an exception handler includes only an OTHERS handler, then the statements within that handler will be executed whenever any exception occurs within an application.

9-3. Creating and Raising Named Programmer-Defined Exceptions

Problem

You want to alert the users of your application when a specific event occurs. The event does not raise an Oracle exception, but it is rather an application-specific exception. You want to associate this event with a custom exception so that it can be raised whenever the event occurs.

Solution

Declare a named user-defined exception, and associate it with the event for which you are interested in raising an exception. In the following example, a user-defined exception is declared and raised within a code block. When the exception is raised, the application control is passed to the statements contained within the exception handler for the named user exception.

```
CREATE OR REPLACE PROCEDURE salary_increase(emp_id IN NUMBER,
                                            pct_increase IN NUMBER) AS

    salary              employees.salary%TYPE;
    max_salary          jobs.max_salary%TYPE;
    INVALID_INCREASE    EXCEPTION;


BEGIN

    SELECT salary, max_salary
    INTO salary, max_salary
    FROM employees, jobs
    WHERE employee_id = emp_id
    AND jobs.job_id = employees.employee_id;


    IF (salary + (salary * pct_increase)) <= max_salary THEN
        UPDATE employees
        SET salary = (salary + (salary * pct_increase))
        WHERE employee_id = emp_id;

        DBMS_OUTPUT.PUT_LINE('SUCCESSFUL SALARY INCREASE FOR EMPLOYEE #: ' ||
                emp_id ||
                '. NEW SALARY = ' || salary + (salary * pct_increase));

    ELSE
        RAISE INVALID_INCREASE;
    END IF;



EXCEPTION
    WHEN NO_DATA_FOUND THEN
        DBMS_OUTPUT.PUT_LINE('UNSUCCESSFUL INCREASE, NO EMPLOYEE RECORD FOUND ' ||
                    'FOR THE GIVEN ID');

    WHEN INVALID_INCREASE THEN
        DBMS_OUTPUT.PUT_LINE('UNSUCCESSFUL INCREASE.  YOU CANNOT INCREASE THE ' ||
                    'EMPLOYEE SALARY BY ' || pct_increase ||
                    'PERCENT...PLEASE ENTER ' ||
                    'A SMALLER INCREASE AMOUNT TO TRY AGAIN');


    WHEN OTHERS THEN
```

```
DBMS_OUTPUT.PUT_LINE('UNSUCCESSFUL INCREASE.  AN UNKNOWN ERROR HAS '||
                'OCCURRED, ' ||
                'PLEASE TRY AGAIN OR CONTACT ADMINISTRATOR' || pct_increase);

END;
```

As you can see from the code, the exception block can accept one or more handlers. The named user exception is declared within the declaration section of the procedure, and the exception can be raised anywhere within the containing block.

■ **Note** In a real-world application, an exception should be manually raised within the OTHERS handler. To learn more about determining the exception that was raised, please see Recipe 9-4.

How It Works

A PL/SQL application can contain any number of custom exceptions. When a developer declares their own exception, it is known as a user-defined exception. A user-defined exception must be declared within the declaration section of a package, function, procedure, or anonymous code block. To declare an exception, use the following:

```
exception_name  EXCEPTION;
```

You can provide any name as long as it applies to the standard naming convention and is not the same as an internally defined exception name. It is a coding convention to code exception names using uppercase lettering, but lowercase would work as well since PL/SQL is not a case-sensitive language.

To raise your exception, type the RAISE keyword followed by the name of the exception that you want to raise. When the code executes the RAISE statement, control is passed to the exception handler that best matches the exception that was named in the statement. If no handler exists for the exception that was raised, then control will be passed to the OTHERS handler, if it exists. In the worst-case scenario, if there are not any exception handlers that match the name that was provided in the RAISE statement and there has not been an OTHERS handler coded, then control will be passed back to the enclosing block, the calling code, or the host environment.

The RAISE statement can also be used in a couple of other ways. It is possible to raise an exception that has been declared within another package. To do so, fully qualify the name of the exception by prefixing it with the package name. The RAISE statement can also be used stand-alone to reraise an exception.

As seen in the solution to this recipe, catching a named user exception is exactly the same as catching an internally defined exception. Code the WHEN..THEN clause, naming the exception that you want to catch. When the exception is raised, any statements contained within that particular exception handler will be executed.

9-4. Determining Which Error Occurred Inside the OTHERS Handler

Problem

Your code is continually failing via an exception, and the OTHERS handler is being invoked. You need to determine the exact cause of the exception so that it can be repaired.

Solution

Code the OTHERS exception handler as indicated by Recipe 9-2, and use the SQLCODE and DBMS_UTILITY.FORMAT_ERROR_STACK functions to return the Oracle error code and message text for the exception that has been raised. The following example demonstrates the usage of these functions, along with the procedure that was used in Recipe 9-3, for obtaining the error code and message when the OTHERS handler is invoked.

```
CREATE OR replace PROCEDURE salary_increase(emp_id       IN NUMBER,
                                            pct_increase IN NUMBER)
AS
  salary              employees.salary%TYPE;
  max_salary          jobs.max_salary%TYPE;
  invalid_increase    EXCEPTION;
  error_number        NUMBER;
  error_message       VARCHAR2(1500);
BEGIN
  SELECT salary,
         max_salary
  INTO   salary, max_salary
  FROM   employees,
         jobs
  WHERE  employee_id = emp_id
         AND jobs.job_id = employees.employee_id;

  IF ( salary + ( salary * pct_increase ) ) <= max_salary THEN
    UPDATE employees
    SET    salary = ( salary + ( salary * pct_increase ) )
    WHERE  employee_id = emp_id;

    dbms_output.Put_line('SUCCESSFUL SALARY INCREASE FOR EMPLOYEE #: '
                         || emp_id
                         || '.  NEW SALARY = '
                         || salary + ( salary * pct_increase ));
  ELSE
    RAISE invalid_increase;
  END IF;
EXCEPTION
  WHEN no_data_found THEN
    dbms_output.Put_line('UNSUCCESSFUL INCREASE, NO EMPLOYEE RECORD FOUND '
                         || 'FOR THE '
                         || 'GIVEN ID'); WHEN invalid_increase THEN
    dbms_output.Put_line('UNSUCCESSFUL INCREASE.  YOU CANNOT INCREASE THE '
                         || 'EMPLOYEE '
```

```
                                || 'SALARY BY '
                                || pct_increase
                                || ' PERCENT...PLEASE ENTER '
                                || 'A SMALLER INCREASE AMOUNT TO TRY AGAIN');
          WHEN OTHERS THEN
                       error_number := SQLCODE;

                       error_message := DBMS_UTILITY.FORMAT_ERROR_STACK;

               dbms_output.Put_line('UNSUCCESSFUL INCREASE.  AN UNKNOWN ERROR HAS '
                                    || 'OCCURRED, '
                                    || 'PLEASE TRY AGAIN OR CONTACT ADMINISTRATOR'
                                    || ' Error #: '
                                    || error_number
                                    || ' - '
                                    || error_message);
          END;
```

When this procedure is executed, the following error will be returned:

```
UNSUCCESSFUL INCREASE.  AN UNKNOWN ERROR HAS OCCURRED, PLEASE TRY AGAIN OR CONTACT
ADMINISTRATOR Error #: -1722 - ORA-01722: invalid number
```

This example intentionally raises an error in order to demonstrate the functionality of these utilities. A reference to the line number that raised the error may also be helpful. To learn more about writing an exception handler that returns line numbers, please see Recipe 9-9.

How It Works

The SQLCODE and DBMS_UTILITY.FORMAT_ERROR_STACK functions provide the means to determine what code and message had caused the last exception that was raised. The SQLCODE function will return the Oracle error number for internal exceptions and +1 for a user-defined exception. The DBMS_UTILITY.FORMAT_ERROR_STACK function will return the Oracle error message for any internal exception that is raised, and it will contain the text User-Defined Exception for any named user exception that is raised. A user-defined exception may receive a custom error number, as you will read about in Recipe 9-9. In such cases, the SQLCODE function will return this custom error number if raised.

To use these functions, you must assign them to a variable because they cannot be called outright. For instance, if you wanted to use the SQLCODE within a CASE statement, you would have to assign the function to a variable first. Once that has been done, you could use the variable that was assigned the SQLCODE in the statement.

Oracle includes DBMS_UTILITY.FORMAT_ERROR_STACK, which can be used to return the error message associated with the current error. DBMS_UTILITY.FORMAT_ERROR_STACK can hold up to 1,899 characters, so there is rarely a need to truncate the message it returns. SQLERRM is a similar function that can be used to return the error message, but it only allows messages up to 512 bytes to be displayed. Oftentimes, SQLERRM messages need to be truncated for display. Oracle recommends using DBMS_UTILITY.FORMAT_ERROR_STACK over SQLERRM because this utility doesn't have such a small message limitation.

However, SQLERRM does have its place, because there are some benefits of using it. A handy feature of SQLERRM is that you can pass an error number to it and retrieve the corresponding error message. Any error number that is passed to SQLERRM should be negative; otherwise, you will receive the message User-defined error. Table 9-2 displays the error number ranges and their corresponding messages using SQLCODE and SQLERRM.

Table 9-2. SQLCODE Return Codes and Meanings

Code	Description
Negative Oracle Error Number	Internal Oracle exception
0	No exceptions raised
+1	User-defined exception
+100	NO_DATA_FOUND
-20000 to -20999	User-defined error with PRAGMA EXCEPTION_INIT

■ **Note** PRAGMA EXCEPTION_INIT is used to associate an Oracle error number with an exception name.

If you choose to use SQLERRM, the code is not much different from using DBMS_UTILITY.FORMAT_ERROR_STACK, but you will probably need to include some code to truncate the result. The next example demonstrates the same example that was used in the solution to this recipe, but it uses SQLERRM instead of DBMS_UTILITY.FORMAT_ERROR_STACK.

```
CREATE OR replace PROCEDURE salary_increase(emp_id       IN NUMBER,
                                            pct_increase IN NUMBER)
AS
  salary               employees.salary%TYPE;
  max_salary           jobs.max_salary%TYPE;
  invalid_increase     EXCEPTION;
  error_number         NUMBER;
  error_message        VARCHAR2(1500);
BEGIN
  SELECT salary,
         max_salary
  INTO   salary, max_salary
  FROM   employees,
         jobs
  WHERE  employee_id = emp_id
         AND jobs.job_id = employees.employee_id;

  IF ( salary + ( salary * pct_increase ) ) <= max_salary THEN
    UPDATE employees
    SET    salary = ( salary + ( salary * pct_increase ) )
    WHERE  employee_id = emp_id;
```

```
        dbms_output.Put_line('SUCCESSFUL SALARY INCREASE FOR EMPLOYEE #: '
                            || emp_id
                            || '.  NEW SALARY = '
                            || salary + ( salary * pct_increase ));
      ELSE
        RAISE invalid_increase;
      END IF;
EXCEPTION
  WHEN no_data_found THEN
      dbms_output.Put_line('UNSUCCESSFUL INCREASE, NO EMPLOYEE RECORD FOUND '
                          || 'FOR THE '
                          || 'GIVEN ID'); WHEN invalid_increase THEN
      dbms_output.Put_line('UNSUCCESSFUL INCREASE.  YOU CANNOT INCREASE THE '
                          || 'EMPLOYEE '
                          || 'SALARY BY '
                          || pct_increase
                          || ' PERCENT...PLEASE ENTER '
                          || 'A SMALLER INCREASE AMOUNT TO TRY AGAIN');
WHEN OTHERS THEN
          error_number := SQLCODE;

          error_message := Substr(sqlerrm, 1, 150);

dbms_output.Put_line('UNSUCCESSFUL INCREASE.  AN UNKNOWN ERROR HAS OCCURRED, '
                    || 'PLEASE TRY AGAIN OR CONTACT ADMINISTRATOR'
                    || ' Error #: '
                    || error_number
                    || ' - '
                    || error_message);
END;
```

There are some other tools that can be used to further diagnose which errors are being raised and even to see the entire stack trace. These tools are further explained within Recipe 9-9. By combining the techniques learned in this recipe with those you will learn about in Recipe 9-9, you are sure to have a better chance of diagnosing your application issues.

9-5. Raising User-Defined Exceptions Without an Exception Handler

Problem

Your application includes some error handling that is specific to your application. For instance, you want to ensure that the input value for a procedure is in the valid format to be an e-mail address. Rather than writing an exception handler for each user-defined exception, you want to simply raise the exception inline and provide an error number as well.

Solution

This scenario is perfect for using the RAISE_APPLICATION_ERROR procedure. Test the e-mail address that is passed into the procedure to ensure that it follows certain criteria. If it does not contain a specific characteristic of a valid e-mail address, use the RAISE_APPLICATION_ERROR procedure to display an exception message to the user. Here's an example:

```
CREATE OR REPLACE PROCEDURE obtain_emp_detail(emp_email IN VARCHAR2) IS
  emp_qry          VARCHAR2(500);
  emp_first        employees.first_name%TYPE;
  emp_last         employees.last_name%TYPE;
  email            employees.email%TYPE;

  valid_id_count       NUMBER := 0;
  valid_flag           BOOLEAN := TRUE;
  temp_emp_info        VARCHAR2(50);

BEGIN
  emp_qry := 'SELECT FIRST_NAME, LAST_NAME, EMAIL FROM EMPLOYEES ';
  IF emp_email LIKE '%@%' THEN
    temp_emp_info := substr(emp_email,0,instr(emp_email,'@')-1);
    emp_qry := emp_qry || 'WHERE EMAIL = :emp_email';
  ELSIF emp_email NOT LIKE '%.mycompany.com' THEN
    RAISE_APPLICATION_ERROR(-20001, 'Not a valid email address from ' ||
                          'this company!');
  ELSE
    RAISE_APPLICATION_ERROR(-20002, 'Not a valid email address!');
  END IF;

  IF valid_flag = TRUE THEN
    EXECUTE IMMEDIATE emp_qry
    INTO emp_first, emp_last, email
    USING temp_emp_info;

    DBMS_OUTPUT.PUT_LINE(emp_first || ' ' || emp_last || ' - ' || email);
  ELSE
    DBMS_OUTPUT.PUT_LINE('THE INFORMATION YOU HAVE USED DOES ' ||
                        'NOT MATCH ANY EMPLOYEE RECORD');
  END IF;

END;
```

As you can see, there is no exception handler in this example. When the conditions are met, an exception is raised inline via RAISE_APPLICATION_EXCEPTION.

How It Works

The RAISE_APPLICATION_EXCEPTION procedure can associate an error number with an error message. The format for calling the RAISE_APPLICATION_EXCEPTION procedure is as follows:

```
RAISE_APPLICATION_EXCEPTION(exception_number,
                          exception_message[, retain_error_stack]);
```

where exception_number is a number within the range of -20000 to -20999, and exception_message is a string of text that is equal to or less than 2KB in length. The optional retain_error_stack is a BOOLEAN value that tells Oracle whether this exception should be added to the existing error stack or whether the error stack should be wiped clean and this exception should be placed into it. By default, the value is FALSE, and all other exceptions are removed from the error stack, leaving this exception as the only one in the stack.

When you invoke the procedure, the current block is halted immediately, and the exception is raised. No further processing takes place within the current block, and control is passed to the program that called the block or an enclosing block if the current block is nested. Therefore, if you need to perform any exception handling, then it needs to take place prior to calling RAISE_APPLICATION_EXCEPTION. There is no commit or rollback, so any updates or changes that have been made will be retained if you decide to issue a commit. Any OUT and IN OUT values, assuming you are in a procedure or a function, will be reverted. This is important to keep in mind, because it will help you determine whether to use an exception handler or issue a call to RAISE_APPLICATION_ERROR.

When calling RAISE_APPLICATION_EXCEPTION, you pass an error number along with an associated exception message. Oracle sets aside the range of numbers from -20000 to -20999 for use by its customers for the purpose of declaring exceptions. Be sure to use a number within this range, or Oracle will raise its own exception to let you know that you are out of line and using one of its proprietary error numbers!

■ **Note** There are some numbers within that range that are still used by Oracle-specific exceptions. Passing a TRUE value as the last argument in a call to RAISE_APPLICATION_EXCEPTION will retain any existing errors in the error stack. Passing TRUE is a good idea for the purposes of debugging so that the stack trace can be used to help find the code that is raising the exception. Otherwise, the exception stack is cleared.

One may choose to create a function or procedure that has the sole purpose of calling RAISE_APPLICATION_EXCEPTION to raise an exception and associate an error number with an exception message. This technique can become quite useful if you are interested in using a custom error number for your exceptions, but you still need to perform proper exception handling when errors occur. You could use the OTHERS exception handler to call the function or procedure that uses RAISE_APPLICATION_EXCEPTION, passing the error number and a proper exception message.

9-6. Redirecting Control After an Exception Is Raised

Problem

After an exception is raised within an application, usually the statements within the exception handler are executed, and then control goes to the next statement in the calling program or outside the current code block. Rather than printing an error message and exiting your code block after an exception, you want to perform some further activity. For instance, let's say you are interested in logging the exception in a database table. You have a procedure for adding entries to the log table, and you want to make use of that procedure.

Solution

Invoke the procedure from within the exception handler. When the exception is raised, program control will be passed to the appropriate handler. The handler itself can provide an exception message for the user, but it will also call the procedure that is to be used for logging the exception in the database. The following example demonstrates this technique:

```
CREATE OR REPLACE PROCEDURE log_error_messages(error_code  IN NUMBER,
                                               message     IN VARCHAR2) AS
PRAGMA AUTONOMOUS_TRANSACTION;
BEGIN
  DBMS_OUTPUT.PUT_LINE(message);
  DBMS_OUTPUT.PUT_LINE('WRITING ERROR MESSAGE TO DATABASE');
END;

CREATE OR REPLACE PROCEDURE obtain_emp_detail(emp_info IN VARCHAR2) IS
  emp_qry                 VARCHAR2(500);
  emp_first                 employees.first_name%TYPE;
  emp_last                   employees.last_name%TYPE;
  email                         employees.email%TYPE;

  valid_id_count          NUMBER := 0;
  valid_flag                  BOOLEAN := TRUE;
  temp_emp_info           VARCHAR2(50);


BEGIN
    emp_qry := 'SELECT FIRST_NAME, LAST_NAME, EMAIL FROM EMPLOYEES ';
    IF emp_info LIKE '%@%' THEN
      temp_emp_info := substr(emp_info,0,instr(emp_info,'@')-1);
      emp_qry := emp_qry || 'WHERE EMAIL = :emp_info';
    ELSE
      SELECT COUNT(*)
      INTO valid_id_count
      FROM employees
      WHERE employee_id = emp_info;

      IF valid_id_count > 0 THEN
          temp_emp_info := emp_info;
          emp_qry := emp_qry || 'WHERE EMPLOYEE_ID = :id';
      ELSE
          valid_flag := FALSE;
      END IF;
    END IF;

    IF valid_flag = TRUE THEN
      EXECUTE IMMEDIATE emp_qry
      INTO emp_first, emp_last, email
      USING temp_emp_info;

      DBMS_OUTPUT.PUT_LINE(emp_first || ' ' || emp_last || ' - ' || email);
    ELSE
```

```
        DBMS_OUTPUT.PUT_LINE('THE INFORMATION YOU HAVE USED DOES ' ||
                             'NOT MATCH ANY EMPLOYEE RECORD');
    END IF;

    EXCEPTION
      WHEN NO_DATA_FOUND THEN

        DBMS_OUTPUT.PUT_LINE('THE INFORMATION YOU HAVE USED DOES ' ||
                             'NOT MATCH ANY EMPLOYEE RECORD');
        log_error_messages(SQLCODE, DBMS_UTILITY.FORMAT_ERROR_STACK);

      WHEN OTHERS THEN
        DBMS_OUTPUT.PUT_LINE('AN UNEXPECTED ERROR HAS OCCURRED, PLEASE ' ||
                             'TRY AGAIN');
        log_error_messages(SQLCODE, DBMS_UTILITY.FORMAT_ERROR_STACK);
    END;
```

In this scenario, the log_error_messages procedure would be called from within each of the exception handlers. Since it is an autonomous transaction, the log_error_messages procedure will execute without affecting the calling procedure. This ensures that no issues will arise if log_error_messages were to raise an exception. Control of the application would be passed to this procedure for the processing, and then the program would exit.

How It Works

It is possible to redirect control of your code after an exception has been raised using various techniques. After an exception is raised and control is redirected to the handler, the statements within the handler are executed, and then that program ends. If the code block that contains the exception handler is contained within enclosing code block, control will be passed to the next statement within the enclosing control block. Otherwise, the program will exit after statements are executed.

To execute a particular action or series of processes after an exception has been raised, it is a useful technique to call a stored procedure or function from within the exception handler. In the solution to this recipe, a logging procedure is called that will insert a row into the logging table after each exception is raised. This allows the program control to be passed to the procedure or function that is called, and when that body of code has completed execution, control is passed back to the exception handler. This is a very useful technique for logging exceptions but can also be used for various other tasks such as sending an e-mail alert or performing some database cleanup.

9-7. Raising Exceptions and Continuing Processing

Problem

The application you are coding requires a series of INSERT, UPDATE, and DELETE statements to be called. You want to add proper exception handling to your code and also ensure that processing continues and all of the statements are executed even if an exception is raised.

Solution

Enclose each statement within its own code block, and provide an exception handler for each of the blocks. When an exception is raised within one of the nested blocks, then control will be passed back to the main code block, and execution will continue. This style of coding is displayed in the following example:

```
CREATE OR REPLACE PROCEDURE delete_employee (in_emp_id   IN NUMBER) AS
  BEGIN
    -- ENTER INITIAL NESTED CODE BLOCK TO PERFORM DELETE
    BEGIN
        -- DELETE EMP
    EXCEPTION
      WHEN NO_DATA_FOUND THEN
        -- perform statements
    END;

    -- ENTER SECOND NESTED CODE BLOCK TO PERFORM LOG ENTRY
    BEGIN
        -- LOG DELETION OF  EMP
    EXCEPTION
      WHEN NO_DATA_FOUND THEN
        -- perform statements
    END;
EXCEPTION WHEN OTHERS THEN
  -- perform statements
END;
```

As this code stands, no exception will go on to become an unhanded exception because the outermost code block contains an exception handler using the OTHERS exception name. Every nested code block contains a handler, so every exception that is encountered in this application will be caught.

How It Works

Scope plays an important role when designing your application's exception-handling system. When doing so, you should think of your application and determine whether portions of the code need to be executed regardless of any exception being raised. If this is the case, then you will need to provide proper exception handling and still ensure that the essential code is executed each run.

The scope of an exception pertains to the code block in which the exception is declared. Once an exception has been encountered, program control halts immediately and is passed to the exception handler for the current block. If there is not an exception handler in the current code block or if no handler matches the exception that was raised, then control passes to the calling program or outer control block. Control is immediately passed to the exception handler of that program. If no exception handler exists or matches the exception being raised, then the execution of that block halts, and the exception is raised to the next calling program or outer code block, and so on.

This pattern can be followed any number of times. That is why the technique used in the solution to this recipe works well. There is one main code block that embodies two nested code blocks. Each of the blocks contains essential statements that need to be run. If an exception is raised within the DELETE block, then program control is passed back to its outer code block, and processing continues. In this case, both essential statements will always be executed, even if exceptions are raised.

9-8. Associating Error Numbers with Exceptions That Have No Name

Problem

You want to associate an error number to those errors that do not have predefined names.

Solution

Make use of PRAGMA EXCEPTION_INIT to tell the compiler to associate an Oracle error number with an exception name. This will allow the use of an easy-to-identify name rather than an obscure error number when working with the exception. The example in this recipe shows how an error number can be associated with an exception name and how the exception can later be raised.

```
CREATE OR REPLACE FUNCTION calculate_salary_hours(salary  IN NUMBER,
                                          hours   IN NUMBER DEFAULT 1)
RETURN NUMBER AS
BEGIN
  RETURN salary/hours;
END;


DECLARE
  DIVISOR_IS_ZERO  EXCEPTION;
  PRAGMA EXCEPTION_INIT(DIVISOR_IS_ZERO, -1476);
  per_hour       NUMBER;
BEGIN
  SELECT calculate_salary_hours(0,0)
  INTO per_hour
  FROM DUAL;
EXCEPTION WHEN DIVISOR_IS_ZERO THEN
  DBMS_OUTPUT.PUT_LINE('You cannot pass a zero for the number of hours');
END;
```

The exception declared within this example is associated with the ORA-01476 error code. When a divide-by-zero exception occurs, then the handler is executed.

How It Works

PRAGMA EXCEPTION_INIT allows an error number to be associated with an error name. Thus, it provides an easy way to handle those exceptions that are available only by default via an error number. It is much easier to identify an exception by name rather than by number, especially when you have been away from the code base for some length of time.

The PRAGMA EXCEPTION_INIT must be declared within the declaration section of your code. The exception that is to be associated with the error number must be declared prior to the PRAGMA declaration. The format for using PRAGMA EXCEPTION_INIT is as follows:

```
DECLARE
  exception_name    EXCEPTION;
  PRAGMA EXCEPTION_INIT(exception_name, <<exception_code>>);
BEGIN
```

```
   -- Perform statements
EXCEPTION
  WHEN exception_name THEN
    -- Perform error handling
END;
```

The exception_name in this pseudocode refers to the name of the exception you are declaring. The <<exception_code>> is the number of the ORA-xxxxx error that you are associating with the exception. In the solution to this recipe, ORA-01476 is associated with the exception. That exception in particular denotes divisor is equal to zero. When this exception is raised, it is easier to identify the cause of the error via the DIVISOR_IS_ZERO identifier than by the -01476 code.

Whenever possible, it is essential to provide an easy means of identification for portions of code that may be difficult to understand. Exception numbers by themselves are not easily identifiable unless you see the exception often enough. Even then, an exception handler with the number -01476 in it seems obscure. In this case, it is always best to associate a more common name to the exception so that the code can instantly have meaning to someone who is unfamiliar with the code or to you when you need to maintain the code for years to come.

9-9. Tracing an Exception to Its Origin

Problem

Your application continues to raise an exception that is being caught with the OTHERS handler. You've used SQLCODE and DBMS_UTILITY.FORMAT_ERROR_STACK to help you find the cause of the exception but are still unable to do so.

Solution

Use the stack trace for the exception to trace the error back to its origination. In particular, use DBMS_UTILITY.FORMAT_ERROR_BACKTRACE and DBMS_UTILITY.FORMAT_CALL_TRACE to help you find the cause of the exception. The following solution demonstrates the use of FORMAT_ERROR_BACKTRACE:

```
CREATE OR REPLACE PROCEDURE obtain_emp_detail(emp_info IN VARCHAR2) IS
   emp_qry            VARCHAR2(500);
   emp_first          employees.first_name%TYPE;
   emp_last           employees.last_name%TYPE;
   email              employees.email%TYPE;

   valid_id_count     NUMBER := 0;
   valid_flag         BOOLEAN := TRUE;
   temp_emp_info      VARCHAR2(50);


BEGIN
   emp_qry := 'SELECT FIRST_NAME, LAST_NAME, EMAIL FROM EMPLOYEES ';
   IF emp_info LIKE '%@%' THEN
     temp_emp_info := substr(emp_info,0,instr(emp_info,'@')-1);
     emp_qry := emp_qry || 'WHERE EMAIL = :emp_info';
   ELSE
     SELECT COUNT(*)
```

```
        INTO valid_id_count
        FROM employees
        WHERE employee_id = emp_info;

        IF valid_id_count > 0 THEN
            temp_emp_info := emp_info;
            emp_qry := emp_qry || 'WHERE EMPLOYEE_ID = :id';
        ELSE
            valid_flag := FALSE;
        END IF;
    END IF;

    IF valid_flag = TRUE THEN
        EXECUTE IMMEDIATE emp_qry
        INTO emp_first, emp_last, email
        USING temp_emp_info;

        DBMS_OUTPUT.PUT_LINE(emp_first || ' ' || emp_last || ' - ' || email);
    ELSE
        DBMS_OUTPUT.PUT_LINE('THE INFORMATION YOU HAVE USED DOES ' ||
                            'NOT MATCH ANY EMPLOYEE RECORD');

    END IF;

    EXCEPTION
        WHEN NO_DATA_FOUND THEN

            DBMS_OUTPUT.PUT_LINE('THE INFORMATION YOU HAVE USED DOES ' ||
                            'NOT MATCH ANY EMPLOYEE RECORD');
            DBMS_OUTPUT.PUT_LINE(DBMS_UTILITY.FORMAT_ERROR_BACKTRACE);

        WHEN OTHERS THEN
            DBMS_OUTPUT.PUT_LINE('AN UNEXPECTED ERROR HAS OCCURRED, PLEASE ' ||
                            'TRY AGAIN');
            DBMS_OUTPUT.PUT_LINE(DBMS_UTILITY.FORMAT_ERROR_BACKTRACE);
END;
```

Here are the results when calling within invalid argument information:

```
SQL> exec obtain_emp_detail('junea@');
THE INFORMATION YOU HAVE USED DOES NOT MATCH ANY EMPLOYEE RECORD
ORA-06512: at "OBTAIN_EMP_DETAIL", line 32


PL/SQL procedure successfully completed.
```

As you can see, the exact line number that caused the exception to be raised is displayed. This is especially useful if you use a development environment that includes line numbering for your source code. If not, then you can certainly count out the line numbers manually.

Similarly, DBMS_UTILITY.FORMAT_CALL_STACK lists the object number, line, and object where the issue had occurred. The following example uses the same procedure as the previous example, but this time DBMS_UTILITY.FORMAT_CALL_STACK is used in the exception handler:

```
CREATE OR REPLACE PROCEDURE obtain_emp_detail(emp_info IN VARCHAR2) IS
  emp_qry                 VARCHAR2(500);
  emp_first               employees.first_name%TYPE;
  emp_last                employees.last_name%TYPE;
  email                   employees.email%TYPE;

  valid_id_count          NUMBER := 0;
  valid_flag              BOOLEAN := TRUE;
  temp_emp_info           VARCHAR2(50);


BEGIN
    emp_qry := 'SELECT FIRST_NAME, LAST_NAME, EMAIL FROM EMPLOYEES ';
    IF emp_info LIKE '%@%' THEN
       temp_emp_info := substr(emp_info,0,instr(emp_info,'@')-1);
       emp_qry := emp_qry || 'WHERE EMAIL = :emp_info';
    ELSE
       SELECT COUNT(*)
       INTO valid_id_count
       FROM employees
       WHERE employee_id = emp_info;

       IF valid_id_count > 0 THEN
           temp_emp_info := emp_info;
           emp_qry := emp_qry || 'WHERE EMPLOYEE_ID = :id';
       ELSE
           valid_flag := FALSE;
       END IF;
    END IF;

    IF valid_flag = TRUE THEN
      EXECUTE IMMEDIATE emp_qry
      INTO emp_first, emp_last, email
      USING temp_emp_info;

      DBMS_OUTPUT.PUT_LINE(emp_first || ' ' || emp_last || ' - ' || email);
    ELSE
      DBMS_OUTPUT.PUT_LINE('THE INFORMATION YOU HAVE USED DOES ' ||
                           'NOT MATCH ANY EMPLOYEE RECORD');
    END IF;

    EXCEPTION
      WHEN NO_DATA_FOUND THEN

        DBMS_OUTPUT.PUT_LINE('THE INFORMATION YOU HAVE USED DOES ' ||
                             'NOT MATCH ANY EMPLOYEE RECORD');
        DBMS_OUTPUT.PUT_LINE(DBMS_UTILITY.FORMAT_CALL_STACK);

      WHEN OTHERS THEN
        DBMS_OUTPUT.PUT_LINE('AN UNEXPECTED ERROR HAS OCCURRED, PLEASE ' ||
                             'TRY AGAIN');
        DBMS_OUTPUT.PUT_LINE(DBMS_UTILITY.FORMAT_CALL_STACK);
```

```
END;
```

Here are the results when calling within invalid argument information:

```
SQL> exec obtain_emp_detail('june@');
THE INFORMATION YOU HAVE USED DOES NOT MATCH ANY EMPLOYEE RECORD
----- PL/SQL Call Stack -----
  object      line  object
  handle    number
name
24DD3280      47   procedure OBTAIN_EMP_DETAIL
273AA66C       1
anonymous block


PL/SQL procedure successfully completed.
```

Each of the two utilities demonstrated in this solution serves an explicit purpose—to assist you in finding the cause of exceptions in your applications.

How It Works

Oracle provides a few different utilities to help diagnose and repair issues with code. The utilities discussed in this recipe provide feedback regarding exceptions that have been raised within application code. DBMS_UTILITY.FORMAT_ERROR_BACKTRACE is used to display the list of lines that goes back to the point at which your application fails. This utility was added in Oracle Database 10g. Its ability to identify the exact line number where the code has failed can save the time of reading through each line to look for the errors. Using this information along with the Oracle exception that is raised should give you enough insight to determine the exact cause of the problem.

The result from DBMS_UTILITY.FORMAT_ERROR_BACKTRACE can be assigned to a variable since it is a function. Most likely a procedure will be used to log the exceptions so that they can be reviewed at a later time. Such a procedure could accept the variable containing the result from DBMS_UTILITY.FORMAT_ERROR_BACKTRACE as input.

The DBMS_UTILITY.FORMAT_CALL_STACK function is used to print out a formatted string of the execution call stack or the sequence of calls for your application. It displays the different objects used, along with line numbers from which calls were made. It can be very useful for pinpointing those errors that you are having trouble resolving. It can also be useful for obtaining information regarding the execution order of your application. If you are unsure of exactly what order processes are being called, this function will give you that information.

Using a combination of these utilities when debugging and developing your code is a good practice. You may find it useful to create helper functions that contain calls to these utilities so that you can easily log all stack traces into a database table or a file for later viewing. These can be of utmost importance when debugging issues or evaluating application execution.

9-10. Displaying PL/SQL Compiler Warnings

Problem

You are interested in making your code more robust by ensuring that no issues will crop up as time goes by and the code evolves. You want to have the PL/SQL compiler alert you of possible issues with your code.

Solution

Use PL/SQL compile-time warnings to alert you of possible issues with your code. Enable warnings for your current session by issuing the proper ALTER SESSION statements or by using the DBMS_WARNING package to do so. This solution will demonstrate each of these techniques to help you decide which will work best for your debugging purposes.

First let's take a look at using ALTER SESSION to enable and configure warnings for your environment. This technique can be very useful when you want to enable warnings for an entire session. The following example shows how to enable warnings and how to display them given a short code block:

```
ALTER SESSION SET PLSQL_WARNINGS = 'ENABLE:ALL';

CREATE OR REPLACE FUNCTION calculate_salary_hours(salary  IN NUMBER,
                                                  hours   IN NUMBER DEFAULT 1)
RETURN NUMBER AS
BEGIN
  RETURN salary/hours;
END;

SHOW ERRORS;
```

Here are the results from running create or replace function with all warnings enabled:

```
Errors for FUNCTION CALCULATE_SALARY_HOURS:

LINE/COL
-------------------------------------------------------------------------------
ERROR
-------------------------------------------------------------------------------
1/1
PLW-05018: unit CALCULATE_SALARY_HOURS omitted optional AUTHID clause;
 default value DEFINER used
```

Next, let's look at the DBMS_WARNINGS package. Use of this technique is more helpful if you are using a development environment such as PL/SQL Developer that compiles your code for you. The following is an example of performing the same CREATE OR REPLACE FUNCTION as earlier, but this time using DBMS_WARNINGS:

```
SQL> CALL DBMS_WARNING.SET_WARNING_SETTING_STRING('ENABLE:ALL','SESSION');

Call completed.
```

```
SQL> CREATE OR REPLACE FUNCTION calculate_salary_hours(salary  IN NUMBER,
                                              hours   IN NUMBER DEFAULT 1)
RETURN NUMBER AS
BEGIN
  RETURN salary/hours;
END;
/  2    3    4    5    6    7

SP2-0806: Function created with compilation warnings

SQL> SHOW ERRORS;
Errors for FUNCTION CALCULATE_SALARY_HOURS:

LINE/COL
--------------------------------------------------------------------------
ERROR
--------------------------------------------------------------------------
1/1
PLW-05018: unit CALCULATE_SALARY_HOURS omitted optional AUTHID clause; default v
alue DEFINER used
```

Both techniques provide similar results, but one can be set at the database level and the other can be more useful for use in a development environment.

How It Works

Learning about warnings against your code can help you solidify your code and repair it so that it can become more robust when it is used in a production environment. Although PL/SQL warnings will not prevent the code from compiling and executing, they can certainly provide good insight to inform you of places in your code that could possibly incur issues at a later time. As you have learned from the solution to this recipe, there are two techniques that can be used to enable warnings for your application. Those are the use of ALTER SESSION statements and the DBMS_WARNINGS package. Both are valid techniques for enabling and disabling warnings, but each has its own set of strong points and drawbacks.

The PLSQL_WARNINGS compilation parameter must be used to enable or disable warnings within a session. By setting it, you can control the types of warnings that are displayed, along with how much information is displayed and even how it is displayed. This parameter can be set using the ALTER SESSION statement. The format for setting this parameter using ALTER SESSION is as follows:

```
ALTER SESSION SET PLSQL_WARNINGS = "[ENABLE/DISABLE:PARAMETER]"
```

The PLSQL_WARNINGS compilation parameter accepts a number of different parameters that each tell the compiler what types of warnings to display and what to ignore. There are three different categories of warnings that can be used. Table 9-3 shows the different types of warnings along with their descriptions.

Table 9-3. Warning Categories

Category	Description
PERFORMANCE	May hinder application performance
INFORMATIONAL	May complicate application maintenance but contains no immediate issues
SECURE	May cause unexpected or incorrect results
ALL	Includes all the categories

The DBMS_WARNINGS package works in a similar fashion: it accepts the same arguments as the PLSQL_WARNINGS parameter. The difference is that you can control when the warnings are enabled or disabled by placing the call to the package in locations that you choose. This does not matter much when working via SQL*Plus, but if you are using a development environment such as Oracle SQL Developer, then DBMS_WARNINGS must be used. The format for calling this procedure is as follows:

```
CALL DBMS_WARNING.SET_WARNING_SETTING_STRING('warning_category:value','scope');
```

The categories are the same as PLSQL_WARNINGS, as are the values of the categories. The scope determines whether the warnings will be used for the duration of the session or for all sessions. There are various other options that can be used with the DBMS_WARNINGS package. To learn more about these options, please see the Oracle Database 11g documentation.

CHAPTER 10

■ ■ ■

PL/SQL Collections and Records

Collections are single-dimensional arrays of data all with the same datatype and are accessed by an index; usually the index is a number, but it can be a string. Collections indexed by strings are commonly known as *hash arrays*.

Records are groups of related data, each with its own field name and datatype, similar to tables stored in the database. The record data structure in PL/SQL allows you to manipulate data at the field or record level. PL/SQL provides an easy method to define a record's structure based on a database table's structure or a cursor. Combining records and collections provide a powerful programming advantage described in the following recipes.

10-1. Creating and Accessing a VARRAY

Problem

You have a small, static list of elements that you initialize once and that would benefit from using in a loop body.

Solution

Place the elements into a varray (or varying array). Once initialized, a varray may be referenced by its index. Begin by declaring a datatype of varray with a fixed number of elements, and then declare the datatype of the elements. Next, declare the variable that will hold the data using the newly defined type. For example, the following code creates a varying array to hold the abbreviations for the days of the week:

```
DECLARE

TYPE    dow_type IS VARRAY(7) OF VARCHAR2(3);
dow     dow_type := dow_type ('Sun', 'Mon', 'Tue', 'Wed', 'Thu', 'Fri', 'Sat');

BEGIN

   FOR i IN 1..dow.COUNT LOOP
      DBMS_OUTPUT.PUT_LINE (dow(i));
   END LOOP;

END;

Results
```

```
Sun
Mon
Tue
Wed
Thu
Fri
Sat
```

How It Works

The type statement dow_type defines a data structure to store seven instances of VARCHAR2(3). This is sufficient space to hold the abbreviations of the seven days of the week. The dow variable is defined as a VARRAY of the dow_type defined in the previous line. That definition invokes a built-in constructor method to initialize values for each of the elements in the VARRAY.

The FOR .. LOOP traverses the dow variable starting at the first element and ending with the last. The COUNT method returns the number of elements defined in a collection; in this recipe, there are seven elements in the VARRAY, so the LOOP increments from one to seven. The DBMS_OUTPUT.PUT_LINE statement displays its value.

A VARRAY is best used when you know the size the array and it will not likely change. The VARRAY construct also allows you to initialize its values in the declaration section.

10-2. Creating and Accessing an Indexed Table

Problem

You need to store a group of numbers for later processing in another procedure.

Solution

Create an indexed table using an integer index to reference the elements. For example, this recipe loads values into an indexed table of numbers.

```
DECLARE

TYPE    num_type IS TABLE OF number INDEX BY BINARY_INTEGER;
nums    num_type;
total   number;

BEGIN

    nums(1) := 127.56;
    nums(2) := 56.79;
    nums(3) := 295.34;

    -- call subroutine to process numbers;
    -- total := total_table (nums);
END;
```

How It Works

PL/SQL tables are indexed collections of data of the same type. The datatype can be any of the built-in datatypes provided by PL/SQL; in this example, the datatype is a number. Here are some things to note about the example:

- The TYPE statement declares a TABLE of numbers.

- The INDEX BY clause defines how the array is accessed, in this case by an INTEGER.

- The array is populated by assigning values to specific indexes.

Because the TABLE is INDEXED BY an INTEGER, there is no predefined limit on the index value, other than those imposed by Oracle, which is $-2^{31} - 2^{31}$. Indexed tables are best suited for collections where the number of elements stored is not known until runtime.

This recipe is an example of a TABLE indexed by an INTEGER. PL/SQL provides for tables indexed by strings as well. See Recipe 10-5 for an example.

10-3. Creating Simple Records

Problem

You need a PL/SQL data structure to group related employee data to make manipulating the group easier.

Solution

Define a record structure of the related employee data, and then create a variable to hold the record structure. In this example, a simple RECORD structure is defined and initialized.

```
DECLARE

TYPE    rec_type IS RECORD (
                last_name       varchar2(25),
                department      varchar2(30),
                salary          number );
rec     rec_type;

begin

    rec.last_name       := 'Juno';
    rec.department      := 'IT';
    rec.salary          := '5000';

END;
```

How It Works

Record structures are created in PL/SQL by using the TYPE statement along with a RECORD structure format. The fields defined in the record structure can be, and often are, of different datatypes. Record structures use dot notation to access individual fields. Once defined, the rec_type record structure in the solution can be used throughout the code to create as many instantiations of data structures as needed.

10-4. Creating and Accessing Record Collections

Problem

You need to load records from a database table or view into a simple data structure that would benefit from use in a loop body or to pass as a parameter to another function or procedure. You want to act upon sets of records as a single unit.

Solution

Use a TYPE to define a TABLE based on the database table structure. The following example declares a cursor and then uses it to declare the table of records. The result is a variable named recs that holds the data fetched by the cursor.

```
DECLARE

CURSOR  driver IS
SELECT  *
FROM    employees;

TYPE    emp_type IS TABLE OF driver%ROWTYPE INDEX BY BINARY_INTEGER;
recs    emp_type;
total   number := 0.0;

BEGIN

    OPEN DRIVER;
    FETCH DRIVER BULK COLLECT INTO recs;
    CLOSE DRIVER;

    DBMS_OUTPUT.PUT_LINE (recs.COUNT || ' records found');

    FOR i in 1..recs.COUNT LOOP
       total := total + recs(i).salary;
    END LOOP;

END;
```

When you execute this block of code, you will see a message such as the following:

```
103 records found
```

How It Works

The TYPE statement defines a data structure using the attributes (columns) of the employees table as elements within the structure. The TABLE OF clause defines multiple instances of the record structure. The INDEX BY clause defines the index method, in this case an integer. Think of this structure as a spreadsheet with the rows being separate records from the database and the columns being the attributes (fields) in the database. The recipe works whether your cursor selects all the fields (SELECT *) or selects just a subset of fields from the table.

The BULK COLLECT portion of the fetch statement is more efficient than looping through the data in a standard cursor loop because PL/SQL switches control to the database just once to retrieve the data as opposed to switching to the database for each record retrieved in a cursor FOR .. LOOP. In a BULK COLLECT, all records meeting the query condition are retrieved and stored in the data structure in a single operation. Once the records are retrieved, processing may occur in a standard FOR .. standard FOR .. LOOP.

10-5. Creating and Accessing Hash Array Collections

Problem

You want to use a single cursor to query employee data and sum the salaries across departments.

Solution

You can use two cursors—one to select all employees and the other to sum the salary grouping by department. However, you can more easily and efficiently accomplish your task by using one cursor and a hashed collection. Define your cursor to select employee data, joined with the department table. Use a hash array collection to total by department by using the INDEX BY option to index your collection based on the department name rather than an integer. The following code example illustrates this more efficient approach:

```
DECLARE

CURSOR  driver IS
SELECT  ee.employee_id, ee.first_name, ee.last_name, ee.salary, d.department_name
FROM    departments    d,
        employees      ee
WHERE   d.department_id = ee.department_id;

TYPE    total_type IS TABLE OF number INDEX BY departments.department_name%TYPE;
totals  total_type;

dept    departments.department_name%TYPE;

BEGIN

   FOR rec IN driver LOOP
      -- process paycheck
      if NOT totals.EXISTS(rec.department_name) then  -- create element in the array
         totals(rec.department_name) := 0; -- initialize to zero
      end if;

      totals(rec.department_name) := totals(rec.department_name) + nvl (rec.salary, 0);
   END LOOP;

   dept := totals.FIRST;
   LOOP
      EXIT WHEN dept IS NULL;
      DBMS_OUTPUT.PUT_LINE (to_char (totals(dept),  '999,999.00') || ' ' || dept);
```

```
      dept := totals.NEXT(dept);
   END LOOP;

END;
```

When you execute this block of code, you will see the following results:

```
20,310.00 Accounting
58,720.00 Executive
51,600.00 Finance
6,500.00 Human Resources
19,000.00 Marketing
2,345.34 Payroll
10,000.00 Public Relations
304,500.00 Sales
156,400.00 Shipping
35,295.00 Web Developments
```

How It Works

The TOTAL_TYPES PL/SQL type is defined as a collection of numbers that is indexed by the department name. Indexing by department name gives the advantage of automatically sorting the results by department name.

As new elements are created, using the EXISTS method, the index keys are automatically sorted by PL/SQL. The totals are accumulated by department name as opposed to a numerical index, such as department ID, which may not be sequential. This approach has the added advantage of not requiring a separate collection for the department names.

Once the employee paychecks are processed, the dept variable is initialized with the first department name from the totals array using the FIRST method. In this example, the first department is accounting. A loop is required to process the remaining records. The NEXT method is used to find the next department name—in alphabetical order—and this process repeats until all departments are displayed.

10-6. Creating and Accessing Complex Collections

Problem

You need a routine to load managers and their corresponding employees from the database and store them in one data structure. The data must be loaded in a manner such that direct reports are associated with their manager. In addition, the number of direct reports for any given manager varies, so your structure to hold the manager/employee relationships must handle any number of subordinates.

Solution

Combine records and collections to define one data structure capable of storing all the data. PL/SQL allows you to use data structures you create via the type statement as datatypes within other collections. Once your data structures are defined, use dot notation to distinguish attributes within the collections. Use the structure's index to reference items within the table. For example:

```
SET SERVEROUT ON SIZE 1000000

DECLARE

TYPE    person_type IS RECORD (
                employee_id       employees.employee_id%TYPE,
                first_name        employees.first_name%TYPE,
                last_name         employees.last_name%TYPE);

  -- a collection of people
TYPE    direct_reports_type IS TABLE OF person_type INDEX BY BINARY_INTEGER;

  -- the main record definition, which contains a collection of records
TYPE    rec_type IS RECORD (
                mgr               person_type,
                emps              direct_reports_type);

TYPE    recs_type IS TABLE OF rec_type INDEX BY BINARY_INTEGER;
recs    recs_type;

CURSOR  mgr_cursor IS  -- finds all managers
SELECT  employee_id, first_name, last_name
FROM    employees
WHERE   employee_id IN
        (     SELECT  distinct manager_id
              FROM    employees)
ORDER BY last_name, first_name;

CURSOR  emp_cursor (mgr_id integer) IS  -- finds all direct reports for a manager
SELECT  employee_id, first_name, last_name
FROM    employees
WHERE   manager_id = mgr_id
ORDER BY last_name, first_name;

  -- temporary collection of records to hold the managers.
TYPE            mgr_recs_type IS TABLE OF emp_cursor%ROWTYPE
                                INDEX BY BINARY_INTEGER;
mgr_recs        mgr_recs_type;

BEGIN

  OPEN mgr_cursor;
  FETCH mgr_cursor BULK COLLECT INTO mgr_recs;
  CLOSE mgr_cursor;

  FOR i IN 1..mgr_recs.COUNT LOOP
    recs(i).mgr := mgr_recs(i);  -- move the manager record into the final structure

      -- moves direct reports directly into the final structure
    OPEN emp_cursor (recs(i).mgr.employee_id);
    FETCH emp_cursor BULK COLLECT INTO recs(i).emps;
    CLOSE emp_cursor;
```

```
     END LOOP;

        -- traverse the data structure to display the manager and direct reports
        -- note the use of dot notation within the data structure
     FOR i IN 1..recs.COUNT LOOP
        DBMS_OUTPUT.PUT_LINE ('Manager: ' || recs(i).mgr.last_name);
        FOR j IN 1..recs(i).emps.count LOOP
           DBMS_OUTPUT.PUT_LINE ('***    Employee: ' || recs(i).emps(j).last_name);
        END LOOP;
     END LOOP;

  END;
```

Executing this code block produces the following results:

```
Manager: Cambrault
***     Employee: Bates
***     Employee: Bloom
***     Employee: Fox
***     Employee: Kumar
***     Employee: Ozer
***     Employee: Smith
...  <<snip>>
Manager: Zlotkey
***     Employee: Abel
***     Employee: Grant
***     Employee: Hutton
***     Employee: Johnson
***     Employee: Livingston
***     Employee: Taylor
```

How It Works

Combining records with collections is one of the most powerful techniques for defining data structures in PL/SQL. It allows you to logically group common data, process large amounts of data efficiently, and seamlessly pass data between procedures and functions.

The data structure contains a collection of managers; each manager contains a collection of direct reports. Managers and direct reports are both person_type. Once your complex structure is defined, you can use the BULK COLLECT feature to quickly fetch data from the database and load it into the structure.

The BULK COLLECT of the MGR_CURSOR selects all persons who are managers at once and then loads them into the temporary structure MGR_RECS. Now that you have retrieved the records, it is easy to move them into your final data structure. Looping through the manager records allows you to move the entire data record for each manager via the RECS(I).MGR := MGR_RECS(I); statement. This statement moves every element (field) from the MGR_RECS into the RECS structure.

The EMP_CURSOR uses the managers' ID to fetch the managers' direct reports. The cursor is opened by passing the managers' ID, and then another BULK COLLECT is used to directly store the fetched data into the data structure; no temporary data structure is needed because the structure of the fetched data exactly matches the target data structure.

Now that the data is stored in the data structure, it can be passed to another routine for processing. Grouping large sets of related data is an efficient method for exchanging data between routines. This helps separate data retrieval routines from business processing routines. It's a very powerful feature in PL/SQL, as you'll see in the next recipe.

10-7. Passing a Collection As a Parameter

Problem

You want to pass a collection as a parameter to a procedure or function. For example, you have a data structure that contains employee data, and you need to pass the data to a routine that prints employee paychecks.

Solution

Create a collection of employee records to hold all employee data, and then pass the data to the subroutine to process the paychecks. The TYPE statement defining the data structure must be visible to the called procedure; therefore, it must be defined globally, prior to defining any procedure or function that uses it.

In this example, employee data is fetched from the database into a collection and then passed to a subroutine for processing.

```
set serverout on size 1000000

DECLARE

CURSOR  driver IS
SELECT  employee_id, first_name, last_name, salary
FROM    employees
ORDER BY last_name, first_name;

TYPE    emps_type IS TABLE OF driver%ROWTYPE;
recs    emps_type;

   PROCEDURE print_paycheck (emp_recs emps_type) IS

   BEGIN

      FOR i IN 1..emp_recs.COUNT LOOP
         DBMS_OUTPUT.PUT ('Pay to the order of: ');
         DBMS_OUTPUT.PUT (emp_recs(i).first_name || ' ' || emp_recs(i).last_name);
         DBMS_OUTPUT.PUT_LINE (' $' || to_char (emp_recs(i).salary, 'FM999,990.00'));
      END LOOP;

   END;

BEGIN

   OPEN driver;
   FETCH driver BULK COLLECT INTO recs;
   CLOSE driver;
```

```
     print_paycheck (recs);

END;

Results

Pay to the order of: Ellen Abel $11,000.00
Pay to the order of: Sundar Ande $6,400.00
Pay to the order of: Mozhe Atkinson $2,800.00
… <<snip>>
Pay to the order of: Alana Walsh $3,100.00
Pay to the order of: Matthew Weiss $8,000.00
Pay to the order of: Eleni Zlotkey $10,500.00
```

How It Works

TYPE globally defines the data structure as a collection of records for use by the PL/SQL block and the enclosed procedure. This declaration of both the type and the procedure at the same level—inside the same code block—is necessary to allow the data to be passed to the function. The type and the procedure are within the same scope, and thus the procedure can reference the type and accept values of the type.

Defining the recs structure as a collection makes it much easier to pass large amounts of data between routines with a single parameter. The data structure emps_type is defined as a collection of employee records that can be passed to any function or procedure that requires employee data for processing. This recipe is especially useful in that the logic of who receives a paycheck can be removed from the routine that does the printing or the routine that archives the payroll data, for example.

10-8. Returning a Collection As a Parameter

Problem

Retrieving a collection of data is a common need. For example, you need a function that returns all employee data and is easily called from any procedure.

Solution

Write a function that returns a complete collection of employee data. In this example, a package is used to globally define a collection of employee records and return all employee data as a collection.

```
CREATE OR REPLACE PACKAGE empData AS

type    emps_type is table of employees%ROWTYPE INDEX BY BINARY_INTEGER;

FUNCTION get_emp_data RETURN emps_type;

END empData;

CREATE OR REPLACE PACKAGE BODY empData as

FUNCTION get_emp_data RETURN emps_type is
```

```
cursor   driver is
select   *
from     employees
order by last_name, first_name;

recs     emps_type;

begin

   open driver;
   FETCH driver BULK COLLECT INTO recs;
   close driver;

   return recs;

end get_emp_data;

end empData;

declare

emp_recs empData.emps_type;

begin

   emp_recs := empData.get_emp_data;
   dbms_output.put_line ('Employee Records: ' || emp_recs.COUNT);

END;
```

Executing this block of code produces the following results.

```
Employee Records: 103
```

How It Works

By defining a PACKAGE, the data structure emps_type is available for use by any package, procedure, or function that has access rights to it.[1] The function get_emp_data within the common package contains all the code necessary to fetch and return the employee data. This common routine can be used by multiple applications that require the employee data for processing. This is a much more efficient method than coding the same select statement in multiple applications.

It is not uncommon to include business rules in this type of function; for example, the routine may fetch only active employees. If the definition of an active employee changes, you need to update only one routine to fix all the applications that use it.

---

[1] To grant access rights, enter the following command: grant execute on empData to SCHEMA, where SCHEMA is the user name that requires access. To grant access to every user in the database, use grant execute on empData to PUBLIC;.

10-9. Counting the Members in a Collection

Problem

You have a collection, and you need to determine the total number of elements in the collection.

Solution

Invoke the built-in COUNT method on the collection. For example, the following code creates two collections: a varying array and an INDEX BY array. The code then invokes the COUNT method on both collections, doing so before and after adding some records to each.

```
DECLARE

TYPE    vtype    IS VARRAY(3) OF DATE;
TYPE    ctype    IS TABLE OF DATE INDEX BY BINARY_INTEGER;

vdates   vtype := vtype (sysdate);
cdates   ctype;

BEGIN

    DBMS_OUTPUT.PUT_LINE ('vdates size is: ' || vdates.COUNT);
    DBMS_OUTPUT.PUT_LINE ('cdates size is: ' || cdates.COUNT);

    FOR i IN 1..3 LOOP
        cdates(i) := SYSDATE + 1;
    END LOOP;

    DBMS_OUTPUT.PUT_LINE ('cdates size is: ' || cdates.COUNT);

END;
```

Executing this block of code produces the following results:

```
vdates size is: 1
cdates size is: 0
cdates size is: 3
```

How It Works

The variable vdates is initialized with one value, so its size is reported as 1 even though it is defined to hold a maximum of three values. The variable cdates is not initialized, so it is first reported with a size of 0. The loop creates and sets three collection values, which increases its count to 3.

Assigning a value directly to cdates(i) is allowed because cdates is an INDEX BY collection. Assigning a value to vdates in the loop would cause an error because the array has only one defined value. See the EXTEND method later in this chapter for more information on assigning values to non-INDEX BY collections.

The COUNT method is especially useful when used on a collection populated with a fetch from BULK COLLECT statement to determine the number of records fetched or to process records in a FOR .. LOOP.

10-10. Deleting a Record from a Collection

Problem

You need to randomly select employees from a collection. Using a random generator may select the same employee more than once, so you need to remove the record from the collection before selecting the next employee.

Solution

Invoke the built-in DELETE method on the collection. For example, the following code creates a collection of employees and then randomly selects one from the collection. The selected employee is removed from the collection using the DELETE method. This process is repeated until three employees have been selected.

```
DECLARE

CURSOR  driver IS
SELECT  last_name
FROM    employees;

TYPE    rec_type IS TABLE OF driver%ROWTYPE INDEX BY BINARY_INTEGER;
recs    rec_type;
j       INTEGER;

BEGIN

   OPEN driver;
   FETCH driver BULK COLLECT INTO recs;
   CLOSE driver;

   DBMS_RANDOM.INITIALIZE(TO_NUMBER (TO_CHAR (SYSDATE, 'SSSSS') ) );

   FOR i IN 1..3 LOOP
--      Randomly select an employee
      j := MOD (ABS (DBMS_RANDOM.RANDom), recs.COUNT) + 1;
      DBMS_OUTPUT.PUT_LINE (recs(j).last_name);

--      Move all employees up one postion in the collection
      FOR k IN j+1..recs.COUNT LOOP
         recs(k-1) := recs(k);
      END LOOP;

--      Remove the last element in the collection
--      so the random number generator has the correct count.
      recs.DELETE(recs.COUNT);
   END LOOP;
```

```
    DBMS_RANDOM.TERMINATE;

END;
```

Executing this block of code produces the following results:

```
Olson
Chung
Seo
```

How It Works

The collection recs is populated with employee names via a BULK COLLECT. The FOR .. LOOP selects three employees at random by generating a random number between 1 and the number of records in the collection. Once an employee is selected, their name is removed from the collection, and the DELETE method is used to reduce the number of elements, which changes the value returned by the COUNT method for the next randomly generated number.

Note: The DELETE method applies only to collections that are indexed. You can invoke DELETE only if the collection's underlying TYPE definition contains the INDEX BY clause.

10-11. Checking Whether an Element Exists

Problem

You are processing elements in a collection but cannot be certain that each element exists. Referencing an element in a collection that does not exist will throw an exception. You want to avoid exceptions by testing for existence before you access an element.

Solution

Use the EXISTS method to test whether a collection has a value for a particular index value. In the following solution, a table collection is created, and then the second element is deleted. It is important to note that a deleted element or an element that was never initialized is not equivalent to an element with a null value.

```
DECLARE

TYPE ctype IS TABLE OF DATE INDEX BY BINARY_INTEGER;

cdates ctype;

BEGIN

    FOR i IN 1..3 LOOP
```

```
      cdates(i) := sysdate + i;
   END LOOP;

   cdates.DELETE(2);

   FOR i IN 1..3 LOOP
      IF cdates.EXISTS(i) then
         DBMS_OUTPUT.PUT_LINE ('cdates(' || i || ')= ' || cdates(i) );
      END IF;
   END LOOP;

END;
```

Executing this block of code produces the following results:

```
cdates(1)= 07-AUG-10
cdates(3)= 09-AUG-10
```

How It Works

The first loop creates and initializes the elements in the collection; the DELETE method removes the second element. Now we're ready to loop through the data. The second loop tests for the existence of the element index before attempting to use the variable. Attempting to access a value to an element in the collection that does not exist throws an exception.

If the first loop initialized the collection elements to NULL, the remaining would execute in exactly the same manner. The only difference would be in the output from running the block of code. In this case, no dates would print. Referencing an element in a collection with a null value does not throw an exception because the indexed element exists, whereas referencing an element that does not exist does throw an exception. Here is the output in this example. Note neither solution prints an element for subscript 2.

```
cdates(1)=
cdates(3)=
```

10-12. Increasing the Size of a Collection

Problem

You have a VARRAY with a defined maximum size, but not all elements are initialized, and you need to add more elements to the collection.

Solution

Use the EXTEND method to create new elements within the predefined boundaries. The following example adds five elements using a loop:

```
DECLARE

TYPE    vtype   IS VARRAY(5) OF DATE;
vdates  vtype := vtype (sysdate, sysdate+1, sysdate+2); -- initialize 3 of the 5 elements
```

```
BEGIN

   DBMS_OUTPUT.PUT_LINE ('vdates size is: ' || vdates.COUNT);

   FOR i IN 1..5 LOOP
      if NOT vdates.EXISTS(i) then
         vdates.EXTEND;
         vdates(i) := SYSDATE + i;
      END IF;
   END LOOP;

   DBMS_OUTPUT.PUT_LINE ('vdates size is: ' || vdates.COUNT);

END;
```

Executing this block of code produces the following results:

```
vdates size is: 3
vdates size is: 5
```

How It Works

The TYPE declaration defines a maximum of five elements in the collection, which is initialized with three values. The loop tests for the existence of the elements by index number. The EXTEND method allocates storage space for the new elements. Without the EXTEND statement preceding the assignment, Oracle will raise an error "ORA-06533: Subscript beyond count." This occurs when the loop attempts to assign a value to the fourth element in the collection.

The EXTEND method applies to TABLE and VARRAY collections that are not indexed. In other words, the EXTEND method applies when the TABLE or VARRAY type definition does not contain the INDEX BY clause. To assign a value to a collection that is indexed, simply reference the collection using the index value.

10-13. Navigating Collections

Problem

You need a routine to display sales totaled by region, which is stored in a collection of numbers, but the collection is indexed by a character string. Using a LOOP from 1 to the maximum size will not work.

Solution

Use the FIRST and LAST method to traverse the collection allowing PL/SQL to supply the proper index values. In this example, sales amounts are stored in a TABLE indexed by a string.

```
DECLARE

TYPE    ntype   IS TABLE OF NUMBER INDEX BY VARCHAR2(5);
nlist   ntype;
idx     VARCHAR2(5);
```

```
total    integer := 0;

BEGIN

   nlist('North') := 100;
   nlist('South') := 125;
   nlist('East')  := 75;
   nlist('West')  := 75;

   idx := nlist.FIRST;
   LOOP
      EXIT WHEN idx is null;
      DBMS_OUTPUT.PUT_LINE (idx || ' = ' || nlist(idx) );
      total := total + nlist(idx);
      idx   := nlist.NEXT(idx);
   END LOOP;

   DBMS_OUTPUT.PUT_LINE ('Total: ' || total);

END;
```

Executing this block of code produces the following results:

```
East = 75
North = 100
South = 125
West = 75
Total: 375
```

How It Works

The FIRST method returns the lowest index value in the collection. In this case, the value is East, because the collection is sorted alphabetically. The loop is entered with idx initialized to the first value in the collection. The NEXT method returns the next index value alphabetically in the collection. The loop continues executing until the NEXT method returns a null value, which occurs after the last index value in the collect is retrieved.

To traverse the collection in reverse alphabetical order, simply initialize the idx value to nlist.LAST. Then replace the nlist.NEXT with nlist.PRIOR.

Note The FIRST, NEXT, PRIOR, and LAST methods are most useful with associative arrays but also work with collections indexed by an integer.

10-14. Trimming a Collection

Problem

You need to remove one or more items from the end of a non-`INDEX BY` collection. The `DELETE` method will not work because it applies only to `INDEX BY` collections.

Solution

Use the `TRIM` method to remove one or more elements from the end of the collection. In this example, a `VARRY` is initialized with five elements. The `TRIM` method is used to remove elements from the end of the collection.

```
DECLARE

TYPE    vtype   IS VARRAY(5) OF DATE;
vdates  vtype := vtype (sysdate, sysdate+1, sysdate+2, sysdate+3, sysdate+4);

BEGIN

    DBMS_OUTPUT.PUT_LINE ('vdates size is: ' || vdates.COUNT);
    vdates.TRIM;
    DBMS_OUTPUT.PUT_LINE ('vdates size is: ' || vdates.COUNT);
    vdates.TRIM(2);
    DBMS_OUTPUT.PUT_LINE ('vdates size is: ' || vdates.COUNT);

END;
```

Executing this block of code produces the following results:

```
vdates size is: 5
vdates size is: 4
vdates size is: 2
```

How It Works

The `TRIM` method deletes elements from the end of the collection including elements not initialized. It accepts an optional parameter for the number of elements to delete; otherwise, it defaults to the last element. The `TRIM` method applies to `TABLE` and `VARRAY` collections that are not indexed. If the underlying `TYPE` definition does not contain the `INDEX BY` clause, then you can invoke `TRIM`.

The `TRIM` method is limited to removing elements from the end of a collection, whereas the `DELETE` method can remove elements anywhere in a collection. If you `DELETE` an element in the middle of a collection, then executing a `FOR .. LOOP` from one to the collection's `COUNT` will not work properly. First, if you attempt to access the element that was deleted without checking whether it `EXISTS`, an exception is thrown. Second, the `COUNT` method will return a value that is less than the collection's maximum index value, which means the `FOR .. LOOP` will not process all elements in the collection.

CHAPTER 11

Automating Routine Tasks

Oracle provides methods to schedule one-time and recurring jobs within the database, which is beneficial when you want to automate repetitive tasks and run them at times when a DBA may not be available. This chapter provides recipes to help you get started scheduling jobs (especially PL/SQL jobs), capturing output, sending e-mail notifications, and keeping data in sync with other databases.

11-1. Scheduling Recurring Jobs

Problem

You want to schedule a PL/SQL procedure to run at a fixed time or at fixed intervals.

Solution

Use the EXEC DBMS_SCHEDULER.CREATE_JOB procedure to create and schedule one-time jobs and jobs that run on a recurring schedule. Suppose, for example, that you need to run a stored procedure named calc_commissions every night at 2:30 a.m. to calculate commissions based on the employees' salaries. Normally, commissions would be based on sales, but the default HR schema doesn't provide that table, so we'll use an alternate calculation for demonstration purposes:

```
EXEC DBMS_SCHEDULER.CREATE_JOB (                  -
             JOB_NAME=>'nighly_commissions',     -
             JOB_TYPE=>'STORED_PROCEDURE',       -
          JOB_ACTION=>'calc_commisions',         -
             ENABLED=>TRUE,                       -
     REPEAT_INTERVAL=>'FREQ=DAILY;INTERVAL=1;BYHOUR=02;BYMINUTE=30');
```

How It Works

The DBMS_SCHEDULER.CREATE_JOB procedure sets up a nightly batch job. JOB_NAME must be unique. The JOB_TYPE, in this example, is STORED_PROCEDURE. This informs the scheduler the job is a PL/SQL procedure stored in the database. In addition to scheduling a stored procedure, the scheduler can also execute a PL/SQL_BLOCK, an external EXECUTABLE program, or a job CHAIN. See Recipe 11-6 for an example on scheduling job chains.

The JOB_ACTION identifies the stored procedure to run. If the procedure is owned by another schema, then include the schema name, for example, HR.calc_commission. If the procedure is part of a larger package, include that as well, for example, HR.my_package.calc_commission.

ENABLED is set to TRUE to tell the scheduler to run at the next scheduled time. By default, the ENABLED parameter is FALSE and would require a call to the DBMS_SCHEDULER.ENABLE procedure to enable the job.

The REPEAT_INTERVAL is an important part of the CREATE_JOB routine. It identifies the frequency, in this case DAILY. The INTERVAL tells scheduler to run the job every day, as opposed to 2 or 3, which would run every other day, or every third day. The BYHOUR and BYMINUTE sections specifies the exact time of the day to run. In this example, the job will run at 2:30 a.m.

The scheduled job, nightly_commissions, runs the stored procedure calc_commission, which reads the data, calculates the commission, and stores the commission records. Running this job nightly keeps the employees' commission data current with respect to daily sales figures.

11-2. E-mailing Output from a Scheduled Job

Problem

You have a scheduled job that runs a stored procedure at a regular interval. The procedure produces output that ordinarily would be sent to the screen via the DBMS_OUTPUT.PUT_LINE procedure, but since it runs as a nightly batch job, you want to send the output to a distribution list as an e-mail message.

Solution

Save the output in a CLOB variable and then send it to the target distribution list using the UTL_MAIL.SEND procedure. For example, suppose you want to audit the employee table periodically to find all employees who have not been assigned to a department within the company. Here's a procedure to do that:

```
CREATE OR REPLACE PROCEDURE employee_audit AS

CURSOR    driver IS    -- find all employees not in a department
SELECT    employee_id, first_name, last_name
FROM      employees
WHERE     department_id is null
ORDER BY  last_name, first_name;

buffer       CLOB := null; -- the e-mail message

BEGIN

    FOR rec IN driver LOOP    -- generate the e-mail message
       buffer := buffer  ||
         rec.employee_id || ' '  ||
         rec.last_name    || ', ' ||
         rec.first_name  || chr(10);
    END LOOP;

--    Send the e-mail
    IF buffer is not null THEN -- there are employees without a department
       buffer := 'Employees with no Department' || CHR(10) || CHR(10) || buffer;

       UTL_MAIL.SEND (
              SENDER=>'someone@mycompany.com',
          RECIPIENTS=>'audit_list@mycompany.com',
            SUBJECT=>'Employee Audit Results',
```

```
            MESSAGE=>buffer);
   END IF;

END;
```

How It Works

The procedure is very straightforward in that it finds all employees with no department. When run as a scheduled job, calls to DBMS_OUTPUT.PUT_LINE won't work because there is no "screen" to view the output. Instead, the output is collected in a CLOB variable to later use in the UTL_MAIL.SEND procedure. The key to remember in this recipe is there is no screen output from a stored procedure while running as a scheduled job. You must store the intended output and either write it to an operating system file or, as in this example, send it to users in an e-mail.

11-3. Using E-mail for Job Status Notification

Problem

You have a scheduled job that is running on a regular basis, and you need to know whether the job fails for any reason.

Solution

Use the ADD_JOB_EMAIL_NOTIFICATION procedure to set up an e-mail notification that sends an e-mail when the job fails to run successfully. Note, this solution builds on Recipe 11-1 where a nightly batch job was set up to calculate commissions.

```
EXEC DBMS_SCHEDULER.ADD_JOB_EMAIL_NOTIFICATION (     -
     JOB_NAME=>'nightly_commissions', -
     RECIPIENTS=> 'me@my_company.com,dist_list@my_company.com');
```

How It Works

The previous recipe is the simplest example of automating e-mail in the event a job fails. The ADD_JOB_EMAIL_NOTIFICATION procedure accepts several parameters; however, the only required parameters are JOB_NAME and RECIPIENTS. The JOB_NAME must already exist from a previous call to the CREATE_JOB procedure (see Recipe 11-1 for an example). The RECIPIENTS is a comma-separated list of e-mail addresses to receive e-mail when an event occurs; by default the events that trigger an e-mail are JOB_FAILED, JOB_BROKEN, JOB_SCH_LIM_REACHED, JOB_CHAIN_STALLED, and JOB_OVER_MAX_DUR. Additional event parameters are JOB_ALL_EVENTS, JOB_COMPLETED, JOB_DISABLED, JOB_RUN_COMPLETED, JOB_STARTED, JOB_STOPPED, AND JOB_SUCCEEDED.

The full format of the ADD_JOB_EMAIL_NOTIFICATION procedure accepts additional parameters, but the default for each is sufficient to keep tabs on the running jobs. The body of the e-mail will return the error messages required to debug the issue that caused the job to fail.

To demonstrate the notification process, the commissions table was dropped after the job was set up to run. The database produced an e-mail with the following subject and body:

```
SUBJECT: Oracle Scheduler Job Notification - HR.NIGHTLY_COMMISSIONS JOB_FAILED
BODY:
Job: JYTHON.NIGHTLY_COMMISSIONS
```

```
Event: JOB_FAILED
Date: 28-AUG-10 03.15.30.102000 PM US/CENTRAL
Log id: 1118
Job class: DEFAULT_JOB_CLASS
Run count: 1
Failure count: 1
Retry count: 0
Error code: 6575
Error message: ORA-06575: Package or function CALC_COMMISSIONS is in an invalid state
```

11-4. Refreshing a Materialized View on a Timed Interval

Problem

You have a materialized view that must be refreshed on a scheduled basis to reflect changes made to the underlying table.

Solution

First, create the materialized view with a CREATE MATERIALIZED VIEW statement. In this example, a materialized view is created consisting of the department and its total salary.:

```
CREATE MATERIALIZED VIEW dept_salaries
BUILD IMMEDIATE
AS
SELECT department_id, SUM(salary) total_salary
FROM employees
GROUP BY department_id;
```

Display the contents of the materialized view:

```
SELECT *
FROM dept_salaries
ORDER BY department_id;
```

DEPARTMENT_ID	TOTAL_SALARY
10	6500
20	20200
30	43500
40	6500
50	297100
60	35000
70	10000
80	305600
90	58000
100	51600
110	20300
	7000

Use the EXEC DBMS_REFRESH.MAKE procedure to set up a refresh of the materialized view:

```
EXEC DBMS_REFRESH.MAKE ('HR_MVs', 'dept_salaries', SYSDATE, 'TRUNC(SYSDATE)+1');
```

Change the underlying data of the view.:

```
UPDATE employees
SET salary = salary * 1.03;

COMMIT;
```

Note that the materialized view has not changed:

```
SELECT *
FROM dept_salaries
ORDER BY department_id;
```

```
DEPARTMENT_ID TOTAL_SALARY
------------- ------------
           10         6500
           20        20200
           30        43500
           40         6500
           50       297100
           60        35000
           70        10000
           80       305600
           90        58000
          100        51600
          110        20300
                      7000
```

Next, manually refresh the materialized view:

```
EXEC DBMS_REFRESH.REFRESH ('HR_MVs');
```

The materialized view now reflects the updated salaries:

```
SELECT *
FROM dept_salaries
ORDER BY department_id;
```

```
DEPARTMENT_ID TOTAL_SALARY
------------- ------------
           10         6695
           20        20806
           30        44805
           40         6695
           50       306013
           60        36050
           70        10300
           80       314768
```

90	59740
100	53148
110	20909
	7210

How It Works

The DBMS_REFRESH.MAKE procedure creates a list of materialized views that refresh at a specified time. Although you could schedule a job that calls the DBMS_REFRESH.REFRESH procedure to refresh the view, the MAKE procedure simplifies this automated task. In addition, once your refresh list is created, you can later add more materialized views to the schedule using the DBMS_REFRESH.ADD procedure.

The first argument of the DBMS_REFRESH.MAKE procedure specifies the name of this list; in this example, the list name is HR_MVs. This name must be unique among lists. The next parameter is a list of all materialized views to refresh. The procedure accepts either a comma-separated string of materialized view names or an INDEX BY table, each containing a view name. If the list contains a view not owned by the schema creating the list, then the view name must be qualified with the owner, for example, HR.dept_salaries. The third parameter specifies the first time the refresh will run. In this example, sysdate is used, so the refresh is immediate. The fourth parameter is the interval, which must be a function that returns a date/time for the next run time. This recipe uses 'TRUNC(SYSDATE)+1', which causes the refresh to run at midnight every night.

In this example, the CREATE MATERIALIZED VIEW statement creates a simple materialized view of the total salary by departments, and the data is selected from the view to verify that it is populated with correct data.

■ **Note** After adding a 3 percent raise to each employee's salary, we continue to see a materialized view that reflects the old data. The DBMS_REFRESH routine solves that problem.

Although the refresh list was created, the content of the materialized view remains unchanged until the automatic update, which occurs every night at midnight. After the refresh occurs, the materialized view will reflect all changes made to employee salary since the last refresh occurred.

The manual call to DBMS_REFRESH.REFRESH demonstrates how the content of the materialized view changes once the view is refreshed. Without the call to the REFRESH procedure, the content of the materialized view remains unchanged until the next automated run of the REFRESH procedure.

11-5. Synchronizing Data with a Remote Data Source

Problem

Your database instance requires data that is readily available in another Oracle instance but cannot be synchronized with a materialized view, and you do not want to duplicate data entry.

Solution

Write a procedure that creates a connection to the remote HR database and performs the steps needed to synchronize the two databases. Then use the EXEC DBMS_SCHEDULER.CREATE_JOB procedure to run the procedure on a regular basis. Suppose, for example, that your Oracle Database instance requires data from the HR employee table, which is in another instance. In addition, your employee table contains tables with foreign key references on the employee_id that prevents you from using a materialized view to keep the HR employee table in synchronization.

Create a database connection to the remote HR database, and then download the data on a regular basis:

```
CREATE DATABASE LINK hr_data
CONNECT TO hr
IDENTIFIED BY hr_password
USING
'(DESCRIPTION=(ADDRESS=(PROTOCOL=TCP)(HOST=node_name)(PORT=1521))(CONNECT_DATA=(SERVICE_NAME=h
r_service_name)))';

CREATE OR REPLACE PROCEDURE sync_hr_data AS

CURSOR    driver IS
SELECT    *
FROM      employees@hr_data;

TYPE      recs_type IS TABLE OF driver%ROWTYPE INDEX BY BINARY_INTEGER;
recs      recs_type;

BEGIN

    OPEN DRIVER;
    FETCH DRIVER BULK COLLECT INTO recs;
    CLOSE DRIVER;

    FOR i IN 1..recs.COUNT LOOP
       UPDATE employees
       SET    first_name      = recs(i).first_name,
         last_name            = recs(i).last_name,
         email                = recs(i).email,
         phone_number         = recs(i).phone_number,
         hire_date            = recs(i).hire_date,
         job_id               = recs(i).job_id,
         salary               = recs(i).salary,
         commission_pct       = recs(i).commission_pct,
         manager_id           = recs(i).manager_id,
         department_id        = recs(i).department_id
       WHERE   employee_id     = recs(i).employee_id
       AND     (    NVL(first_name,'~')    <> NVL(recs(i).first_name,'~')
         OR     last_name                  <> recs(i).last_name
         OR     email                      <> recs(i).email
         OR     NVL(phone_number,'~')      <> NVL(recs(i).phone_number,'~')
         OR     hire_date                  <> recs(i).hire_date
         OR     job_id                     <> recs(i).job_id
         OR     NVL(salary,-1)             <> NVL(recs(i).salary,-1)
         OR     NVL(commission_pct,-1)     <> NVL(recs(i).commission_pct,-1)
         OR     NVL(manager_id,-1)         <> NVL(recs(i).manager_id,-1)
         OR     NVL(department_id,-1)      <> NVL(recs(i).department_id,-1)
```

```
        );

   END LOOP;

-- find all new rows in the HR database since the last refresh
   INSERT INTO employees
   SELECT *
   FROM    employees@hr_data
   WHERE   employee_id NOT IN (
    SELECT    employee_id
    FROM       employees);

END sync_hr_data;

EXEC DBMS_SCHEDULER.CREATE_JOB (            -
        JOB_NAME=>'sync_HR_employees',     -
        JOB_TYPE=>'STORED_PROCEDURE',      -
      JOB_ACTION=>'sync_hr_data',          -
          ENABLED=>TRUE,                   -
   REPEAT_INTERVAL=>'FREQ=DAILY;INTERVAL=1;BYHOUR=00;BYMINUTE=30');
```

How It Works

A database link is required to access the data. This recipe focuses more on the synchronization process, but the creation of the database link is demonstrated here. This link, when used, will remotely log into the HR instance as the HR schema owner.

The procedure sync_hr_data reads all records from the HR instances. It does so in a BULK COLLECT statement, because this is the most efficient method to read large chunks of data, especially over a remote connection. The procedure then loops through each of the employee records updating the local records, but only if the data changed, because there is no need to issue the UPDATE unless something has changed. The NVL is required in the WHERE clause to accommodate values that are NULL and change to a non-NULL value, or vice versa.

The final step is to schedule the nightly job. The CREATE_JOB procedure of the DBMS_SCHEDULER package completes this recipe. The stored procedure sync_hr_data is executed nightly at 12:30 a.m. See Recipe 11-1 for more information on scheduling a nightly batch job.

11-6. Scheduling a Job Chain

Problem

You have several PL/SQL procedures that must run in a fixed sequence—some steps sequentially, others in parallel. If one step fails, processing should stop.

Solution

Use the DBMS_SCHEDULER _CHAIN commands to create and define the order of execution of the chained procedures. Figure 11-1 depicts a simple example of a chain of procedures where the successful completion of step 1 kicks off parallel executions of two additional steps. When the two parallel steps compete successfully, the final step runs.

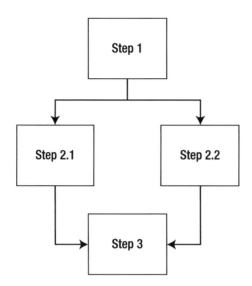

Figure 11-1. *Flowchart representation of a job chain.*

The following code shows how you can use the CREATE_CHAIN, CREATE_PROGRAM, DEFINE_CHAIN_STEP, and DEFINE_CHAIN_RULE options to implement the order of execution shown in Figure 11-1.

```
-- Define the Chain
BEGIN
   DBMS_SCHEDULER.CREATE_CHAIN (
    CHAIN_NAME     => 'Chain1');
END;

-- Create/define the program to run in each step
BEGIN
   DBMS_SCHEDULER.CREATE_PROGRAM (
    PROGRAM_NAME     => 'Program1',
    PROGRAM_TYPE     => 'STORED_PROCEDURE',
    PROGRAM_ACTION   => 'Procedure1',
    ENABLED          => true);
END;

BEGIN
   DBMS_SCHEDULER.CREATE_PROGRAM (
    PROGRAM_NAME     => 'Program2',
    PROGRAM_TYPE     => 'STORED_PROCEDURE',
    PROGRAM_ACTION   => 'Procedure2',
    ENABLED          => true);
END;

BEGIN
   DBMS_SCHEDULER.CREATE_PROGRAM (
```

```
      PROGRAM_NAME     => 'Program3',
      PROGRAM_TYPE     => 'STORED_PROCEDURE',
      PROGRAM_ACTION   => 'Procedure3',
      ENABLED          => true);
END;

BEGIN
    DBMS_SCHEDULER.CREATE_PROGRAM (
      PROGRAM_NAME     => 'Program4',
      PROGRAM_TYPE     => 'STORED_PROCEDURE',
      PROGRAM_ACTION   => 'Procedure4',
      ENABLED          => true);
END;

-- Create each step using a unique name
BEGIN
    DBMS_SCHEDULER.DEFINE_CHAIN_STEP (
      CHAIN_NAME    => 'Chain1',
      STEP_NAME     => 'Step1',
      PROGRAM_NAME  => 'Program1');
END;

BEGIN
    DBMS_SCHEDULER.DEFINE_CHAIN_STEP (
      CHAIN_NAME    => 'Chain1',
      STEP_NAME     => 'Step2_1',
      PROGRAM_NAME  => 'Program2');
END;

BEGIN
    DBMS_SCHEDULER.DEFINE_CHAIN_STEP (
      CHAIN_NAME    => 'Chain1',
      STEP_NAME     => 'Step2_2',
      PROGRAM_NAME  => 'Program3');
END;

BEGIN
    DBMS_SCHEDULER.DEFINE_CHAIN_STEP (
      CHAIN_NAME    => 'Chain1',
      STEP_NAME     => 'Step3',
      PROGRAM_NAME  => 'Program4');
END;

-- Define the step rules; which step runs first and their order
BEGIN
    DBMS_SCHEDULER.DEFINE_CHAIN_RULE (
      CHAIN_NAME    => 'Chain1',
      CONDITION     => 'TRUE',
      ACTION        => 'START Step1');

END;
```

```
BEGIN
   DBMS_SCHEDULER.DEFINE_CHAIN_RULE (
   CHAIN_NAME   => 'Chain1',
   CONDITION    => 'Step1 COMPLETED',
   ACTION       => 'START Step2_1, Step2_2');
END;

BEGIN
   DBMS_SCHEDULER.DEFINE_CHAIN_RULE (
   CHAIN_NAME   => 'Chain1',
   CONDITION    => 'Step2_1 COMPLETED AND Step2_2 COMPLETED',
   ACTION       => 'START Step3');
END;

BEGIN
   DBMS_SCHEDULER.DEFINE_CHAIN_RULE (
   CHAIN_NAME   => 'Chain1',
   CONDITION    => 'Step3 COMPLETED',
   ACTION       => 'END');
END;

-- Enable the chain
BEGIN
   DBMS_SCHEDULER.ENABLE ('Chain1');
END;
/

-- Schedule a Job to run the chain every night
BEGIN
   DBMS_SCHEDULE.CREATE_JOB (
   JOB_NAME         => 'chain1_Job',
   JOB_TYPE         => 'CHAIN',
   JOB_ACTION       => 'Chain1',
   REPEAT_INTERVAL  => 'freq=daily;byhour=3;byminute=0;bysecond=0',
   enabled          => TRUE);
END;
```

How It Works

Defining and scheduling a job chain may seem daunting at first but can be broken down into the following steps:

Create the chain.

Define each program that will run.

Create each step in the chain.

Create the rules that link the chain together.

Enable the chain.

Schedule the chain as a job to run a specific time or interval.

The DBMS_SCHEDULER.CREATE_CHAIN procedure creates a chain named as Chain1.

■ **Note** The chain_name must be unique and will be used in subsequent steps.

The DBMS_SCHEDULER.CREATE_PROGRAM procedure defines the executable code that will run. The programs defined here are run when a chain step is executed. The procedure accepts the following parameters:

- PROGRAM_NAME: A unique name to identify the program.

- PROGRAM_TYPE : Valid values are plsql_block, stored_procedure, and executable.

- PROGRAM_ACTION : Defines what code actually runs when executed based on the value for PROGRAM_TYPE. For a PROGRAM_TYPE of PLSQL_BLOCK, it is a text string of the PL/SQL code to run. For a STORED_PROCEDURE, it is the name of an internal PL/SQL procedure. For an EXECUTABLE, it is the name of an external program.

- ENABLE : Determines whether the program can be executed; the default is FALSE if not specified.

The DBMS_SCHEDULER.DEFINE_CHAIN_STEP procedure defines each step in the chain. You must supply the chain's name as its first parameters, which was created in the DBMS_SCHEDULER.CREATE_CHAIN procedure, along with a unique name for the step in the chained process and the name of the PL/SQL program to execute during the step. Note that the program is the name assigned in the DBMS_SCHEDULER.CREATE_PROGRAM procedure; it is not the name of your PL/SQL program.

The DBMS_SCHEDULER.DEFINE_CHAIN_RULE procedure defines how each step in the chain is linked together. Arguably, this is the most difficult step in the process because you must define the starting and ending steps in the chain properly. In addition, you must take care in defining links between sequential steps and parallel steps. Sketching a flow chart like the one shown in Figure 11-1 can aid in the sequencing of the chain steps.

The DBMS_SCHEDULER.DEFINE_CHAIN_RULE procedure accepts the following parameters:

- CHAIN_NAME: The name used when you created the chain.

- CONDITION: An expression that must evaluate to a boolean expression and must evaluate to true to perform the action. Possible test conditions are NOT_STARTED, SCHEDULED, RUNNING, PAUSED, STALLED, SUCCEEDED, FAILED, and STOPPED.

- ACTION: The action to perform when the condition evaluates to true. Possible actions are start a step, stop a step, or end the chain.

- RULE_NAME: The name you want to give to the rule being created. If omitted, Oracle will generate a unique name.

- COMMENTS : Optional text to describe the rule.

In this example, the first call to the DBMS_SCHEDULER.DEFINE_CHAIN_RULE procedure sets the condition to TRUE and the action to START Step1. This causes step 1 to run immediately when the chain starts. The next call to the DBMS_SCHEDULER.DEFINE_CHAIN_RULE procedure defines the action to take when step 1 completes successfully. In this example, steps 2.1 and 2.2 are started. Starting multiple steps simultaneously allows you to schedule steps to run in parallel. In the third call to the `DBMS_SCHEDULER.DEFINE_CHAIN_RULE` procedure, the condition waits for the successful completion of steps 2.1 and 2.2 and then starts step 3 as its `action`. The final call to the `DBMS_SCHEDULER.DEFINE_CHAIN_RULE` procedure waits for the successful completion of step 3 and then ends the chain.

If any step in the chain fails, the entire chained process stops at its next condition test. For example, if step 1 fails, steps 2.1 and 2.2 are never started. However, if steps 2.1 and 2.2 are running and step 2.1 fails, step 2.2 will continue to run and may complete successfully, but step 3 will never run. You can account for chain failures and other conditions by testing for a `condition` such as `NOT_STARTED`, `SCHEDULED`, `RUNNING`, `PAUSED`, `STALLED`, `FAILED`, and `STOPPED`.

The call to the procedure `DBMS_SCHEDULER.ENABLE` does just what you expect; it enables the chain to run. It is best to keep the chain disabled while defining the steps and rules. You can run the chain manually with a call to the `DBMS_SCHEDULE.RUN_CHAIN` procedure or, as shown in this example, with a call to the `DBMS_SCHEDULE.CREATE_JOB` procedure. See Recipe 11-1 for more information on scheduling a job.

■ ■ ■

CHAPTER 12

Oracle SQL Developer

Tools can be useful for increasing productivity while developing code. They oftentimes allow you to take shortcuts when coding by providing templates to start from or by providing autocompletion as words are typed. A good development tool can also be useful by incorporating several different utilities and functions into one development environment. Oracle SQL Developer is no exception, because it provides functionality for database administrators and PL/SQL developers alike. Functionalities include creating database tables, importing and exporting data, managing and administering multiple databases, and using robust PL/SQL development tools.

Oracle SQL Developer is an enterprise-level development environment, and it would take an entire book to document each of its features. Rather than attempting to cover each of the available options, this chapter will focus on developing and maintaining Oracle PL/SQL code using the tool. Along the way, you will learn how to configure database connections and obtain information from database objects. In the end, you should feel comfortable developing PL/SQL applications using the Oracle SQL Developer environment.

12-1. Creating Standard and Privileged Database Connections

Problem

You want to create a persistent connection to your database from within Oracle SQL Developer using both privileged and standard accounts so that you can work with your database.

Solution

Open Oracle SQL Developer, and select New from the File menu. This will open the Create a New window. Select the Database Connection option, and click OK. A New/Select Database Connection window opens, which has a list of existing database connections on the left side and an input form for creating a new connection on the right side, as shown in Figure 12-1.

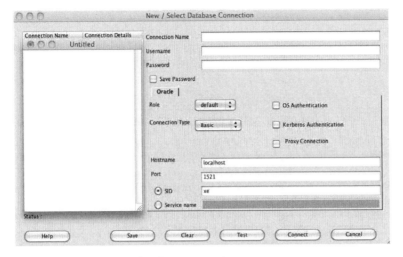

Figure 12-1. Creating a database connection

If you are creating a standard connection, choose the Basic connection type. If you are creating a privileged connection as SYS, then choose the SYSDBA connection type. Once you have created a connection, then you will be able to connect to the database via the user for which you have made a connection and browse the objects belonging to that user's schema.

How It Works

Before you can begin working with PL/SQL code in Oracle SQL Developer, you must create a database connection. Once created, this connection will remain in the database list that is located on the left side of the Oracle SQL Developer environment. During the process of creating the connection, you can either select the box to allow the password to be cached or keep it deselected so that you will be prompted to authenticate each time you want to use the connection. From a security standpoint, it is advised that you leave the box unchecked so that you are prompted to authenticate for each use.

Once the connection has been successfully established and you are authenticated, the world of Oracle SQL Developer is opened up, and you have a plethora of options available. At this point, you have the ability to browse through all the database tables, views, stored programs, and other objects that are available to the user account that you used to initiate the connection to the database by simply using the tree menu located within the left pane of the environment. Figure 12-2 shows a sample of what you will see when your database connection has been established.

Figure 12-2. Database connection in the navigator

■ **Note** If you plan to develop PL/SQL code for system events such as an AFTER LOGON trigger, you should create a separate connection for the privileged user using SYSDBA. This will allow you to traverse the privileged database objects.

As mentioned in the introduction to this chapter, you will learn how to use those features provided by Oracle SQL Developer that are useful for PL/SQL application development. This does not mean the other features offered by the environment are not useful, but it would take an entire book to cover each feature that Oracle SQL Developer has to offer. Indeed, there are entire books on the topic. This book strives to provide you with the education and concepts that you will need to know to develop complete and robust PL/SQL applications using Oracle SQL Developer.

12-2. Obtaining Information About Tables

Problem

You are interested in learning more about a particular database table. You also want to look at system triggers and other privileged PL/SQL objects.

Solution

Use the Oracle SQL Developer navigator to select the table that you want to view information about, as demonstrated in Figure 12-3.

Figure 12-3. *Viewing table information*

The editor window will then populate with a tab that consists of a worksheet and several subtabs. Each of these tabs provides different information about the table you are inspecting. Figure 12-4 shows the Columns tab of the Table Editor.

COLUMN_NAME	DATA_TYPE	NULLABLE	DATA_DEFAULT	COLUMN_ID	COMMENTS
EMPLOYEE_ID	NUMBER(6,0)	No	(null)	1	Primary key of employees
FIRST_NAME	VARCHAR2(20 BYTE)	Yes	(null)	2	First name of the emplo
LAST_NAME	VARCHAR2(25 BYTE)	No	(null)	3	Last name of the employ
EMAIL	VARCHAR2(25 BYTE)	No	(null)	4	Email id of the employe
PHONE_NUMBER	VARCHAR2(20 BYTE)	Yes	(null)	5	Phone number of the emp
HIRE_DATE	DATE	No	(null)	6	Date when the employee
JOB_ID	VARCHAR2(10 BYTE)	No	(null)	7	Current job of the empl
SALARY	NUMBER(8,2)	Yes	(null)	8	Monthly salary of the e
COMMISSION_PCT	NUMBER(2,2)	Yes	(null)	9	Commission percentage o
MANAGER_ID	NUMBER(6,0)	Yes	(null)	10	Manager id of the emplo

Figure 12-4. *Table Editor*

How It Works

Oracle SQL Developer provides an excellent means for examining table metadata. When a table is selected within the database connection navigator, a worksheet becomes available that includes detailed information pertaining to the table characteristics and data. The first tab, which is labeled Columns, includes information about the table columns and each of their datatypes. This is most likely the tab that you will spend the most time in. It includes toolbar buttons that allow you to perform editing on the table and to refresh the table view in the editor, and it even includes an extensive table manipulation menu labeled Action that is a database administrator's dream come true.

Next, the Data tab provides a live view of the data that exists within the table. It also includes toolbar buttons for inserting and deleting rows. This tab resembles a spreadsheet, and it allows different columns to be edited and then committed to the database. For a PL/SQL developer, it is most useful for editing data within a table that is being used for application debugging or testing purposes.

The Triggers tab will be useful to PL/SQL developers because it displays a selectable list of all table triggers. You can also create new triggers from the tab. Figure 12-5 shows the Triggers tab.

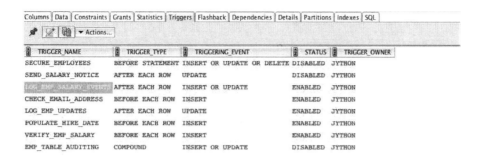

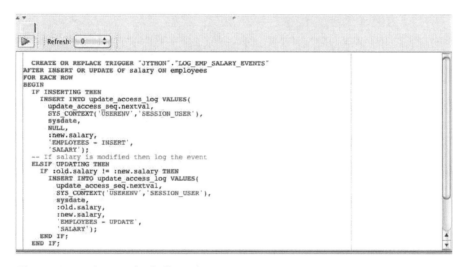

Figure 12-5. *Triggers tab of editor*

When a trigger is selected on the Triggers tab, its DDL is displayed in a panel on the bottom half of the window. The green arrow button will allow the trigger to be executed, and the refresh specifies an interval of time. You will learn more about trigger development in Recipe 12-11.

Oracle SQL Developer provides very useful information regarding database tables for PL/SQL developers. It also provides convenient access for trigger development and manipulation.

12-3. Enabling Output to Be Displayed

Problem

You want to display the results of DBMS_OUTPUT within Oracle SQL Developer.

Solution

Enable DBMS_OUTPUT for your connection via the Dbms Output pane. This pane resides on the lower-right side of the IDE. Do so by selecting the green plus icon within the pane and then choosing the desired connection from the resulting dialog box. Figure 12-6 shows the connection dialog box. After selecting the desired connection and then clicking the OK button, you will be prompted for a password for the connection if you are not already connected. Once a successful password has been entered, then DBMS_OUTPUT will be enabled for the specified connection.

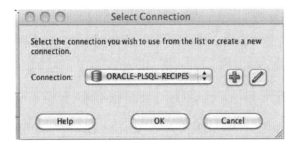

Figure 12-6. Select Connection dialog box

After enabling the DBMS_OUTPUT option, you will be able to see the output from DBMS_OUTPUT within Oracle SQL Developer. This can be very useful, especially for testing purposes.

How It Works

The easiest way to enable SERVEROUTPUT for a particular database connection is to enable DBMS_OUTPUT from within the Dbms Output window. Doing so will enable output to be displayed within the pane when the code is executed.

■ **Note** For more information on the DBMS_OUTPUT package, please see Recipe 1-6.

Selecting the Dbms Output option from the View menu will open the DBMS_OUTPUT pane. This pane gives you several options that include the ability to save the script output, change the buffer size, and even print the output. To enable SERVEROUTPUT via the pane, you must select the green plus symbol and choose a database connection. You will see the correct script output if you run the script again after enabling DBMS_OUTPUT via one of the two options we have discussed. Figure 12-7 shows the Dbms Output pane.

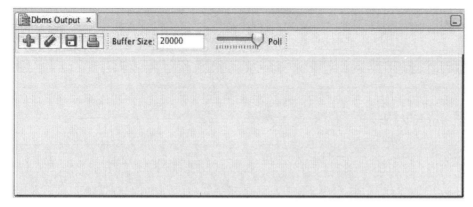

Figure 12-7. *Dbms Output pane*

Once a connection has been established using the Dbms Output pane, all `DBMS_OUTPUT` code that is executed against that connection will be displayed within the pane. It is possible to have more than one connection established within the pane, and in this case different tabs can be used to select the connection of your choice.

12-4. Writing and Executing PL/SQL

Problem

You want to use Oracle SQL Developer to execute an anonymous block of code.

Solution

Establish a connection to the database of your choice, and the SQL worksheet will automatically open. Once the worksheet has opened, you can type the code directly into it. For the purposes of this recipe, type or copy/paste the following anonymous block into a SQL worksheet:

```
DECLARE
  CURSOR emp_cur IS
  SELECT * FROM employees;

  emp_rec emp_cur%ROWTYPE;
BEGIN
  FOR emp_rec IN emp_cur LOOP
    DBMS_OUTPUT.PUT_LINE(emp_rec.first_name || ' ' || emp_rec.last_name);
  END LOOP;
END;
```

Figure 12-8 shows the Oracle SQL Developer worksheet after this anonymous block has been written into it.

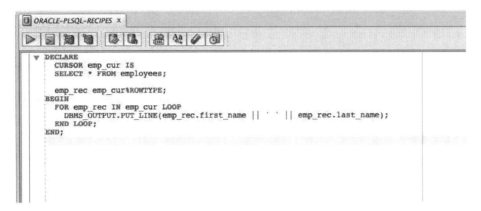

Figure 12-8. Oracle SQL Developer worksheet with PL/SQL anonymous block

How It Works

By default, when you establish a connection within Oracle SQL Developer, a SQL worksheet for that connection is opened. This worksheet can be used to create anonymous code blocks, run SQL statements, and create PL/SQL code objects. The SQL worksheet is analogous to the SQL*Plus command prompt, although it does not allow all the same commands that are available using SQL*Plus.

If you want to open more than one SQL worksheet or a new worksheet for a connection, this can be done in various ways. You can right-click (Ctrl+click) the database connection of your choice and then select Open SQL Worksheet from the menu. Another way to open a new worksheet is to use the SQL Worksheet option within the Tools menu. This will allow you to specify the connection of your choice to open a worksheet against.

As you type, you will notice that the worksheet will place all Oracle keywords into a different color. This helps distinguish between keywords and defined variables or stored programs. By default, the keywords are placed into a bold blue text, but this color can be adjusted within the user Preferences window that can be accessed from the Tools drop-down menu. Similarly, any text placed within single quotes will appear in a different color. By default, this is also blue, except it is not bold.

Besides the syntax coloring, there are some other features of the SQL worksheet that can help make your programming life easier. Oracle SQL Developer will provide autocompletion for some SQL and PL/SQL statements. For instance, if you enter a package name and type a dot, all the package members will be displayed in the drop-down list. You can also press Ctrl+spacebar to manually activate the autocomplete drop-down list. After the drop-down list appears, you can use the arrow keys to choose the option you want to use and then hit the Tab key. Oracle SQL Developer provides similar autocompletion for table and column names and even SQL statement GROUP BY and ORDER BY clauses. Take a look at Figure 12-9 to see the autocomplete feature in action.

Figure 12-9. Autocomplete drop-down list

Another feature that helps productivity is to use Oracle SQL Developer snippets. To learn more about snippets, please see Recipe 12-7. Within the SQL worksheet toolbar, there is a group of buttons that can be used to help increase programmer productivity. The group of buttons at the far-right side of the toolbar contains a button for making highlighted words uppercase, lowercase, and initial-cap. The button that has an eraser on it can be used to quickly clear the SQL worksheet. There is also button that can be used to display the SQL History panel. This SQL History panel opens along the bottom of the Oracle SQL Developer environment, and it contains all the SQL that has been entered into the worksheet. Double-clicking any line of the history will automatically add that SQL to the current worksheet. Figure 12-10 shows the SQL History window.

SQL	Connection	TimeSta..
CREATE OR REPLACE PROCEDURE INCREASE_WAGE (empno_i...	FESSDEV-JYT...	03-AUG-
file:/Users/juneau/Documents/PLSQL_Recipes/sources/12...	FESSDEV-JYT...	01-AUG-
DECLARE CURSOR emp_cur IS SELECT * FROM employees...	FESSDEV-JYT...	31-JUL-1
file:/Users/juneau/Documents/PLSQL_Recipes/sources/12...	FESSDEV-JYT...	31-JUL-1
file:/Users/juneau/Documents/PLSQL_Recipes/sources/12...	FESSDEV-JYT...	30-JUL-1

Figure 12-10. SQL History window

To execute the SQL or PL/SQL that is contained within the script, you can use the first two toolbar icons. The first icon in the toolbar (as shown in Figure 12-8) is a green arrow will execute the code that is in the worksheet and display the result in a separate pane. The second icon in the toolbar (as shown in Figure 12-8) that resembles a piece of paper with a green arrow in front will execute the code within the worksheet and then display the output in a pane that can be saved as script output.

■ **Note** It is possible to have more than one SQL statement or PL/SQL block within the SQL worksheet at the same time. In doing so, only the highlighted code will be executed when the green arrow button is selected. If all the code is selected, then a separate output pane will appear for the output of each block or statement. However, if the Script icon (paper with green arrow) is selected, then all the highlighted code will have its output displayed in the resulting script output pane.

Other toolbar options within the SQL worksheet include the ability to COMMIT or ROLLBACK changes that are made, run an explain plan on the current code, or set up autotrace. The SQL worksheet is like SQL*Plus with many additional features. It provides the power of many tools in one easy-to-use environment.

12-5. Creating and Executing a Script

Problem

You are interested in creating a PL/SQL script using Oracle SQL Developer that will run against your database. Once it has been created, you want to save it and then execute it.

Solution

Establish a connection to the database for which you want to create a script. By default, the SQL worksheet for the selected database will open. To create a script, choose New from the File menu or select the first icon on the left side of the toolbar that resembles a piece of paper with a plus sign. Next, select the SQL File option from the Create a New window. When the Create SQL File window opens, type in a file name for your script, and choose a directory in which to store it. For the purposes of this demonstration, choose the file name select_employees, browse and choose the desired storage location, and click OK. At this point, a new tab opens in the Oracle SQL Developer editor. This tab represents the SQL file you have just created. Type the following script into the editor for demonstration purposes:

```
DECLARE
  CURSOR emp_cur IS
  SELECT * FROM employees;

  emp_rec emp_cur%ROWTYPE;
BEGIN
  FOR emp_rec IN emp_cur LOOP
    DBMS_OUTPUT.PUT_LINE(emp_rec.first_name || ' ' || emp_rec.last_name);
  END LOOP;
END;
```

After the script has been typed into the editor, your Oracle SQL Developer editor should resemble that shown in Figure 12-11. Save your script by clicking the Save icon that looks like a disk, or choose Save from the File menu.

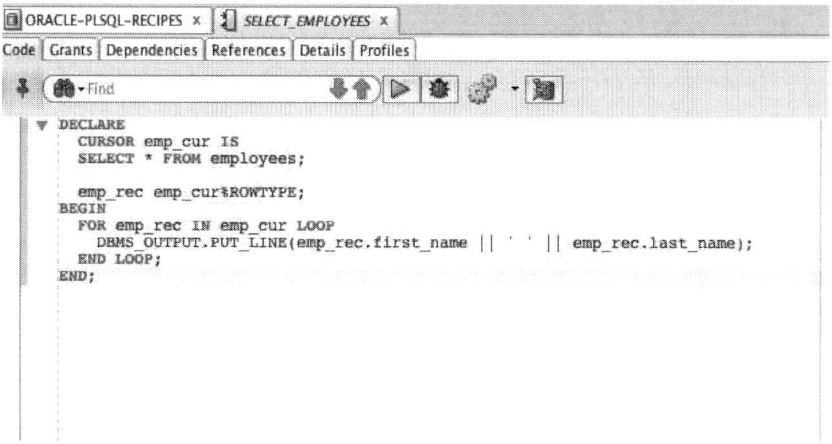

Figure 12-11. *Typing a script into the SQL editor*

To execute the script, click the Run Script icon that is the second icon from the left above the editor, or press the F5 function key. You will be prompted to select a database connection. At this point, you can choose an existing connection, create a new connection, or edit an existing connection. Choose the database connection that coincides with the schema for this book. Once you select the connection, the script will execute against the database, and you will see another pane appear in the lower half of the Oracle SQL Developer window. This is the Script Output pane, and you should see a message that states "anonymous block completed." The editor should now look like Figure 12-12.

Figure 12-12. *Anonymous block completed*

How It Works

In the solution to this recipe, you learned how to create and execute a script using Oracle SQL Developer. As you were typing the script, you may have noticed that the text being typed is color-coded. Oracle SQL Developer places PL/SQL and SQL keywords into a different color text that can be chosen from within the preferences window, which is located within the Tools menu. The default color for keywords is blue.

When the script is executed, it prompts for a database connection to use. Once that connection has been selected and established, then the script is run against the database. The script may not display any useful results by default, unless the SERVEROUTPUT has been enabled via the Dbms Output pane. To learn more about enabling DBMS_OUTPUT, please see Recipe 12-3.

When you select the Save option, the script is written to disk to a file having the name you specified earlier. To execute a saved script, open the File menu, and then select the Open option. A dialog box will open that allows you to browse your file system for the script that you want to open. Once you have found the script and opened it, a new tab is opened, and the script is loaded into that tab along with all the options of an ordinary SQL worksheet (see Figure 12-13).

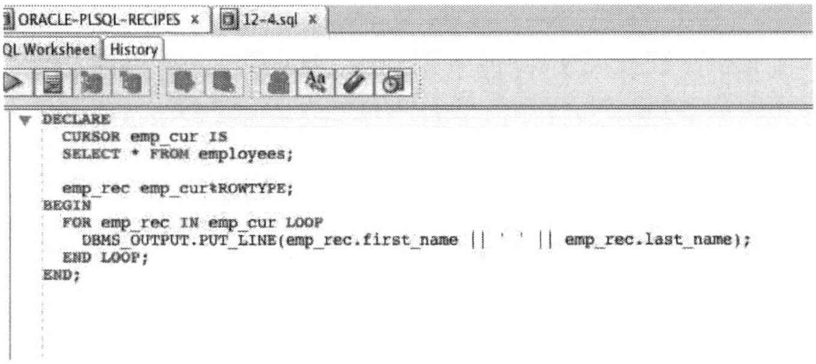

Figure 12-13. Loaded script

12-6. Accepting User Input for Substitution Variables

Problem

You want to create a PL/SQL application that accepts user input from the keyboard. To test the input, you want to have Oracle SQL Developer prompt you for input.

Solution

Use an ampersand in front of a text string just like in SQL*Plus. Assign the resulting user variable to a PL/SQL variable, or use the value inline.

How It Works

Just as SQL*Plus treats the ampersand as a token to denote user input, Oracle SQL Developer does the same. When an ampersand is encountered, Oracle SQL Developer will display a pop-up box to prompt the user for the input. For example, type or copy and paste the following code into the SQL worksheet, and then select the Run Statement toolbar button.

```
DECLARE
    email       VARCHAR2(25);
BEGIN
  SELECT   email
  INTO   email
  FROM employees
  WHERE employee_id = &emp_id;

  DBMS_OUTPUT.PUT_LINE('Email Address for ID: ' || email);
```

```
EXCEPTION
  WHEN OTHERS THEN
    DBMS_OUTPUT.PUT_LINE('An unknown error has occured, please try again.');
END;
```

When the code is executed, you will be prompted to provide a value for the emp_id variable. A separate dialog box that looks like the one shown in Figure 12-14 is displayed.

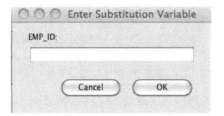

Figure 12-14. *Entering substitution variable*

If the value being accepted from the user is a string, then the ampersand-variable must be placed within single quotes. For example, &last_name would be used to prompt for user entry of a string value.

12-7. Saving Pieces of Code for Quick Access

Problem

You want to save a portion of code so that it can be made easily reusable by other PL/SQL programs.

■ **Tip** This recipe also works for frequently used bits of SQL.

Solution

Use the Snippets window to create the reusable piece of code and use it for access at a later time.

How It Works

The Snippets window can be accessed by selecting the View menu and then choosing the Snippets option. The Snippets window will open as a pane on the far-right side of the Oracle SQL Developer environment. The pane consists of a toolbar that includes a button used for creating a new snippet and a button for editing an existing snippet. There is also a drop-down menu that consists of several menu options that organize each of the snippets into a different category. Figure 12-15 shows the Snippets pane.

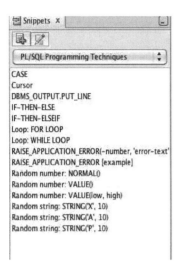

Figure 12-15. Snippets

The snippet is used by dragging its text onto a SQL worksheet or script. Once dragged onto the worksheet, the actual code is displayed in a template fashion. In some cases, you will need to change a bit of the text to make it usable, but the reusable code that is provided by the snippet can greatly reduce development time.

You can add your own snippet by selecting the icon that resembles a piece of paper with a plus sign on it from the Snippets panel. This opens the Save Snippet window (as shown in Figure 12-16) that gives you the option of using one of the existing categories or typing a new one. You can also type a name and tooltip for the snippet. The name of the snippet will appear in the Snippets panel after it has been saved. The text of the snippet itself will be placed into the worksheet once you drag the name of your snippet to a worksheet or script.

Figure 12-16. Save Snippet pane

The Edit Snippet icon (the one with the pencil through it) brings up another window that allows you to choose an existing snippet to edit, create a new snippet, or delete a snippet. Only those snippets that you have created are available for editing. Figure 12-17 displays the Edit Snippets window.

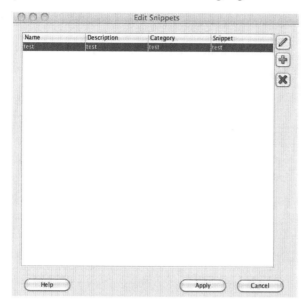

Figure 12-17. Edit Snippets window

The snippets are actually saved within an XML file named UserSnippets.xml. This file is located in your user sqldeveloper directory. This file can be transported to another machine and placed into the sqldeveloper directory so that the snippets can be made available in more than one place. This can be useful if you have a group of developers who may want to share snippets. The ability to copy the UserSnippets.xml file into other user sqldeveloper directories and make the snippets available to other users can certainly be advantageous.

Snippets can be useful for saving the time of typing a SQL or PL/SQL construct. They can also be beneficial if you do not remember the exact syntax of a particular piece of code. They provide quick access to template-based solutions.

12-8. Creating a Function

Problem

You want to create a function using Oracle SQL Developer.

Solution

You can manually create the function by typing the code into the SQL worksheet for the database connection for which you want to create. You can also use the Create Function Wizard within Oracle SQL Developer to provide some assistance throughout the function creation process. There are a couple of different ways to invoke the Create Function Wizard. If you go to the File menu and select New, the Create a New window opens, and Function is one of the available options. You can also reach the same menu by selecting the New toolbar button. Both of these paths will lead you to the same window because after clicking OK, the Create PL/SQL Function window will appear (Figure 12-18).

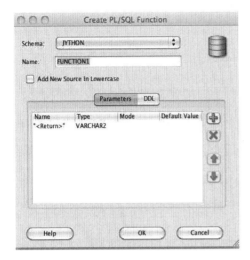

Figure 12-18. *Create PL/SQL Function window*

A final way to invoke this same window is to establish a database connection and then expand the connection navigator to list all subfolders and then right-click the Functions subfolder. One of the available options after doing so will be New Function.

How It Works

If using the SQL worksheet to create a function, you will need to type the code for creating your function into the editor and then click the Run button to compile and save the object. If any errors are encountered while compiling, they will appear in the Messages window along with the line number that they occurred on. The SQL worksheet works very well for those who are well accustomed to creating functions. The Create Function Wizard may be the best choice for creating a function or those who like to write less code.

■ **Note** Using the Connections pane, you are able to browse both valid and invalid objects. An object may become invalid if it is not compilable, becomes stale, or because of issues with other dependencies.

Once within the Create PL/SQL Function window, you will be able to name the function and specify any parameters that will need to be used. The first parameter in the list is already defined by default, and it represents the function's return value. You can change the return type by selecting from the list of datatype options within the Type column of the parameter listing.

To add a new parameter, click the plus symbol on the right side of the window, and a new line will be added to the parameter-listing table. You can then populate the name of the parameter, select a datatype and mode, and designate a default value if one should exist. After all parameters have been declared, click the OK button to continue.

The function editor window will open, and it will contain the code that needs to be used for creation of the function that you have defined. All that is left to code will be any declarations and then the actual function code. The editor window contains a toolbar of options along with several tabs that can be used to find out more information about a function once it has been created (Figure 12-19).

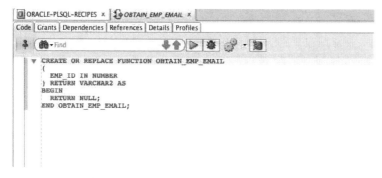

Figure 12-19. The Function Editor window

The remaining function declarations and code should be typed into the editor, and when completed, the Save toolbar button or menu option can be used to compile and save the function into the database. If there are compilation errors upon saving, the errors will be displayed in a Compiler – Log window along with the line number on which the error occurred. By clicking the error in the window, your cursor will be placed on the line of code that needs to be repaired. Figure 12-20 shows the Compiler – Log window including a reference to an error in the code.

Figure 12-20. Compilation errors in Function Editor

Once you have successfully compiled and saved the function into the database, it can be executed for testing purposes using the green arrow icon within the Function Editor window. When you execute the function, the Run PL/SQL window will be displayed. If you defined any parameters for the function, you can supply values for them within the PL/SQL Block portion of the window. You can then click OK to execute the function using the value(s) you have defined within the window, and the results will be displayed in the Run Log window. The Run PL/SQL window can also be used to save your test case to a file or restore a test case from disk. The test case incorporates all the text that is contained within the PL/SQL block portion of the Run PL/SQL window. This window is displayed in Figure 12-21.

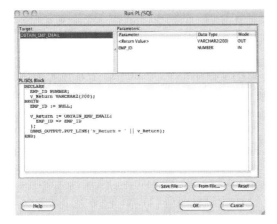

Figure 12-21. *Run PL/SQL window*

You can use the database navigator to display the functions contained within a particular database connection. If you highlight a particular trigger and right-click it, then a menu containing several options will be displayed. This is shown in Figure 12-22.

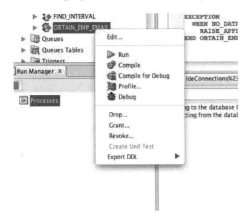

Figure 12-22. *Using the navigator with functions*

The options provided can be used for administering or editing the selected function. The Edit option will open the Function Editor, and it will contain the code for the selected function. If the selected function is not compiled successfully, then you can make changes to it and choose the Compile option within the right-click contextual menu to recompile the code. Similarly, the menu can be used to invoke the profiler, debug, or administer privileges for the function.

12-9. Creating a Stored Procedure

Problem

You want to create a stored procedure using Oracle SQL Developer.

Solution

You can manually create a stored procedure by typing the code for creating your procedure into a SQL worksheet and executing it. You can also use the Create Procedure Wizard. To start the wizard, go to the File menu and select the New option. Once the Create a New dialog box opens (Figure 12-23), select Procedure.

Figure 12-23. *Create a New dialog box*

Once you click OK, you will be prompted to select a database connection. Doing so will open the Create PL/SQL Procedure Wizard. Alternatively, you can connect to the database of your choice and then expand the navigator so that all the objects within the database are available. Right-click the Procedures submenu, and select New Procedure, as shown in Figure 12-24.

Figure 12-24. *Right-click the Procedures submenu within a designated database connection.*

How It Works

You can use the Create a New Wizard or SQL worksheet to create a new stored procedure. The wizard is best suited for those who are new to PL/SQL or not very familiar with the overall syntax for creating a stored procedure. To use the wizard, select the File menu followed by the New option. At this point, you will be presented with the Create a New window that allows several options for creating new database objects or code. Select the Procedure option, and click OK. Oracle SQL Developer will now prompt you to select a database connection for which you will create the stored procedure. Select the connection of your choice, and click OK. The Create PL/SQL Procedure window will open, and it will resemble Figure 12-25.

Figure 12-25. *Create PL/SQL Procedure window*

The Create PL/SQL Procedure window provides a window that can be used to create a procedure. You can select a schema and name the procedure. There is a check box that allows you to create your code using all lowercase if you want. Using the green plus symbol on the right side of the window, you can add a row of text to the Parameters window. By default, the parameter will be named PARAM1, and it will be given a datatype of VARCHAR2 with a mode of IN. All of these options can be changed, including the name. You can add zero or more parameters to the list, and you can rearrange their order by selecting a parameter from the list and using the arrow buttons on the right side of the window. You can select the DDL tab to see the actual code for creating the stored procedure, along with all the parameters you have defined. When finished, you can optionally choose to save your code to disk using the Save button and then click OK to create the procedure.

Once you have completed and saved the Create PL/SQL Procedure form, the code is transferred to a SQL worksheet that is a procedure editor that contains buttons and tabs for working with the stored procedure, as shown in Figure 12-26.

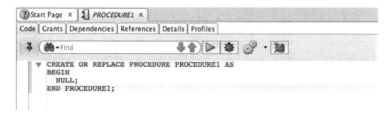

Figure 12-26. Stored Procedure Wizard

The worksheet contains six tabs that can be used to find out more information about the stored procedure that it contains. This information includes the grants that have been made on the procedure. Other information includes dependencies, references, details, and profiles. You can add code to the procedure by typing into the editor. The editor will perform autocompletion where appropriate, and snippets can be dragged into the editor.

Next, copy the following procedure into the editor for testing purposes:

```
CREATE OR REPLACE PROCEDURE INCREASE_WAGE
(
  EMPNO_IN IN NUMBER,
 PCT_INCREASE IN NUMBER
) AS
  emp_count     NUMBER := 0;
  Results    VARCHAR2(50);
BEGIN

  SELECT count(*)
  INTO EMP_COUNT
  FROM EMPLOYEES
  WHERE employee_id = empno_in;

  IF emp_count > 0 THEN
    UPDATE EMP
    SET salary = salary + (salary * PCT_INCREASE)
    WHERE employee_id = empno_in;
    Results := 'SUCCESSFUL INCREASE';
  ELSE
    Results := 'NO EMPLOYEE FOUND';
  END IF;

  DBMS_OUTPUT.PUT_LINE(RESULTS);
END;
```

Once the procedure has been coded, select the Save option from the File menu, or click the Save icon that contains an image of a disk. This will compile and store the procedure into the database. You can alternatively use the Gears button to compile and save, which will produce the same results. If any compilation errors are found, they will be displayed in a pane below the editor along with the line number on which the error was found (Figure 12-27).

❌ Error(16,5): PL/SQL: SQL Statement ignored

❌ Error(16,12): PL/SQL: ORA-00942: table or view does not exist

Figure 12-27. Compilation errors

If you double-click the error message, the cursor will be placed into the line of code that contains the error. In this case, you can see that the EMP table does not exist. Replace it with EMPLOYEES, and then click the Save button again. The procedure should now be successfully compiled and saved into the database. If you select the Refresh icon above the navigator, the new procedure will appear within the list of procedures for the database connection.

To execute the procedure, right-click it within the navigator, and choose the Run option; this will cause the Run PL/SQL window to open. This window is shown in Figure 12-28.

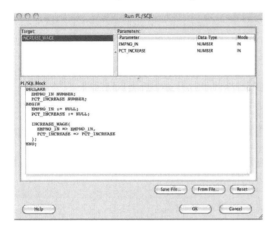

Figure 12-28. Run PL/SQL procedure window

At this point, you have the option to save the file to disk or open another SQL file. If you want to test the procedure, then you can assign some values to the parameters within this window. Assign the values directly within the code that is listed in the PL/SQL Block section of the Run PL/SQL window. When you click OK, then the procedure will be executed. The results of the execution will be displayed in the log pane that is located below the editor pane.

12-10. Creating a Package Header and Body

Problem

You want to create a package and store it into the database using Oracle SQL Developer.

Solution

Use the Create Package Wizard, or type the PL/SQL package code into a SQL worksheet. To start the wizard, go to the File menu, and select the New option. Once the Create a New dialog box opens, select Package, as shown in Figure 12-29.

Figure 12-29. *Creating a new package*

Once you click OK, you will be prompted to select a database connection. This will open the Create PL/SQL Package Wizard. Alternatively, you can connect to the database of your choice and then expand the navigator so that all the objects within the database are available. Right-click (Ctrl+click) the Packages submenu and select New Package.

How It Works

Creating a new package with Oracle SQL Developer is much the same as creating other code objects using this tool. You can develop using the manual technique of writing all code using the SQL worksheet, or you can use the creation wizards that are provided by the tool. You can type the example code into a SQL worksheet for your data connection and click the Run Statement toolbar button to compile and save the package into the database. You can also issue a Save As and save the code to a file on your workstation when writing code using the SQL worksheet.

Alternatively, the wizard is useful for quickly creating the standard code for a package, and you can use the editor to add the details that are specific to your package. Once you have opened the New Package Wizard, you will be prompted to enter a package name. For the purposes of this recipe, enter the name PROCESS_EMPLOYEE_TIME, and click OK. If there is an existing object that has the same name, then you will be alerted via a red pop-up message (Figure 12-30).

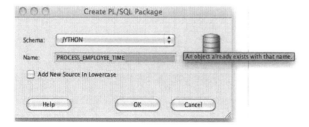

Figure 12-30. *Naming the PL/SQL package using creation wizard*

■ **Note** If you want to enter all code in lowercase for readability within the tool, you can select the check box before clicking OK once the package has been named. PL/SQL is *not* a case-sensitive language, so case does not affect code execution.

After proceeding, the package editor is opened, and it contains some standard package creation code using the name that you placed into the wizard. As you can see from Figure 12-31, the package editor contains several tabs, along with a search bar and Run, Debug, Compile, and Profile buttons. Enter the following example code into the text box on the Code tab:

```
CREATE OR REPLACE PACKAGE process_employee_time IS
    total_employee_salary               NUMBER;
    PROCEDURE grant_raises(pct_increase IN NUMBER);
    PROCEDURE INCREASE_WAGE (empno_in IN NUMBER,
                            Pct_increase IN NUMBER) ;
END;
```

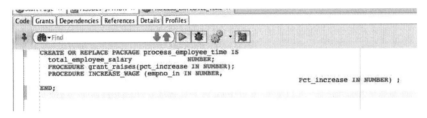

Figure 12-31. Package editor window

Click the Save button to compile and store the package into the database. Once this has been completed, then the package header should be successfully stored in the database. Next, a package body will need to be added in order to make the package functional. This can be done by expanding the Package subfolder within the navigator. Once expanded, select the package for which you want to create a body. Right-click the selected package, and select the Create Body option (Figure 12-32).

Figure 12-32. Creating a package body

Next, the standard package body creation code will be added to an editor much like the SQL worksheet. You can now edit this code accordingly to ensure that it performs the correct actions. Type the following package body into the editor, and then click the Save button to compile and store the package body:

```
CREATE OR REPLACE PACKAGE BODY process_employee_time AS
  PROCEDURE grant_raises (
    pct_increase IN NUMBER) as
      CURSOR emp_cur is
      SELECT employee_id
      FROM employees;
    BEGIN
      FOR emp_rec IN emp_cur LOOP
        increase_wage(emp_rec.employee_id, pct_increase);
      END LOOP;
      DBMS_OUTPUT.PUT_LINE('All employees have received the salary increase');
  END grant_raises;

 PROCEDURE increase_wage (
  empno_in IN NUMBER,
  Pct_increase IN NUMBER) as
  Emp_count    NUMBER := 0;
  Results    VARCHAR2(50);
BEGIN
  SELECT count(*)
  INTO emp_count
  FROM employees
  WHERE employee_id = empno_in;

  IF emp_count > 0 THEN
    UPDATE employees
    SET salary = salary + (salary * pct_increase)
    WHERE employee_id = empno_in;

    SELECT salary
    INTO total_employee_salary
    FROM employees
    WHERE employee_id = empno_in;

    Results := 'SUCCESSFUL INCREASE';
  ELSE
    Results := 'NO EMPLOYEE FOUND';
  END IF;
  DBMS_OUTPUT.PUT_LINE(results);

 END increase_wage;
END process_employee_time;
```

If any compilation errors are encountered, an error window will be displayed providing the line number and specific error message that needs to be addressed. After any compile errors are repaired, the package body will be successfully created. You can then use the navigator to expand the package name and see the package body listed within it. Right-clicking the package body in the navigator offers some options such as Edit, Run, Compile, Profile, and Debug. You will learn more about debugging in Recipe 12-12. The Edit option will open the package body editor if it is not already open. The Run option will open the Run PL/SQL window, which allows you to select a procedure or function to execute from the chosen package (Figure 12-33).

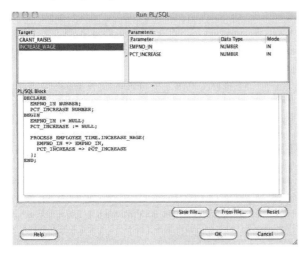

Figure 12-33. Running the PL/SQL package

Once a function or procedure is chosen from the Run PL/SQL window, it is executed using the values that are assigned to the variables within the PL/SQL Block panel of the window (this code is automatically generated by SQL*Developer). These values can be changed prior to running the package by editing the code that is displayed within the panel. This window also provides the opportunity to save the code to a file or load code from an existing file.

Oracle SQL Developer makes developing PL/SQL packages easy. All the tools that are needed to successfully create, edit, and manage packages are available within the environment. Whether you are a beginner or seasoned expert, these tools will make package development and maintenance a breeze.

12-11. Creating a Trigger

Problem

You need to create a DML database trigger that validates data prior to inserting it into a table, and you want to use Oracle SQL Developer to do so. For instance, you want to create a trigger that will validate an e-mail address prior to inserting a row into the EMPLOYEES table.

Solution

Use the Create Trigger Wizard, type the PL/SQL trigger code into a SQL worksheet, or use the trigger options that are available from the database table worksheet. To start the wizard, go to the File menu and select the New option. Once the Create a New dialog box opens, select Trigger. This will open the Create Trigger window, as shown in Figure 12-34.

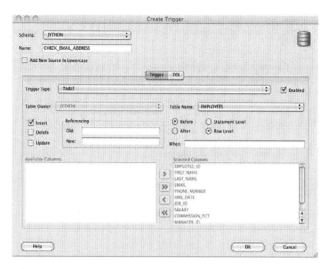

Figure 12-34. Creating a new trigger

The Create Trigger window simplifies the process of creating a trigger because it provides all the essential details that are required up front. Once the information has been completed, the trigger code can be developed using the trigger editor window.

How It Works

As with all the other code creation techniques available in Oracle SQL Developer, there are various different ways to create a trigger. Using the SQL worksheet for a database connection is the best way to manually create a trigger. To do so, you will need to open the SQL worksheet, type the trigger creation code, and click the Run toolbar button to compile and save the code. The many wizards that are available for trigger creation can greatly simplify the process, especially if you are new to PL/SQL or rusty on the details of trigger creation.

As mentioned in the solution to the recipe, the Create Trigger window allows you to specify all the details for creating a trigger. You choose the type of trigger by selecting one of the options available from the drop-down menu. Different options become available in the window depending upon the type of trigger you choose to create. By default, a table trigger is chosen. Using that option, you can select the table from another drop-down list and choose whether the trigger should be executed on INSERT, UPDATE, or DELETE from the specified table. The wizard allows you to specify your own variable names for representing old and new table values. The timing for trigger execution is determined by selecting Before, Statement Level, After, or Row Level and specifying an optional WHEN clause. You can even specify whether the trigger is to be executed based upon a specific column.

If you attempt to enter a trigger name that matches an existing object in the database within the specified schema, you will receive an error message, as shown in Figure 12-35.

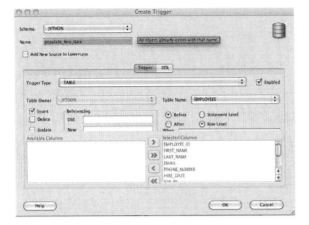

Figure 12-35. Create Trigger window—object already exists

After finishing with the Create Trigger Wizard and clicking the OK button, the initial trigger creation code will be displayed in an editor (Figure 12-36).

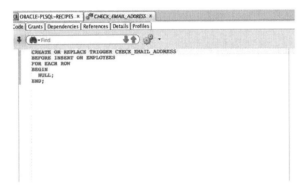

Figure 12-36. Trigger Editor

Type the following code into the editor, and hit the Save button to compile the code and save it into the database:

```
TRIGGER CHECK_EMAIL_ADDRESS
BEFORE INSERT ON employees
FOR EACH ROW
BEGIN
  IF NOT INSTR(:new.email,'@') > 0 THEN
    RAISE_APPLICATION_ERROR(-20001, 'INVALID EMAIL ADDRESS');
  END IF;
END;
```

The Save button will automatically compile the code, and the output will appear in the Messages pane below the editor, as shown in Figure 12-37.

Figure 12-37. Messages log

After the trigger has been successfully compiled and stored into the database, it can be highlighted in the navigator, and right-clicking it will reveal several options (Figure 12-38).

Figure 12-38. Trigger options

These options help allow easy access for dropping, disabling, or enabling the trigger. Choosing the Edit option from this submenu will open the trigger in the editor window to allow for code modifications.

Using the Create Trigger Wizard in Oracle SQL Developer can greatly reduce the time it takes to create a database trigger. By selecting the appropriate options within the wizard, you will be left with only the trigger functionality to code.

12-12. Debugging Stored Code

Problem

One of your stored procedures contains logical errors, and you want to use Oracle SQL Developer to help you find the cause.

Solution

A few different options are available for debugging stored code within Oracle SQL Developer. The environment includes a complete debugger that provides the ability to set breakpoints within the code and modify variable values at runtime to investigate a problem with your code. There are several ways to invoke the debugger for a particular piece of code. When a code object is opened within the editor, the toolbar will contain a red "bug" icon that can be used to invoke the debugger (Figure 12-39).

***Figure 12-39.** Debugger icon*

The right-click contextual menu within the navigator also contains a Debug option for procedures and packages (Figure 12-40).

***Figure 12-40.** Debugger option in Navigator*

How It Works

Using the debugger is a great way to find issues with your code. The debugger enables the application to halt processing at the designated breakpoints so that you can inspect the current values of variables and step through each line of code so that issues can be pinpointed. Debugging PL/SQL programs is a multistep process that consists of first setting breakpoints in code, followed by compiling the code for debug, and lastly running the actual debugger. To use the debugger, the user who is running the debugger must be granted some database permissions. The user must be granted the DEBUG ANY PROCEDURE privilege to have debug capabilities on any procedure or DEBUG <procedure name> to allow debugging capabilities on a single procedure. The DEBUG CONNECT SESSION privilege must also be granted in order to allow access to the debugging session.

After a user has been granted the proper permissions for debugging, the next step is to place a breakpoint (or several) into the code that will be debugged. For the purposes of this recipe, the INCREASE_WAGE procedure will be loaded into the procedure editor, and a breakpoint will be set by placing the mouse cursor on the left margin of the editor window next to the line of code that you want the debugger to pause execution at. Once the cursor is in the desired location, click in the left margin to place the breakpoint. Figure 12-41 shows a breakpoint that has been placed at the beginning of a SELECT statement within the INCREASE_WAGE procedure.

Figure 12-41. *Setting a breakpoint*

After one or more breakpoints have been placed, the code needs to be compiled for debug. To do so, use the icon in the editor toolbar for compiling, and select the Compile for Debug option. Once the code has been compiled for debug, its icon in the navigator will adopt a green bug to indicate that it is ready for debugging (Figure 12-42).

Figure 12-42. *Code ready for debug*

Next, the debugger can be started by selecting the debug icon within the editor or by right-clicking the code within the navigator and selecting the Debug option. If the user who is debugging the code does not have appropriate permissions to debug, then error messages such as those shown in Figure 12-43 will be displayed.

Figure 12-43. *User not granted necessary permissions*

Assuming that the user has the correct permissions to debug, the Debug PL/SQL window will be displayed. This window provides information about the code that is being debugged including the target name, the parameters, and a PL/SQL block that will be executed in order to debug the code. The code that is contained within the PL/SQL block portion of the screen can be modified so that the parameters being passed into the code (if any) can be set to the values you choose (Figure 12-44). In Figure 12-44, the values have been set to an EMPNO_IN value of 10 and a PCT_INCREASE value of .03.

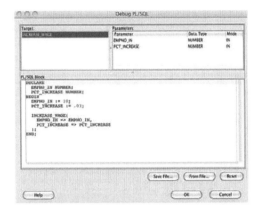

Figure 12-44. *Debug PL/SQL window*

Once the Debug PL/SQL window has been completed with the desired values, click OK to begin the debugger. This will cause Oracle SQL Developer to issue the DBMS_DEBUG_JDWP.CONNECT_TCP (hostname, port) command and start the debugging session. The debugger will start, and it will provide a number of different options, allowing you to step through the code one line at a time and see what the variable values are at any given point in time. You will see three tabs on the debugger: Data, Smart Data, and Watches. The Data tab is used for watching all the variables and their values as you walk through your code using the debugger. The Smart Data tab will keep track of only those variables that are part of the current piece of code that is being executed. You can set watches to determine which variables that you would like to keep track of. The inspector can be used to see the values within those variables you are watching. You are also given the very powerful ability to modify the values at runtime as the code is executing. This provides the capability of determining how code will react to different values that are passed into it.

The Oracle SQL Developer debugger is a useful tool and provides an intuitive user interface over the DBMS_DEBUG_JDWP utility. Although this recipe covers only the basics to get you started, if you spend time using each feature of the debugger, then you will learn more powerful ways to help you maintain and debug issues found in your code.

12-13. Compiling Code Within the Navigator

Problem

You want to compile some PL/SQL code within Oracle SQL Developer. In this solution, the navigation menu of your Oracle SQL Developer environment contains code that has a red *X* on it. This means the code needs to be compiled or that it contains an error.

Solution

Select the code that needs to be compiled, and right-click (Ctrl+click) it. A menu will be displayed that lists several options. Select the Compile option from that menu (Figure 12-45).

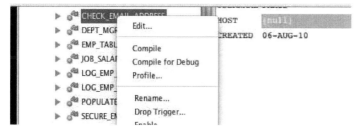

Figure 12-45. *Compile option*

How It Works

The Oracle SQL Developer navigation menu is very handy for quickly glancing at the code that a database contains. All the code that is successfully loaded into the database will contain a green check mark, whereas any code that has a compilation error will contain a red *X* label. Sometimes code needs to simply be recompiled in order to validate it and make it usable once again. This is most often the case after a database has just recently been migrated or updated. This can also occur if a particular piece of code depends upon another piece of code that has recently been modified, although Oracle Database 11gR2 includes fine-grained dependencies that help alleviate this issue. Another event that may cause code to require recompilation is if an object that the code references such as a table or view has been changed. Whatever the case, Oracle SQL Developer makes it easy to recompile code by right-clicking it within the navigator and selecting Compile from the pop-up menu.

■ **Note** Oracle Database 11g introduced the idea of fine-grained dependencies. This allows PL/SQL objects to remain valid even if an object that they depend upon has changed, as long as the changes do not affect the PL/SQL object. For instance, if a column has been removed from a table and object A depends upon that table but not the specific column that was removed, then object A will remain valid.

Once the compile task has been completed, a message will be displayed within the Messages panel to note whether the compilation was successful. If there were any issues encountered, they will be listed, each on a separate line, within the Messages window. The messages will contain the error code, as well as the line number that caused the exception to be raised. Double-clicking each error message will take you directly to the line of code that raised the exception so that you can begin working on repairs.

CHAPTER 13

■ ■ ■

Analyzing and Improving Performance

This chapter introduces several methods to help you analyze your code to improve its performance in terms of runtime or memory usage. Many recipes use the DBMS_PROFILE package, which is supplied by Oracle, to help in the analysis. It is a useful tool for identifying which lines of code consume the most execution time.

13-1. Installing DBMS_PROFILER

Problem

You want to analyze and diagnose your code to find bottlenecks and areas where excess execution time is being spent, but the DBMS_PROFILER package is not installed.

Solution

Install the DBMS_PROFILER packages, and then create the tables and the Oracle sequence object they need in order to run. Once installed, you can use the DBMS_PROFILER package to help diagnose application performance issues.

Installing the Packages

To install the DBMS_PROFILER packages, follow these steps:

> The packages are owned by the SYS account; therefore, it requires DBA login access. Start by opening a SQL Plus connect with the connect sys command. If the operation is successful, the system will respond with the message "Connected."

```
connect sys/sys_pwd as sysdba
Connected.
```

> Once connected, run the profload.sql script that can be found within the RDBMS/ADMIN directory contained in your Oracle Database home. The system will respond with a series of messages like those shown next.

```
@[Oracle_Home]/RDBMS/ADMIN/profload.sql
```

You should see the following output after executing the script:

```
Package created.
Grant succeeded.
Synonym created.
Library created.
Package body created.
Testing for correct installation
SYS.DBMS_PROFILER successfully loaded.
PL/SQL procedure successfully completed.
```

Finally, enter the grant execute command to ensure that all schemas within the database have access to the DBMS_PROFILER package.

```
grant execute on DBMS_PROFILER to PUBLIC;
Grant succeeded.
```

Creating the Profiler Tables and Sequence Object

Create the tables and Oracle sequence object you need for the profiler to run. Log into the account that wants to use the profiler, and enter the following. The system will respond as follows:

```
@[Oracle_Home]/RDBMS/ADMIN/proftab.sql
```

How It Works

The first step creates the packages and makes them available for public access. The second creates the required tables in the schema that wants to use the profiler. There are alternatives to this installation method based on needs and preferences.

The DBA may, for example, want to grant execution privileges to specific users instead of everyone. Step 2 must be repeated for every user who wants to use the profiling tools. An alternative is for the DBA to create public synonyms for the tables and sequence created, thereby having only one copy of the profiler table, in which case the solution changes as in the following example. In the following recipe, replace [Oracle_Home] with the exact path used to install the database software on your system.

```
connect sys/sys_pwd as sysdba
@[Oracle_Home]/RDBMS/ADMIN/profload.sql
grant execute on DBMS_PROFILER to USER1, USER2, USER3;
@[Oracle_Home]/RDBMS/ADMIN/proftab.sql

CREATE PUBLIC SYNONYM plsql_profiler_data FOR plsql_profiler_data;
CREATE PUBLIC SYNONYM plsql_profiler_units FOR plsql_profiler_units;
CREATE PUBLIC SYNONYM plsql_profiler_runs FOR plsql_profiler_runs;
CREATE PUBLIC SYNONYM plsql_profiler_runnumber FOR plsql_profiler_runnumber;
```

13-2. Identifying Bottlenecks

Problem

You notice that a PL/SQL program is running slowly, and you need to identify what sections of the code are causing it to perform poorly.

Solution

Use the DBMS_PROFILER routines to analyze the code and find potential bottlenecks. In the following example, the profiler is used to collect statistics on a run of a program, and then a query displays the statistics.

```
EXEC DBMS_PROFILER.START_PROFILER ('Test1', 'Testing One');
EXEC sync_hr_data;    -- the procedure identifed has having a bottleneck
EXEC DBMS_PROFILER.FLUSH_DATA;
EXEC DBMS_PROFILER.STOP_PROFILER;
```

Now that the profile data is collected, you can query the underlying tables to see the results of the analysis:

```
COL line# FORMAT 999
COL hundredth FORMAT a6

SELECT     d.line#,
           to_char (d.total_time/10000000, '999.00') hundredth,
           s.text
FROM       user_source       s,
           plsql_profiler_data   d,
           plsql_profiler_units  u,
           plsql_profiler_runs   r
WHERE  r.run_comment      = 'Test1' -- run_comment matches the text in START_PROFILER
AND    u.runid            = r.runid
AND    u.unit_owner       = r.run_owner
AND    d.runid            = r.runid
AND    d.unit_number      = u.unit_number
AND    s.name             = u.unit_name
AND    s.line             = d.line#
ORDER BY d.line#;
```

Here are the results of the previous query:

```
1     .00 PROCEDURE sync_hr_data AS
3     .00 CURSOR     driver is
4   11.58 SELECT     *
5     .00 FROM       employees@hr_data;
9    2.25    FOR recs IN driver LOOP
10   1.64       UPDATE      employees
15    .01 END sync_hr_data;
```

Here is the complete source code for the sync_hr_data procedure:

```
CREATE OR REPLACE PROCEDURE sync_hr_data AS

CURSOR    driver IS
SELECT    *
FROM      employees@hr_data;

BEGIN

   FOR recs IN driver LOOP
      UPDATE employees
      SET    first_name = recs.first_name
      WHERE  employee_id = recs.employee_id;
   END LOOP;

END sync_hr_data;
```

How It Works

There are four steps necessary to collect statistics on a running procedure:

1. Call the DBMS_PROFILER.START_PROFILER routine to begin the process of collecting statistics. The two parameters allow you to give the run a name and a comment. Unique names are not required, but that will make it easier to query the results later.

2. Execute the program you suspect has bottleneck issues; in this example, we run the sync_hr_data program.

3. Execute DBMS_PROFILER.FLUSH_DATA to write the data collected to the profiler tables.

4. Call the DBMS_PROFILER.STOP_PROFILER routine to, as the name implies, stop the collection of statistics.

The query joins the profiler data with the source code lines to display executable lines and the execution time, in hundredths of a second. The raw data stores time in nanoseconds. The query results show three lines of code with actual execution time.

The SELECT statement from the program unit in question, in which Oracle must establish a remote connection via a database link, consumes the majority of the execution time. The remainder of the time is consumed by the FOR statement, which fetches each record from the remote database connection, and the UPDATE statement, which writes the data to the local database.

Selecting records in the loop and then updating them causes the program to switch context between PL/SQL and the database engine. Each iteration of the LOOP causes this switch to occur. In this example, there were 107 employee records updated. The next recipe shows you how to improve the performance of this procedure.

13-3. Speeding Up Read/Write Loops

Problem

You have identified a loop that reads and writes large batches of data. You want to speed it up.

Solution

Use a BULK COLLECT statement to fetch the target data records, and then use a FORALL loop to update the local database. For example, suppose you want to speed up the sync_hr_data procedure demonstrated in Chapter 11:

```
CREATE OR REPLACE PROCEDURE sync_hr_data AS

CURSOR    driver IS
SELECT    *
FROM      employees@hr_data;

TYPE      recs_type IS TABLE OF driver%ROWTYPE INDEX BY BINARY_INTEGER;
recs      recs_type;

BEGIN

    OPEN driver;
    FETCH driver BULK COLLECT INTO recs;
    CLOSE driver;

    FORALL i IN 1..recs.COUNT
       UPDATE     employees
       SET        first_name  = recs(i).first_name
       WHERE      employee_id = recs(i).employee_id;

END sync_hr_data;
```

Run the profiler procedures to collect additional statistics:

```
EXEC DBMS_PROFILER.START_PROFILER ('Test2', 'Testing Two');
EXEC sync_hr_data;
EXEC DBMS_PROFILER.FLUSH_DATA;
EXEC DBMS_PROFILER.STOP_PROFILER;
```

Query the underlying tables to see the results of the analysis:

```
COL line# FORMAT 999
COL hundreth FORMAT A6

SELECT    d.line#,
          TO_CHAR (d.total_time/10000000, '999.00') hundreths,
          s.text
```

```
FROM     user_source          s,
         plsql_profiler_data    d,
         plsql_profiler_units   u,
         plsql_profiler_runs    r
WHERE    r.run_comment      = 'Test2'
AND      u.runid            = r.runid
AND      u.unit_owner       = r.run_owner
AND      d.runid            = r.runid
AND      d.unit_number      = u.unit_number
AND      s.name             = u.unit_name
AND      s.line             = d.line#
ORDER BY d.line#;
```

```
1      .00 PROCEDURE sync_hr_data AS
3      .00 CURSOR    driver is
4    11.54 SELECT    *
5      .00 FROM      employees@hr_data;
12     .00     OPEN driver;
13    1.61     FETCH driver BULK COLLECT INTO recs;
14     .01     CLOSE driver;
16    1.15     FORALL i IN 1..recs.COUNT
21     .00 END sync_hr_data;
```

How It Works

The procedure is updated from the previous recipe to use a BULK COLLECT statement to gather the data into a collection. The update statement uses the FORALL command to pass the entire collection of data to the Oracle engine for processing rather than updating one row at a time. BULK COLLECT and FORALL loops pass the entire dataset of the collections to the database engine for processing, unlike the loop in recipe 13-2, where each iteration passes only one record at a time from the collection to the database. The constant switching back and forth between PL/SQL and the database engine creates unnecessary overhead.

Perform the following steps to collect statistics on the update procedure:

1. Run the DBMS_PROFILER.START_PROFILER routine to begin the process of collecting statistics. You use the two parameters of the routine to give the run a name and to post a comment. Unique names are not required, but doing so will make it easier to query the results later.

2. Run the sync_hr_data program to collect statistics.

3. Run the DBMS_PROFILER.FLUSH_DATA procedure to write the data collected to the tables.

4. Run the DBMS_PROFILER.STOP_PROFILER routine to, as the name implies, stop the collection of statistics.

The query joins the profiler data, using the run name of Test2, with the source code lines to display executable lines and the execution time, in hundredths of a second. The raw data stores time in nanoseconds. The query results show three lines of code with actual execution time.

Comparing these results with the previous recipe, we note a 28 percent improvement, 2.25 to 1.61, in fetching the records via the BULK COLLECT statement, and a 30 percent improvement, 1.64 to 1.15, in the writing of the records via the FORALL statements. This improvement is realized while processing only

107 records. Greater gains can be realized with larger data sets, especially when selecting records via a remote database link as there are fewer context switches between PL/SQL and the Oracle engine.

13-4. Passing Large or Complex Collections as OUT Parameters

Problem

You have a procedure or function that accepts one or more large or complex collections that are also OUT parameters, and you need a more efficient method to pass these variables.

Solution

Pass the parameters to your procedure or function by reference using the NOCOPY option on the procedure or function declaration.

```
CREATE OR REPLACE PACKAGE no_copy_test AS

   TYPE rec_type IS TABLE OF all_objects%ROWTYPE INDEX BY BINARY_INTEGER;
   PROCEDURE test;

END no_copy_test;
/
show error

CREATE OR REPLACE PACKAGE BODY no_copy_test AS

PROCEDURE proc1 (rec_list IN OUT rec_type) IS
BEGIN
   FOR i IN 1..rec_list.COUNT LOOP
      rec_list(i) := rec_list(i);
   END LOOP;
END;

PROCEDURE proc2 (rec_list IN OUT NOCOPY rec_type) IS
BEGIN
   FOR i IN 1..rec_list.COUNT LOOP
      rec_list(i) := rec_list(i);
   END LOOP;
END;

PROCEDURE test IS

CURSOR  driver IS
SELECT  *
FROM    all_objects;

recs        rec_type;
rec_count   integer;

BEGIN
```

```
    OPEN driver;
    FETCH DRIVER BULK COLLECT INTO recs;
    CLOSE driver;

    rec_count := recs.COUNT;

    DBMS_OUTPUT.PUT_LINE (systimestamp);
    proc1 (recs); -- parameter passed by value
    DBMS_OUTPUT.PUT_LINE (systimestamp);
    proc2 (recs); -- paramter passed by reference
    DBMS_OUTPUT.PUT_LINE (systimestamp);
END test;

END no_copy_test;

set serverout on  -- Enable output from DBMS_OUTPUT statements
EXEC no_copy_test.test;
```

Running the procedure produced the following output:

```
03-NOV-10 05.05.14.865000000 PM -05:00
03-NOV-10 05.05.14.880000000 PM -05:00
03-NOV-10 05.05.14.880000000 PM -05:00
```

How It Works

The recipe utilizes the NOCOPY feature within PL/SQL. It begins by defining two procedures within the test package. The first procedure, PROC1, accepts a collection of records using the default parameter-passing method, which is by VALUE. The second procedure, PROC2, is an exact copy of PROC1; however, its parameter is passed using the NOCOPY option. In PROC1, the parameter is passed in by VALUE, which means a copy of the entire collection is created in the REC_LIST variable within PROC1. In PROC2, the parameter data is passed by REFERENCE. Passing a parameter by reference does not copy the data; rather, it uses the existing data structure passed to it by the calling program. This method is more efficient for very large collections in both running time and in memory usage.

The output from the test shows the first procedure, which passed its parameter by VALUE took longer to run than the second procedure, which passed its parameter by REFERENCE. In this example, the USER_OBJECTS table was used as the data for the parameter, which retrieved only 6,570 records. Larger performance gains can be realized with more records and more complex data structures.

13-5. Optimizing Computationally Intensive Code

Problem

You have computationally intensive code that you want to optimize to decrease its running time.

Solution

Recompile the package, procedure, or function in native mode using the NATIVE setting:

```
ALTER PACKAGE my_package COMPILE BODY PLSQL_CODE_TYPE=NATIVE REUSE SETTINGS;
ALTER PROCEDURE my_procedure COMPILE PLSQL_CODE_TYPE=NATIVE REUSE SETTINGS;
ALTER FUNCTION my_function COMPILE PLSQL_CODE_TYPE=NATIVE REUSE SETTINGS;
```

Here is an example of a computationally intensive procedure. It uses the factorial function from Recipe 17-4.

```
CREATE OR REPLACE PROCEDURE factorial_test as

fact    NUMBER;

BEGIN

    FOR i IN 1..100 LOOP
        fact := factorial(33);
    END LOOP;

END factorial_test;

  -- enable display of execution time
SET TIMING ON

  -- run the test
EXEC factorial_test

PL/SQL procedure successfully completed.
Elapsed: 00:00:01.18
```

Now, recompile the code using the NATIVE option and rerun the test, noting any change in running time:

```
ALTER PROCEDURE factorial_test COMPILE PLSQL_CODE_TYPE=NATIVE REUSE SETTINGS;

EXEC factorial_test

PL/SQL procedure successfully completed.
Elapsed: 00:00:00.42
```

How It Works

The ALTER. . .COMPILE command invokes the compiler on the named object. The syntax differs slightly when recompiling a PACKAGE body in that the BODY clause follows the COMPILE statement. The PLSQL_CODE_TYPE=NATIVE clause compiles the code in NATIVE format, which runs faster than interpreted code. The REUSE SETTINGS clause ensures the code will be recompiled in the same mode if it later becomes invalid and requires automatic recompilation.

Native mode realizes the most benefit from computational intensive code; it has little effect on DML statements (in other words, SELECT, INSERT, UPDATE, and DELETE). In the previous example, the factorial function is called repeatedly to simulate a computationally intensive procedure. When the procedure is compiled in the default, interpretive method, it completes its run in 1.18 seconds. When compiled in NATIVE mode, it completes in 0.42 seconds. This is a 64 percent improvement in running time!

13-6. Improving Initial Execution Running Time

Problem

You have a procedure that you run frequently, and you want to improve its overall running time by minimizing its startup time.

Solution

Use the DBMS_SHAPRED_POOL.KEEP procedure to keep a permanent copy of your code in the shared memory pool. For example, the following statement pins the procedure my_large_procedure in the database's shared memory pool:

```
DBMS_SHARED_POOL.KEEP (
   Name => 'my_large_procedure',
   flag => 'P');
```

How It Works

The DBMS_SHARED_POOL.KEEP procedure permanently keeps your code in the shared memory pool. By default, when PL/SQL code is executed, Oracle must first read the entire block of code into memory if it isn't already there from a previous execution. As additional procedures are executed, less recently used code in the shared memory pool begins to age. If there isn't sufficient free space in the shared memory pool, older code is removed to make room.

If large procedures are run frequently and are aging out of the shared memory pool, then pinning the procedure in the shared memory pool can improve performance by removing the overhead necessary to reload the procedure again and again.

The first parameter of the DBMS_SHARED_POOL.KEEP procedure is the name of the object you want to pin in the shared memory pool. The second parameter identifies the object type of the first parameter. The most commonly used values for FLAG are as follows:

- P: The default, which specifies the object is a package, procedure, or function

- T: Specifies the object is a trigger

- Q: Specifies the object is a sequence

You must have execute privileges on the DBMS_SHARED_POOL package to pin your code. An account with SYSDBA privileges must grant execute on DBMS_SHARED_POOL to your schema or to public.

CHAPTER 14

■■■

Using PL/SQL on the Web

Oracle's Application Server provides a powerful gateway that exposes your PL/SQL procedures to web browsers. The gateway is defined using a Data Access Descriptor (DAD) that runs PL/SQL code as either the user defined in the DAD or as the user running the web application.

Oracle provides a PL/SQL Web Toolkit, which is a set of procedures and functions that generate HTML tags. In addition to making your code easier to read and manage, the toolkit sends the HTML code through Apache directly to the client web browser.

The following recipes teach you how to write PL/SQL procedures that produce interactive web pages. These recipes can be combined to create solutions for complex business applications.

14-1. Running a PL/SQL Procedure on the Web

Problem

You'd like to make your PL/SQL procedures accessible to users in a web browser via the Oracle Application Server.

Solution

To run a PL/SQL procedure on the Web, you must first configure a Data Access Descriptor (DAD) within the Oracle Application Server to define the connection information required between mod_plsql within the Oracle Application Server and the Oracle database that holds the PL/SQL procedures you wish to run. In this example the mod_plsql configuration file dads.conf (located in [Oracle_Home]\Apache\ modplsql\conf) is edited to define the DAD.

```
<Location /DAD_NAME>
    SetHandler pls_handler
    Order deny,allow
    Deny from all
    Allow from localhost node1.mycompany.com node2.mycompany.com
    AllowOverride None

    PlsqlDatabaseUsername ORACLE_SCHEMA_NAME
    PlsqlDatabasePassword PASSWORD
    PlsqlDatabaseConnectString TNS_ENTRY
    PlsqlSessionStateManagement StatelessWithResetPackageState
    PlsqlMaxRequestsPerSession 1000
    PlsqlFetchBufferSize 128
    PlsqlCGIEnvironmentList QUERY_STRING
    PlsqlErrorStyle DebugStyle
```

```
</Location>
```

You may repeat the `<Location>` data for additional DADs as required; perhaps one DAD for every major application. You must restart the Oracle Application Server for changes to the DAD configuration file to take effect.

How It Works

To verify that your DAD is configured properly and will run your PL/SQL code, log into the Oracle database defined in your DAD. The Oracle database account is defined in the `PlsqlDatabaseUsername`, `PlsqlDatabasePassword` and `PlsqlDatabaseConnectString` statements. Next, compile the following test procedure.

```
create or replace procedure test as
begin
    htp.p ('Hello World!');
end;
```

Finally, point your web browser to http://node_name/DAD_NAME/test. Where node_name is the name of the machine where the Oracle Application Server is installed and `DAD_NAME` is the name assigned your DAD in the `<Location>` tag within the `mod_plsql` configuration file and test is the name of the PL/SQL procedure create for this test. Your browser should respond with the text "Hello World!"

The `<Location>` tag within the `dads.conf` file defines the equivalent of a virtual directory within Apache. When a request reaches the Oracle iAS Apache web server containing the location name defined in the DAD, the PL/SQL package or procedure specified in the remaining portion of the URL is executed. For example, if the URL is http://node.my_company.com/plsqlcgi/employee.rpt, plsqlcgi is the `DAD_NAME`, then `employee` is the package name and `rpt` is the procedure name. Calls to the PLSQL Web Toolkit within the `employee.rpt` procedure send output directly to the client's web browser.

The `SetHandler` directive invokes `mod_plsql` within Apache to handle requests for the virtual path defined by the `<Location>` tag. This directive is required to run PL/SQL packages and procedures through the Apache web server.

The next three directives restrict access to the virtual path to the nodes specified on the `Allow from` line. To allow access from any web browser in the world, replace these three directives with the following two.

- `Order allow,deny`

- `Allow from all`

The `PlsqlDatabase` directives define the connection information `mod_plsql` needs to log into the database. If the `PlsqlDatabasePassword` directive is supplied, Apache will automatically log into the database when requests from web clients are processed. The `TNS_ENTRY` is used to complete the login information. If the `PlsqlDatabasePassword` directive is omitted, the Web browser prompts the user for a username and password. The username entered by the user must exist in the database specified by the `TNS_ENTRY` name and the user must have execute privileges to the requested procedure. The procedure must be accessible to the `ORACLE_SCHEMA_NAME` specified in `PlsqlDatabaseUsername`. In other words, the schema must own the procedure or, if owned by another schema, it must have execute privileges to the procedure.

14-2. Creating a Common Set of HTML Page Generation Procedures

Problem

Every web page you generate with a PL/SQL procedure requires a common HTML tag to start and another to finish every web page, and you do not wish to repeat the code to add those tags in every procedure you write for the Web.

Solution

Create a package that contains calls to the PL/SQL Web Toolkit procedures that produce the HTML code necessary to properly display a well-formed,[1] HTML web page. In this example a package is created with two procedures, one to generate the HTML tags required to start a page and one to generate the closing HTML tags to finish a page.

```
CREATE OR REPLACE PACKAGE common AS

    PROCEDURE header (title VARCHAR2);
    PROCEDURE footer;

END common;

CREATE OR REPLACE PACKAGE BODY common AS

PROCEDURE header (title VARCHAR2) IS

BEGIN

    htp.p ('<!DOCTYPE HTML PUBLIC "-//W3C//DTD HTML 4.0 Transitional//EN" ' ||
          '"http://www.w3.org/TR/REC-html40/loose.dtd">');
    htp.htmlOpen;
    htp.headOpen;
    htp.meta ('Content-Type', null, 'text/html;' ||
            owa_util.get_cgi_env('REQUEST_IANA_CHARSET') );
    htp.meta ('Pragma', null, 'no-cache');
    htp.Title (title);
    htp.headClose;
    htp.bodyOpen;
    htp.header (2, title);

END HEADER;

PROCEDURE footer IS

BEGIN
```

---

[1] A well-formed HTML web page conforms to the standards defined by The World Wide Web Consortium (W3C). You can validate your HTML web pages at http://validator.w3.org/.

```
-- This is a great place to add legal disclaimers, about us, contact us, etc. links
   htp.hr;  -- horizontal line
   htp.anchor ('http://www.mynode.com/legal_statement.html', 'Disclaimer');
   htp.anchor ('http://www.mynode.com/About.html', 'About Us');
   htp.bodyClose;
   htp.htmlClose;

END footer;

END common;
```

How It Works

Recipe 14-1 includes a test procedure to verify the DAD is setup correctly; however the test procedure does not produce a well-formed HTML page. Here is the updated example from Recipe 14-1, this time with calls to the common header and footer procedures.

```
create or replace procedure test as
begin
    common.header ('Test Page');
    htp.p ('Hello World!');
    common.footer;
end;
```

This procedure, when called from a web browser, produces the following HTML code.

```
<!DOCTYPE HTML PUBLIC "-//W3C//DTD HTML 4.0 Transitional//EN" "http://www.w3.org/↵
TR/REC-html40/loose.dtd">
<HTML>
<HEAD>
<META HTTP-EQUIV="Content-Type" NAME="" CONTENT="text/html;WINDOWS-1252">
<META HTTP-EQUIV="Pragma" NAME="" CONTENT="no-cache">
<TITLE>Test Page</TITLE>
<BODY>
<H2>Test Page</H2>
Hello World!
</BODY>
</HTML>
```

The header routine generates the necessary opening HTML code to properly display a web page. It begins by setting the document type, then sending the opening <HTML> and <HEAD> tags. It sets the content-type to the character set defined in the Apache environment variable, which is retrieved using a call to the PL/SQL Web Toolkit's owa_util.get_cgi_env routine. The Pragma <META> tag tells the browser not to store the page's content in its internal cache. This is useful when the PL/SQL routine returns time-sensitive data because the users need to see real-time data. The remaining code sets the title in the user's browser, opens the <BODY> tag and displays the title on the user's web browser.

The footer routine closes the <BODY> and <HTML> tags. As stated in the code's comments, this is a good place to include any legal disclaimers or other useful text or links required for every web page generated.

Oftentimes when creating an application, you will create several procedures that will make use of the same code. You could copy the code throughout your procedures, but it is more efficient and safer to write once and use in many different places. The creation of a common codebase that is accessible to each PL/SQL object within a schema can be quite an effective solution for storing such code.

14-3 Creating an Input Form

Problem

You require a web page that accepts and processes data entered by users. The data should be collected on the opening page and processed (stored in a table, used to update rows in a table, etc.) when the user clicks the Submit button.

Solution

Create a package using the Oracle PL/SQL Web Toolkit to display a data entry form and process the results. In this example a simple data entry form is created to collect employee information and send the user's input to a second procedure for processing.

■ **Note** See Recipe 14-2 for more information on the common package, which is used in this recipe.

```
CREATE OR REPLACE PACKAGE input_form AS

    null_array OWA_UTIL.IDENT_ARR;

    PROCEDURE html;
    PROCEDURE submit (emp_id     VARCHAR2,
                      gender     VARCHAR2 DEFAULT NULL,
                      options    OWA_UTIL.IDENT_ARR DEFAULT null_array,
                      comments   varchar2);

END input_form;

CREATE OR REPLACE PACKAGE BODY input_form AS

PROCEDURE html IS

type    options_type is varray(3) of varchar2(50);
options options_type := options_type ('I will attend the Team Meeting',
                        'I will attend the social event',
                        'I will attend the company tour');

BEGIN

    common.header ('Input Form');
    htp.formOpen ('input_form.submit', 'POST');

    htp.p ('Employee ID: ');
```

```
    htp.formText ('emp_id', 9, 9);
    htp.br;

    htp.p ('Gender: ');
    htp.formRadio ('gender', 'M');
    htp.p ('Male');
    htp.formRadio ('gender', 'F');
    htp.p ('Female');
    htp.br;

    FOR i IN 1..10 LOOP
        htp.formCheckBox ('options', i);
        htp.p (options(i));
        htp.br;
    END LOOP;
    htp.br;

    htp.p ('COMMENTS: ');
    htp.formTextArea ('comments', 5, 50);
    htp.br;

    htp.formSubmit;
    htp.formClose;
    common.footer;

END html;

PROCEDURE submit (emp_id      VARCHAR2,
                  gender      VARCHAR2 DEFAULT NULL,
                  options     OWA_UTIL.IDENT_ARR DEFAULT null_array,
                  comments    varchar2) is

BEGIN

    common.header ('Input Results');
    htp.bold ('You entered the following...');
    htp.br;

    htp.p ('Employee ID: ' || emp_id);
    htp.br;
    htp.p ('Gender: ' || gender);
    htp.br;
    htp.p ('Comments: ' || comments);
    htp.br;

    htp.bold ('Options Selected...');
    htp.br;
    FOR i IN 1..options.COUNT LOOP
        htp.p (options(i));
        htp.br;
    END LOOP;
```

```
    common.footer;

END submit;

END input_form;
```

How It Works

Access the web page using a link with an HTML anchor URL of http://node.mycompany.com/DAD_NAME/
input_form.html.

▨ **Note** See Recipe 14-1 to define the DAD_NAME.

The input_form package specification defines an empty collection named null_array as the type
OWA_UTIL.IDENT_ARR. It is used as the default value in the event the web form is submitted without
checking at least one of the check boxes. Without the default value for the input parameter options, the
call to input_form.submit will not work and returns an error to the user if no boxes are checked.

▨ **Note** See Recipe 14-9 for more information on viewing errors.

The two procedures, html and submit, exposed in the package specification, are required to make
them visible to the PL/SQL module within the Apache web server. It is important to note that it is not
possible to call procedures via a URL if they are not defined in the package specification.

The html procedure generates the data entry form shown in Figure 14-1. It begins with a call to
header common procedure, which generates the opening HTML tags. The htp.formOpen call generates
the <FORM> tag with the destination of the submit button to the submit procedure within the input_form
package.

The htp.p procedure call sends the data passed to it directly to the client's web browser, this
procedure should not be confused with the htp.para, which produces the <P> tag. The htp.br call sends
the <BR> tag to the client's web browser.

The remainder of the procedure generates several form elements that accept user input. The
htp.formText call generates a simple text box that accepts nine bytes. The htp.formRadio routine is called
twice with the same variable name in the first parameter. This defines the variable gender with one of
two possible values, M or F. The call to htp.formCheckBox within the FOR…LOOP generates the checkboxes,
each having a unique value returned if checked by the user. Only the values checked are sent in a
collection to the submit routine. The call to htp.formTextArea creates a multi-line, text box 50 characters
wide and 5 lines deep. See Table 14-1 for a list of common PL/SQL Web Toolkit procedures that generate
HTML form tags.

The procedure ends with a calls to htp.formSubmit and htp.formClose, which generate the form's
submit button and the closing </FORM> tag. When the user clicks the submit button, the client's web
browser sends the data entered into the form to the submit routine within the input_form package.

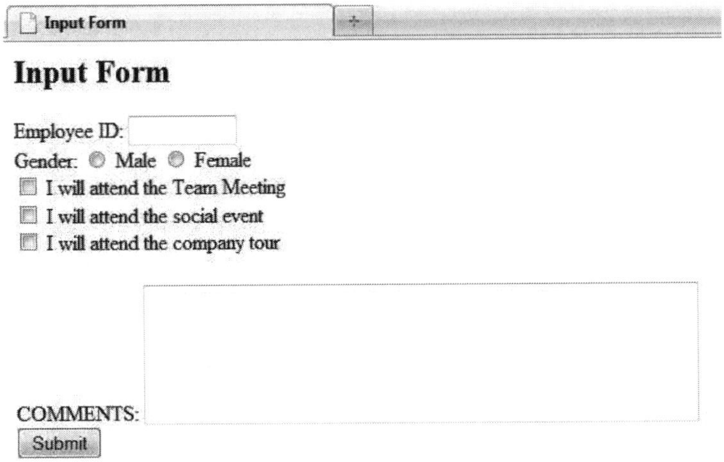

Figure 14-1. *Form generated by the input_form.html procedure*

Table 14-1. *Common form procedures in the PL/SQL Web Toolkit*

Toolkit Procedure	HTML Tag
htp.formCheckbox	<INPUT TYPE="CHECKBOX">
htp.formClose	</FORM>
htp.formHidden	<INPUT TYPE="HIDDEN">
htp.formImage	<IPUT TYPE="IMAGE">
htp.formOpen	<FORM>
htp.formPassword	<INPUT TYPE="PASSWORD">
htp.formRadio	<INPUT TYPE="RADIO">
htp.formReset	<INPUT TYPE="RESET">
htp.formSelectClose	</SELECT>
htp.formSelectOpen	<SELECT>
htp.formSelectOption	<OPTION>
htp.formSubmit	<INPUT TYPE="SUBMIT">

Toolkit Procedure	HTML Tag
htp.formText	<INPUT TYPE="TEXT">
htp.formTextarea	<TEXTAREA></TEXTAREA>
htp.formTextareaClose	</TEXTAREA>
htp.formTextareaOpen	<TEXTAREA>

14-4. Creating a Web–based Report Using PL/SQL Procedures

Problem

You need to generate a web page report that displays the results of a database query.

Solution

Create a package with two procedures, one to accept a user's input, and another to query the database and display the results. Suppose, for example, that you need a report that displays information for an employee whose employee ID has been entered by an authorized user. This recipe uses the employee table in the HR schema.

> ■ **Note** When defining packages that contain procedures you wish to access via web browsers, you must include each procedure you wish to access in the package specification.

> ■ **Note** See Recipe 14-2 for more information on the common package, which is used in this recipe.

```
CREATE OR REPLACE PACKAGE emp_rpt AS

   PROCEDURE html;
   PROCEDURE rpt (emp_id VARCHAR2);

END emp_rpt;

CREATE OR REPLACE PACKAGE BODY emp_rpt AS

PROCEDURE html IS

BEGIN
```

```
    common.header ('Employee Report');
    htp.formOpen ('emp_rpt.rpt', 'POST');
    htp.p ('Employee ID:');
    htp.formText ('emp_id', 6, 6);
    htp.formSubmit;
    htp.formClose;
    common.footer;  -- See recipe 14-2 for the common package.


END html;

PROCEDURE show_row (label VARCHAR2, value VARCHAR2) IS

BEGIN

    htp.tableRowOpen ('LEFT', 'TOP');
    htp.tableHeader (label, 'RIGHT');
    htp.tableData (value);
    htp.tableRowClose;

END show_row;

PROCEDURE rpt (emp_id VARCHAR2) IS

CURSOR  driver IS
SELECT  *
FROM    employees
WHERE   employee_id = emp_id;

rec             driver%ROWTYPE;
rec_found       BOOLEAN;

BEGIN

    common.header ('Employee Report');

    OPEN driver;
    FETCH driver INTO rec;
    rec_found := driver%FOUND;
    CLOSE driver;

    IF rec_found THEN
        htp.tableOpen;
        show_row ('Employee ID', rec.employee_id);
        show_row ('First Name', rec.first_name);
        show_row ('Last Name', rec.last_name);
        show_row ('Email', rec.email);
        show_row ('Phone', rec.phone_number);
        show_row ('Hire Date', rec.hire_date);
        show_row ('Salary', rec.salary);
        show_row ('Commission %', rec.commission_pct);
        htp.tableClose;
```

```
ELSE
   htp.header (3, 'No such employee ID ' || emp_id);
END IF;

common.footer; -- See recipe 14-2 for the common package.

EXCEPTION
   WHEN OTHERS THEN
   htp.header (3, 'Invalid employee ID. Click your browser''s back button and try again.');
   common.footer;

END rpt;

END emp_rpt;
```

How It Works

Users access the web page using the URL http://node.mycompany.com/DAD_NAME/emp_rpt.html.

■ **Note** See Recipe 14-1 for more on how to define the DAD_NAME.

The package specification is defined with two procedures, html and rpt. Exposing these procedures in the specification is required to make the PL/SQL procedures available within Apache.

Next, the package body is defined. The html procedure generates the data entry form. It generates the opening HTML code by calling the common.header routine defined in recipe 14-2. Next, it calls the htp.formOpen to set the form's action, which is to run the PL/SQL procedure emp_rpt.rpt, when the user clicks the submit button and to send the form data in a POST method, as opposed to GET. A simple prompt and a text box follows to allow the user to enter an employee ID. A call to form.submit, form.close and common.footer complete the HTML code.

The show_row procedure is a handy subroutine to output one table row with two data cells. It displays data on the client's browser in a formatted table, making it more visually appealing.

The rpt procedure accepts the user's input in the emp_id parameter and uses it to query the employee record. The common.header routine generates the opening HTML code. The cursor is opened and the data is fetched into the rec data structure. The rec_found variable stores the flag that identifies if a record was fetched. It needs to be referenced after the fetch and before the close. If a record is found, the employee data is displayed in a two-column table, shown in Figure 14-2, otherwise a message is sent to the user that the employee ID is not valid.

The exception is necessary to trap the error generated if the user enters a non-numeric employee ID. Another option is to validate the user's input prior to using it in the cursor query.

■ **Note** See recipe 14-10 for an example of validating user input.

Employee Report

Employee ID 200

First Name Jennifer

Last Name Whalen

Email JWHALEN

Phone 515.123.4444

Hire Date 17-SEP-87

Salary 6501

Commission %

Figure 14-2. Results from entering employee ID 200 on the previous data entry screen

14-5. Displaying Data from Tables

Problem

You wish to provide the results from an SQL SELECT statement to the users via a web browser.

Solution

Use the Oracle PL/SQL Web Toolkit to SELECT and display data. The owa_util.tablePrint procedure accepts any table name for the ctable parameter. When this procedure is compiled in a schema with a DAD it can be accessed via the Web. This example displays information similar to the describe feature within SQL*Plus.

■ **Note** See Recipe 14-1 to define a DAD and direct your browser to run your procedure.

■ **Note** See Recipe 14-2 for more information on the common package, which is used in this recipe.

```
CREATE OR REPLACE PROCEDURE descr_emp IS

BEGIN

    common.header ('The Employees Table');

    IF owa_util.tablePrint (
            ctable=>'user_tab_columns',
        cattributes=>'BORDER',
```

```
                 ccolumns=>'column_name, data_type, data_length, data_precision, nullable',
                 cclauses=>'WHERE table_name=''EMPLOYEES'' ORDER BY column_id') then
       NULL;
   END IF;

   common.footer;

END descr_emp;
```

How It Works

Users access the web page using the URL http://node.mycompany.com/DAD_NAME/emp_rpt.html. The descr_emp procedure calls the owa_util.tablePrint procedure, which is included in the PL/SQL Web Toolkit. The ctable parameter defines the table the owa_util.tablePrint procedure accesses to read the data. The cattributes parameter accepts options for the HTML <TABLE> tag. The ccolumns parameter allows you to specify which columns to select from the named table. If no columns are specified, then the procedure shows all columns. The cclauses parameter allows you to add a where clause and/or an order by statement. If no where clause is specified, all rows are returned. The output is shown in Figure 14-3.

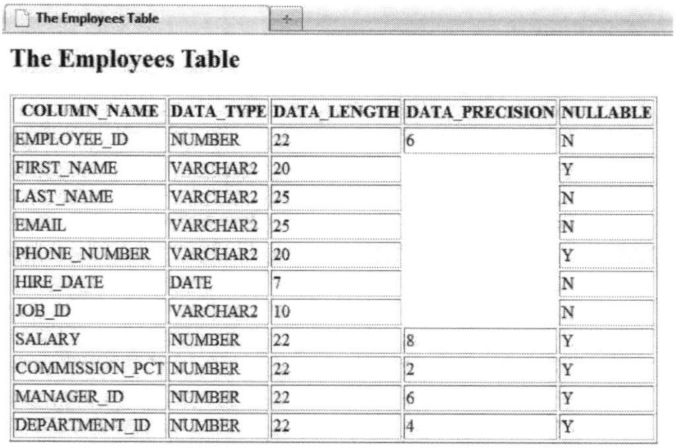

The Employees Table

COLUMN_NAME	DATA_TYPE	DATA_LENGTH	DATA_PRECISION	NULLABLE
EMPLOYEE_ID	NUMBER	22	6	N
FIRST_NAME	VARCHAR2	20		Y
LAST_NAME	VARCHAR2	25		N
EMAIL	VARCHAR2	25		N
PHONE_NUMBER	VARCHAR2	20		Y
HIRE_DATE	DATE	7		N
JOB_ID	VARCHAR2	10		N
SALARY	NUMBER	22	8	Y
COMMISSION_PCT	NUMBER	22	2	Y
MANAGER_ID	NUMBER	22	6	Y
DEPARTMENT_ID	NUMBER	22	4	Y

Figure 14-3. Results of the descr_emp procedure

14-6. Creating a Web Form Dropdown List from a Database Query

Problem

Your web form requires a dropdown list whose elements are drawn from a database table.

Solution

Use the `htp.formSelectOpen`, `htp.formSelectOption` and `htp.formSelectClose` procedures in the PL/SQL Web Toolkit to generate the required HTML tags. For example, suppose you need to use the HR schema to create a dropdown list of job titles from the JOBS table. Here's how you'd do it.

```
create or replace procedure job_list as

cursor  driver is
select  job_id, job_title
from    jobs
order by job_title;

begin

    common.header ('Job Title');
    htp.formSelectOpen ('id', 'Job Title: ');
    htp.formSelectOption ('', 'SELECTED');

    for rec in driver LOOP
        htp.formSelectOption (rec.job_title, cattributes=>'VALUE="' || rec.job_id || '"');
    end LOOP;

    htp.formSelectClose;
    common.footer;

end job_list;
```

This procedure produces the following web page.

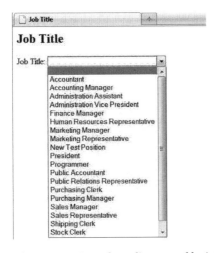

Figure 14-4. Dropdown list created by job_list procedure

How It Works

The `htp.formSelectOpen` procedure generates the HTML `<SELECT NAME="id">`, which defines the dropdown list in the web browser. In addition the procedure uses the second parameter as the prompt for the dropdown list. In this example the prompt is `Job Title:`.

The call to `htp.formSelectOption` procedure defines the elements of the dropdown list. The first parameter is the text displayed in the list and the second parameter preselects the element in the list when it is first displayed. In this example the first call to the `htp.formSelectOption` procedure defines the default selected element in the list to an empty value.

The subsequent calls to `htp.formSelectOption` that appear in the cursor for loop define the remaining elements in the dropdown list using the data selected from the `JOBS` table. The `cattributes` parameter is used to change the default value returned by the web browser when the element is selected from the list.

The call to `htp.formSelectClose` generates the `</SELECT>` HTML tag to close the dropdown list. Dropdown lists usually appear within the `<FORM>` tags to accept user input and process that input on a subsequent page.

■ **Note** See Recipe 14-3 for more information on creating an input form.

14-7. Creating a Sortable Web Report

Problem

You need a report that displays data that is sorted by a field the user selects.

Solution

Create a package that prompts the user for a sort field, then generates the sorted output using the sort field parameter in the `ORDER BY` section of the `SELECT` statement. In this example the user is prompted to select a sort option on the `EMPLOYEES` table. The options are to sort by last name, hire date, salary, or employee ID.

■ **Note** See Recipe 14-1 to define a DAD and direct your browser to run your procedure.

■ **Note** See Recipe 14-2 for more information on the common package, which is used in this recipe.

```
CREATE OR REPLACE PACKAGE sorted AS

    PROCEDURE html;
```

```
    PROCEDURE rpt (sort_order VARCHAR2);

END sorted;

CREATE OR REPLACE PACKAGE BODY sorted AS

PROCEDURE html IS

BEGIN

    common.header ('Sorted Report');
    htp.formOpen ('sorted.rpt', 'POST');
    htp.formSelectOpen ('sort_order', 'Select a Sort Order: ');
    htp.formSelectOption ('Last Name');
    htp.formSelectOption ('Hire Date');
    htp.formSelectOption ('Salary');
    htp.formSelectOption ('Employee ID');
    htp.formSelectClose;
    htp.formSubmit;
    htp.formClose;
    common.footer;
END html;

PROCEDURE rpt (sort_order VARCHAR2) IS

CURSOR  driver IS
SELECT  *
FROM    employees
ORDER BY DECODE (sort_order,
                 'Last Name',   last_name,
                 'Hire Date',   TO_CHAR (hire_date, 'YYYYMMDD'),
                 'Salary',      TO_CHAR (salary, '00000'),
                 'Employee ID', TO_CHAR (employee_id, '00000') );

BEGIN

    common.header ('Sorted Report by '||sort_order); -- See recipe 14-2.
    htp.tableOpen ('BORDER');
    htp.tableRowOpen ('LEFT', 'BOTTOM');
    htp.tableHeader ('Name');
    htp.tableHeader ('Hired');
    htp.tableHeader ('Salary');
    htp.tableHeader ('ID');
    htp.tableRowClose;

    FOR rec IN driver LOOP
        htp.tableRowOpen ('LEFT', 'TOP');
        htp.tableData (rec.last_name);
        htp.tableData (rec.hire_date);
        htp.tableData (rec.salary);
        htp.tableData (rec.employee_id);
        htp.tableRowClose;
```

```
  END LOOP;

  htp.tableClose;
  common.footer;

END rpt;

END sorted;
```

How It Works

Users access the web page using the URL http://node.mycompany.com/DAD_NAME/sorted.html.

■ **Note** See Recipe 14-1 for more on how to to define the DAD_NAME.

The package specification is defined by exposing two procedures, html and rpt. You must define these procedures in the specification to make the PL/SQL procedures available within Apache.

Next, the package body is defined. The html procedure generates the data entry form. It generates the opening HTML code by calling the common.header routine defined in Recipe 14-2. Next, it calls the htp.formOpen to set the form's action when the user clicks the Submit button. The calls to htp.formSelectOpen, htp.formSelectOption and htp.formSelectClose procedures create the dropdown list for the user to select a sort order.

■ **Note** See Recipe 14-6 for more information on how to create dropdown lists.

A call to form.submit, form.close and common.footer complete the necessary HTML code. The form generated is shown in Figure 14-5.

The rpt procedure accepts the sort_order parameter, which is used in the cursor to dynamically determine the sort order on the EMPLOYEES table. The order by option in the select statement uses the decode function to return the proper string needed for ordering based on the user's input.

The first set of parameters sent to the decode function, namely the first_name field, defines the data type returned by the decode function. This is important to note as the remaining data types returned from the decode function will be converted to strings to match the first_name. It is necessary to convert the numeric and date fields to strings that sort properly. For example, if the default date string format is dd-Mon-yy, then the hire dates will sort by the day of the month first, then by the month's abbreviation and year. The desired sort order is year, month, then day.

Figure 14-5. Initial data entry screen showing the sort options

14-8. Passing Data Between Web Pages

Problem

You have a multi-page data entry form in which the final page requires data entered on pages that precede it. You need to pass the data gathered on previous pages to the current page.

Solution

Pass the name/value pairs from previous pages using the htp.formHidden procedure in the PL/SQL Web Toolkit. In this recipe each parameter is passed to the next form using hidden HTML elements.

```
CREATE OR REPLACE PACKAGE multi AS

    PROCEDURE page1;
    PROCEDURE page2 (var1 varchar2);
    PROCEDURE page3 (var1 varchar2, var2 varchar2);
    PROCEDURE process (var1 varchar2, var2 varchar2, var3 varchar2);

END multi;

CREATE OR REPLACE PACKAGE BODY multi AS

PROCEDURE page1 IS

begin

    htp.formOpen ('multi.page2', 'POST');
    htp.p ('Enter First Value:');
    htp.formText ('var1', 10, 10);
    htp.formSubmit;
    htp.formClose;

END page1;

PROCEDURE page2 (var1 VARCHAR2) IS
```

```
begin

    htp.formOpen ('multi.page3', 'POST');
    htp.formHidden ('var1', var1);
    htp.p ('Enter Second Value:');
    htp.formText ('var2', 10, 10);
    htp.formSubmit;
    htp.formClose;

END page2;

PROCEDURE page3 (var1 VARCHAR2, var2 VARCHAR2) IS

begin

    htp.formOpen ('multi.process', 'POST');
    htp.formHidden ('var1', var1);
    htp.formHidden ('var2', var2);
    htp.p ('Enter Third Value:');
    htp.formText ('var3', 10, 10);
    htp.formSubmit;
    htp.formClose;

END page3;

PROCEDURE process (var1 varchar2, var2 varchar2, var3 varchar2) is

BEGIN

  htp.p ('The three variables entered are...');
  htp.br;

  htp.p ('1=' || var1);
  htp.br;
  htp.p ('2=' || var2);
  htp.br;
  htp.p ('3=' || var3);

END process;

END multi;
```

How It Works

Users access the web page using the URL http://node.mycompany.com/DAD_NAME/multi.page1.

■ **Note** See Recipe 14.1 to define the DAD_NAME.

The page1 procedure within the mulit package prompts the user for an input value, which is passed to procedure page2 as its parameter, var1. The htp.formHidden call in the page2 procedure produces an HTML <INPUT> tag of type HIDDEN. In this recipe it produces the following HTML code in the client's web browser: <INPUT TYPE="hidden" NAME="var1" VALUE="xxx">, where xxx is the text the user entered on the first page of this multi-part form.

The page2 procedure then accepts more user input into the form variable var2, which is passed to page3 along with var1 collected on the first input page. The third page accepts the final user input and passes it to the process procedure, where final processing occurs.

14-9. Viewing Errors for Debugging Web Apps

Problem

You have a PL/SQL package or procedure called from a web client that generates errors and you need to view the error message.

Solution

Choose one of the following two solutions, depending on your circumstances.

Solution #1

If the package is in use in a production environment, then check the output of the Apache error log file. The log file location is defined in the httpd.conf configuration file. The default log file location is [oracle_home]\Apache\Apache\logs directory. Open the log file and search for the errors generated with a timestamp that corresponds to the approximate time the error was generated.

Solution #2

If the application is in development or running in a non-production environment, change the default error style within the DAD used to produce the web page that failed. The error style is defined in the DADS.CONF file located in [oracle_homme]\Apache\modplsql\conf. Set the PlsqlErrorStyle to DebugStyle.

■ **Note** See recipe 14-1 for more information on defining DADs.

How It Works

Solution #1

The PL/SQL module within Apache logs all errors, complete with timestamps. New errors are written to the end of the error log. This solution is recommended for production environments where the display of Apache environment variables may pose security issues.

Here's an example of an error message written to the error log. In this example, a procedure was called from the Web but was missing required parameters.

```
[error] [client 127.0.0.1] mod_plsql: /DAD_NAME/class_sched.list HTTP-404

class_sched.list: SIGNATURE (parameter names) MISMATCH
VARIABLES IN FORM NOT IN PROCEDURE:
NON-DEFAULT VARIABLES IN PROCEDURE NOT IN FORM: THIS_ID, THIS_ID_TYPE
```

Solution #2

Setting the PlsqlErrorStyle to DebugStyle causes Apache to display all PL/SQL error messages on the client's web browser when the PL/SQL routine fails. It displays the same error messages normally found in the Apache log file plus a list of all Apache environment variables and their values. This solution is recommended for non-production environments where errors are more likely to occur during development and testing. It has the advantage of immediate, onscreen feedback for developers and testers.

The following is an example of an error message written to the web browser.

```
class_sched.list: SIGNATURE (parameter names) MISMATCH
VARIABLES IN FORM NOT IN PROCEDURE:
NON-DEFAULT VARIABLES IN PROCEDURE NOT IN FORM: THIS_ID, THIS_ID_TYPE

  DAD name: default
  PROCEDURE  : class_sched.list
  URL        : http://node.mycomp.com/DAD_NAME/class_sched.list
  PARAMETERS :
  ===========

  ENVIRONMENT:
  ============
    PLSQL_GATEWAY=WebDb
    GATEWAY_IVERSION=3
        << snip >>
```

14-10. Generating JavaScript via PL/SQL

Problem

Your procedure requires JavaScript but you do not have access to the Oracle application server to store the script file to make it accessible from Apache.

Solution

Use the Oracle PL/SQLWeb Toolkit to output JavaScript within your PL/SQL procedure. There are two steps to define and enable a JavaScript within your PL/SQL procedure.

First, define the JavaScript source on the web page that requires access to your JavaScript routine using the HTML tag <SCRIPT>.

Define a PL/SQL procedure to match the name of the <SCRIPT> tag's source (SRC) property.

In the following example the html procedure defines the <SCRIPT> tag with the source set to empID.js and the js procedure generates the JavaScript code.

```
CREATE OR REPLACE PACKAGE empID IS

    PROCEDURE html;
    PROCEdURE js;

END empID;

CREATE OR REPLACE PACKAGE BODY empID IS

PROCEDURE html is

BEGIN

    common.header ('Employee Report'); -- See recipe 14-2 for the common package.
    htp.p ('<SCRIPT LANGUAGE="JavaScript" SRC="'               ||
                owa_util.get_cgi_env ('REQUEST_PROTOCOL')      || '://'        ||
                owa_util.get_cgi_env ('HTTP_HOST')             ||
                owa_util.get_cgi_env ('SCRIPT_NAME')           || '/empID.js"></SCRIPT>');

    htp.formOpen ('emp_rpt.rpt', 'POST'); -- See recipe 14-4 for the emp_rpt pacakge.
    htp.p ('Employee ID:');
    htp.formText ('emp_id', 6, 6, cattributes=>'onChange="validateNumber(this.value);"');

    htp.formSubmit;
    htp.formClose;
    common.footer; -- See recipe 14-2 for the common package.


END html;

PROCEDURE js is

BEGIN

    htp.p ('

function validateNumber (theNumber) {

    if ( isNaN (theNumber) ) {
        alert ("You must enter a number for the Employee ID");
        return false; }

    return true;
```

```
}');

END js;

END empID;
```

How It Works

Begin by creating the package specification for empID, which exposes the html and js procedures. Next create the package body with two procedures, html and js.

The html procedure generates the opening HTML code with a call to common.header. Next, the procedure generates a <SCRIPT> tag that identifies the location of the JavaScript to include in the user's browser. The <SCRIPT> tag of this form is one of the few HTML tags not predefined in the PL/SQL Web Toolkit.

The <SCRIPT> tag takes advantage of the owa_util package, which is also part of the PL/SQL Web Toolkit, to dynamically generate the web address of the JavaScript using the settings of the Apache environment values. This method avoids your having to hard-code the URL of the script into the procedure and allows it to run in any environment—development, integration, production, etc. The URL generated references the JavaScript package defined later in the package body.

Next, the html procedure generates the <FORM> tag with emp_rpt.rpt as its target. When the user clicks the Submit button the form will call the PL/SQL procedure emp_rpt.rpt defined in Recipe 14-4. It will not call a procedure within the empID package.

The htp.formText routine contains an extra parameter to include the JavaScript necessary to run when the user changes the value in the emp_id field. Nearly every procedure in the htp package includes the cattributes parameter, which provides for any additional option needed within the tag that is not already defined in the existing parameters. Figure 14-6 shows the data entry form with a non-numeric employee ID; in this example the letter "o" was used instead of a zero. JavaScript pops up the error message shown.

The js procedure consists of a simple print statement that contains the entire contents of the JavaScript code. JavaScript allows either single or double quotes for character strings. Using double quotes in the JavaScript code avoids conflicts with the single quote requirements of PL/SQL.

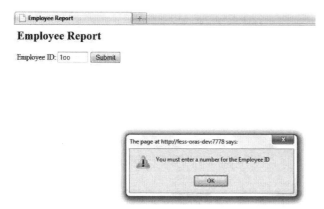

Figure 14-6. *Error message generated by JavaScript when a non-numeric employee ID is entered*

14-11. Generating XML Output

Problem

You need to provide XML data for PL/SQL or other consumers of data from your Oracle database.

Solution

Use Oracle's built-in DBMS_XMLGEN package to extract data from the database in standard XML format and then output the data through the Apache web server. In this example a generic procedure builds and outputs XML formatted data based on the SQL query statement passed to it. This procedure can be used in any application that requires XML output extracted from database tables.

```
CREATE OR REPLACE PROCEDURE gen_xml (sql_stmt VARCHAR2) IS

string          VARCHAR2(4000);
ipos            INTEGER;
offset          INTEGER;
n               INTEGER := 1;

qryctx          dbms_xmlgen.ctxhandle;
result          CLOB;

BEGIN

    qryctx := dbms_xmlgen.newcontext (sql_stmt);
    result := dbms_xmlgen.getxml (qryctx);
    dbms_xmlgen.closecontext (qryctx);

    owa_util.mime_header ('text/xml', true);
    LOOP
        EXIT WHEN result IS NULL;
        ipos := dbms_lob.instr (result, CHR(10), 1, n);
        EXIT WHEN ipos = 0;

        string := dbms_lob.substr (result, ipos-offset, offset);
        htp.p (string);

        offset      := ipos + 1;
        n           := n + 1;
    END LOOP;

    IF result IS NULL THEN
        htp.p ('<ROWSET>');
        htp.p ('</ROWSET>');
    END IF;

END gen_xml;
```

How It Works

The `newcontext` procedure in the `dbms_xmlgen` package executes the query passed to it in the first parameter. The `getxml` procedure returns the data in XML format. Each row of data from the select statement is enclosed in the XML tags `<ROW>`. Each field in the row is enclosed by its attribute (field) name in the database. For example, the employee ID is enclosed in the XML tag `<EMPLOYEE_ID>`.

The `owa_util.mime_header` is called to output the proper string to the client's browser, indicating the content of the web page is in standard XML format. At this point it is sufficient to simply output the XML data returned by the call to `xmlgen` with an `htp.p` statement. However, this approach works only if the length in bytes of the XML data does not exceed the maximum allowed by the `htp.p` procedure, which is 32k. The `LOOP` breaks apart the XML data into smaller segments at each line break, `CHR(10)`, insuring no call to `htp.p` exceeds the maximum length.

The final `IF` statement returns an empty XML tag set if the result of the query returns no rows. Without the empty tag set your Ajax call will fail because the Ajax call to parse the data from the XML structure requires the `<ROWSET>` tags.

Here is an example of the XML output produced from Recipe 14-12. Only the first two data rows retrieved are displayed.

```
<ROWSET>
 <ROW>
  <EMPLOYEE_ID>101</EMPLOYEE_ID>
  <LAST_NAME>Kochhar</LAST_NAME>
 </ROW>
 <ROW>
  <EMPLOYEE_ID>102</EMPLOYEE_ID>
  <LAST_NAME>De Haan</LAST_NAME>
 </ROW>
</ROWSET>
```

14-12. Creating an Input Form with AJAX

Problem

You need a web application that can interactively retrieve data based on partial data entered by the user. The data must be retrieved before the user clicks the Submit button to process the page.

Solution

Use JavaScript and Ajax to dynamically retrieve data as the user enters data into the web form. This recipe uses the EMPLOYEES table in the HR schema.

The data entry screen is built with all managers in a single dropdown list, which includes a call to a JavaScript procedure that invokes Ajax to retrieve subordinate data. Once the user selects a manager, the employee dropdown list populates with the manager's subordinates. The subordinates' dropdown list is defined with an ID, which is required by JavaScript to access the list and load the manager's subordinates.

The package contains the procedure `xml`, which is required to produce the XML data required by the Ajax call. The PL/SQL procedure `ajax.xml` is called by the web browser within the `AjaxMgr.js` procedure.

```
CREATE OR REPLACE PACKAGE ajax IS
```

```
    PROCEDURE html;
    PROCEDURE xml (ID INTEGER);

END ajax;

CREATE OR REPLACE PACKAGE BODY ajax IS

PROCEDURE html is

CURSOR  driver IS
SELECT  employee_id, last_name
FROM    employees
WHERE   employee_id in
(        SELECT  DISTINCT manager_id
         FROM    employees)
ORDER BY last_name;

BEGIN

    common.header ('Manager/Employee Example'); -- See recipe 14-2 for the common package.
    htp.p ('<SCRIPT LANGUAGE="JavaScript" SRC="'          ||
              owa_util.get_cgi_env ('REQUEST_PROTOCOL')      || '://'          ||
              owa_util.get_cgi_env ('HTTP_HOST')             ||
                            '/js/AjaxMgr.js"></SCRIPT>');

    htp.formOpen ('#', 'POST');
    htp.p ('Select a Manager:');
    htp.formSelectOpen ('mgr', cattributes=>'onChange="loadEmployees(this.value);"');
    htp.formSelectOption ('', 'SELECTED');

    FOR rec IN driver LOOP
        htp.formSelectOption (rec.last_name, cattributes=>'VALUE="'||rec.employee_id||'"');
    END LOOP;

    htp.formSelectClose;
    htp.br;

    htp.p ('Select a Subordinate:');
    htp.formSelectOpen ('emp', cattributes=>'ID="emp_list"');
    htp.formSelectClose;
    htp.br;

    htp.formSubmit;
    htp.formClose;
    common.footer;

END html;

PROCEDURE xml (ID INTEGER) IS

BEGIN
```

```
-- see recipe 14-11 for more information on the gen_xml procedure.
   gen_xml ('SELECT employee_id, last_name '    ||
           'FROM employees '                    ||
           'WHERE manager_id = ' || ID           ||
           ' ORDER by 1');

END xml;

END ajax;
```

How It Works

The recipe begins by defining the package specification with two packages, html and xml. The html package generates the HTML data entry form and the xml procedure generates the XML data required by the call to Ajax.

The html procedure generates the opening HTML code with a call to common.header. Next, the procedure generates a <SCRIPT> tag that identifies the location of the JavaScript to include in the user's browser. The <SCRIPT> tag of this form is one of the few HTML tags not pre-defined in the PL/SQL Web Toolkit.

The <SCRIPT> tag takes advantage of the owa_util package, which is also part of the PL/SQL Web Toolkit. It dynamically generates the web address of the JavaScript based on Apache environment values. This method avoids hard-coding the URL into the procedure and allows it to run in any environment—development, integration, production, etc.

▓ **Note** The JavaScript, AjaxMgr.js, is included in the media but not reproduced here.

An HTML form is opened with two dropdown lists defined. The first list is populated with the names of all managers from the employees table. The second dropdown list is intentionally left empty. It will be populated at runtime when the user selects a manager from the first dropdown list. Figure 14-7 shows the initial data entry screen generated by the html procedure, prior to the user selecting a manager from the manager's dropdown list.

The manager's dropdown list, mgr, is created using the htp.formSelectOpen procedure with an additional parameter to define the JavaScript to execute when the selected item in the list changes. A change to the manager's dropdown list invokes the JavaScript procedure loadEmployees, which was defined earlier in the <SCRIPT> tag.

The employee's dropdown list, emp, is also created using the htp.formSelectOpen procedure with an additional parameter to define the ID name of the object in the Web browser's DOM[2]. This ID is required by the JavaScript to dynamically rebuild the employee dropdown list if the value in the manager dropdown list changes. Figure 14-8 shows the data entry form after a Manager is selected by the user. Note the Subordinate list is now populated.

---

[2] A DOM (Document Object Model) "is a cross-platform and language-independent convention for representing and interacting with objects in HTML, XHTML and XML documents." – Wikipedia.

The xml procedure calls the gen_xml procedure, created in Recipe 14-11, to generate the data required to populate the employee dropdown list via the Ajax call. The gen_xml procedure is generic in that it only requires the select statement need to produce the XML output.

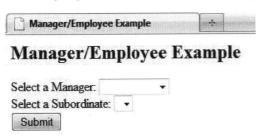

Figure 14-7. Manager dropdown list with empty subordinate dropdown list

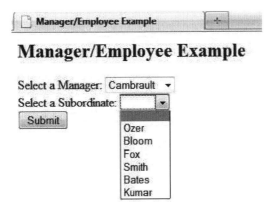

Figure 14-8. Subordinate list after being populated by Ajax

▪▪▪

CHAPTER 15

Java in the Database

Java plays an important role in the application development space today. It has become increasingly popular over the years, because it is cross-platform, powerful, and easy to learn. Although Java development is not directly related to PL/SQL, it is important for a PL/SQL developer to learn a bit about Java since there are some major benefits to using it to perform database tasks. Integrating the two languages when you're building Oracle Database applications is a seamless effort. Oracle Database 11g contains JVM compatibility with Java 1.5, which includes substantial changes to the Java language, making it an even more complementary development platform. Also starting with Oracle 11g, the database includes a just-in-time compiler, which compiles Java bytecode into machine language instructions, making Java in the database run much faster. In 2010, Oracle acquired Sun Microsystems, so it now owns Java. This may help the database JVM compatibility remain in concert with the latest releases.

In this chapter, you will learn how to combine the power of PL/SQL development with Java code that is stored within the database. You will learn how to create stored procedures, functions, and triggers using the Java language. Running Java in the database is a substantial topic that has filled entire books, but in this chapter, we will focus only on using the Java types in conjunction with PL/SQL applications—which, after all, is the subject of this book. For complete documentation on using Java inside Oracle Database, please see the Oracle Java developers guide at
`http://download.oracle.com/docs/cd/E11882_01/java.112/e10588/toc.htm`.

15-1. Creating a Java Database Class

Problem

You want to write a Java class that will query the database and return a result.

Solution

Create a Java class that uses the Java Database Connectivity (JDBC) API to query the Oracle Database. For example, the Java class in the following example will query the EMPLOYEES table for all employees who belong to the IT department. The example entails a complete Java class that is named Employees. This class contains a method named getItEmps() that will become a Java stored procedure. The Employees class shown here will be stored into a file named Employees.java.

```
import java.sql.*;
import oracle.jdbc.*;

public class Employees {
  public static void getItEmps(){
```

```
        String firstName = null;
        String lastName = null;
        String email = null;
        try {
            Connection conn = DriverManager.
                        getConnection("jdbc:default:connection:");
            String sql = "SELECT FIRST_NAME, LAST_NAME, EMAIL " +
                        "FROM EMPLOYEES " +
                        "WHERE DEPARTMENT_ID = 60";

            PreparedStatement pstmt = conn.prepareStatement(sql);
            ResultSet rset = pstmt.executeQuery();
            while(rset.next()) {
              firstName = rset.getString(1);
              lastName = rset.getString(2);
              email = rset.getString(3);
              System.out.println(firstName + " " + lastName + " " +
                                email);
            }
            pstmt.close();
            rset.close();
        } catch (SQLException ex){
            System.err.println("ERROR: " + ex);
        }
    };
```

The following lines from SQL*Plus show how to execute this Java in the database, followed by the output from the program. Prior to executing the code, you must load it into the database and compile it. You will learn more about doing this in the next recipe. To learn more about executing Java in the database, please see Recipe 15-5. For now, it is important to see the output that will result from a successful call to this Java program.

```
SQL> exec get_it_emps;
Alexander Hunold AHUNOLD
Bruce Ernst BERNST
David Austin DAUSTIN
Valli Pataballa VPATABAL
Diana Lorentz DLORENTZ

PL/SQL procedure successfully completed.
```

The Java class in this example performs a simple query and then prints the result. Although this class does not demonstrate the full potential of using Java, it is a good segue into Java database development.

How It Works

Java is a mature language that can be used in conjunction with PL/SQL. Sometimes it makes sense to code portions of your application in Java, while in other instances it may make sense to code the entire application in Java. Both PL/SQL and Java can coexist in the same application, and you must use PL/SQL to access Java via the database.

This recipe demonstrates how to create a simple Java class that queries the database for EMPLOYEE records. The JDBC APIs provide a way for Java programs to methodically perform the tasks you will typically want to complete whenever you access a database, whether it's querying data, updating records, or deleting rows.

A Java class that you will use to access an Oracle Database as a stored procedure must adhere to a few standards. The class must be public, and each of its methods must be public and static. Failure to follow these standards will render the class methods inaccessible for use as stored procedures.

The first step taken in the solution to this recipe is to obtain a connection to the database. In a Java class that lives outside the database, obtaining a connection is a performance-intensive operation, and you must pass a user name and password along with the database host name. However, obtaining a connection using stored procedures is a bit different since they reside within the database itself. The only requirement is that you pass jdbc:default:connection to the getConnection() method.

Next, the SQL query (sql) is formed as a String, and a PreparedStatement object (pstmt) is then created from it using the prepareStatement method. The prepared statement is what actually queries the database. The next line of code in the solution issues the query by calling the executeQuery() method on the prepared statement object, which returns a result set. The result set is what you need to use in order to access the rows that have been returned via the query. Use a simple while loop to traverse the rows, and obtain each of the values from the result set within each iteration of the loop by indicating the position of the column you want to retrieve. For instance, to obtain the FIRST_NAME, you will call rset.getString(1) because FIRST_NAME is the first column that is listed within the query.

Lastly, the class in the solution closes the prepared statement and result set objects. Not doing so may cause issues such as memory leaks, although Java has a very efficient garbage collection system, so it should take care of this for you. Again, closing the objects is a form of good practice to ensure that resources can be reallocated.

The Oracle Java virtual machine (JVM) also supports the use of SQLJ for database access. Use of SQLJ is beyond the scope of this book, but if you are interested in learning about it JVM, then please refer to the Oracle Java Developer Guide, which can be found at http://download.oracle.com/docs/cd/E11882_01/java.112/e10588/toc.htm.

15-2. Loading a Java Database Class into a Database

Problem

You want to load a Java class into a schema within your Oracle Database.

Solution #1

You can use the CREATE JAVA command to load the Java source into the database by copying and pasting the Java source into a SQL file. This is the easiest way to create a Java class and then load it into the database if you are not working directly on the database server but rather remotely using an editor or SQL*Plus. The following lines of SQL code will load the Java class that was created in Recipe 15-1 into the database using the CREATE JAVA command:

```
CREATE OR REPLACE JAVA SOURCE NAMED "Employees" AS
import java.sql.*;
import oracle.jdbc.*;
```

```java
public class Employees {
  public static void getItEmps(){
      String firstName = null;
      String lastName = null;
      String email = null;
      try {
          Connection conn = DriverManager.
                        getConnection("jdbc:default:connection:");
          String sql = "SELECT FIRST_NAME, LAST_NAME, EMAIL " +
                        "FROM EMPLOYEES " +
                        "WHERE DEPARTMENT_ID = 60";

          PreparedStatement pstmt = conn.prepareStatement(sql);
          ResultSet rset = pstmt.executeQuery();
          while(rset.next()) {
             firstName = rset.getString(1);
             lastName = rset.getString(2);
             email = rset.getString(3);
             System.out.println(firstName + " " + lastName + " " +
                              email);
          }
          pstmt.close();
          rset.close();
      } catch (SQLException ex){
          System.err.println("ERROR: " + ex);
          }
      }
  };
```

Next, you need to compile the code. To do so, use the ALTER JAVA CLASS <name> RESOLVE command. The following line of code compiles the Employees Java source:

```
ALTER JAVA CLASS "Employees" RESOLVE;
```

Solution #2

You can use the loadjava utility that is provided by Oracle in order to load Java code into the database. This situation works best if you are working directly on the database server and have access to the loadjava utility that is installed in the Oracle Database home. This utility is also nice to use if you already have the Java code stored in a file and do not want to copy and paste code into an editor or SQL*Plus. The following code demonstrates loading a Java source file named Employees.java using the loadjava utility:

```
loadjava -user dbuser Employees.java
```

After the command is issued, you will be prompted for the password to the user who you named using the –user option. By issuing the –resolve option, you will be loading the Java into the database and compiling at the same time. This saves you the step of issuing the ALTER JAVA CLASS <name> RESOLVE command.

How It Works

You can load Java source code into the database directly using the CREATE JAVA SOURCE command. This will load the source and make it accessible to the schema in which it was loaded. Once loaded, you can create a *call specification f*or any of the class methods that you want to make into a stored procedure or function. The call specification maps the Java method names, parameter types, and return types to their SQL counterparts. You will learn more about creating call specifications in Recipe 15-4. We recommend compiling the source using the RESOLVE command before attempting to invoke any of its methods. However, if you do not issue the RESOLVE command, then Oracle Database will attempt to compile the Java source dynamically at runtime.

■ **Note** A class name can be a maximum of 30 characters in length. If the specified name is more than 30 characters in length, then Oracle will automatically shorten it for you and create and use a map to correlate the long name with the shortened name. You can still specify the long name in most cases, and Oracle will automatically convert that name to the shortened name for you. However, in some cases you will need to use the DBMS_JAVA.SHORTNAME('long_classname') function to map the name for you. Conversely, if you want to retrieve the long name by using its corresponding short name, you can use the DBMS_JAVA.LONGNAME('short_classname') function.

The loadjava utility, which is the tool you use to implement the second solution, uses the CREATE JAVA command to load the Java into the database. It also allows you to specify the –resolve option, which will compile the code once it has been loaded. The advantage to using loadjava is that you can load Java source files directly into the database without the need to create a separate SQL file containing the CREATE JAVA command or copy and paste the Java class into SQL*Plus. The downside is that you must have access to the loadjava binary executable that resides on the Oracle Database server. This utility can also be used to load files of type .class, .sqlj., .properties, and .ser.

If your code is unable to compile because of errors, then it will not execute if you attempt to invoke one of its methods. You must repair the error(s) and ensure that the code compiles successfully before it can be used. If your code does not compile, then you can check the USER_ERRORS table to see what issue(s) are preventing the code from compiling successfully. The USER_ERRORS table describes the current errors on all the objects that are contained within the user's schema. To learn more about querying the USER_ERRORS table, please refer to Recipe 15-15.

15-3. Loading a Compiled Java Class Into the Database

Problem

You want to load a compiled Java class into the database so that you can use one or more of its methods as stored procedures.

Solution

Use the loadjava command-line utility to load the compiled Java class into the database. The following line of code demonstrates how to use the loadjava utility to load a compiled Java class file named Employees.class into the database.

```
loadjava -user dbuser -resolve Employees.class
```

You will be prompted to enter the password for the database user who you designated when issuing the command.

How It Works

The loadjava utility can be used to load compiled Java class files into the database. To do so, you have access to the binary loadjava utility executable. Usually this means you are located directly on the Oracle Database server hosting the database that you want to load the Java into. Before you can invoke the loadjava utility, you should be sure that the ORACLE_SID for the target database has been set. If the server on which you are located contains more than one Oracle home, then it is a good idea to also set the ORACLE_HOME environment variable to be sure you will be invoking the correct version of the loadjava utility for your database. The loadjava utility is located within the bin directory of the Oracle Database home. The following statements show how to set these two environment variables on a Windows machine:

```
SET ORACLE_SID=MYDATABASE
SET ORACLE_HOME=<PATH_TO_ORACLE_HOME>
```

If you happen to be working on a Unix or Linux machine, the equivalent commands would be as follows:

```
setenv ORACLE_SID = MYDATABASE
setenv ORACLE_HOME= <PATH_TO_ORACLE_HOME>
```

You must have the following permissions in order to use the loadjava utility:
- CREATE PROCEDURE
- CREATE TABLE
- Oracle.aurora.security.JServerPermission.loadLibraryInClass.classname

Several options are at your disposal when using loadjava to load source or compiled class files into the database. The -resolve option can be used to compile Java source and mark it as VALID within the Oracle Database. The -resolver option can be used for locating other Java class files that your code is dependant upon. For a complete listing of loadjava options, please see the online Oracle documentation, which can be found at http://download.oracle.com/docs/cd/E11882_01/java.112/e10588/cheleven.htm#CACFHDJE.

The loadjava utility is a member of the DBMS_JAVA package, and it can be invoked directly from within your PL/SQL code as well. To do this, issue a call to DBMS_JAVA.loadjava, and pass the options separated by spaces. This is demonstrated by the following lines of text in SQL*Plus:

```
call dbms_java.loadjava('Employees.class');
```

15-4. Exposing a Java Class As a Stored Procedure

Problem

You have created a Java stored procedure and loaded it into the database, and now you want to access it via PL/SQL.

Solution

Create a PL/SQL call specification for the Java class. The PL/SQL call specification will essentially wrap the call to the Java class, enabling you to have access to the class from PL/SQL. The following code demonstrates the creation of a call specification for the Java class that was created in Recipe 15-1 and loaded into the database in Recipe 15-2.

```
CREATE OR REPLACE PROCEDURE get_it_emps AS LANGUAGE JAVA
NAME 'Employees.getItEmps()';
```

How It Works

To make the Java class accessible from the database, you must create a PL/SQL *call specification* (sometimes known as PL/SQL wrapper) for the stored Java code. A call specification maps a Java method call to a PL/SQL procedure so that the Java code can be called from the database directly. A call specification also maps any parameters and return type to the Java code. To learn more about mapping parameters and return types, please see Recipe 15-7.

The call specification for a Java stored procedure is a PL/SQL procedure itself that specifies AS LANGUAGE JAVA, followed by the name of the Java class and method that will be mapped to the procedure name. The name of the Java method to be invoked must be preceded by the Java class name that contains it. This is because the method has been defined as static, meaning it is a class method rather than an instance method. When a call to the specification is made, Oracle will automatically call the underlying Java class method.

■ **Note** Two types of methods can be created in a Java class: class methods and instance methods. Class methods belong to the class, rather than to an instance of the class. This means the methods are instantiated once for each class. Instance methods belong to an instance of the class. This means that if a new instance of the class is created, a new method will be created with that instance. Class methods have access to class variables (otherwise known as *static*), whereas instance methods have access only to instance variables.

15-5. Executing a Java Stored Procedure

Problem

You want to execute a Java stored procedure that you have created from within SQL*Plus.

Solution

Call the PL/SQL call specification that maps to the Java stored procedure. The following SQL*Plus code demonstrates how to execute the Java class for which you created a call specification in Recipe 15-3.

```
SQL> set serveroutput on
SQL> call dbms_java.set_output(2000);

Call completed.

SQL> exec get_it_emps;
Alexander Hunold AHUNOLD
Bruce Ernst BERNST
David Austin DAUSTIN
Valli Pataballa VPATABAL
Diana Lorentz DLORENTZ

PL/SQL procedure successfully completed.
```

As you can see, when the code is executed, the results are returned to SQL*Plus and displayed as if it were the output of a PL/SQL procedure or function.

How It Works

Java can be executed directly from within the database once a call specification has been made for the corresponding Java method. Since the call specification is a PL/SQL procedure itself, you can invoke the underlying Java just as if it were PL/SQL using the EXEC command from SQL*Plus or call it from any other PL/SQL block as if it were PL/SQL as illustrated in Recipe 15-6. To see any output from the Java, you must set the buffer size appropriately to display it. If the buffer size is not set, then no output will be displayed. Similarly, if the buffer size is set too small, then only a portion of the output will be displayed. Personally, we recommend setting the output size to 2000 and moving up from there if needed. To set the buffer size, issue this command:

```
CALL DBMS_JAVA.SET_OUTPUT(buffer_size);
```

The Java will be executed seamlessly and display the result, if any, just as if it were a PL/SQL response. In the solution to this recipe, the get_it_emps PL/SQL procedure is called. Since get_it_emps is a call specification, it will invoke the underlying Java class method getItEmps() that actually performs the query and displays the content.

15-6. Calling a Java Stored Procedure from PL/SQL

Problem

You want to access a Java stored procedure from within one of your PL/SQL applications. For instance, you are creating a PL/SQL procedure, and you want to make a call to a Java stored procedure from within it.

Solution

Make a call to the Java stored procedure using the call specification that you created for it. The following code demonstrates a PL/SQL package that makes a call to a Java stored procedure and then resumes PL/SQL execution once the call has been made.

```
CREATE OR REPLACE PROCEDURE employee_reports AS
  CURSOR emp_cur IS
  SELECT first_name, last_name, email
  FROM employees
  WHERE department_id = 50;

  emp_rec     emp_cur%ROWTYPE;
BEGIN
  DBMS_OUTPUT.PUT_LINE('Employees from Shipping Department');
  DBMS_OUTPUT.PUT_LINE('----------------------------------');
  FOR emp_rec IN emp_cur LOOP
    DBMS_OUTPUT.PUT_LINE(emp_rec.first_name || ' ' ||
                         emp_rec.last_name || ' ' ||
                         emp_rec.email);
  END LOOP;

  DBMS_OUTPUT.PUT_LINE('=========================================');
  DBMS_OUTPUT.PUT_LINE('Employees from IT Department');
  DBMS_OUTPUT.PUT_LINE('----------------------------');
  get_it_emps;
END;
```

This results in the following output:

```
SQL> EXEC EMPLOYEE_REPORTS
Employees from Shipping Department
----------------------------------
Matthew Weiss MWEISS
Adam Fripp AFRIPP
...
Alana Walsh AWALSH
Kevin Feeney KFEENEY
Donald OConnell DOCONNEL
Douglas Grant DGRANT
=========================================
Employees from IT Department
----------------------------
Alexander Hunold AHUNOLD
Bruce Ernst BERNST
David Austin DAUSTIN
Valli Pataballa VPATABAL
Diana Lorentz DLORENTZ

PL/SQL procedure successfully completed.
```

The call to the Java stored procedure from within the PL/SQL procedure is seamless. It is integrated into the PL/SQL procedure body and invoked as if it were PL/SQL.

How It Works

The call specification publishes the Java stored procedure as if it were a PL/SQL procedure. This allows for seamless integration of Java stored procedures and PL/SQL. In the solution to this recipe, the EMPLOYEES table is queried via a PL/SQL cursor for all employees who belong to department 50. That cursor is then parsed, and the results are displayed. After the cursor results have been processed, a call is made to the Java stored procedure getItEmps() using the call specification get_it_emps. The Java stored procedure is executed, and its results are displayed along with those from the PL/SQL cursor processing.

As you can see, Java can be executed from PL/SQL just as if it were native PL/SQL code. It can be very useful to create database jobs utilizing Java stored procedures by developing a PL/SQL stored procedure or anonymous block that makes a series of calls to different Java stored procedures or functions that perform the actual processing. PL/SQL and Java in the database can be very complementary to each other.

15-7. Passing Parameters Between PL/SQL and Java

Problem

You want to pass parameters from PL/SQL to a Java stored procedure that expects them.

Solution

Create a call specification that accepts the same number of parameters as the number the Java stored procedure expects. For this example, an additional method will be added to the Employee Java class that was created in Recipe 15-1. This method will be an enhanced version of the original method that will accept a department ID as an input argument. It will then query the database for the employees who belong to that department and display them.

The following code is the enhanced Java method that will be added the Employees class contained within the Employees.java file:

```java
public static void getItEmpsByDept(int departmentId){
     String firstName = null;
     String lastName = null;
     String email = null;
     try {
          Connection conn = DriverManager.
                    getConnection("jdbc:default:connection:");
          String sql = "SELECT FIRST_NAME, LAST_NAME, EMAIL " +
                    "FROM EMPLOYEES " +
                    "WHERE DEPARTMENT_ID = ?";

          PreparedStatement pstmt = conn.prepareStatement(sql);
          pstmt.setInt(1, departmentId);
          ResultSet rset = pstmt.executeQuery();
          while(rset.next()) {
            firstName = rset.getString(1);
            lastName = rset.getString(2);
```

```
            email = rset.getString(3);
            System.out.println(firstName + " " + lastName + " " +
                              email);
        }
        pstmt.close();
        rset.close();
    } catch (SQLException ex){
        System.err.println("ERROR: " + ex);
        }
    }
}
```

Once this method has been added to the Employees class, then the Java source should be loaded into the database using the technique demonstrated in Recipe 15-2.

■ **Note** You must include the OR REPLACE clause of the CREATE JAVA statement if the Employees source is already contained in the database. If you do not include this clause, then you will receive an Oracle error.

Once the Java has been loaded into the database and compiled, you will need to create the call specification that will be used by PL/SQL for accessing the Java stored procedure. The following code demonstrates a call specification that will accept a parameter when invoked and pass it to the Java stored procedure:

```
CREATE OR REPLACE PROCEDURE get_it_emps_by_dept(dept_id IN NUMBER)
 AS LANGUAGE JAVA
NAME 'Employees.getItEmpsByDept(int)';
```

The procedure can now be called by passing a department ID value as such:

```
SQL> exec get_it_emps_by_dept(60);
Alexander Hunold AHUNOLD
Bruce Ernst BERNST
David Austin DAUSTIN
Valli Pataballa VPATABAL
Diana Lorentz DLORENTZ

PL/SQL procedure successfully completed.
```

How It Works

The call specification is what determines how a Java stored procedure or function's arguments are mapped to PL/SQL arguments. To implement parameters, the call specification must match each parameter in the stored procedure or function to an argument in the specification. As mentioned in previous recipes, the call specification is a PL/SQL procedure itself, and each argument that is coded in the specification matches an argument that is coded within the Java stored procedure.

The datatypes that Java uses do not match those used in PL/SQL. In fact, a translation must take place when passing parameters listed as a PL/SQL datatype to a Java stored procedure that accepts parameters as a Java datatype. If you are familiar enough with each of the two languages, the translation is fairly straightforward. However, there are always those cases where one is not sure what datatype to match against. Table 15-1 lists some of the most common datatypes and how they map between Java and PL/SQL. For a complete datatype map, please refer to the Oracle documentation at http://download.oracle.com/docs/cd/B28359_01/java.111/b31225/chsix.htm#CHDFACEE.

Table 15-1. Datatype Map

SQL Datatype	Java Type
CHAR	oracle.sql.CHAR
VARCHAR	java.lang.String
LONG	java.lang.String
NUMBER	java.lang.Integer,Java.lang.Float,Java.lang.Double,Java.math.BigDecimal,Java.lang.Byte,Oracle.sql.NUMBER,Java.lang.Short,
DATE	oracle.sql.DATE
TIMESTAMP	oracle.sql.TIMESTAMP
TIMESTAMP WITH TIME ZONE	oracle.sql.TIMESTAMPTZ
TIMESTAMP WITH LOCAL TIME ZONE	oracle.sql.TIMESTAMPLTZ
BLOB	oracle.sql.BLOB
CLOB	oracle.sql.CLOB

Creating a PL/SQL call specification that includes parameters must use the fully qualified Java class name when specifying the parameter datatypes in the Java class method signature. If an incorrect datatype is specified, then an exception will be thrown. For instance, if you want to pass a VARCHAR2 from PL/SQL to a Java stored procedure, the signature for the Java class method must accept an argument of type java.lang.String. The following pseudocode demonstrates this type of call specification:

```
CREATE OR REPLACE PROCEDURE procedure_name(value    VARCHAR2)
AS LANGUAGE JAVA
NAME 'JavaClass.javaMethod(java.lang.String)';
```

15-8. Creating and Calling a Java Database Function

Problem

You want to create a database function using the Java language.

Solution

Create a function written in Java, and then create a call specification for the function. Ensure that the call specification allows for the same number of parameters to pair up with the Java function and allows for a returning result. For this recipe, you will add a function to the Employees Java class that will accept an employee ID and return that employee's job title. The following code is the Java source for the function named getEmpJobTitle:

```
public static String getEmpJobTitle(int empId){
    String jobTitle = null;
    try {
        Connection conn = DriverManager.
                    getConnection("jdbc:default:connection:");
        String sql = "SELECT JOB_TITLE " +
                    "FROM EMPLOYEES EMP, " +
          "JOBS JOBS " +
                    "WHERE EMP.EMPLOYEE_ID = ? " +
                    "AND JOBS.JOB_ID = EMP.JOB_ID";

        PreparedStatement pstmt = conn.prepareStatement(sql);
        pstmt.setInt(1, empId);
        ResultSet rset = pstmt.executeQuery();
        while(rset.next()) {
          jobTitle = rset.getString(1);
        }
        pstmt.close();
        rset.close();
                    } catch (SQLException ex){
                            System.err.println("ERROR: " + ex);
                            jobTitle = "N/A";
    }
            if (jobTitle == null){
                jobTitle = "N/A";
            }
                            return jobTitle;
}
```

Next is the call specification for the function:

```
CREATE OR REPLACE FUNCTION get_emp_job_title(emp_id IN NUMBER)
RETURN VARCHAR2 AS LANGUAGE JAVA
NAME 'Employees.getEmpJobTitle(int) return java.lang.String';
```

The function can now be called just like a PL/SQL function would. The following lines of code show a SQL SELECT statement that calls the function passing an employee ID number of 200.

```
SQL> select get_emp_job_title(200) from dual;

GET_EMP_JOB_TITLE(200)
-----------------------------------------------------------------------------
Administration Assistant
```

How It Works

The difference between a stored procedure and a stored function is that a function always returns a value. In the Java language, a method may or may not return a value. The difference between a PL/SQL call specification for a Java stored procedure and a PL/SQL call specifcation for a Java function is that the PL/SQL call specification will specify a return value if it is being used to invoke an underlying function. In the solution to this recipe, the example PL/SQL call specification returns a VARCHAR2 data type because the Java function that is being called will return a Java String.

15-9. Creating a Java Database Trigger

Problem

You want to create a database trigger that uses a Java stored procedure to do its work.

Solution

Create a Java stored procedure that does the work you require, and publish it as a Java stored procedure, making it accessible to PL/SQL. Once it's published, write a standard PL/SQL trigger that calls the Java stored procedure.

For example, suppose you need a trigger to audit INSERT events on the EMPLOYEES table and record them in another table. First, you must create the table that will be used to record each of the logged events. The following DDL creates one:

```
CREATE TABLE EMPLOYEE_AUDIT_LOG (
employee_id     NUMBER,
enter_date      DATE);
```

Next, you will need to code the Java stored procedure that you want to have executed each time an INSERT occurs on the EMPLOYEES table. Add the following Java method to the Employees class of previous recipes in this chapter:

```java
public static void employeeAudit(int empId){
    try {
        Connection conn = DriverManager.
                    getConnection("jdbc:default:connection:");
        String sql = "INSERT INTO EMPLOYEE_AUDIT_LOG VALUES(" +
                "?, sysdate)";
        PreparedStatement pstmt = conn.prepareStatement(sql);
        pstmt.setInt(1, empId);
        pstmt.executeUpdate();
    pstmt.close();
    conn.commit();

    } catch (SQLException ex){
        System.err.println("ERROR: " + ex);
        }

}
```

Next, the PL/SQL call specification for the Java stored procedure must be created. The following is the code to implement the call specification:

```
CREATE OR REPLACE PROCEDURE emp_audit(emp_id NUMBER)
AS LANGUAGE JAVA
NAME 'Employees.employeeAudit(int)';
```

Finally, a trigger to call the EMP_AUDIT procedure must be created. The trigger will be executed on INSERT to the EMPLOYEES table. The following code will generate the trigger to call EMP_AUDIT:

```
CREATE OR REPLACE TRIGGER emp_audit_ins
AFTER INSERT ON EMPLOYEES
FOR EACH ROW
CALL emp_audit(:new.employee_id);
```

Once all these pieces have been successfully created within the database, the EMP_AUDIT_INS trigger will be executed each time there is an INSERT made to the EMPLOYEES table. In turn, the trigger will call the EMP_AUDIT PL/SQL procedure, which calls the Java method contained within the Employees class. The SQL*Plus output shown here demonstrates an INSERT into the EMPLOYEES table, followed by a query on the EMPLOYEE_AUDIT_LOG table to show that the trigger has been invoked:

```
SQL> insert into employees values(
    employees_seq.nextval,
    'Jane',
    'Doe',
    'jane.doe@mycompany.com',
    null,
    sysdate,
    'FI_MGR',
    null,
    null,
    null,
    null);

1 row created.

SQL> select * from employee_audit_log;

EMPLOYEE_ID ENTER_DAT
----------- ---------
        265 02-NOV-10
```

How It Works

A Java-based trigger combines the power of Java code with the native ease of performing data manipulation using PL/SQL triggers. Although creating a Java trigger requires more steps than using native PL/SQL, the Java code is portable. If your application is supported on more than one database platform, this lets you write code once and deploy it in many environments. It also makes sense to code a trigger using Java if you require the use of Java libraries or technologies that are unavailable to PL/SQL.

In the solution to this recipe, a trigger was created that will insert a row into an audit table each time an INSERT is made on the EMPLOYEES table. The actual work is performed within a Java method that is added to a Java class and loaded into the database. For more information on loading Java into the database, please see Recipe 15-2. To invoke the stored Java method, you must create a PL/SQL call specification, which maps the Java method to a PL/SQL stored procedure. The call specification can accept zero, one, or many parameters, and it will seamlessly pass the parameters to the underlying Java method. The final step to creating a Java trigger is to code a PL/SQL trigger that invokes the PL/SQL stored procedure that was created.

Creating a Java-based trigger entails a series of steps. Each piece of code depends upon the others, and like a domino effect, the trigger will call the procedure that in turn executes the Java method. This solution opens the world of Java libraries and thousands of possibilities to the standard PL/SQL trigger.

15-10. Passing Data Objects from PL/SQL to Java

Problem

You have retrieved a row of data from the database using PL/SQL, and you want to populate a PL/SQL object type with that data and then pass the populated data object to a Java procedure.

Solution

Create a PL/SQL object type, along with a call specification for the Java stored procedure that you want to pass the object to. Ensure that the Java stored procedure accepts an object of type oracle.sql.STRUCT and that the call specification accepts the PL/SQL object type you have created. For this recipe, the example will demonstrate the creation of a Java method that will accept an Employee object and return that employee's corresponding department name. The Java code will be invoked from within a PL/SQL anonymous block that queries each employee, loads an Employee object with the data, passes the object to the Java method, and returns the result.

First, add the following Java method to the Employees class you've used with previous recipes in this chapter:

```
public static String getEmpDepartment(oracle.sql.STRUCT emp) {

    String deptName = null;
    BigDecimal employeeId = null;
    try {
        Object[] attribs = emp.getAttributes();
        // Use indexes to grab individual attributes.
        Object empId = attribs[0];
        try{
            employeeId = (BigDecimal) empId;
        } catch (ClassCastException cce) {
            System.out.println(cce);
        }
        Connection conn = DriverManager.
                    getConnection("jdbc:default:connection:");
            String sql = "SELECT DEPARTMENT_NAME " +
                        "FROM DEPARTMENTS DEPT, " +
            "EMPLOYEES EMP " +
                        "WHERE EMP.EMPLOYEE_ID = ? " +
```

```
        "AND DEPT.DEPARTMENT_ID = EMP.DEPARTMENT_ID";

        PreparedStatement pstmt = conn.prepareStatement(sql);
        pstmt.setInt(1, employeeId.intValue());
        ResultSet rset = pstmt.executeQuery();
        while(rset.next()) {
          deptName = rset.getString(1);
        }
        pstmt.close();
        rset.close();
    } catch (java.sql.SQLException ex){
        System.err.println("ERROR: " + ex);
        deptName = "N/A";
        }
    if (deptName == null){
      deptName = "N/A";
    }
    return deptName;
}
```

Next, create the PL/SQL object that will contain employee information. The following SQL statement will create this object:

```
CREATE TYPE Employee AS OBJECT (
emp_id NUMBER(6),
first VARCHAR2(20),
last  VARCHAR2(25),
email VARCHAR2(25),
job VARCHAR2(10),
dept NUMBER(4)
);
```

Now you need to create the call specification for the Java method. Since the method is returning a value, the call specification needs to be a PL/SQL function that accepts an Employee object and returns a String value. The following code demonstrates such a call specification for the getEmpDepartment Java method:

```
CREATE OR REPLACE FUNCTION get_emp_department (emp Employee) RETURN VARCHAR2 AS
LANGUAGE JAVA
NAME 'Employees.getEmpDepartment(oracle.sql.STRUCT) return java.lang.String';
```

Finally, call the new Java function from within an anonymous block. The following PL/SQL block uses a cursor to traverse the EMPLOYEES table and populates an Employee object with each iteration. In turn, the object is passed to the Java stored procedure via the PL/SQL function GET_EMP_DEPARTMENT, and the corresponding DEPARTMENT_NAME is returned.

```
DECLARE
  CURSOR emp_cur IS
  SELECT * FROM EMPLOYEES;

  emp_rec     emp_cur%ROWTYPE;
```

```
  emp        Employee;
BEGIN
  FOR emp_rec IN emp_cur LOOP
    emp := Employee(emp_rec.employee_id,
                    emp_rec.first_name,
                    emp_rec.last_name,
                    emp_rec.email,
                    emp_rec.job_id,
                    emp_rec.department_id);
    DBMS_OUTPUT.PUT_LINE(emp.first || ' ' || emp.last || ' - ' ||
            get_emp_department(emp));
  END LOOP;
END;
```

How It Works

Passing objects to Java code should be second nature to you since Java is an object-oriented language. You can create PL/SQL objects as well and use them within your PL/SQL and Java mashup applications. The solution to this recipe demonstrated the creation of an Employee object in PL/SQL that was passed to Java.

To accept a PL/SQL object type, Java code must use a parameter of type oracle.sql.STRUCT in place of the object. The STRUCT object is basically a container that allows the contents to be accessed by calling the getAttributes method. In the solution to this recipe, the oracle.sql.STRUCT object is accepted in the Java class as a parameter, and then the getAttributes method is called on it. This creates an array of objects that contains the data. The Java stored procedure accesses the object using the 0 index position, which is the first placeholder from the PL/SQL object. This position maps to the emp_id field in the PL/SQL object. The Java class then uses that emp_id to query the database and retrieve a corresponding DEPARTMENT_ID if it exists.

The call specification must accept the PL/SQL object type as a parameter but use the oracle.sql.STRUCT object as the parameter in the Java source signature. When the object is passed to the PL/SQL call specification procedure, it will be converted into an oracle.sql.STRUCT object, which is a datatype that a Java class can accept.

Organizing your data into objects can be useful, especially when the object you are creating does not match a table definition exactly. For instance, you could create an object that contains employee information along with region information. There are no tables that contain both of these fields, so in order to retrieve the information together, you are forced into either using a SQL query that contains table joins or creating a database view. In such a case, it may be easier to populate the object using PL/SQL and then hand it off to the Java program for processing.

15-11. Embedding a Java Class Into a PL/SQL Package

Problem

You are interested in creating a Java class and making each of its methods and attributes available to PL/SQL in an organized unit of code.

Solution

Use a PL/SQL package to declare each of the attributes and methods that reside within the Java class, and then create separate call specifications for each of the Java methods within the PL/SQL package body. The following code demonstrates the creation of a PL/SQL package named EMP_PKG, which declares each of the methods that reside within the Employee Java class and makes them available to PL/SQL via call specifications that are implemented within the package body.

First, create the package header as follows:

```
CREATE OR REPLACE PACKAGE EMP_PKG AS

    PROCEDURE get_it_emps;
    PROCEDURE get_it_emps_by_dept(dept_id IN NUMBER);
    PROCEDURE emp_audit(emp_id NUMBER);

    FUNCTION get_emp_job_title(emp_id IN NUMBER) RETURN VARCHAR2;
    FUNCTION get_emp_department (emp Employee) RETURN VARCHAR2;

END;
```

Next, create the package body as follows, adding a call specification for each Java method or attribute you plan to use:

```
CREATE PACKAGE BODY EMP_PKG AS

    PROCEDURE get_it_emps
    AS LANGUAGE JAVA
    NAME 'Employees.getItEmps()';

    PROCEDURE get_it_emps_by_dept(dept_id IN NUMBER)
    AS LANGUAGE JAVA
    NAME 'Employees.getItEmpsByDept(int)';

    PROCEDURE emp_audit(emp_id NUMBER)
    AS LANGUAGE JAVA
    NAME 'Employees.employeeAudit(int)';

    FUNCTION get_emp_job_title(emp_id IN NUMBER) RETURN VARCHAR2
    AS LANGUAGE JAVA
    NAME 'Employees.getEmpJobTitle(int) return String';

    FUNCTION get_emp_department (emp Employee) RETURN VARCHAR2
    AS LANGUAGE JAVA
    NAME 'Employees.getEmpDepartment(oracle.sql.STRUCT) return java.lang.String';

END;
```

Now the package can be used to call each of the underlying Java stored procedures instead of having separate PL/SQL procedures and functions for each. The following anonymous block has been modified to make use of the PL/SQL package for calling GET_EMP_DEPARTMENT rather than a stand-alone function.

```
DECLARE
  CURSOR emp_cur IS
  SELECT * FROM EMPLOYEES;
```

```
  emp_rec    emp_cur%ROWTYPE;
  emp        Employee;
BEGIN
  FOR emp_rec IN emp_cur LOOP
    emp := Employee(emp_rec.employee_id,
                    emp_rec.first_name,
                    emp_rec.last_name,
                    emp_rec.email,
                    emp_rec.job_id,
                    emp_rec.department_id);
    DBMS_OUTPUT.PUT_LINE(emp.first || ' ' || emp.last || ' - ' ||
            emp_pkg.get_emp_department(emp));
  END LOOP;
END;
```

How It Works

In programming, it is a best practice to organize code in a way that makes it easy to maintain. Placing related procedures and functions inside a single PL/SQL package is one such application of that approach. The same can be said for working with Java code in the database. A few Java stored procedures or functions will not cause much trouble to maintain. However, once you start to accumulate more than a handful within the same underlying Java class, then it is a good idea to consolidate the call specifications into a single PL/SQL package.

In the solution to this recipe, all the Java stored procedures that are contained within the Employees Java class have call specifications that are grouped into a single PL/SQL package. If you create one PL/SQL package containing call specifications per each Java class that is loaded into the database, you will have a nicely organized environment. In some cases, you may have more than one Java class that contains the implementations that are to be used within a single PL/SQL application. In those cases, it may make more sense to combine all call specifications into a single PL/SQL package.

Using PL/SQL package to group call specifications is a good idea. Not only will this technique make for easier maintenance, but it also makes for more uniform applications with consistent interfaces.

15-12. Loading Java Libraries Into the Database

Problem

You want to create a Java class that utilizes some external Java libraries. To do so, you must load those external libraries into the database.

Solution

Use the loadjava utility to store the external libraries into the database. In this example, a Java utility class containing a method that uses the JavaMail API to send e-mail will be loaded into the database. The method relies on some external Java libraries to use the JavaMail API. The following loadjava commands demonstrate the loading of three essential JAR files for using the JavaMail API:

```
loadjava -u <username> mail.jar
loadjava -u <username> standard.jar
loadjava -u <username> activation.jar
```

Next, load the Java source for the JavaUtils class into the database:

```
CREATE OR REPLACE JAVA SOURCE NAMED "JavaUtils" AS
import java.util.*;
import java.util.logging.Level;
import java.util.logging.Logger;
import javax.activation.*;
import javax.mail.*;
import javax.mail.internet.*;
import javax.naming.*;

public class JavaUtils {

 public static void sendMail(String subject,
            String recipient,
            String message) {
      try {

            Properties props = System.getProperties();
            props.put("mail.from", "me@mycompany.com");
            props.put("mail.smtp.host","company.smtp.server");
            Session session = Session.getDefaultInstance(props,null);
            Message msg = new MimeMessage(session);
            msg = new MimeMessage(session);
            msg.setSubject(subject);
            msg.setSentDate(new java.util.Date());
            msg.setFrom();

            msg.setRecipients(Message.RecipientType.TO, InternetAddress.parse(recipient,
false));

            MimeBodyPart body = new MimeBodyPart();
            body.setText(message);
            Multipart mp = new MimeMultipart();
            mp.addBodyPart(body);
            msg.setContent(mp);

            Transport.send(msg);
      } catch (MessagingException ex) {
            Logger.getLogger(JavaUtils.class.getName()).log(Level.SEVERE, null, ex);
      }
   };
```

Compile the Java sources using the ALTER JAVA SOURCE command. The sources should compile without issues since the JAR files containing the required library references have been loaded into the database. If the JAR files had not been loaded, then the class would not compile successfully.

```
ALTER JAVA SOURCE "JavaUtils" RESOLVE;
```

Lastly, create the call specification for the sendMail Java stored procedure. In this case, a PL/SQL package will be created that contains the call specification for sendMail.

```
CREATE OR REPLACE PACKAGE JAVA_UTILS AS
    PROCEDURE send_mail(subject VARCHAR2,
                        recipient VARCHAR2,
                        message VARCHAR2);

END;

CREATE OR REPLACE PACKAGE BODY JAVA_UTILS AS

    PROCEDURE send_mail(subject VARCHAR2,
                        recipient VARCHAR2,
                        message VARCHAR2)
    AS LANGUAGE JAVA
    NAME 'JavaUtils.sendMail(java.lang.String, java.lang.String, java.lang.String)';

END;
```

The stored procedure can now be executed using the following command:

```
EXEC java_utils.send_mail('Test','myemail@mycompany.com','Test Message');
```

If the message is sucessfully sent, you will see the following output:

```
PL/SQL procedure successfully completed.
```

How It Works

Java libraries are packaged into JAR files so that they can be easily distributed. The loadjava utility can be used to load Java libraries into the database. To use the utility, download the JAR files that you want to load into the database, and place them into a directory that can be accessed by the database server. Open the command prompt or terminal, traverse into that directory, and execute the loadjava utility, using the –u flag to specify the database user and passing the name of the JAR file to load. If successful, the JAR file will be loaded into the schema that you indicated with the –u flag, and you may begin to use the libraries contained in the JAR file within your stored Java code.

The loadjava utility contains a number of options. For a complete listing of loadjava options, please see the online Oracle documentation at
http://download.oracle.com/docs/cd/B28359_01/java.111/b31225/cheleven.htm.

Additional options are not necessary to load a JAR file into the schema that you indicate with the -u flag. Since the JAR file consists of compiled Java libraries, there is no need to resolve the library once loaded. As indicated in the solution to this recipe, you can begin to import classes from the libraries as soon as they have been loaded.

15-13. Removing a Java Class

Problem

You want to drop a Java class from your database.

Solution

Issue the SQL DROP JAVA command along with the schema and object name you want to drop. For instance, you want to drop the Java source for the Employees class. In this case, you would issue the following command:

```
DROP JAVA SOURCE "Employees";
```

How It Works

There may come a time when you need to drop a Java class or sources from the database. For instance, if you no longer want to maintain or allow access to a particular Java class, it may make sense to drop it. The DROP JAVA SOURCE command does this by passing the name of the class or source as demonstrated within the solution to this recipe.

■ **Note** Be careful not to drop a Java class if other Java procedures or PL/SQL call specifications depend upon it. Doing so will invalidate any dependent code, and you will receive an error if you try to execute. The data dictionary provides views, such as DBA_DEPENDENCIES, that can be queried in order to find dependent objects.

Alternately, if you are on the database server, there is a dropjava utility that works in the same fashion as the loadjava utility that was demonstrated in Recipe 15-3. To use the dropjava utility, issue the dropjava command at the command line, and pass the database connect string using the –u flag along with the name of the Java class or source you want to drop. The following example demonstrates the command to drop the Employees Java class using the dropjava utility.

```
dropjava –u username/password@database_host:port:database_name Employees.class
```

The dropjava utility actually invokes the DROP JAVA SOURCE command. The downside to using the utility is that you must be located on the database server to use it. I recommend using the DROP JAVA SOURCE command from SQL*Plus if possible because it tends to make life easier if you are working within SQL*Plus on a machine that is remote from the server.

15-14. Retrieving Database Metadata with Java

Problem

You are interested in retrieving some metadata regarding the database from within your Java stored procedure. In this recipe, you want to list all the schemas within the database.

Solution

Create a Java stored procedure that utilizes the OracleDatabaseMetaData object to pull information from the connection. In the following example, a Java stored procedure is created that utilizes the

OracleDatabaseMetaData object to retrieve schema names from the Oracle connection. This Java method will be added to the JavaUtils class.

```
public static void listDatabaseSchemas() {
        Connection conn = null;
        try {
            conn = DriverManager.getConnection("jdbc:default:connection:");
            OracleDatabaseMetaData meta = (OracleDatabaseMetaData) conn.getMetaData();

            if (meta == null) {
                System.out.println("Database metadata is unavailable");
            } else {
                ResultSet rs = meta.getSchemas();
                while (rs.next()) {
                    System.out.println(rs.getString(1));
                }
            }
        } catch (SQLException ex) {
            System.out.println(ex);
        }
    }
```

The output from the execution of this Java method will be a list of all database schemas.

How It Works

Sometimes it may be useful to use Java code for obtaining database metadata. One such instance might arise when you are developing a Java class that needs to access database metadata. Your code will be easier to maintain and read if you use Java to obtain the metadata rather than a PL/SQL procedure. The OracleDatabaseMetaData object was created for that purpose. In the solution to this recipe, the metadata object is used to retrieve a listing of all database schemas. However, several other methods can be called on the OracleDatabaseMetaData object to obtain other useful database metadata. For instance, information about the underlying database tables or columns can also be obtained using this resource. For a complete listing of the different options available via the OracleDatabaseMetaData object, please refer to the online documentation at www.oracle.com/technology/docs/tech/java/sqlj_jdbc/doc_library/javadoc/oracle.jdbc.driver.OracleDatabaseMetaData.html.

In the solution to this recipe, a Java Connection object is obtained using jdbc:default:connection. The getMetaData method can be called on a Connection object and casted to an OracleDatabaseMetaData object type. This solution demonstrates this technique and then uses the object to retrieve information about the database.

15-15. Querying the Database to Help Resolve Java Compilation Issues

Problem

You are attempting to compile Java source within the database, and you are receiving an unsuccessful result. You need to determine the underlying issue to the problem that is preventing the Java source from compiling correctly.

Solution

Query the USER_ERRORS table to determine the cause of the compilation issue. For example, suppose the JavaUtils class source is loaded into the database with an incorrect variable name. This will cause a compiler error that will be displayed within the USER_ERRORS table. The following is an excerpt from a SQL*Plus session where an attempt has been made to compile the code:

```
SQL> ALTER JAVA SOURCE "JavaUtils" RESOLVE;

Warning: Java altered with compilation errors.
```

Since compilation errors have occurred, query the USER_ERRORS table to determine the exact cause of the error so that it can be repaired. The following query demonstrates this technique:

```
SQL> COL TEXT FOR A25
SQL> SELECT NAME, TYPE, LINE, TEXT
  2  FROM USER_ERRORS
  3  WHERE TYPE LIKE 'JAVA%';

NAME                         TYPE           LINE TEXT
---------------------------- ------------ ---------- -------------------------
JavaUtils                    JAVA CLASS        0 ORA-29535: source require
                                    s recompilation

JavaUtils                    JAVA SOURCE       0 JavaUtils:51: cannot find
                                 symbol

JavaUtils                    JAVA SOURCE       0 symbol  : variable me
JavaUtils                    JAVA SOURCE       0 location: class JavaUtils
JavaUtils                    JAVA SOURCE       0             ResultSet
                              rs = me.getSchemas();


NAME                         TYPE           LINE TEXT
---------------------------- ------------ ---------- -------------------------
JavaUtils                    JAVA SOURCE       0
                                 ^

JavaUtils                    JAVA SOURCE       0 1 error
```

```
7 rows selected.
```

How It Works

The USER_ERRORS table contains the most recent errors generated by PL/SQL or Java code. It is the most useful way to determine the issues that are causing compilation errors when attempting to resolve Java source errors. Unlike PL/SQL, you are unable to issue the SHOW ERRORS command to display the most recent compiler errors. The Java compiler, as well as the PL/SQL compiler, writes output to the USER_ERRORS table, making it a beneficial tool when writing Java code for the database.

■ ■ ■

CHAPTER 16

Accessing PL/SQL from JDBC, HTTP, Groovy, and Jython

Java programs run on a virtual machine known as the Java virtual machine (JVM). A version of the JVM is available for most operating systems and is deployed on millions of servers, desktops, phones, and even Blu-ray players throughout the world. Because of the widespread availability of the JVM, Java is considered a portable language: you can essentially write Java code once and run it just about anywhere, whether it's on a Linux box, a Mac, Android phone, or a Windows desktop.

The JVM has evolved over time, and Java is no longer the only language that can run on it. There have been many languages implemented in Java that provide different features for those who enjoy developing applications for the JVM. Each of these languages has its own syntax and constructs, and many of them can be viable alternatives for developing scripts, desktop applications, or enterprise-level web applications. As such, this chapter not only covers the ins and outs of accessing PL/SQL from Java application code but also includes recipes for working with two popular dynamic languages that run on the JVM: Jython and Groovy.

This chapter is not intended to be an overall instruction set for using Java or any other language on the JVM. It is meant for the purpose of demonstrating how to access PL/SQL code from within these languages. The Java online community is outstanding, and a plethora of resources are available on the Web for learning about Java or other languages on the JVM. For more detailed information, please consult those resources, because this chapter will only provide solutions targeting PL/SQL integration.

16-1. Accessing a PL/SQL Stored Procedure via JDBC

Problem

You are writing a Java application that uses JDBC to access data, but you also want to call some PL/SQL stored procedures from within your Java application.

Solution

Use the JDBC API to connect to the database, and then execute prepareCall(), passing a string to it that consists of a PL/SQL code block that calls the stored procedure. For example, consider a stand-alone Java class that contains a method named increaseWage(). This method uses JDBC to obtain a database connection, create a CallableStatement, and then invoke the PL/SQL stored procedure that passes in the required variables.

```
import java.sql.*;
import oracle.jdbc.*;
```

```
public class EmployeeFacade {

 public void increaseWage()
 throws SQLException {
  int ret_code;
  Connection conn = null;
  try {
     //Load Oracle driver
     DriverManager.registerDriver(new oracle.jdbc.driver.OracleDriver());
     //Obtain a connection

     conn = DriverManager.getConnection("jdbc:oracle:thin:@hostname:port_number:mydb",
                                                                 "user",
"password");
     int emp_id = 199;
     double increase_pct = .02;
     int upper_bound = 10000;
     CallableStatement pstmt =
     conn.prepareCall("begin increase_wage(?,?,?); end;");
     pstmt.setInt(1, emp_id);
     pstmt.setDouble(2, increase_pct);
     pstmt.setInt(3, upper_bound);
     pstmt.executeUpdate();

     pstmt.close();
     conn.commit();
     conn.close();
     System.out.println("Increase successful");
  } catch (SQLException e) {ret_code = e.getErrorCode();
     System.err.println(ret_code + e.getMessage()); conn.close();}
  }

  public static void main(String[] args){
      EmployeeFacade facade = new EmployeeFacade();
      try {
          facade.increaseWage();
      } catch (SQLException e){
          System.err.println("A database exception has occurred.");
      }
  }
}
```

Running this code within an integrated development environment such as NetBeans would result in
the following output:

```
run:
Increase successful
BUILD SUCCESSFUL (total time: 4 seconds)
```

The EmployeeFacade class contains a main() method that is used to initiate the execution of the
increaseWage() method. The increaseWage() method initializes three variables that are passed to the
increase_wage PL/SQL stored procedure using a CallableStatement.

How It Works

It is possible to invoke a PL/SQL stored procedure from a JDBC call just as if you were issuing a call from PL/SQL. You can do so by passing a PL/SQL code block that contains the procedure call as a string to the JDBC connection. In the solution to the example we've chosen for this recipe, a Java class named EmployeeFacade contains a method that makes a JDBC call to invoke a stored procedure. If you are unfamiliar with Java and database connectivity, you can see that using JDBC is very methodical. There are several steps that need to be taken in order to obtain a connection to the database, followed by the steps to perform the database transaction and lastly to commit the changes and close all of the JDBC constructs.

Any Java work that is done using the JDBC API must include an exception handler for the java.sql.SQLException. As the increaseWage() method demonstrates, the SQLException is handled using a Java try-catch block. Prior to the try-catch block, a couple of variables are created that the rest of the method will use. One of the variables is the java.sql.Connection, which is to be used to make a connection to the database, execute the call, and then finally close the connection. In the next couple of lines, a try-catch block is started, and a connection is obtained to the Oracle Database using the DriverManager class. The getConnection() method accepts a JDBC URL pertaining to a database as well as a user name and password.

■ **Note** It is important to maintain a close watch on JDBC connections. They can be costly for performance, and only a limited number of connections is usually available for use. For this reason, a connection should always be obtained, used, and then closed.

If a connection is successfully made to the database, then a CallableStatement is created that performs all the work against the database. If you wanted to issue a query, then you would use a PreparedStatement instead because CallableStatements are most useful for making PL/SQL calls. A string containing a PL/SQL code block is used to invoke the call to the PL/SQL stored procedure. The call is a bit different from native PL/SQL because it includes Java bind variables that represent the parameters that need to be passed into the procedure. A bind variable is represented by a question mark (?) character, and subsequent setter methods will be used to set values for each bind variable. After the CallableStatement's prepareCall() method is invoked, variables are passed to the procedure using a series of setXXX() methods on the CallableStatement. The set methods correlate with the type of data that is being passed to the stored procedure, and they provide a positional parameter that maps the variable to the bind variable position in the call. For instance, the first setInt(1, emp_id) method contains an integer variable, emp_id, and it will be passed to the bind variable in the first position within the call.

After all the variables have been set, the executeUpdate() method is called in order to execute the call to the procedure. If successful, program execution will continue. However, if unsuccessful for some reason, then a java.sql.SQLException will be thrown that will cause the execution of the Java program to be passed to the catch block. Finally, if the transaction was a success, then the connection commits the transaction, and the CallableStatement is closed, followed by the closing of the connection. You will notice that the throws SQLException clause has been placed within the method declaration. When any Java method contains a throws clause within the declaration, then you must code an exception handler for any Java code that calls the method. In this solution, the throws clause has been put into place to handle any exceptions that may be raised when closing the connection within the exception-handling catch block. For more information on Java exception handling, please see the online documentation available at http://download.oracle.com/javase/tutorial/essential/exceptions/handling.html.

The JDBC API can be used to call PL/SQL stored procedures by passing a PL/SQL code block in the form of a Java String to a CallableStatement object. The majority of the code using JDBC is spent creating and closing the database connections as well as the CallableStatements. If you are unfamiliar with JDBC, then you can learn more about it at www.oracle.com/technetwork/java/overview-141217.html. It can be used for creating small Java programs or enterprise-level Java applications. The JDBC API has been around since the early days of Java, so it is quite mature and allows you to access the database and your PL/SQL programs directly.

16-2. Accessing a PL/SQL Stored Function from JDBC

Problem

You want to utilize a PL/SQL function from a Java application that uses the JDBC API to connect to an Oracle Database and returns a value to the Java application.

Solution

Use the JDBC API and a CallableStatement to invoke the PL/SQL function by passing a Java String containing the function call to the CallableStatement. The following example demonstrates a Java method that accepts a parameter of type double and then makes a JDBC call to the PL/SQL function calc_quarter_hour using the parameter. It is assumed that this Java method is to be added into the class that was created in Recipe 16-1.

```java
public void calcQuarterHour(double hours)
            throws SQLException {
        float returnValue;
        int ret_code;
        Connection conn = null;
        try {
            //Load Oracle driver
            DriverManager.registerDriver(new oracle.jdbc.driver.OracleDriver());
            //Obtain a connection

            conn = DriverManager.getConnection("jdbc:oracle:thin:@hostname:1521:mydb",
                    "user", "password");

            CallableStatement pstmt =
                    conn.prepareCall("{? = call calc_quarter_hour(?)}");

            pstmt.registerOutParameter(1, java.sql.Types.FLOAT);
            pstmt.setDouble(2, hours);
            pstmt.execute();
            returnValue = pstmt.getFloat(1);
            pstmt.close();
            conn.commit();
            conn.close();
            System.out.println("The calculated value: " + returnValue);
        } catch (SQLException e) {
```

```
            ret_code = e.getErrorCode();
            System.err.println(ret_code + e.getMessage());
            conn.close();
        }
    }
```

Update the main method from the class that was created in Recipe 16-1 to the following code in order to make a call to the new calcQuarterHour method.

```
public static void main(String[] args) {
        EmployeeFacade facade = new EmployeeFacade();
        try {
            facade.calcQuarterHour(7.667);
        } catch (SQLException e) {
            System.err.println("A database exception has occurred.");
        }
    }
```

Running this code within an integrated development environment such as NetBeans would result in the following output:

```
run:
The calculated value: 7.75
BUILD SUCCESSFUL (total time: 1 second)
```

Values can be passed as parameters from Java to PL/SQL, and in turn, PL/SQL can pass return values back to Java. This helps form a seamless integration between the two languages.

How It Works

Calling a PL/SQL function from a JDBC application is not very much different from using native PL/SQL. The biggest difference is that you need to use the JDBC API to make the database call and to set and retrieve values from the database. The solution to this recipe contains a Java method that accepts a double value representing a number of hours. The method connects to the Oracle Database using the JDBC, calls the PL/SQL function using a CallableStatement, and then returns the results.

To make the connection, the database driver is first registered using the DriverManager.registerDriver() method and passing the appropriate driver for Oracle Database. Next, a connection is obtained using the DriverManager.getConnection() method by passing the URL for the Oracle Database that will be used, along with the appropriate user name and password. In Recipe 16-1, obtaining JDBC connections is discussed in more detail. If you haven't yet read Recipe 16-1 and are unfamiliar with JDBC, we recommend you read it for more information on this important aspect of using the JDBC API.

Once a connection has been obtained, a CallableStatement is created by calling the java.sql.Connection prepareCall() method and passing a Java String that contains the call to the PL/SQL function. The function call is in the following format:

```
{? = call calc_quarter_hour(?)}
```

The String is surrounded by curly braces ({}), and the call to the PL/SQL function is preceded by the ? = characters. The question mark (?) character represents a bind variable in a Java prepared statement. Bind variables are used to represent the returning value as well as the parameter value that will be passed into the function. The first ? character represents the returning value, whereas the ? character within the parentheses correlates to the parameter being passed to the function. The PL/SQL function is invoked using the `call` keyword followed by the function name.

The next line of code registers the return value using the CallableStatement `registerOutParameter()` method. This method accepts the bind variable position as its first argument and accepts the datatype of the value as the second argument. In this example, the datatype is `java.sql.Types.FLOAT`, which correlates to a PL/SQL float type. Many different types are available within `java.sql.Types`, and if you are using a Java integrated development environment (IDE) that contains code completion, then you should see a list of all available types after you type the trailing dot when declaring `java.sql.Type`. Next, the parameter that will be passed into the PL/SQL function is set by calling the `setDouble()` method and passing the bind variable position along with the value. Lastly, the `CallableStatement` is executed by invoking the `execute()` method.

If the function call is successful, then the return value of the function can be obtained by calling the `getFloat()` method on the `CallableStatement` and passing the bind variable position. If you were calling a PL/SQL function that had a different return type, then you would use the getter method that correlates to the return type. This method will return the value of the call, so it should be assigned to a Java variable. In the solution, `returnValue` is the variable that is used to hold the value returned from the function call. Finally, the `CallableStatement` is closed, and the transaction is committed by calling the `commit()` method on the `java.sql.Connection`.

The entire method is enclosed within a Java exception-handling `try-catch` block. Code that is contained within the `try` block may or may not throw an exception. If an exception is thrown, then it can be caught by a subsequent `catch` block. For more information on Java exception handling, please see the documentation at http://download.oracle.com/javase/tutorial/essential/exceptions/handling.html.

Interacting with PL/SQL functions from within a Java application can be quite powerful. You will gain the most benefit if the function that you are calling is working with the data. Any application that is not stored in the database will incur at least a minor performance hit when working with the database because of connections and round-trips to and from the database server. If you have a PL/SQL function that works with the database, then it can be more efficient to call the PL/SQL function from your Java application rather than reproducing that function in Java code.

16-3. Accessing PL/SQL Web Procedures with HTTP

Problem

You are developing a Java web application that uses an Oracle Database. You have already created a PL/SQL web application that displays some particular data from your database that is generated from an input identifier. You want to use the PL/SQL web application to display that data by passing the necessary input from the Java web application.

Solution

Write your PL/SQL web program to accept parameter values within a URL. Pass the values from your Java web application to the PL/SQL application by embedding them within the URL that calls it. When the URL is clicked, then it will redirect control to the PL/SQL application, passing the parameters that are required to display the correct data. Suppose, for example, that you are writing a Java web application that generates a list of employees on a web page. Suppose further that you have already written PL/SQL web application that, given an `employee_id`, displays employee record details in a browser. You want to combine that functionality with your Java program so that when you click one of the employees in the list generated by the Java web program, it passes the selected employee's ID to the

PL/SQL web program. In turn, the PL/SQL program will display the detail for that ticket. In the following example, the EMP_RPT package that was introduced in Recipe 14-4 is accessed via a Java Server Faces page.

■ **Note** JSF is the Java standard for creation of server-side user interfaces. To learn more about this technology, please see the online documentation at www.oracle.com/technetwork/java/javaee/javaserverfaces-139869.html.

```xml
<?xml version='1.0' encoding='UTF-8' ?>
<!DOCTYPE html PUBLIC "-//W3C//DTD XHTML 1.0 Transitional//EN"
"http://www.w3.org/TR/xhtml1/DTD/xhtml1-transitional.dtd">
<html xmlns="http://www.w3.org/1999/xhtml"
     xmlns:ui="http://java.sun.com/jsf/facelets"
     xmlns:f="http://java.sun.com/jsf/core"
     xmlns:h="http://java.sun.com/jsf/html">

  <body>

     <ui:composition template="layout/my_layout.xhtml">

        <ui:define name="body">
           <f:view id="employeeView">
              <h:form id="employeeResults">
                 <center>

                    <br/>
                    <h:messages id="messages"
                             errorClass="error"
                             infoClass="info" />
                    <br/>
                    <span class="sub_head_sub">
                       Employee Listing
                    </span>
                    <br/>
                    <br/>

                    <h:dataTable id="employeeList"
                             rows="20"
                             value="#{employeeList}"
                             var="emp">
                       <f:facet name="header">
                          <h:column >
                             <h:outputText value="First Name"/>
                          </h:column>
                          <h:column >
                             <h:outputText value="Last Name"/>
```

```
                              </h:column>
                              <h:column >
                                  <h:outputText value="Email"/>
                              </h:column>
                          </f:facet>

                          <h:column id="firstNameCol">
                              <h:outputText id="firstName" value="#{emp.firstName}"/>
                          </h:column>
                          <h:column id="lastNameCol">
                              <h:outputText id="lastName" value="#{emp.lastName}"/>
                          </h:column>

                          <h:column id="emailCol">
                              <h:outputLink value="http://my-oracle-application-
server:7778/DAD/emp_rpt.rpt"

                                      target="_blank">
                                  <f:param name="emp_id" value="#{emp.employeeId}"/>
                                  <h:outputText id="email" value="#{emp.email}"/>
                              </h:outputLink>
                          </h:column>


                      </h:dataTable>


                  </center>
              </h:form>

          </f:view>

      </ui:define>

   </ui:composition>

 </body>
</html>
```

The JSF tags in this example would generate a web page that looks similar to Figure 16-1. However, it is important to note that JSF contains template functionality, so the look and feel of the user interface can be changed significantly if a different template were applied.

Employee Listing

First Name	Last Name	Email
Steven	King	SKING
Neena	Kochhar	NKOCHHAR
Lex	De Haan	LDEHAAN
Alexander	Hunold	AHUNOLD
Bruce	Ernst	BERNST
David	Austin	DAUSTIN
Valli	Pataballa	VPATABAL
Diana	Lorentz	DLORENTZ
Nancy	Greenberg	NGREENBE
Daniel	Faviet	DFAVIET
John	Chen	JCHEN
Ismael	Sciarra	ISCIARRA
Jose Manuel	Urman	JMURMAN
Luis	Popp	LPOPP
Den	Raphaely	DRAPHEAL
Alexander	Khoo	AKHOO
Shelli	Baida	SBAIDA
Sigal	Tobias	STOBIAS
Guy	Himuro	GHIMURO
Karen	Colmenares	KCOLMENA

Figure 16-1. Employee listing JSF web page

For the sake of brevity, the Java code will not be displayed, because it is not essential for this solution. However, if you want to learn more about writing Java web applications utilizing the Java Server Faces web framework, please see the online documentation available at www.oracle.com/technetwork/java/javaee/javaserverfaces-139869.html.

When you look at the JSF page output on your monitor, you'll see that the EMAIL column values are blue. This signifies that they are links that will take you to another page when selected with the mouse. In this case, the link will redirect users to a PL/SQL application that accepts the employee ID as input and in turn displays a result. Figure 16-2 shows the output from the PL/SQL web application when the e-mail user name SKING is selected from the JSF page.

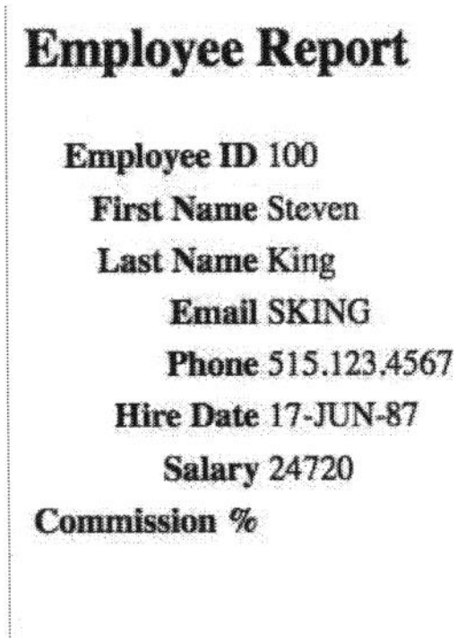

Employee Report

Employee ID 100
First Name Steven
Last Name King
Email SKING
Phone 515.123.4567
Hire Date 17-JUN-87
Salary 24720
Commission %

Figure 16-2. PL/SQL web application output

How It Works

Developing Java web applications and PL/SQL web applications can be quite different. However, accessing one from the other can be quite easy and can create powerful solutions. In this recipe, a mashup consisting of a standard web URL passes data from a Java application to a PL/SQL stored procedure, and then the PL/SQL stored procedure displays content via a web page.

The PL/SQL stored procedure in this recipe utilizes the built-in UTL_HTTP package to display content in HTML format via the Web. The procedure accepts one argument, an EMPLOYEE_ID. The given EMPLOYEE_ID field is used to query the database, and the content that is retrieved is displayed. The procedure is accessible from the Web because a Data Access Descriptor (DAD) has been created on the web server, which allows access to a particular schema's web-accessible content. Using the DAD, a URL incorporating the host name, the DAD, and the procedure to be used can access the stored procedure. Please see Recipe 14-1 to learn more about creating DADs. For more details regarding the creation of web content using PL/SQL, please refer to Chapter 14.

The Java application Extensible Hypertext Markup Language (XHTML) page that is displayed in the solution to this recipe creates a listing of employee names by querying the database using EJB technology. Enterprise Java Beans (EJB) is part of the Java Enterprise Edition stack that is used for object relational mapping of Java code and database entities. For more information regarding EJB technology, please refer to the documentation at www.oracle.com/technetwork/java/index-jsp-140203.html.

The important code for this particular recipe is the web page code that resides within the Java Server Faces XHTML page. The generated list of employee names is a list of URLs that contain the host name of the Oracle Application Server, the DAD for the schema containing the PL/SQL you want to access, and the name of the PL/SQL stored procedure, which is EMP_RPT.RPT in this case. The URL also contains an embedded parameter that is passed to the stored procedure upon invocation. The following code shows an example of a URL that is generated by the Java application:

```
<a href="http://my-web-server:port/hr/EMP_RPT.RPT?emp_id=200">
```

The code that generates this URL is written in Java Server Faces using Facelets markup, as shown here:

```
<h:outputLink value="http://my-oracle-application-server:port/DAD/emp_rpt.rpt"
                              target="_blank">
```

```
                <f:param name="emp_id" value="#{emp.employeeId}"/>
                <h:outputText id="email" value="#{emp.email}"/>
</h:outputLink>
```

The &emp_id=200 portion of the URL is the parameter name and value that is passed to the EMP_RPT.RPT procedure when called. In the case of the JSF markup, #{emp.employeeId} will pass this value as a parameter to the URL. In turn, the EMP_RPT.RPT procedure queries the EMPLOYEES table for the given EMPLOYEE_ID and displays the record data. In a sense, the Java application performs a redirect to the PL/SQL stored procedure, as illustrated by Figure 16-3.

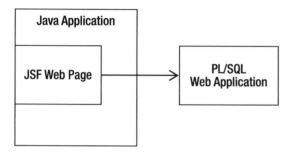

Figure 16-3. *JSF to PL/SQL web redirect*

■ **Note** Facelets is an open source web framework that is the default view handler technology for JSF.

Any two languages that can be used to develop web applications can be used to create mashups in a similar fashion. A regular HTML page can include links to any PL/SQL stored procedure that has been deployed and made available using a DAD. This is a simple technique that can be used to allow applications to use data that resides in a remote database.

16-4. Accessing PL/SQL from Jython

Problem

You are working with a Jython program and want to call some PL/SQL stored procedures or functions from it.

Solution #1

Use Jython's zxJDBC API to obtain a connection to the Oracle Database, and then call the PL/SQL stored procedure passing parameters as required. The following code is an example of a Jython script that performs these tasks:

```
from __future__ import with_statement
from com.ziclix.python.sql import zxJDBC

# Set up connection variables
jdbc_url = "jdbc:oracle:thin:@host:1521:dbname"
username = "user"
password = "password"
driver = "oracle.jdbc.driver.OracleDriver"

# obtain a connection using the with-statment
with zxJDBC.connect(jdbc_url, username, password, driver) as conn:
    with conn:
        with conn.cursor() as c:
            c.callproc('increase_wage',[199,.03,10000])
            print 'Procedure call complete'
            conn.commit()
```

This example does not display any real output; it only calls the INCREASE_WAGE procedure and performs a commit. After the procedure is called, a line of text is printed to alert the user that the procedure call is complete.

Solution #2

Use a Python web framework, such as Django, along with Jython to create a web application for deployment to a Java application server. Use the selected web framework's built-in syntax to invoke the stored procedure or function call.

DJANGO

Django is a popular web framework that is used with the Python programming language. Django has worked with Jython since the release of Jython 2.5. Django takes a model-view-controller approach to web design, whereas all code is separated from web pages. The web pages use templating that makes it easy to create dynamic and expressive web pages. Django uses an object-oriented approach to working with the database that is known as object relational mapping. For more information on the Django framework, please visit the Django web site at www.djangoproject.com/ and the Django-Jython project that is located at http://code.google.com/p/django-jython/.

For example, here's how you might use the Django web framework to create a call to the PL/SQL stored procedure CALC_QUARTER_HOUR that was demonstrated in Recipe 4-1. The following code demonstrates an excerpt taken from a Django view to make a call to an Oracle PL/SQL function:

```
# Views.py
from django.db import connection

def calc_hours(self, hours_in):
```

```
cursor = connection.cursor()
ret = cursor.callproc("CALC_QUARTER_HOUR", (hours_in))# calls PROCEDURE OR FUNCTION
cursor.close()
return ret
```

This view code only demonstrates a function written in Python or Jython that will perform the call to the database and return a result.

How It Works

The Jython language is an incarnation of the Python language that has been implemented on the JVM. Using Jython provides a developer with all the corresponding syntax and language constructs that the Python language has to offer and allows them to be used to write applications running on the JVM. Furthermore, Jython applications have access to all the underlying libraries that the Java platform has to offer, which is a tremendous asset to any developer. Jython is one of the first additional languages developed to run on the JVM. It has matured over the years, although it remains a bit behind its sister language Python in release number. Jython can be used for developing scripts, desktop applications, and enterprise-level web applications.

Using the zxJDBC API to Solve the Problem

In the first solution to this recipe, Jython's zxJDBC API is used to perform tasks against an Oracle Database. zxJDBC is an extension of the Java JDBC API that allows Jython developers to program JDBC calls in a Python-like syntax. Working with zxJDBC can be very efficient. It is similar to working with regular Java JDBC code, except the syntax makes development a bit easier since there are fewer lines of code to maintain. zxJDBC contains the function callproc() that can be used to make calls to PL/SQL procedures or functions. Once you have obtained a database connection, you allocate a cursor from the connection and invoke that cursor's callproc() function. The callproc() function accepts one argument, which is the name of the PL/SQL procedure to be called. The called procedure or function will return the results to the caller in a seamless manner.

The zxJDBC API is useful for writing stand-alone Jython applications or scripts. Many developers and database administrators use Jython to script their nightly jobs, allowing zxJDBC to invoke PL/SQL functions and stored procedures. This is one alternative to using Oracle Scheduler for executing database tasks, and it can allow for much more flexibility because all the libraries available for use on the JVM are at your disposal.

Using Django to Solve the Problem

Although zxJDBC is a great way to work with the database, there are other techniques that can be used for creation of web content that accesses PL/SQL. Many Jython users create web applications using different Python web frameworks. One such Python web framework is Django, and it can be used along with Jython to productively create web applications that run on the Java platform. The Django framework uses an object-oriented approach to work with the database. In other terms, Django provides an object-relational mapping solution that allows developers to work with Python objects representing database tables rather than working directly with SQL.

Django uses a model.py file to map a database table to a Python object. A views.py file is used to implement separate views for the web site, and a urls.py file is used to contain the valid URL mappings for a Django application. In the solution to this recipe, a Python function that would go into the `views.py` file is displayed. The purpose of this function is to make a connection to the database and invoke a PL/SQL function call. The Django framework handles database connections for you by declaring some parameters for the database connection within a `settings.py` file for the project. As you can see from the example, obtaining a connection is trivial because you merely import it from the `django.db` package. The code is similar to using zxJDBC for calling a PL/SQL stored procedure or function. The cursor's `callProc()` function is used to make the function call, and the syntax for performing that task is as follows:

```
cursor.callProc(function_or_procedure_name,(parameter_one, parameter_two, etc))
```

The function or procedure name should be a string value, and the parameters can passed as a tuple or listed one by one, separated by commas. If calling a PL/SQL function, the `callProc()` function should be assigned to a variable because there will be a return result. Lastly, the cursor should be closed in order to release resources. Again, when using the Django framework connections to the database will be handled for you, so there is no need to worry about closing connections after a database call has been made.

For more information on using the Django web framework, please visit the project home page at `www.djangoproject.com`. To use the Django web framework with Jython, you will also need to include the django-jython site package at `http://code.google.com/p/django-jython/`.

16-5. Accessing PL/SQL from Groovy

Problem

You are writing a Groovy program and want to call some PL/SQL stored procedures or functions from it.

Solution

Use `GroovySQL` to establish a database connection, and make the call to the PL/SQL stored program. For example, here's how you would use of `GroovySQL` to connect to an Oracle Database and call a PL/SQL function:

```
import groovy.sql.Sql
import oracle.jdbc.driver.OracleTypes

Sql sql = Sql.newInstance("jdbc:oracle:thin:@hostname:1521:dbname",

"username","password","oracle.jdbc.driver.OracleDriver")
dept_id = 50

sql.call('{? = call calc_quarter_hour(?)}', [Sql.DOUBLE, 6.35]) { qtr_hour->
  println qtr_hour
}
```

Short and to the point, the Groovy script in this example connects to an Oracle Database, executes a PL/SQL function call, returns a value, and prints the result.

How It Works

Groovy is a unique JVM language that is useful for developing productive and efficient applications. It can be used for developing a wide variety of applications, from scripts to enterprise-level web applications. The syntax of the Groovy language is unlike that of other languages on the JVM because the Groovy compiler allows you to write Java code and it will be deemed as valid Groovy. However, Groovy also has its own syntax that can be combined with Java syntax if you want to do so. Its flexibility allows for beginners to pick up the language as they go and allows advanced Groovy coders to write code in Groovy syntax that is magnitudes smaller than the amount of lines taken to write the same code in Java.

In the solution to this example, the Groovy SQL API is used to connect to an Oracle Database and issue a PL/SQL function call. The top of the script contains import statements. The imports in Groovy work in the same manner as Java imports. The groovy.sql.Sql import pulls all the Groovy SQL functionality into the script. The second import is used to pull in the Oracle driver.

The database connection is made by using the Sql.newInstance method and passing the JDBC URL for the database along with the user name, password, and database driver class. The actual PL/SQL function call occurs with the Sql instance's call() method, and the syntax is very similar to that of Java's JDBC API, whereas you pass a string that is enclosed in curly braces in the following format. The following example demonstrates a call to the CALC_QUARTER_HOUR PL/SQL function that was written in Recipe 4-1:

```
{? = call calc_quarter_hour(?)}
```

The question mark characters (?) correlate to bind variables. The second argument that is passed to the call() method is a list of parameters including the return type and value of the parameter that will be passed to the PL/SQL function. In this case, the PL/SQL function's return type is groovy.sql.Sql.DOUBLE, and the value that will be passed to the function is 6.35. The code that follows the call is some Groovy syntactic sugar and is otherwise known as a *closure*. By specifying curly braces ({}) after the function call, you are telling Groovy to pass any return values to the variable contained within the braces. In this case, qtr_hour will contain the result from the PL/SQL function call, and it prints the result upon return via use of the closure -> notation and then specifying a print statement afterward.

If you have never seen Groovy code before, this syntax will seem a bit awkward. However, once you become used to the syntax, it will become a powerful asset to your tool box. It is easy to see that taking standard Java JDBC implementations for accessing PL/SQL and translating them into a different language will allow for the same PL/SQL connectivity across most languages that run on the JVM. For more information regarding the use of Groovy, Groovy SQL, or closures in Groovy, please see the online documentation at http://groovy.codehaus.org/Beginners+Tutorial.

CHAPTER 17

■ ■ ■

Unit Testing With utPLSQL

Testing is a necessary evil of the application development process. Sadly, testing is oftentimes overlooked or bypassed when time is short. Distribution of untested or undertested code can lead to code that is riddled with bugs and to disappointed users. Unit testing with a well-constructed framework can help to alleviate some of the time that it takes to conform to a well-tested development process.

There are a few different options available to you for testing your PL/SQL code. SQL Developer provides some good debugging options that you can read about in Recipe 12-12. You can also use DBMS_OUTPUT statements within your code to display the results of variables as your code executes. This is a good technique for helping to pinpoint issues in your code and one you can read about in Recipe 17-1. There are also unit-testing frameworks available that will help you to write unit tests for your PL/SQL code objects. Although not covered in this book, the PLUTO (PL/SQL Unit Testing for Oracle) framework (http://code.google.com/p/pluto-test-framework/) is one such framework. Another is the utPLSQL unit-testing framework, and this chapter will focus on utPLSQL since it is more widely adopted than the others.

The utPLSQL unit-testing framework can alleviate some of the pain of unit testing. The framework is easy to use and performs nicely for testing code under every circumstance that can be imagined. There are also many options in utPLSQL that can be used to enhance your unit testing process. This chapter includes recipes that show how to use the framework for testing PL/SQL objects, how to create test suites, and how to automate your unit tests. In the end, you will learn to make the unit testing process a functional part of your development process. As a result of using unit testing, your applications will be successful, and you will spend much less time maintaining the code base.

17-1. Testing Stored PL/SQL Code Without Unit Tests

Problem

You want to ensure that a block of PL/SQL code is working properly, but don't want to take the time to write a unit test.

Solution

Wrap the code in DBMS_OUTPUT statements that display or print the results of intermediate and final computations and the results of complex conditional steps and branches. This will enable you to see the path that the code is taking when the function is called with specified parameters. The following example demonstrates this tactic for placing comments into strategic locations within a PL/SQL code block in order to help determine if code is functioning as expected. For example, suppose you wish to quickly test the function we introduced in the example for Recipe 4-1. Here's how you'd modify it to quickly test the correctness of its results.

```
CREATE OR REPLACE
FUNCTION CALC_QUARTER_HOUR(HOURS IN NUMBER) RETURN NUMBER AS
  CALCULATED_HOURS NUMBER := 0;
BEGIN

  -- if HOURS is greater than one, then calculate the decimal portion
 -- based upon quarterly hours
 IF HOURS > 1 THEN
  -- calculate the modulus of the HOURS variable and compare it to
  DBMS_OUTPUT.Put_LINE('The value passed in was greater than one hour...');
  -- fractional values
    IF MOD(HOURS, 1) <=.125 THEN
       DBMS_OUTPUT.Put_LINE('The decimal portion < .125');
       CALCULATED_HOURS := substr(to_char(HOURS),0,1);
    ELSIF MOD(HOURS, 1) > .125 AND MOD(HOURS,1) <= .375 THEN
       DBMS_OUTPUT.Put_LINE('The decimal portion <= .375');
       CALCULATED_HOURS := substr(to_char(HOURS),0,1) + MOD(.25,1);
    ELSIF MOD(HOURS, 1) > .375 AND MOD(HOURS,1) <= .625 THEN
       DBMS_OUTPUT.Put_LINE('The decimal portion <= .625');
       CALCULATED_HOURS := substr(to_char(HOURS),0,1) + MOD(.50,1);
    ELSIF MOD(HOURS, 1) > .63 AND MOD(HOURS,1) <= .825 THEN
       DBMS_OUTPUT.Put_LINE('The decimal portion <= .825');
       CALCULATED_HOURS := SUBSTR(TO_CHAR(HOURS),0,1) + MOD(.75,1);
    ELSIF MOD(HOURS, 1) > .825 AND MOD(HOURS,1) <= .999 THEN
       DBMS_OUTPUT.Put_LINE('The decimal portion <= .999');
       CALCULATED_HOURS := (substr(to_char(HOURS),0,1) + 1) + MOD(.00,1);
    ELSE
       DBMS_OUTPUT.Put_LINE('The hours passed in will use standard rounding');
       CALCULATED_HOURS := ROUND(HOURS,1);

    END IF;

  ELSE
     -- if HOURS is less than one, then calculate the entire value
     DBMS_OUTPUT.Put_LINE('Less than 1 hour was passed in...');
     -- based upon quarterly hours
     IF HOURS > 0 AND HOURS <=.375 THEN
        DBMS_OUTPUT.Put_LINE('The decimal portion < .125');
        CALCULATED_HOURS := .25;
     ELSIF HOURS > .375 AND HOURS <= .625 THEN
        DBMS_OUTPUT.Put_LINE('The decimal portion <= .625');
        CALCULATED_HOURS := .5;
     ELSIF HOURS > .625 AND HOURS <= .825 THEN
        DBMS_OUTPUT.Put_LINE('The decimal portion <= .825');
        CALCULATED_HOURS := .75;
     ELSIF HOURS > .825 AND HOURS <= .999 THEN
        DBMS_OUTPUT.Put_LINE('The decimal portion <= .999');
        CALCULATED_HOURS := 1;
     ELSE
        DBMS_OUTPUT.Put_LINE('The hours passed in will use standard rounding');
        CALCULATED_HOURS := ROUND(HOURS,1);
     END IF;
```

```
  END IF;

  RETURN CALCULATED_HOURS;

END CALC_QUARTER_HOUR;
```

When the CALC_QUARTER_HOUR function is executed with a value of 7.34, the comments will be displayed as seen in the next snippet from a SQL*Plus session.

```
SQL> set serveroutput on
SQL> select calc_quarter_hour(7.34) from dual;

CALC_QUARTER_HOUR(7.34)
-----------------------
                   7.25

The value passed in was greater than one hour...
The decimal portion <= .375
```

How It Works

The use of DBMS_OUTPUT statements within PL/SQL code for displaying data or information pertaining to the functionality of the code has been a great tactic for testing code in any language. As a matter of fact, it is probably one of the most widely used techniques for debugging code. The ability to see values as they are calculated or to determine how a condition is being handled can be very useful for determining whether your code is executing as it should.

In order to use DBMS_OUTPUT statements for testing your code, you must place them in strategic locations. In the example for this recipe, comments have been placed within each of the IF-ELSE blocks to display a bit of text that will tell the developer how the values are being processed within the function. This can be very useful when testing the code because a series of numbers can be passed into the function in order to determine whether the correct result is being returned. If not, then you will be able to see exactly where the code is being evaluated incorrectly.

Although using DBMS_OUTPUT statements in code can be very useful for determining where code is functioning properly, it can cause clutter, and can also create its own issues. For example, if you forget to place a quote after one of the DBMS_OUTPUT statements that you place into your code, then the code will not compile correctly, causing you to hunt for the cause of yet another issue. Also, it is a good idea to remove the output statements before code is released into production. This can take some time, which could be better spent on development. As a means for testing small units of code, using DBMS_OUTPUT statements works quite well. However, if you wish to develop entire test suites and automated unit testing then you should go on to read Recipe 17-2 regarding utPLSQL.

17-2. Installing the utPLSQL Unit Testing Framework

Problem

You've chosen the utPLSQL unit-testing framework for PL/SQL for your work, and you want to install it.

Solution

First, download the utPLSQL sources from `http://utplsql.sourceforge.net/`. Once you have obtained the sources, use the following steps to install the utPLSQL package into the database for which you wish to write unit tests, and make it available for all schemas.

> Create a user to host the utPLSQL tables, packages, and other objects. In this example, the user will be named UTP, and the default permanent and temporary tablespaces will be used.

```
SQL> create user utp identified by abc123;
```

> Grant privileges to the newly created UTP user using the `GRANT privilege_name TO user_name` statement, replacing values with the appropriate privilege and username. The user will require the following privileges:

> > Create session

> > Create procedure

> > Create table

> > Create view

> > Create sequence

> > Create public synonym

> > Drop public synonym

> Install the objects by running the `ut_i_do.sql` script.

```
SQL> @ut_i_do install
```

Once these steps have been completed then you will have the ability to run unit tests on packages that are loaded into different schemas within the database.

How It Works

Before you can begin to write and run unit tests within the utPLSQL framework for the PL/SQL contained within your database, you must install the utPLSQL package into a database schema. While the utPLSQL framework can be loaded into the SYSTEM schema, it is better to separate the framework into its own schema by creating a separate user and installing the packages, tables, and other objects into it. The solution to this recipe steps through the recommended approach taken to install the utPLSQL framework into the database of your choice.

Once you have created a user schema in which to install the utPLSQL framework objects, you must grant it the appropriate privileges. The majority of the privileges are used to create the objects that are required to make the framework functional. Public synonyms are created for many of the framework objects, and this allows them to be accessible to other database user accounts. After all privileges have been granted, running the `ut_i_do.sql` script and passing the install parameter will complete the installation of the framework. After completion, you can begin to build unit test packages and install them into different schemas within the database, depending on which PL/SQL objects that you wish to test.

■ **Note** Unit tests will be executed from the same schema in which the PL/SQL object that is being tested resides, not from the schema that contains the utPLSQL framework objects.

17-3. Building a utPLSQL Test Package

Problem

You would like to build a unit test package for one or more of the PL/SQL objects in your database schema.

Solution

You want to build a utPLSQL *test package* to test an object in your database. A test package consists of two separate files, a package header and a package body.

> Create a header for the test package and save it in a file with the same name you have given the header and with a `.pks` suffix. A header file contains three procedures: ut_setup, ut_teardown, and the procedure that performs the unit tests of the target object in your database. For example, suppose you want to create a unit test package to test the code for the CALC_QUARTERLY_HOURS function of Recipe 17-1. This package header should be stored into a file named ut_calc_quarter_hour.pks and loaded into the database whose objects you are testing.

```
CREATE OR REPLACE PACKAGE ut_calc_quarter_hour
IS
  PROCEDURE ut_setup;
  PROCEDURE ut_teardown;

  PROCEDURE ut_calc_quarter_hour;
END ut_calc_quarter_hour;
```

> Create the package body that implements the procedures specified by the unit test package header and save it as a file with the same name as the header, but this time with a `.pkb` suffix. The following package body should be stored into a file named ut_calc_quarter_hour.pkb and loaded into the database.

```
CREATE OR REPLACE PACKAGE BODY ut_calc_quarter_hour
IS

PROCEDURE ut_setup IS
BEGIN
  NULL;
END;

PROCEDURE ut_teardown IS
BEGIN
  NULL;
END;
```

```
PROCEDURE ut_calc_quarter_hour IS
BEGIN

  -- Perform unit tests here
  NULL;

END ut_calc_quarter_hour;

END ut_calc_quarter_hour;
```

The package body in this example conforms to the format that must be used for testing packages using the utPLSQL framework.

■ **Note** The .pks and .pkb suffixes could be changed to something different, like .sql, if you wish. You could also store both the package header and body in the same file. However, utPLSQL framework will look for the .pks and .pkb suffixes in order to automatically recompile your test packages before each test. It is best to follow the utPLSQL convention to ensure that your test packages are always valid.

How It Works

A unit test package for the utPLSQL framework consists of a package header and a body. The package header declares a setup procedure, a teardown procedure, and a unit testing procedure. The package body consists of the PL/SQL code that implements the unit test. When you create a ut_PLSQL package, its name must be prefixed with ut_, followed by the procedure or function name for which you are writing the unit test. The unit test prefix can be changed, but ut_ is the default. For more information on changing the unit test prefix, please see Recipe 12-8.

The test package body must contain both a setup and teardown procedure. These procedures must also be given names that use the same prefix you have chosen for your unit testing. Therefore, as you can see in the solution to this recipe, the package header declares ut_setup and ut_teardown procedures. The ut_setup procedure is to initialize the variables or data structures the unit test procedure uses. When a unit test is executed, ut_setup is always the first procedure to execute. The ut_teardown procedure is used to clean up after all of the tests have been run. You should use this procedure to destroy all of the data structures and variables created to support your unit tests. The ut_teardown procedure is always executed last, after all unit tests have been run.

■ **Note** If you are choosing to use manual registration for your tests, you will be required to register each test procedure in the ut_setup procedure as well. By default, registration of unit test procedures occurs automatically, so you do not need to register them within ut_setup. If you are interested in learning more about manual unit test registration, please see the online documentation that can be found at: http://utplsql.oracledeveloper.nl/

The package must also contain an implementation for your unit test procedures. The unit test procedure names should begin with the ut_ prefix followed by the name of the PL/SQL object that you are testing. In the case of the solution for this recipe, the procedure name is ut_calc_quarter_hour. The solution to this recipe does not contain any unit tests per se, but in order to perform a valid unit test of the PL/SQL object, you must define a test case for each possible scenario using the assertion routines that are made available by utAssert. To learn more about the different assertion routines, please see Recipe 17-4.

17-4. Writing a utPLSQL Unit Test Procedure

Problem

You have a PL/SQL object that you'd like to test to verify it returns the expected values.

Solution

Create a utPLSQL test package to test every code branch and computation within your function. Use utPLSQL assertion statements to test every foreseeable use case for the function. For example, suppose you wish to test a simple factorial function that contains four code branches, each of which returns a value. Here's the target function:

```
CREATE OR REPLACE FUNCTION factorial (fact INTEGER) RETURN INTEGER is

BEGIN

    IF fact < 0 THEN RETURN NULL;
    ELSIF fact = 0 THEN RETURN 1;
    ELSIF fact = 1 THEN RETURN fact;
    ELSE RETURN fact * factorial (fact-1);
    END IF;

END factorial;
```

Next, create the unit test package to test the factorial function. Name the package using the same name as the function to be tested and adding the prefix ut_ to it In this example, you'll name the package ut_factorial. Create the three required procedures within the package for setup, teardown, and testing. Remember to save the file as a PKS file (i.e., one with a .pks file extension).

```
CREATE OR REPLACE PACKAGE ut_factorial IS

    PROCEDURE ut_setup;
    PROCEDURE ut_teardown;
    PROCEDURE ut_factorial;

END ut_factorial;
```

Now create the unit testing package body. No code is required for the ut_setup or the ut_teardown procedures as these are usually reserved for code that updates the database prior to or after running the tests. For example, the setup procedure may insert records that are required only by the unit test, which means that the teardown routine must clean up any data the test leaves behind. The ut_factorial procedure is built with a series of assert statements that test each code branch in the factorial function. Remember to save the file as a PKB file (i.e., one with a .pkb file extension).

```
CREATE OR REPLACE PACKAGE BODY ut_factorial IS

PROCEDURE ut_setup IS
BEGIN
    NULL;
END ut_setup;

PROCEDURE ut_teardown IS
BEGIN
    NULL;
END ut_teardown;

PROCEDURE ut_factorial IS
BEGIN
    utAssert.isnull ('is NULL test', factorial(-1));
    utAssert.eqQuery ('0! Test', 'select factorial(0) from dual', 'select 1 from dual');
    utAssert.eqQuery ('1! Test', 'select factorial(1) from dual', 'select 1 from dual');
    utAssert.eqQuery ('N! Test', 'select FACTORIAL(5) from dual', 'select 120 from dual');
END ut_factorial;

END ut_factorial;
```

How It Works

The utPLSQL package contains a number of tests that can be used to ensure that your code is working properly. Each of these tests is an *assertion*, which is a statement that evaluates to either true or false depending on whether its conditions are met. The solution to this recipe uses four tests to determine whether the function returns an appropriate result for each scenario. The utAssert.isnull procedure verifies the second parameter returns a null value when executed. The utAssert.eqQuery procedure uses the select statements in parameter positions two and three to determine if the unit test succeeds or fails. Each select statement must return the same value when executed to succeed. The three calls to utAssert.eqQuery procedure in the ut_factorial procedure tests one branch (if statement) within the factorial function. The expected return value from the factorial is used in the select statement of the third parameter to retrieve the value from dual. If the factorial is updated in such a way that any code branch no longer returns the expected value, the unit test will fail. This test should be performed after modifying the factorial function to test for bugs introduced by the update. Table 17-1 lists the different assertion tests that are part of the utAssert package.

Table 17-1. utPLSQL Assertion Tests

Assertion Name	Description
utAssert.eq	Checks equality of scalar values
utAssert.eq_refc_query	Checks equality of RefCursor and Query
utAssert.eq_refc_table	Checks equality of RefCursor and Database Tables

Assertion Name	Description
utAssert.eqcoll	Checks equality of collections
utAssert.eqcollapi	Checks equality of collections
utAssert.eqfile	Checks equality of files
utAssert.eqoutput	Checks equality of DBMS_OUTPUT values
utAssert.eqpipe	Checks equality of database pipes
utAssert.eqquery	Checks equality of different queries
utAssert.eqqueryvalue	Checks equality of query against a value
utAssert.eqtabcount	Checks equality of table counts
utAssert.eqtable	Checks equality of different database tables
UTASSERT.isnotnull	Checks for NOT NULL values
utAssert.isnull	Checks for NULL values
utAssert.objexists	Checks for the existence of database objects
utAssert.objnotexists	Checks for the existence of database objects
utAssert.previous_failed	Checks if the previous assertion failed
utAssert.previous_passed	Checks if the previous assertion passed
utAssert.this	Generic "this" procedure
utAssert.throws	Checks if a procedure or function throws an exception

There are many other tests that can also be used to help build your unit test packages. For an entire list of the tests that are available, please see the documentation that can be found online at: http://utplsql.oracledeveloper.nl/.

17-5. Running a utPLSQL Test

Problem

With a unit test package defined, you want to run it to verify that a function returns the values you expect under a variety of scenarios.

Solution

Use the utPLSQL.test procedure to run your test package. For example, suppose you want to run the unit test you built in 17-4. To do so, enter the following commands.

```
set serverout on
exec utPLSQL.test('factorial', recompile_in => FALSE)
```

Executing the commands above produces the following output.

```
.

> SSSS   U    U  CCC    CCC   EEEEEE  SSSS    SSSS

> S    S  U    U  C   C   C   C E       S   S   S    S

> S       U    U  C     C  C   C E       S       S

> S       U    U  C      C     E       S       S

> SSSS   U    U  C      C     EEEE    SSSS    SSSS

>     S  U    U  C      C     E           S       S

>      S  U    U  C    C C    C E           S       S

> S    S  U    U  C   C   C   C E       S   S   S    S

> SSSS     UUU    CCC    CCC   EEEEEE  SSSS    SSSS

.

SUCCESS: "factorial"

.

> Individual Test Case Results:

>

SUCCESS - factorial.UT_FACTORIAL: ISNULL "is NULL test" Expected "" and got ""

>

SUCCESS - factorial.UT_FACTORIAL: EQQUERY "0! Test" Result: Result set for "select
factorial(0) from dual does match that of "select 1 from dual"
```

```
>

SUCCESS - factorial.UT_FACTORIAL: EQQUERY "1! Test" Result: Result set for "select
factorial(1) from dual does match that of "select 1 from dual"

>

SUCCESS - factorial.UT_FACTORIAL: EQQUERY "N! Test" Result: Result set for "select
FACTORIAL(5) from dual does match that of "select 120 from dual"

>

>

> Errors recorded in utPLSQL Error Log:

>

> NONE FOUND



PL/SQL procedure successfully completed.



SQL> spool off
```

What if one of your test cases fails? Suppose that one of the test cases for the FACTORIAL test has been modified so that a failure will result. Following is the resulting output from a failed unit test.

```
SQL> exec utPLSQL.test('factorial', recompile_in => FALSE)

.

>   FFFFFFF   AA      III  L      U      U RRRRR    EEEEEEE

>   F         A A     I    L      U      U R    R   E

>   F        A   A    I    L      U      U R    R   E

>   F        A     A  I    L      U      U R    R   E

>   FFFF     A     A  I    L      U      U RRRRRR   EEEE
```

```
>  F     AAAAAAAA  I  L     U     U R   R   E
>  F     A    A  I  L     U     U R   R   E
>  F     A    A  I  L       U  U R     R  E
>  F     A    A  III  LLLLLLL  UUU   R     R EEEEEEE
.
FAILURE: "factorial"
.
> Individual Test Case Results:
>
SUCCESS - factorial.UT_FACTORIAL: ISNULL "is NULL test" Expected "" and got ""
>
SUCCESS - factorial.UT_FACTORIAL: EQQUERY "0! Test" Result: Result set for
"select factorial(0) from dual does match that of "select 1 from dual"
>
SUCCESS - factorial.UT_FACTORIAL: EQQUERY "1! Test" Result: Result set for
"select factorial(1) from dual does match that of "select 1 from dual"
>
FAILURE - factorial.UT_FACTORIAL: EQQUERY "N! Test" Result: Result set for
"select FACTORIAL(5) from dual does  not match that of "select 121 from dual"
>
>
> Errors recorded in utPLSQL Error Log:
>
```

```
> NONE FOUND
```

```
PL/SQL procedure successfully completed.
```

How It Works

The utPLSQL framework makes it easy to execute all of the tests that you have setup within a unit test package; you need only to enter a utPLSQL.test command. In the solution to this recipe, the SET SERVEROUT ON command enables output from the DBMS_OUTPUT statements within the utPLSQL.test procedure. Without this command you cannot view the results of the unit test. The call to the utPLSQL.test procedure passes two parameters, the first is the name of the unit test to run. Notice that you do not specify the name of the package built for the unit test. Instead, you pass the name of the function being tested. The second parameter tells the utPLSQL.test procedure not to recompile any of the code before running the test.

17-6. Building a utPLSQL Test Suite

Problem

You have created numerous unit test procedures that you must run every time you modify your code. Running each test individually is both time-consuming and error-prone, as you may forget to run a test or two. You need a simple method to run all of your tests at once.

Solution

Use the utsuite.add command of utPLSQL to build a test suite, use the utPackage.add command to add individual unit tests to it, and then run the result. For example, here's how to build a suite to run the unit tests you developed in Recipes 17-3 and 17-4.

Create the test suite.
```
exec utSuite.add ('My Test Suite', 'Test all my functions');
```

Add individual unit tests to the suite.
```
exec utPackage.add ('My Test Suite', 'calc_quarter_hour');
exec utPackage.add ('My Test Suite', 'factorial');
```

Run the test suite. See recipe 17-7.

How It Works

The utSuite.add routine creates a new test suite using the text in the first parameter as its unique name. Note that the utPLSQL utility uppercases the suite name before saving, so take that into consideration, as suite names must be unique. The second parameter is descriptive text for your test suite.

Once the suite is created, use the utPackage.add procedure to add existing unit tests to the suite. The first parameter must match the name of an existing test suite. The second parameter is the name of the unit test to run. As more unit tests are developed, they can be added to the suite to provide an easy method to run all tests at once.

17-7. Running a utPLSQL Test Suite

Problem

You have defined a test suite and now wish to run the tests.

Solution

Use the utPLSQL.testSuite routine to run your tests. For example, here's how run the test suite defined in Recipe 17-6.

```
exec utPLSQL.testSuite ('My Test Suite', recompile_in=>false);
```

Executing the above test suite produces the following results.

```
SQL> exec utPLSQL.testSuite ('My Test Suite', recompile_in=>false);

.

>    SSSS   U    U  CCC    CCC   EEEEEEE  SSSS    SSSS

>   S    S U   U C  C  C  C  E        S   S   S    S

>   S       U    U C   C C     C E        S       S

>   S       U    U C      C    E          S       S

>    SSSS   U    U C      C     EEEE    SSSS    SSSS

>       S U   U C      C    E              S       S

>        S U   U C   C C     C E              S       S

>   S    S U   U C  C  C  C  E          S   S   S    S

>    SSSS    UUU   CCC    CCC  EEEEEEE  SSSS    SSSS

.

SUCCESS: "FACTORIAL"

.

> Individual Test Case Results:

>
```

SUCCESS - FACTORIAL.UT_FACTORIAL: ISNULL "is NULL test" Expected "" and got ""

>

SUCCESS - FACTORIAL.UT_FACTORIAL: EQQUERY "0! Test" Result: Result set for "select factorial(0) from dual does match that of "select 1 from dual"

>

SUCCESS - FACTORIAL.UT_FACTORIAL: EQQUERY "1! Test" Result: Result set for "select factorial(1) from dual does match that of "select 1 from dual"

>

SUCCESS - FACTORIAL.UT_FACTORIAL: EQQUERY "N! Test" Result: Result set for "select FACTORIAL(5) from dual does match that of "select 120 from dual"

>

>

> Errors recorded in utPLSQL Error Log:

>

> NONE FOUND

.

```
>    SSSS   U    U  CCC     CCC   EEEEEE   SSSS      SSSS
>   S    S U    U C  C   C   C E        S    S   S    S
>   S        U    U C     C C    C E        S         S
>   S        U    U C         C        E        S         S
>    SSSS  U    U C         C        EEEE     SSSS      SSSS
>        S U    U C         C        E              S         S
>         S U    U C     C C    C E              S         S
>   S    S U    U  C    C   C   C E        S    S   S    S
>    SSSS     UUU    CCC     CCC   EEEEEE   SSSS      SSSS
```

.

SUCCESS: "CALC_QUARTER_HOUR"

.

> Individual Test Case Results:

>

SUCCESS - CALC_QUARTER_HOUR.UT_CALC_QUARTER_HOUR: ISNULL "NULL value" Expected "" and got ""

>

SUCCESS - CALC_QUARTER_HOUR.UT_CALC_QUARTER_HOUR: EQQUERY "Check that .10 rounds down" Result: Result set for "select calc_quarter_hour(6.10) from dual does match that of "select 6 from dual"

>

SUCCESS - CALC_QUARTER_HOUR.UT_CALC_QUARTER_HOUR: EQQUERY "Check that .15 rounds up" Result: Result set for "select calc_quarter_hour(6.15) from dual does match that of "select 6.25 from dual"

>

SUCCESS - CALC_QUARTER_HOUR.UT_CALC_QUARTER_HOUR: EQQUERY "Check that .35 rounds down" Result: Result set for "select calc_quarter_hour(6.35) from dual does match that of "select 6.25 from dual"

>

SUCCESS - CALC_QUARTER_HOUR.UT_CALC_QUARTER_HOUR: EQQUERY "Check that .40 rounds up" Result: Result set for "select calc_quarter_hour(6.40) from dual does match that of "select 6.5 from dual"

>

SUCCESS - CALC_QUARTER_HOUR.UT_CALC_QUARTER_HOUR: EQQUERY "Check that .65 rounds up" Result: Result set for "select calc_quarter_hour(6.65) from dual does match that of "select 6.75 from dual"

>

SUCCESS - CALC_QUARTER_HOUR.UT_CALC_QUARTER_HOUR: EQQUERY "Check that .83 rounds down" Result: Result set for "select calc_quarter_hour(6.83) from dual does match that of "select 7 from dual"

```
>

SUCCESS - CALC_QUARTER_HOUR.UT_CALC_QUARTER_HOUR: EQQUERY "Check that .92 rounds up" Result:
Result set for "select calc_quarter_hour(6.92) from dual does match that of "select 7 from
dual"

>

>

> Errors recorded in utPLSQL Error Log:

>

> NONE FOUND
```

If you happen to have a test fail, then the output of the test suite will display a failure message for the unit test that failed. In the following output, one of the test cases for the FACTORIAL unit test fails.

```
>   FFFFFFF    AA      III  L       U      U RRRRR    EEEEEEE

> F          A  A     I    L       U      U R    R  E

> F           A    A  I    L       U      U R     R E

> F          A     A  I    L       U      U R     R E

> FFFF       A     A  I    L       U      U RRRRRR  EEEE

> F          AAAAAAAA I    L       U      U R   R   E

> F          A     A  I    L       U      U R    R  E

> F          A     A  I    L        U    U R     R E

> F          A     A  III  LLLLLLL  UUU    R      R EEEEEEE

.

FAILURE: "FACTORIAL"

.

> Individual Test Case Results:
```

```
>

SUCCESS - FACTORIAL.UT_FACTORIAL: ISNULL "is NULL test" Expected "" and got ""

>

SUCCESS - FACTORIAL.UT_FACTORIAL: EQQUERY "0! Test" Result: Result set for

"select factorial(0) from dual does match that of "select 1 from dual"

>

SUCCESS - FACTORIAL.UT_FACTORIAL: EQQUERY "1! Test" Result: Result set for

"select factorial(1) from dual does match that of "select 1 from dual"

>

FAILURE - FACTORIAL.UT_FACTORIAL: EQQUERY "N! Test" Result: Result set for

"select FACTORIAL(5) from dual does  not match that of "select 121 from dual"

>

>

> Errors recorded in utPLSQL Error Log:

>

> NONE FOUND

.

>    SSSS   U    U  CCC     CCC   EEEEEEE   SSSS     SSSS

> S    S U    U C   C   C   C E        S    S   S    S

> S        U    U C    C C     C E      S         S

> S        U    U C      C      E      S         S

>    SSSS   U    U C      C      EEEE      SSSS     SSSS

>         S U    U C      C      E              S         S
```

```
>        S U    U C    C C    C E          S      S
>   S    S   U   U   C    C    C   C E        S    S    S    S
>   SSSS      UUU      CCC      CCC    EEEEEE    SSSS      SSSS
.
SUCCESS: "CALC_QUARTER_HOUR"
.
> Individual Test Case Results:
>
SUCCESS - CALC_QUARTER_HOUR.UT_CALC_QUARTER_HOUR: ISNULL "NULL value" Expected
"" and got ""
>
SUCCESS - CALC_QUARTER_HOUR.UT_CALC_QUARTER_HOUR: EQQUERY "Check that .10 rounds
down" Result: Result set for "select calc_quarter_hour(6.10) from dual does
match that of "select 6 from dual"
>
SUCCESS - CALC_QUARTER_HOUR.UT_CALC_QUARTER_HOUR: EQQUERY "Check that .15 rounds
up" Result: Result set for "select calc_quarter_hour(6.15) from dual does match
that of "select 6.25 from dual"
>
SUCCESS - CALC_QUARTER_HOUR.UT_CALC_QUARTER_HOUR: EQQUERY "Check that .35 rounds
down" Result: Result set for "select calc_quarter_hour(6.35) from dual does
match that of "select 6.25 from dual"
>
```

SUCCESS - CALC_QUARTER_HOUR.UT_CALC_QUARTER_HOUR: EQQUERY "Check that .40 rounds

up" Result: Result set for "select calc_quarter_hour(6.40) from dual does match

that of "select 6.5 from dual"

>

SUCCESS - CALC_QUARTER_HOUR.UT_CALC_QUARTER_HOUR: EQQUERY "Check that .65 rounds

up" Result: Result set for "select calc_quarter_hour(6.65) from dual does match

that of "select 6.75 from dual"

>

SUCCESS - CALC_QUARTER_HOUR.UT_CALC_QUARTER_HOUR: EQQUERY "Check that .83 rounds

down" Result: Result set for "select calc_quarter_hour(6.83) from dual does

match that of "select 7 from dual"

>

SUCCESS - CALC_QUARTER_HOUR.UT_CALC_QUARTER_HOUR: EQQUERY "Check that .92 rounds

up" Result: Result set for "select calc_quarter_hour(6.92) from dual does match

that of "select 7 from dual"

>

>

> Errors recorded in utPLSQL Error Log:

>

> NONE FOUND

PL/SQL procedure successfully completed.

How It Works

The utPLSQL.testSuite procedure steps though each unit test added using the utPackage.add procedure and executes each test. In turn, each test executes and sends its results to the screen. This is a quick method to run all tests and see the output on one screen capture. If one of the test cases within a unit test fails, all of the remaining tests in the suite will continue to execute, and the test that failed will be noted in the output. This is very useful as it will allow tests of many PL/SQL objects at once, and you will be able to see which tests had issues and which did not.

▧ **Hint** Spool the output to a file if the number of tests exceeds the screen buffer's capacity.

17-8. Reconfiguring utPLSQL Parameters

Problem

You would like to change some of the configurations for your utPLSQL install. For instance, you would like to change the prefix for all of your unit test packages so that, instead of beginning with ut_, they all start with test_.

Solution

Use the utConfig package to alter the configurations for utPLSQL. For this solution, you will see how utConfig can be used to change the prefix that is used for all of your test packages. For example, here's how to change the prefix for your test packages from ut_ to test_ using the utConfig package for the current schema.

```
SQL> exec utConfig.setPrefix('test_');

PL/SQL procedure successfully completed.
```

After executing the statement in the example, the utPLSQL unit test framework will look for test packages beginning with the test_ prefix rather than ut_ within the current schema, until the prefix is changed again using the utConfig package.

How It Works

The utPLSQL test framework can be configured to operate differently from its default manner by changing options using the utConfig package. Changes can be made for the current schema only, or for all schemas within the database. In the solution to this recipe, you have seen that the prefix for test packages is configurable. To change the prefix, pass the desired prefix in string format to utConfig.setPrefix(). The setPrefix() procedure also accepts an additional schema name that will specify the schema to which the configuration option will be applied. If you do not pass a schema name, the changes will occur within the current schema. The actual format for executing the utConfig.setPrefix procedure is as follows:

```
exec utConfig.setPrefix(desired_prefix, [schema]);
```

There are many configurable options that can be changed using the utConfig package. Table 17-2 shows the complete list of options.

Table 17-2. utConfig Configuration Options

Option	Description
utConfig.autocompile	Configure autocompile feature
utConfig.registertest	Configure the registration mode (manual or automatic)
utConfig.setdateformat	Configure the date format for the date portion of output file names
utConfig.setdelimiter	Configure the V2 delimiter
utConfig.setdir	Configure the directory containing the test package code
utConfig.setfiledir	Configure the directory for file output
utConfig.setfileextension	Configure the file extension for output file names
utConfig.setfileinfo	Configure all of the above file output related items
utConfig.setincludeprogname	Configure whether to include the name of the program being tested within output file names
utConfig.setprefix	Configure the default unit test prefix
utConfig.setreporter	Configure the default Output Reporter
utConfig.settester	Configure whose configuration is used
utConfig.setuserprefix	Configure the user prefix for output file names
utConfig.showfailuresonly	Switch off the display for successful tests

You can set of the options shown here using a syntax similar to that shown for the setPrefix() procedure that was demonstrated in the solution to this recipe. For more information on using the configurations listed in Table 17-2, please see the online documentation that can be found at: http://utplsql.oracledeveloper.nl/. Along with configurable options, the utConfig package includes some functions that can be called to retrieve information regarding the unit test configuration for the database or for a particular schema. Table 17-3 contains a listing of the options that utConfig makes available for obtaining information.

Table 17-3. utConfig Informational Options

Option Name	Description
utConfig.autocompiling	Returns autocompile flag value
utConfig.dateformat	Returns date format used to construct output file names
utConfig.delimiter	Returns V2 delimiter
utConfig.dir	Returns directory containing the test package code
utConfig.filedir	Returns file output directory
utConfig.fileextension	Returns output file name extension
utConfig.fileinfo	Returns all file output—related items
utConfig.getreporter	Obtains name of the default Output Reporter to use
utConfig.includeprogname	Returns whether to include the name of the program being tested within file names
utConfig.prefix	Returns default unit test prefix for your code
utConfig.registering	Returns registration mode
utConfig.showconfig	Displays a schema configuration
utConfig.showingfailuresonly	Returns whether successful test results are displayed
utConfig.tester	Returns the schema whose configuration is used
utConfig.userprefix	Returns the user prefix for output files

The functions can be called just as if they were standard functions within your schema. Some, such as the utConfig.showconfig procedure, require you to set serveroutput on in order to display the output. The following excerpt from a SQL*Plus session shows a call to utConfig.showconfig.

```
SQL> set serveroutput on
SQL> exec utconfig.showconfig
============================================================
utPLSQL Configuration for USERNAME
Directory:
Autcompile?
Manual test registration?
Prefix =
```

```
Default reporter    =
----- File Output settings:
Output directory:
User prefix    =
Include progname?
Date format    =
File extension  =
----- End File Output settings
===========================================================

PL/SQL procedure successfully completed.
```

The utConfig package contains a variety of configurable options that will allow you to adjust unit testing according to your specific needs. Out of the box, the utPLSQL testing framework contains default values for each of these options, so you may never need to touch utConfig, but the option is available if you need it. Another nice feature is that you can set configurable options for a specific schema. Doing so will allow different schemas in the database to act differently when performing unit testing.

17-9. Redirecting utPLSQL Test Results to a File

Problem

You are interested in writing the results of a unit test to a file.

Solution

Change the setting of the setreporter option of utPLSQL so that output is redirected to a file instead of DBMS_OUTPUT. Once the configuration has been altered, execute the unit tests for which you would like to have the output captured to the file. After you've run your tests, close the file and change the configuration back to its default. In the following lines of code, all of the steps that are necessary for redirecting test results to a file are exhibited. For example, suppose that the database has a directory that has already been enabled for use with the database named FILE_SYSTEM.

```
SQL>  BEGIN
  utconfig.setfiledir('FILE_SYSTEM');
  -- Causes output to be redirected to file system
  utconfig.setreporter('File');
  utPLSQL.test('calc_quarter_hour');
  -- Closes the fle
  utfilereporter.close();
  -- Returns output redirection to DBMS_OUTPUT
  utconfig.setreporter('Output');
END;

PL/SQL procedure successfully completed.
```

When the code block in this example is executed, a file will be created within the directory represented by FILE_SYSTEM. The unit test for CALC_QUARTER_HOUR will then be executed and the results will be redirected to the newly created file. Lastly, the file will be closed and the output will be redirected back to DBMS_OUTPUT.

How It Works

One of the configurable options of utPLSQL allows for the output of your unit tests to be redirected. The choices for displaying unit test results include Output, File, and HTML. The standard Output option is Output , which causes output to be displayed within the SQL*Plus environment using DBMS_OUTPUT. The File option allows for a file to be created and unit test results to be written to that file. Lastly, the HTML option allows for unit test results to be formatted into file in the format of an HTML table. In the solution to this recipe, the use of the File output reporter is demonstrated.

Prior to redirecting unit test output to a file, you must create a database directory using the CREATE DIRECTORY statement with a privileged account. For more information about creating directories, please see the Oracle documentation that can be found at: http://download.oracle.com/docs/cd/E11882_01/server.112/e17118/statements_5007.htm#SQLRF01207. Once you have created a database directory, you can use it to write the results of unit tests by setting the file directory using the utConfig.setfiledir() procedure. This procedure accepts the name of the database directory as a parameter. In the solution to this recipe, the directory is named FILE_SYSTEM. To redirect the unit test output from utPLSQL, you must use the utConfig.setreporter() procedure. This procedure accepts the name of the reporter that you would like to use for displaying output. As you can see from the solution to this recipe, the File reporter is chosen to redirect the output to a file on the file system. It is also possible to create a custom reporter configuration that you can pass to the utConfig.setreporter() procedure. For more information about creating customized reporters, please see the utPLSQL documentation that can be found at: http://utplsql.sourceforge.net/Doc/reporter.html.

After the output has been redirected using utConfig.setreporter(), you can run as many tests as you wish and all of the output will be directed to a file instead of to the SQL*Plus command prompt. In the solution to this recipe, the CALC_QUARTER_HOUR function is tested. Once you have finished running your tests, you must close the output file in order to make it available for you to use. If you fail to close the file, you will be unable to open it or use it because the database will maintain a lock on the file. To close the file, use issue utfilereporter.close(). Lastly, I recommend redirecting unit test output to the default Ouput option, which will cause it to be sent to DBMS_OUTPUT. By doing so, the next person who runs a unit test will receive the functionality that he or she expects by default, as the output will be directed to the screen. It is a good idea to set the default output at the beginning of all test suites just to ensure that you know where the output will be directed. However, if you are the only person running unit tests, or if you prefer to maintain the File reporter as your default, then omit the final call to utConfig.setreporter() that is shown in this solution.

Many times it can be useful to have unit test results redirected to an output file rather than displayed within the SQL*Plus environment. For instance, if you are running unit tests during off hours and would like to see the output, then it would be helpful to have it recorded to a file that can be viewed at a later time. Similarly, if you are running several unit tests, it may be easier to read through a file rather than scrolling through SQL*Plus output. Whatever the requirement may be, utPLSQL makes it easy to redirect unit test output to a file or another device by creating a custom reporter.

17-10. Automating Unit Tests for PL/SQL and Java Stored Procedures Using Ant

Problem

You wish to automatically run your unit tests for PL/SQL code and Java stored procedures each day and to write the results of the unit test to a file.

Solution

Use Apache's Ant build system to perform unit testing on your PL/SQL code. At the same time, Ant can build and compile any Java code that you will be using for your stored procedures. To do so, develop an Ant build script that will execute some SQL statements, automate your unit tests, and compile Java source into a directory. For example, the following build.xml file is an example of such a build that can be used to compile Java sources and execute unit tests on PL/SQL within a single Ant run.

```xml
<project name="MyPLSQLProject" default="unitTest" basedir=".">
    <description>
        PLSQL Unit Test and Application Builder
    </description>
  <!-- set global properties for this build -->
  <property name="src" location="src"/>
  <property name="build" location="build" value="build"/>
  <property name="user" value="myuser"/>
  <property name="db_password" value="mypassword"/>
  <property name="database.jdbc.url" value="jdbc:oracle:thin:@hostname:1521:database"/>

  <target name="init">
    <!-- Create the time stamp -->
    <tstamp/>
    <mkdir dir="${build}"/>
  </target>

  <target name="compile" depends="init"
        description="compile the source " >
    <!-- Compile the java code from ${src} into ${build} -->
    <!-- This is where you place the code for your java stored procedures -->
    <javac srcdir="${src}" destdir="${build}"/>
  </target>

  <target name="unitTest" depends="compile"
        description="Execute PLSQL Unit Tests" >
    <sql
     driver = "oracle.jdbc.driver.OracleDriver"
     url = "${database.jdbc.url}"
     userid = "${user}"
     password = "${db_password}"
     print="true"
    >
      call utconfig.setfiledir('FILE_SYSTEM');
      call utconfig.setreporter('File');
      call utPLSQL.test('calc_quarter_hour');
      -- Closes the fle
      call utfilereporter.close();
      -- Returns output redirection to DBMS_OUTPUT
      call utconfig.setreporter('Output');

    </sql>

  </target>
```

```
</project>
```

This build script can be executed by issuing the ant command from within the terminal or command prompt. The results will resemble the following output.

```
juneau$ ant

Buildfile: /Users/juneau/Documents/PLSQL_Recipes/sources/17/build.xml


init:


compile:

    [javac] /Users/juneau/Documents/PLSQL_Recipes/sources/17/build.xml:22: warning:
'includeantruntime' was not set, defaulting to build.sysclasspath=last; set to false for
repeatable builds


unitTest:

     [sql] Executing commands

     [sql] 0 rows affected

     [sql] 0 rows affected

     [sql] 0 rows affected

     [sql] 0 rows affected

     [sql] 0 rows affected

     [sql] 5 of 5 SQL statements executed successfully


BUILD SUCCESSFUL

Total time: 4 seconds
```

How It Works

Automating unit tests can be very helpful, especially if you are working on a project where there may be more than one developer contributing code. The Apache Ant build system is useful for automating builds and unit tests for Java projects. However, it can also be used to perform a myriad of other tasks, including issuing SQL statements, as seen in the solution to this recipe. Ant provides an entire build and unit test solution that is easy to use. To set up a build, all you need to do is install Ant on your machine and then create a build.xml file that consists of targets that Ant will use to build the project. Once you have created a build file, then simply open a command prompt or terminal and traverse into the directory containing your build file. Once in the directory, issue the ant command and it will automatically look for a file named build.xml that will provide Ant the sequence used for the build.

Ant uses simple logic to determine the order of sequence that will be used to execute the targets that are listed within the build.xml file. In the solution to this recipe, the build file contains three targets, init, compile, and unitTest. Ant will start the build by executing the target listed within the <project> tag as the default. In this case, the default target is unitTest.

```
<project name="MyPLSQLProject" default="unitTest" basedir=".">
```

The unitTest target contains a depends attribute, which lists the compile target. This tells Ant that the compile target should be executed first because unitTest depends upon its outcome.

```
<target name="unitTest" depends="compile"
        description="Execute PLSQL Unit Tests" >
```

Consequently, the compile target depends upon the init target, so init will be executed before compile.

```
<target name="compile" depends="init"
        description="compile the source " >
```

The order of target execution for the solution to this recipe will be the init target first, followed by the compile target, and lastly the unitTest target. The project tag also contains an attribute named basedir. This attribute tells Ant where the build files should be located. In the solution to this recipe, basedir contains a period "." that tells Ant to use the current directory.

At the top of the build file, you can see that there is a <description> tag. This is used to provide a brief description of the tasks completed by the build file. There are also several <property> tags. These tags are used to define the variables that will be used within the build file. Each <property> tag contains a name attribute and either a value or location attribute.

```
<property name="src" location="src"/>
<property name="build" location="build" value="build"/>
<property name="user" value="myuser"/>
<property name="db_password" value="mypassword"/>
<property name="database.jdbc.url" value="jdbc:oracle:thin:@hostname:1521:database"/>
```

The properties that use a value attribute are used to assign values to the property name, whereas the properties that contain location attributes are used to assign a location to the property name. Properties can be referenced within the build file by using the following syntax: "${property_name}". As you can see from the solution to this recipe, each target within the build file consists of a number of tasks in the form of XML tags. The init target creates a timestamp by using the <tstamp/> tag, and it creates a directory using the <mkdir/> tag and passing the name of a directory to be created. In this case, the directory name will be named the same as the value that is assigned to the <property> tag that is named build.

```
<target name="init">
    <!-- Create the time stamp -->
    <tstamp/>
    <mkdir dir="${build}"/>
  </target>
```

The compile target is used to compile all of the Java sources contained in the project. All of the sources should reside within a named directory that is located in the base directory of the Ant project. The compile target contains a single task using the <javac> tag. This tag contains a src attribute that defines the location of the sources to be compiled, and a destdir attribute that tells Ant where to place the resulting Java class files. An Ant project that builds a Java project may contain only this task, but can build several hundred Java class files. In the solution to this recipe, and for most Ant uses with PL/SQL projects, however, the project will probably contain no Java source files or only a few at most. If a project contains no Java source files, then the target will be executed, but the <javac> task will do nothing since there are not any sources to be compiled.

```
<target name="compile" depends="init"
        description="compile the source " >
    <!-- Compile the java code from ${src} into ${build} -->
    <!-- This is where you place the code for your java stored procedures -->
    <javac srcdir="${src}" destdir="${build}"/>
  </target>
```

The most important target in the solution to this recipe is the unitTest target. It consists of a single task using the <sql> tag. The sole purpose of the <sql> task is to execute SQL within a designated database. The <sql> tag contains a driver attribute that is used to list the JDBC driver for the target database, a url attribute used to define the JDBC URL for the target database, a userid and password attribute for defining the database username and password, and a print attribute that tells Ant whether to print the result sets from the SQL statements. In the solution to this recipe, the SQL that is required to execute the unit tests is contained within the <sql> opening and closing tags. This causes the unit tests to be executed as if you were issuing these statements at the SQL*Plus command prompt.

```
<target name="unitTest" depends="compile"
        description="Execute PLSQL Unit Tests" >
    <sql
     driver = "oracle.jdbc.driver.OracleDriver"
     url = "${database.jdbc.url}"
     userid = "${user}"
     password = "${db_password}"
     print="true"
    >
      call utconfig.setfiledir('FILE_SYSTEM');
      call utconfig.setreporter('File');
      call utPLSQL.test('calc_quarter_hour');
      -- Closes the fle
      call utfilereporter.close();
      -- Returns output redirection to DBMS_OUTPUT
      call utconfig.setreporter('Output');
```

```
</sql>

</target>
```

To automate your Ant build, you will need to set up an operating system task that starts the Ant build. The task is very simple and needs to contain only very few lines. The following lines of code contain batch script for the Windows operating system that can be used to invoke the Ant build. This assumes that the java.exe executable is contained within the PATH environment variable.

```
cd C:/path_to_project_directory
ant
```

You will also need to ensure that the JDBC driver for the Oracle database is contained within your CLASSPATH. If you do not include the JDBC driver in the CLASSPATH, then you will receive an error when you try to execute the build. When the Ant build is executed, a file will be placed onto the database server in the location designated by the FILE_SYSTEM database directory. The file will contain the results of the unit test execution.

Ant is a complex build system that can be used for configuration and preparation of your builds and unit tests. It is a widely used build system, especially for organizations that do lots of Java development. As you can see, it is easy to use, but does contain complexity in that there are a number of different tasks and attributes that can be used. This recipe does not even scratch the surface of everything that Ant can do. However, there are lots of sources for documentation on Ant that can be found online as well as in book format. To learn more about Ant, you can start by reading the online documentation that can be found at: http://ant.apache.org/manual/.

Index

Special Characters

A

B